BRITISH HEROES

IN

FOREIGN WARS.

DISCOVERY OF THE BODY OF MARSHAL KEITH.

BRITISH HEROES

IN

FOREIGN WARS

OR

THE CAVALIERS OF FORTUNE

By JAMES GRANT
AUTHOR OF "THE ROMANCE OF WAR"

The Naval & Military Press Ltd
in association with
The National Army Museum, London

Published jointly by

The Naval & Military Press Ltd
Unit 10 Ridgewood Industrial Park,
Uckfield, East Sussex,
TN22 5QE England

Tel: +44 (0) 1825 749494
Fax: +44 (0) 1825 765701

www.naval-military-press.com
www.military-genealogy.com
www.militarymaproom.com

and

The National Army Museum, London
www.national-army-museum.ac.uk

In reprinting in facsimile from the original, any imperfections are inevitably reproduced and the quality may fall short of modern type and cartographic standards.

PREFACE.

The biographies or sketches which compose this volume are prepared from memoranda, the result of historical reading for my military romances.

The Memoir of Colonel John Cameron first appeared, with that of Count Lally, &c., in the *Dublin University Magazine* for 1854; and though he cannot strictly be considered a Soldier of Fortune, it is given here with the rest. It was carefully compiled from a mass of private papers and letters submitted to me by his brother, Sir Duncan Cameron, Bart.; from several letters written to me by his brother officers; the MSS. Records of the 92nd Highlanders; and—like the sketch of Count O'Connell—from information readily afforded to me by the authorities at the War-Office and Horse Guards.

In several instances, the brief *Biographie Universelle*, edited by Michaud, has been of service to me in fixing dates—especially in the account of the Lacys.

The Thirty Years' War, the Septennial War, and the War of the Spanish Succession formed an ample field of enterprise for those Scots and Irish who, having nothing better to do at home, sold their swords and their valour to the highest bidder; and who, having but little hope of attaining rank in the service of Britain, sought fortune, fame, and a new home in the camp of the stranger. Thus many of the military wanderers who form the subject of these detached Memoirs belonged to the Sister Isle.

The Irish troops in the service of France covered themselves with glory, as the Scots had done under Gustavus of Sweden; and by the Memoir of their last Colonel, Count O'Connell, it will be seen that they were faithful and true, as they had been valiant, to the end. They filled Europe with the fame of their exploits, and have left their bones on many a hard-fought battle-field; and, as their song has it,—

> "They who survived fought and drank as of yore,
> But the land of their heart's hope they never saw more;
> For on far foreign fields, from Dunkirk to Belgrade,
> Lie the soldiers and chiefs of the IRISH BRIGADE!"

Under the happier influences of the present time, our people are no longer forced to seek their bread in foreign camps. The restless military spirit which produced the Soldier of Fortune is now on the wane; yet it is impossible, without emotion, to look back on the exploits of those brave fellows who led the armies of Europe in so many "king-making victories," and won by their swords those honours which were denied them in the land of their forefathers.

26, *Danube Street*,
   EDINBURGH, 1858.

CONTENTS.

	PAGE
ARTHUR COUNT DE LALLY, GENERAL OF THE TROOPS OF LOUIS XV. IN INDIA	1
COLONEL JOHN CAMERON, OF THE GORDON HIGHLANDERS, SLAIN AT QUATRE BRAS	44
ADMIRAL SIR SAMUEL GREIG, "FATHER OF THE RUSSIAN NAVY"	85
ULYSSES COUNT BROWN, MARSHAL OF THE ARMIES OF MARIA THERESA	112
MARSHAL LACY, THE CONQUEROR OF THE CRIMEA	142
COUNT LACY, MARSHAL OF THE IMPERIAL ARMIES	164
COUNT LACY, CAPTAIN GENERAL OF CATALONIA	168
LOUIS LACY, MARISCAL DE CAMPO AND COMMANDER OF LEON	169
COLONEL BUTLER, OF THE IRISH MUSKETEERS UNDER THE EMPEROR FERDINAND	178
MARSHAL CLARKE, DUC DE FELTRE, AND GOVERNOR OF VIENNA	192
GENERAL KILMAINE, COMMANDER OF LOMBARDY, AND THE ARMEE D'ANGLETERRE	213
COUNTS O'REILLY, O'DONNEL, AND THE IRISH IN SPAIN	233
BARON LOUDON, MARSHAL OF THE AUSTRIAN ARMY	263
COUNT O'REILLY, CHAMBERLAIN OF THE EMPIRE	292
COUNT O'CONNELL, KNIGHT OF ST. LOUIS, AND COLONEL OF THE IRISH BRIGADE	293
MARSHAL MACDONALD, DUKE OF TARENTUM	308
THOMAS DALYELL, OF BINNS, GENERAL OF THE SCOTTISH ARMY, AND FIRST COLONEL OF THE SCOTS GREY DRAGOONS	356

THE
CAVALIERS OF FORTUNE.

Life of the Count de Lally,

GENERAL OF THE TROOPS OF LOUIS XV. IN THE EAST INDIES.

AMONG the many gallant Irishmen, and those descended from the Irish race, who served in the armies of France, and sought there those honours and distinctions which political misfortune and studied misrule denied them at home, I know of none more distinguished, and of none whose name is more worthy of being rescued from oblivion, than General the Count de Lally, the ill-requited leader of the troops of Louis XV. in the wars of India.

Arthur Lally was the son of Captain O'Lally, of Tulloch na Daly, in Galway, who passed over to France soon after Limerick capitulated to Goderdt de Ginckel, the Dutch Earl of Athlone, and at the close of that disastrous war in which the Irish troops withstood the army of King William. Captain Lally obtained a commission in the regiment of the Hon. Arthur Dillon, the same battalion in which the great Marshal Macdonald, Duke of Tarentum, commenced his military career as a sub-lieutenant.

Soon after he settled in France, Captain Lally married a French lady of distinction. They had two children, the eldest of whom, Arthur, was soon after his birth enrolled—according to a custom then prevailing in the

French army—as a private soldier in the company of his father. In this capacity he served at the famous siege of Barcelona under the Maréchal Duke of Berwick in 1714. His father being an officer of distinguished merit, and his mother being by blood allied to some of the most noble families in France, afforded young Lally every opportunity for the improvement of his mind and person; thus at the age of nineteen he was considered one of the handsomest and most accomplished chevaliers in Paris.

Without having seen much active service, he had then been appointed to a company in that gallant band of exiles whose valour contributed to win many a victory for the House of Bourbon—the *Irish Brigade*. His regiment—every member of which knew his father's worth and merit—received him with satisfaction, and his *reception* took place early in 1718.

In the old French service this was an indispensable ceremony when an officer first joined. His company was drawn up in front of the regiment, with the drummers beating on the flanks. Dressed in full uniform, with his scarf, sword, and gorget, Arthur Lally was led forward by the general of division, who, when the drums ceased, raised his cocked hat, and said :—

"De par le Roi ! Soldats, vous reconnoitrez Monsieur de Lally, votre capitaine de la compagnie, et vous lui obeirez en tout ce qu'il vous ordonnera pour le service du Roi, en cette qualité."

Another ruffle on the drums, the company fell back to its place in the line of the regiment of Dillon, and Arthur Lally was formally installed its captain.

Though he was known by his education and spirit to have possessed all those qualities which were requisite for the perfect soldier, uniting a clear head and solid judgment to a light and joyous, but intrepid heart, he was found to be equally qualified for the civil service of the State ; thus at the age of five-and-twenty he was sent by Louis XV. to the court of Russia on a political mission of importance. On this duty he acquitted himself ably, his fidelity on one hand securing the confidence of the king his master, by his address and winning manner; on the other, obtaining the esteem and admiration of the Empress Catharine, whose husband, Peter the Great, had died about a year before. On his return to France in 1725 he proceeded to Versailles, where Louis XV., who had then attained his majority, and taken the reins of government from the Regent Duke of Orleans, received him in the most gracious manner, and promoted him to the rank of colonel of infantry; and at the head of his regiment he had the good fortune to acquit himself with distinction wherever he was employed.

He stood high in the favour of the two ministers who succeeded the Duke of Orleans, namely, the Duke de Bourbon and Cardinal Fleury, then in his seventy-third year, a mild and amiable prelate, under whose moderate and conciliatory counsels France enjoyed many years of peace and tranquillity. During service in France, Lally, though somewhat proud and lofty in his manner, succeeded in gaining the esteem and affection of the officers of his regiment, among whom—even in those days of incessant duelling—he was fortunately successful in maintaining the most perfect union and harmony, while by his unalterable firmness subordination was equally maintained.

Thus had passed the time until 1745, when Prince Charles Edward Stuart projected his gallant and unfortunate rising among the clans in the Scottish Highlands. Entering warmly into the design of restoring the hapless House of Stuart, under which his father had served long and faithfully, and with whom he had eaten the bread of exile, Colonel Lally came boldly over to London. While his ostensible object was to recover certain lands in Ireland, to which he averred his father had a claim, his real errand was to serve the young Prince of Scotland, to animate his friends, to excite the malcontents, to promise money, titles, and prepare the Jacobites of South Britain for the tempest that was gathering among the mountains of the north. By his boldness and determination Lally met with the utmost success in London; but being somewhat unwary, his plans and presence were discovered and revealed by a spy to the Duke of Cumberland, who procured immediate orders for his arrest.

Fortunately, however, Lally escaped those shambles to which "the butcher" of the clans had doomed him, and escaping to France about the time Culloden was fought, resumed the command of his regiment.

A war was then waging between France and Britain, and the fleets of the latter had swept those of the former from the ocean. Admiral Hawke had destroyed the French fleet at Belleisle, and in that year upwards of six hundred prizes were taken by our cruisers.

Though the French armies performed some brilliant actions in the Netherlands, where the Marshal-General, Maurice Count de Saxe, defeated and covered with disgrace the troops of the Duke of Cumberland, Louis XV. was compelled by naval disasters, and the internal distresses of France, to conclude a peace, a congress for which met at Aix-la-Chapelle in April, 1748; and the definitive treaty was signed in the following October.

During this period, and until his promotion to the rank of lieutenant-general and commander-in-chief in the East Indies, the life of Lally—who had now been created a peer of France—does not present any circumstance or incident worthy of attention. In 1749 he married.

In 1750 a dispute pregnant with hostility ensued between France and Britain respecting their mutual claims in North America; various circumstances which occurred in the East Indies about the same time confirmed the idea that the short peace concluded in 1748 was about to end. Each country prepared for war; but though many unfriendly acts were committed, and bitter recriminations exchanged between the Courts of London and Versailles, until Britain was threatened with invasion, as a curb on her aggressive spirit, hostilities were not formally denounced until the month of June, 1756. The declaration made by George II. was mild and moderate in tenor and language, but the declaration promulgated by Louis XV. was full of severity and opprobrium. Prussia became the ally of the former; Sweden and Russia joined the latter. In distant regions as well as at home the sanguinary struggle was maintained, and in America France was stripped of all her possessions by the army of the heroic Wolfe.

Immediately after the declaration of war, in the month of August, 1756, the Count de Lally, as Lieutenant-General and Commander-in-Chief of all his Most Christian Majesty's forces in India, was appointed to conduct an expedition destined for those burning shores, so far distant, and even at that period comparatively so little known to Europeans.

In support of this expedition the Court had destined six millions of livres, six strong battalions of infantry, and three ships of war, which were to co-operate with such an armament as the French India Company could furnish; but the whole of the troops did not embark.

On the 20th February, 1757, the Count de Lally, accompanied by his brother Michael, marched to Brest at the head of two battalions; and though having only two millions of livres in the military chest, embarked on board the ships of the Count d'Aché, who immediately put to sea; but being driven into port again by contrary winds, the squadron was detained until the 2nd of May.

Meanwhile, Major-General the Chevalier des Soupirs, Lally's second in command, had already reached the Indian Ocean, having departed from L'Orient, the principal port of the India Company, on the 30th of the preceding December, with two battalions and two millions of livres, with which he touched at the Isle of France, without accident.

The general had very ample and important instructions given to him by the India Company. Some of these were to the following effect:—

"The Sieur de Lally is authorized to destroy the fortifications of all maritime settlements which may be taken from the English; it may, however, be proper to except Vizagapatam, by reason of its being so nearly situated to Bemelipatana, which in that case would be enriched by the ruin of Vizagapatam; but as to that, and the demolition of all other places, the Sieur de Lally is to consult the Governor and Superior Council of Pondicherry, and to have their opinion in writing; but, notwithstanding, he is to destroy such places as he shall think proper, unless strong and sufficient arguments are made use of to the contrary; such, for example, as the Company being apprehensive for some of their settlements, and that it would then be thought prudent and necessary to reserve the power of exchange in case any of them should be lost. Nevertheless, if the Sieur de Lally should think it too hazardous to keep a place, or could not do so without dividing or weakening his army, then his Majesty leaves him to act as he may deem proper for the good of the service.

"The Sieur de Lally is to allow of no English settlement being ransomed, as we may well remember that, after the taking of Madras last war, the English Company in their Council of the 14th of July, 1747, determined that all ransoms made in India should be annulled. In regard to the English troops, both officers and writers belonging to the Company, and to the inhabitants of that nation, the Sieur de Lally is to permit none of them to remain on the coast of Coromandel; he may, if he pleases, permit the inhabitants to go to England, and order them to be conducted in armed vessels to St. Helena. But as to the officers, soldiers, writers, and sailors belonging to the East India Company, he is to conduct them as soon as possible to the Isle de Bourbon, where the soldiers and sailors will be permitted to work for the inhabitants of that place, according to mutual agreement. It is by no means his Majesty's intention that the English officers, soldiers, and sailors should be ransomed, as none are to be delivered up but by exchange, man for man, according to their different ranks and stations.

"If the exchange of prisoners should by chance be settled at home between the two nations, of which proper notice will be given to the Sieur de Lally, and that the islands of France and Bourbon should have more prisoners than it would be convenient to provide for, in that case it will be permitted to send a certain number to England, in a vessel armed for the purpose. No English officers, soldiers, &c., are to be permitted to remain in a place after it is taken; neither are they to retire to any other of their settlements.

"The Sieur de Lally is not in the least to deviate from the above instructions and regulations, unless there shall be a stipulation to the contrary; in which case the Sieur de Lally is faithfully and honestly to adhere to the capitulation.

"The whole of what has been said before concerns only natives of England; but as they have in their settlements merchants from all nations, such as Moors, Armenians, Jews, Pattaners, &c., the Sieur de Lally is ordered to treat them with humanity, and endeavour by fair means to engage them to retire to Pondicherry, or any other of the Company's acquisitions, assuring them at the same time that they will be protected, and that the same liberty and privileges which they before possessed among the English will be granted them.

"Among the recruits furnished to complete the regiments of Lorrain and Berry, there are three hundred men from Fisher's corps, lately raised, and as it is feared there will be considerable desertions among these new recruits, the Sieur de Lally may, if he pleases, leave them on the Isle de France, and replace them from the troops of that island."*

Before leaving France, Lally had placed his son, Trophine Gerard, who had been born at Paris on the 5th March, 1751, at the College of Harcourt, intending that he should ultimately follow the profession of arms.

Though impetuous and at times apt to be somewhat overbearing, Lally was eminently fitted for command. He possessed secrecy, with a ready facility for quick and judicious decision. His talent was evinced by the manner in which he established magazines, extended his posts and defences, and made himself acquainted with the character and features of the country which was to be the scene of his future operations. His lofty demeanour, talent, tact,

---

* The MS. original of these interesting instructions was presented to Charles Grant, Viscount de Vaux, by the directors of the English East India Company.

and bravery inspired his troops with confidence and an assurance of conquest. If Lally was fond of glory, he was also fond of flattery; and though a strict disciplinarian, he was somewhat too partial, perhaps, to levying contribution on the conquered provinces; but while his enemies in after years averred that he was grasping, they never denied that he was lavish and liberal when the king's service required him by spies to obtain intelligence of the strength and designs of the enemy.

The Count d'Aché, Chef d'Escadre, encountered such adverse winds that he was nearly twelve months on his voyage; thus the Chevalier des Soupirs, having wearied of waiting at the Mauritius, sailed towards the coast of Hindostan, and reaching Pondicherry (or *Puducheri*), disembarked his troops.

This town was the capital of the French settlements in India, being restored to them by the Dutch after the Treaty of Ryswick. It occupied a good position in the rich, fertile, and populous Carnatic, a country studded by an incredible number of forts and strongholds. Their erection was an indispensable necessity in a level district full of open towns, subject to the sudden attacks of hordes of native cavalry. The sovereigns of the Carnatic must have possessed at one period immense wealth and power, for the number and magnitude of their pagodas, and the indications that remain of ancient riches, grandeur, population, industry and art, impress the mind with wonder.

At this crisis the funds and forces of the British in that part of India were so small, that they could scarcely bring one hundred soldiers into the field. Madras, one of their principal places, sixty-three miles distant, was an open town; Fort St. David was in ruins, with a garrison of only sixty invalids. A fortnight would have enabled the Chevalier, with his 2000 men, to reduce the whole coast of Coromandel; but M. des Soupirs was quite unskilled in the art of carrying on war in a country so new to him, and remained inactive, though the French had many losses to repair, having been recently driven from all their wealthy settlements in Bengal by the victorious English.

Eight months after his arrival, on the 25th April, 1758, the Chef d'Escadre anchored in the roadstead before the sandy plain occupied by Pondicherry, and Lally disembarking his troops and treasure, marched into the town, the governor of which, M. de Leyrit, received him with a salute of cannon. At the peace of Amiens, the French population of Pondicherry amounted to 25,000, exclusive of the blacks, who were treble that number. Its revenue was then 40,000 pagodas; but it was a place destitute of natural advantages, its vicinity producing only palm-trees, millet, and a few herbs.

Weary of his long voyage, and anxious to fulfil his orders, which comprehended the total destruction of every British fortification that fell into his power, the ardent and gallant Lally lost not an hour in preparing for active operations. Next day, the 26th, he returned on board to sail for Cudalore, and in one hour after a powerful British fleet assailed the ships of Count d'Aché in the roadstead, where a French 74-gun ship was taken; but the rest fought a passage to the seaward, and favoured by the wind, and by superior sailing, anchored off Cudalore, a town situated fifteen miles from Pondicherry, on the western shore of the Bay of Bengal.

This little town, which occupies the banks of the Pennar, had been obtained by the English East India Company from the Rajah of Gingee, so early as 1681, for the site of a factory, and had been fortified. Its garrison consisted only of ten invalids; but being assisted by the inhabitants, these brave fellows made so stout a resistance, that Lally was occupied three days in taking it. From thence he marched to Fort St. David, a settlement on the Carnatic coast, obtained by the English from a Mahratta rajah in 1691, and besieging it, after being seventeen days in open trenches, exposed to the broiling sun by noon and the baleful dews by night, gained it by capitulation on the 2nd of June, and levelled all its fortifications to the ground.

On the 10th he marched back to Pondicherry, and having resolved to assail Madras, despatched an officer in a small vessel to his naval Chef d'Escadre, with instructions to return and co-operate with him. But Admiral Pocock, who commanded the British squadron in those seas, had defeated M. d'Aché in two engagements, and by driving him sixty miles to the windward, had nearly cut off all communication between him and the army. And now the governor of Pondicherry announced that the town and its vicinity could not subsist Lally's 4000 Frenchmen for more than fifteen days. On this he was compelled to march into the little kingdom of Tanjore (or Tanjowar), which lay one hundred and fifty miles southward, and there quarter his troops during the stormy and rainy season, while the naval squadron took refuge in port. The advance into Tanjowar was not made without a due pretence of wrong to adjust, for the rajah had refused to pay a government debt, which M. de Leyrit assured Count Lally to be more than due.

The discharge of five pieces of cannon against his little capital compelled the rajah to pay down treasure to the amount of 440,000 livres, and afford free-quarters to the French troops for two months, until tidings arrived that 800 British were marching against Pondicherry; upon which Lally immediately abandoned Tanjowar, and advanced to the relief of the Chevalier des Soupirs, who with a slender force was timidly preparing to evacuate the capital of French India.

On Lally approaching, on the 31st of August, the British detachment fell back on Madras, and now our indefatigable Irishman, full of the most sanguine hopes of expelling them from the vast peninsula of Hindostan, at once made new preparations for investing Fort St. George, their principal settlement on the coast of Coromandel; but scarcity of money, and the improper conduct of the naval Chef d'Escadre, retarded the operations, frustrated the bold intentions of Lally, and ultimately betrayed them to the enemy.

While sparing no exertions to officer and equip a body of sepoy infantry, he seized a Dutch ship, in which he found a sufficient quantity of specie to enable him to attack Madras; he then sent a message to the Count d'Aché not to leave the coast; but the count replied, that he required a recruit of seamen, and must return to France. Alarmed by such a threat, Lally offered him half of his soldiers for the marine service; but deaf alike to threats and entreaties, the count sailed for the Straits of Madagascar on the 1st of September, and left Lally to cope single handed with the British forces.

On summoning to his presence M. de Bussy, who commanded the French troops in that extensive region named the Deccan (or Country of the South), and M. Moracin, who commanded at the seaport of Masulipatnam, he found these officers were somewhat influenced by the same pride and disobedience which characterized the conduct of Count d'Aché; and thus, before they would obey, and march against Madras, they required that Lally should embody an additional thousand men. He immediately ordered M. Moracin to return to his post, which the British were approaching. M. Moracin dared to refuse or delay, and taken by surprise during his absence, Masulipatnam was lost to France for ever.

In the month of October, Lally, with his slender force, the flower of which was the valiant Regiment de Lorraine, marched without opposition into the extensive district of Arcot (which seven years before had been overrun by Colonel Clive), and after remaining there at free-quarters for five days, marched back to Pondicherry.

The army was now totally destitute of pay, and the commissariat had no supply but plunder, while the departure of the Count d'Aché cut off all succour or retreat by the seaward. Though numerous, the troubles of Lally were just commencing. Discouraged and disunited by the naval disasters of d'Aché, the French officers were alternately fired with ardour and depressed by despair. M. de Bussy offered to raise 400,000 livres in three hours, if he was permitted to re-enter the Deccan with a body of troops; but being loth to divide his little force, and believing the result to be incredible, Lally wisely declined. De Bussy then informed him that he had 240,000 livres belonging to the East India Company, which were at his service if *he* would be responsible for them; but Lally still more wisely declined to compromise his honour by appropriating the money of the merchants to the service of the nation. He resumed his preparations for the siege of Madras while the British fleet was absent from its shore; but this measure was vehemently opposed by the Governor of Pondicherry, M. Duval de Leyrit, who urged the wretched state of the commissariat and the empty military chest. Lally's Irish spirit could ill brook such disputations, and, "pay or no pay," he was for marching at once.

However, he was compelled to take the opinion of the General Council of Pondicherry, some of whom adhered to De Leyrit; but five, headed by M. le Comte d'Estaigne, offered their plate, to the value of 80,000 livres, towards the expense of the expedition. The true and generous Lally gave, from his private purse, 140,000 livres; and having thus in some measure collected the sinews of war, with his small head-quarter force, 2700 French, and a body of sepoys, he advanced towards Madras early in December.

A march of sixty-three miles brought Lally, on the 12th day of the month, in sight of the town, which, by its strength, wealth, and annual revenue in calicos and muslins, was of such great consequence, even then, to the growing English East India Company. The diamond mines were only a week's journey distant, and the rumour of their priceless wealth, and splendid wonders, animated the French soldiers, as in three divisions they marched across the sunny plains of Choultry.

Madras, or Fort St George, was divided into two parts; one called *the Black*, and the other *the White* town. The former, Madraspatam, had been totally destroyed by the French in 1744, when they levelled to the ground every building that stood within three hundred yards of the fort. The walls of the latter, which rose above the centre of the English town were—as dispatches relate—all built of hard, iron-coloured stone. and defended by four gigantic bastions. The inner fort, or citadel, had a front of one hundred and eight yards; the outer fort consisted of half-moons, curtain-walls, and flankers, which, like the rusty-coloured ramparts of the town were studded by an incredible number of cannon. In short, the aspect of Madras, with its mansions covered by snow-white *chunam*, is delightful from the ocean, and magnificent from the land. On the latter, its walls are moated by a river, which falls into the sea on that flat and sandy shore, where a white and furious surf is ever rolling in mountains of foam.

As he crossed the plains, Lally was briskly cannonaded by the field-pieces of the enemy, and lost many officers and men; but, advancing steadily, took possession of Ogmore and Meliapore (or San Thomé), an old town of the Portuguese, who had built there a large church above a grave reputed to be that of St. Thomas, who had been murdered by a tribe that dwelt in the vicinity, and whose *right legs*, after that sacrilegious act, were, according to Dr. Fryar, swollen to the size of those of elephants.

Colonel Lawrence, a gallant and resolute officer, who commanded the garrison of Madras, was ably seconded by Pigot the governor, by Colonel Draper, Major Caillaud, and other gentlemen. Thus Lally encountered the most determined resistance. The garrison consisted of 5000 men; of these, 1600 were regular troops of the British line, 300 were sepoys, and 400 were servants of the East India Company. Lawrence retired to the island in order to prevent the French from obtaining possession of the island bridge, and ordered all the posts to be occupied in the Black Town, which was triangularly shaped, and surrounded by a fortified wall.

At daybreak, on the morning of the 14th December, Lally sent forward M. de Rillon at the head of his regiment, which assailed the Black Town with great spirit, and after giving and receiving several severe discharges of musketry, during a contest of some hours, gained the place, driving back the British, who retired by detachments into the fort or citadel of Madras. This successful movement was followed by an advance of the Regiment de Lorraine, to keep the ground De Rillon had won; but within an hour, a grand *sortie* was made upon them by a body of British infantry, led by Colonel Draper, who behaved with great personal bravery.

Shrouded in smoke, he led a charge of bayonets against the Regiment de Lorraine; a furious *mêlée* ensued, and the French must have been driven back, or cut off, had not Lally sent forward another detachment, with some sepoys, to sustain the troops of M. de Rillon. A great number of officers and men were shot or bayoneted on both sides; but Colonel Draper was compelled to retreat, for his grenadiers gave way in a somewhat discreditable manner. After this, the garrison of Madras contented themselves by defending their works, being too weak to engage in *sorties* beyond them.

Colonel, afterwards Sir William Draper, was that *preux chevalier* who afterwards conquered Manilla, and became a paramount judge in all matters of military etiquette, and who, in his celebrated letter to JUNIUS, expressed a hope that he would never see officers pushed into the British army who had nothing to lose but their *swords*.

Thus encouraged, by hemming in the enemy, Lally continued to push his approaches, and build batteries. Meanwhile M. de Lequille, another Chef d'Escadre, had arrived at the Isle de France, with four ships of war and three millions of livres, destined for the service of the French India Company. When about to leave the isle for the roads of Pondicherry, he unfortunately met the discomfited fleet of the Count d'Aché, who, being his superior officer, prevented him from proceeding, and removed the treasure on board his own ship, taking upon himself to send only *one* million of livres to the Count de Lally, in a small frigate, which reached Pondicherry on the 21st December, 1758.

This supply enabled Lally to press the siege with greater vigour, and to pay his French soldiers and Indian levies a portion of their arrears; but the blacks were of little service to him during the operations. M. Lally erected several batteries against the Black Town and Fort St. George; one of these, called the Grand Battery, was 450 yards distance from the glacis. They opened on the 6th January, 1759; after which they maintained a continued discharge of shot and shells for twenty days, the pioneers pushing on the trenches until their sap had reached the base of the glacis, within pistol-shot of the parapets. Then Lally formed another and loftier battery, on which he placed four pieces of heavy cannon. It opened on the 31st of January; but for five consecutive days the artillerists were compelled to close up their embrasures with fascines and earth, for the superior fire of the fort was not to be withstood, and it soon compelled them to abandon their redoubt. The Grand Battery, however, still continued a fire, which was so well directed, that it dismounted or broke twenty-six pieces of cannon and three mortars, beating down the wall and effecting a considerable breach.

During these operations, Lally had somewhat needlessly bombarded the town, to terrify the inhabitants, and demolished a number of their houses; but the precautions of Governor Pigot, the vigilance, valour, and experience of Colonels Draper, Lawrence, and Major Brereton repelled every attack; and thus, after the 5th of February, the fire of Lally's batteries gradually diminished from twenty-three to six pieces of cannon. Money, powder, and shot became scarce together; he had lost many of his bravest men; two months had elapsed, and still the British standard waved above the fort of Madras. During this period the remonstrances which Lally sent frequently to France for succour, describe the deep anxiety he felt for the success of a cause in which his honour was implicated; and so keen and bitter did this feeling become, that at times, when aggravated by an illness incident to the climate, his reports and dispatches are remarkable for containing occasional sentences expressive of horror and distraction.

His general chagrin at the conduct of Count d'Aché and others is strongly portrayed in the following letter, which he addressed from the trenches at Madras to the Governor of Pondicherry, and which had been intercepted :—

"M. DUVAL DE LEYRIT,—A good blow might be struck here; there is in the roads a 20-gun ship laden with all the riches of Madras; she will remain there till the 20th. The *Expedition* is just arrived, but M. Gerlin is not a man to attack her, for she made him run away once before. The *Bristol*, on the other hand, did but just make her appearance before San Thomé, and on the vague report of thirteen ships coming from Porto Nova, she took fright, and, after landing the provisions with which she was laden, she would not stay even long enough to take on board twelve of her own guns, which she had lent us for the siege (of Madras).

"If I was to judge of the point of honour of the Company's officers, I would break him like glass, as well as some others of them.

"The *Fidele*, or the *Haerlem*, or even the aforesaid *Bristol*, with her twelve guns restored to her, would be sufficient to make themselves masters of the British ship, if they could get to windward of her in the night. Maugendre and Tremillier are said to be good men, and were they employed to transport 200 wounded we have here, their service would be of importance. We remain in the same position; the breach made these fifteen days; all the time within fifteen toises of the place, and never holding up our heads to look at it. I believe we must, on our return to Pondicherry, learn some *other trade*, for this of war requires too much patience.

"Of the 1500 sepoys who attended our army, I believe nearly 800 are employed upon the road to Pondicherry, laden with pepper, sugar, and other goods; and as for the coolies, they have been employed for the same purpose since the first days we came here. I am taking my measures from this day to set fire to the Black Town and to blow up the powder-mills.

"You will never imagine that fifty French deserters and 100 Swiss are actually stopping the progress of 2000 men of the king's and Company's troops, which are still here existing, notwithstanding the exaggerated accounts that every one makes, according to his own fancy, of the slaughter that has been made among them; and you will be still more surprised if I tell you that, were it not for the combats and four battles we sustained, and for the batteries which failed, or (to speak more properly) which were unskilfully made, we should not have lost fifty men from the commencement of the siege to this day. I have written to M. de Larche, that if he persists in not coming here, let who will raise money upon the Poleagers for me, I will not do it! And I renounce—as I informed you a month ago—meddling directly or indirectly with anything whatever that may relate to your administration, civil or military. For I would rather go and command the Caffres of Madagascar than remain in this Sodom, which the fire of the English must sooner or later destroy, if that from heaven should not. I have the honour to be, &c., "LALLY.

"P.S.—I think it necessary to apprise you that, as M. des Soupirs has refused to take upon him the command of this army, which I have offered him, and which he is empowered to accept, by having received from the Court a duplicate of my commission, you must necessarily, with the council, take it upon you. For my part, I undertake only to bring it back either to Arcot or Sadraste. Send, therefore, your orders, or come yourselves to command it, for I shall quit it upon my arrival there.—L."

Though his cannonade had been diminished to only six pieces, Lally had advanced his sap along the seashore by cutting a trench about ten feet broad, with traverses to cover the soldiers, until he embraced the whole north-east angle of the covered way, from whence the Regiment de Lorraine, by a well directed mousquetade, drove the besieged in disorder. An attempt to open a passage into the ditch by mining failed, for the mine was sprung without effect.

Meanwhile Major Caillaud and Captain Preston, a Scottish officer, with a body of sepoys, another of Indian cavalry, and some European soldiers drawn from the British garrisons at Trinchinopoli and Chingalaput (which Clive when a captain had taken from the French in 1752), hovered on the roads a few miles from Madras, blocking up the avenues, cutting off succour and provisions from Pondicherry, thus compelling Lally four times (as his letter states) to drive them back by detachments. These measures successfully retarded the siege until the 16th February, when, at the very time he was preparing for a grand assault at point of the bayonet, his Britannic Majesty's ship *Queensberry*, commanded by Captain Kempenfeldt, the Company's ship *Revenge*, and four other vessels, having on board 600 men of the 79th, or Colonel Draper's regiment, with a great supply of provision of every kind, came to anchor in the roadstead, and the troops were immediately disembarked and marched into Madras. The rage and mortification of Lally were now complete!

He had encountered innumerable difficulties occasioned by the scarcity of money and munition, by the wretched supplies of the Government commissaries and contractors, by the conduct of Count d'Aché and others, by the sinking of his soldiers' courage before the obstinate defence of the besieged; and now, with Kempenfeldt's arrival all hope of success vanished. After maintaining a smart cannonade until the night of the 16th closed over Madras, Lally abandoned his trenches, and was compelled by scarcity of horses to leave forty pieces of cannon behind him: he blew up the powder-mills of Ogmore and retreated into Arcot.

Soon after this siege had been abandoned, the British received from home another reinforcement of 600 infantry, and on the 16th April the main body of their troops, which had been centred at Madras for its protection, took the field in three divisions against Lally, under the command of Major Brereton. The Chevalier des Soupirs felt the first brunt of this movement, being driven by the Major from Conjeveram, a large and handsome town, principally inhabited by Brahmins, which lies forty-four miles from Madras, and had the chief manufacture of turbans and red handkerchiefs. Major Forde, with another division, took by assault the town of Masulipatnam, the governor of which, M. Moracin, was still absent, as before related. The garrison, which was commanded by the Marquis de Conflans, had been weakened by the withdrawal of its soldiers to the siege of Madras. Thus the commerce of Britain secured a sea-coast of at least eight hundred miles in length along a country teeming with wealth and commerce, while that of France was almost confined to the narrow limits of Pondicherry. The third division of British under Colonel Clive was meanwhile advancing from the province of Bengal to assist the Rajah of Visanapore, who had driven the French out of Vizagapatam, and hoisted thereon the British flag.

The first severe shock sustained by the arms of Britain in the East was given by the gallant Lally in person. Sensible of the importance of such a place as Conjeveram, which with the fort of Chingelpel, commanded all the adjacent country and secured the British conquests to the northward, he marched towards Major Brereton, and took up a strong position at Vandivash. There he cantoned his troops until the month of September, when Brereton, on receiving 300 men under Major Gordon, from Colonel Coote's Bengalese force, resolved on beating up the French in their quarters. Accordingly, on the 14th March he advanced from Conjeveram, at the head of 400 European infantry, 7000 sepoys, seventy European and 300 native horsemen, with fourteen pieces of artillery.

After capturing the fort of Trivitar, he advanced against the village of Vandivash, where Lally, although still struggling with a severe illness, had formed a strong intrenched camp, the lines of which were protected by a redoubt commanded by a rajah, and mounted with twenty pieces of cannon worked by Indians, under the directions of a single French cannonier.

At two on the morning of the 30th September the British attacked the village on three points, and on all with equal fury and determination. The French infantry, 1000 strong, made a spirited resistance; and the moment daylight broke, the guns of the rajah poured a storm of grape-shot upon the ranks of the enemy.

Lally did all that ability and gallantry could inspire to animate his troops; but being deserted by his black pioneers, who (like those of Brereton) fled at the moment of attack, the French were discouraged, and retired beyond a deep dry ditch, from whence the regiments of Lally and Lorraine made a succession of desperate sallies on the British, until, seeing that the column of Anglo-Indian horse were watching for an opportunity to fall upon his flanks, Lally, to preserve his little force from utter ruin, brought up his reserve to cover the retreat, and fell back, after the loss of many gallant chevaliers and 400 soldiers. Brereton and Gordon remained encamped in sight of the fort for some days; but the approach of the rainy season compelled them to retire into Conjeveram.

The Fort of Vandivash was afterwards garrisoned by French and sepoys, while another column of King Louis's troops assembled in Arcot, under Brigadier-General the Marquis de Bussy, who endeavoured to levy as many sepoys as possible. These native troops, whose now familiar name is derived from *Sepahe*, the Indian word for a feudatory chief or military tenant, have ever made excellent soldiers, having an inborn predilection for arms. The success at Vandivash, for giving the British even a *check* was now deemed almost equal to a victory, made Lally conceive the idea of besieging Trinchinopoli; but again the folly or the treachery of the naval Chef d'Escadre baffled his intentions.

After having a third engagement with the British fleet on the 4th September, when with eleven ships of the line he was as usual defeated by Admiral Pocock with nine, the Count d'Aché, on the 17th, reached the roads of Pondicherry, from whence he wrote to the Count de Lally, then in position before Vandivash, offering to place at his disposal, for the king's service, 800,000 livres in piastres and diamonds, being the plunder of a British ship which he had taken at sea, and which he begged the lieutenant-general to receive as part payment of the two millions so improperly detained in the preceding year at the Isle of France. He concluded his dispatch by a notification that on the following day, the 18th September, he would sail towards Madagascar.

At this time, when British valour was bearing all

before it; when the powerful fortress of Karical (which the King of Tanjowar had ceded to France in 1739) was about to fall, and he lost, with all the fertile district around it; when the united fleets of Admirals Pocock, K.B., and Sir Samuel Cornish were sweeping along the shores of the Carnatic, reducing many places of minor importance, and by their cannon everywhere beating down the *Fleur-de-lys* of France; when Colonel Eyre Coote was pressing the French and their allies along the frontier of Bengal, and when the Prince of Vizanapore and other native rajahs were in open revolt against King Louis,—the announcement of the Chef d'Escadre filled the colonists with fear and confusion. Indignant and exasperated, Lally would have left the camp and sought Count d'Aché in person; but at that crisis, being so reduced by sickness that he could not quit his bed, he sent a deputation of field officers to represent the necessity of his remaining in the immediate vicinity of the Carnatic coast; of his co-operating with the land forces, and conjuring him by all means to suspend the execution of a design so pregnant with disaster to the Indian interests of his Most Christian Majesty. But nothing that these officers could urge, or their united eloquence suggest, would avert the fatal purpose of the Count d'Aché, who put to sea, and once more left the disheartened soldiers of King Louis to their fate.

Immediately upon this Lally assembled the Council and drew up a solemn PROTEST against the unaccountable conduct and sudden departure of the Chef d'Escadre and his fleet, proclaiming that he—and *he alone*—would be responsible if Pondicherry, the capital of French India, with all its territory fell into the hands of the British army and revolted rajahs. The "protest" was dated on the 17th of September, 1759, and was unanimously signed in the Hall of Fort Lewis, at Pondicherry, by Lally himself and the following gentlemen:—

"Duval de Leyrit, Renaut, Barthelmy, Chevalier des Soupirs, Michael Lally, Bussy, Du Bois, Carrière, Verdières, Duré, Gaddeville, Du Passage, Beausset, Renaut, De la Salle, Guillart, Porcher, Père Dominique, *Capucin Prêtre* de la Paroisse de Notre Dame des Anges, F. S. Lavacier, Supérieur Général des Jesuites Français dans les Indes, L. Rathon, Supérieur Général des Missions Etrangères, Poitier de Lorme, Duchatel, Audouart, Aimar, Combaut d'Authenil, Goupil, Keisses, J. C. Bon, De Wilst, Banal, Rauly, Termelin, Sainte Paul, J. B. Launay, Deshayes, Fischer, Du Laurent, Audager du Petit Val, D'Arcy, Medin, Dioré, Bertrand, Legris, Miran, Bourville, F. Nicolas, Du Plan, De Laval, Borée, D. l'Arché, Bayelleon de Guillette."

The count had already sailed; but strong currents and adverse winds, however, met his fleet, which was driven far to the north; thus the protest of Lally overtook him at sea. Influenced by its tenor, he returned to Pondicherry, and after remaining one week in the roadstead, again departed for his favourite island of Madagascar, and for *sixteen months* Lally and his soldiers heard no more of him.

The Governor and Council of the British India Company at Madras having heard that Lally had sent a detachment of his forces southward and threatened Trinchinopoli, determined that Colonel Eyre Coote, who had recently arrived in the East, should take the field and drive it back.

The French officers had been fortunate in acquiring the favour of many of the Indian chiefs. Thus in 1755 the King of Travancore employed M. de Launay to discipline 10,000 Naires of Malabar in the mode of the European infantry; and thus M. de Lally, who had won the alliance of Salubetzingue, sovereign of the whole country, expected the arrival of his brother Bassuletzingue with a column of 12,000 Indians. When more than a hundred miles distant from the French army, the prince sent a Rissaldar to request that an officer of rank with a body of French should be sent to facilitate their junction. Lally immediately despatched the Marquis de Bussy on this service, with a detachment which joined the prince beneath the walls of Arcot. In twelve days all that was necessary might have been done; but the loitering marquis spun out the time to no less than two-and-forty.

While Lally was totally unable to account for his absence, a dangerous ferment arose in the camp of Prince Bassuletzingue, there being no pay for his soldiers, as M. d'Aché's diamonds were yet unsold; and during the delay the British troops under Colonel Coote (aware that Lally could not begin a campaign without cavalry) suddenly made themselves masters of Vandivash on the 30th November, after having breached the walls. Thus, by the indolence of M. de Bussy one of the most important fortresses on the coast was lost, and its garrison of 900 men taken, with forty-nine pieces of cannon and a vast quantity of ammunition.

On the 10th December they took Cosangoli, which was bravely defended by a mixed garrison of French and sepoys under Colonel O'Kennely, an Irish officer; who, after his guns were dismounted, capitulated and marched out with all the honours of war. With 100 Frenchmen he joined Lally, but 500 of his sepoys were disarmed and dismissed by Coote.

The double and dangerous success of this vigilant and enterprising officer compelled Lally to attempt a decisive demonstration for the recapture of Vandivash; but Coote, who had completely superseded Brereton in the command, was an officer who ably defended the conquests his bravery had made.

Having now somewhat recovered his health and strength, on the 10th January, 1760, the Lieutenant-General du Roi marched towards the captured fortress at the head of 2200 Frenchmen, and about 10,000 native troops. Among the latter were 1800 blacks called the Regiment de Bussy, 300 Caffres, and 2000 cavalry obtained from a Mahratta chief, with whom Lally had concluded a treaty, as soon as he found himself disappointed by Prince Bassuletzingue. They were all clothed and armed after the picturesque fashion of their native country (which extends across the whole peninsula of Hindostan) and were led by a Rissaldar, or commander of independent horse. He had twenty-five pieces of cannon with him.

He came in sight of the British on the banks of the

Poliar, a broad and sandy river, the bed of which was quite dry; though in the middle of October, when the winter usually commences, and the rain descends in torrents, the river is sometimes half-a-mile broad, and flows towards the ocean with the greatest fury. There the adverse hosts hovered in sight of each other, until after succeeding in destroying some magazines which were in Colonel Coote's rear (the loss of which prevented his troops from acting in the field for some days after), Lally with his 12,000 men suddenly invested Vandivash, against which his batteries opened with such effect, that a broad and practicable breach was soon made in the outer bastion, and now it was hoped that by one bold assault the captured fortress would be re-won, and with it the entire disputed territory.

But at the very time when Lally was about to lead on the assault, Coote with 1700 European and 3000 black troops, fourteen pieces of cannon, and one howitzer, came suddenly upon his rear to relieve the garrison.

Exposed to the cannon of the fort on one side, and to the troops of Coote on the other, Lally found himself critically situated; but, turning like a lion at bay, he drew off from his trenches, and rapidly formed in order of battle to face this new enemy, on the 21st of January.

Both armies were in high spirits and eager to engage.

About nine in the morning they were two miles apart. Coote having advanced with his cavalry and five companies of sepoys, Lally sent forward his Mahratta horse to meet them; but these, on being galled by two pieces of cannon, retired with precipitation. During this the colonel had succeeded in completely reconnoitring the position of Count Lally, whose forces were ably and judiciously placed, till the British made a movement to the right, which obliged him to alter and extend his left flank.

While the lines were three-quarters of a mile apart the cannonading began on both sides, and was continued with deadly precision and effect until noon, when Lally sent forward a small party of his European cavalry to charge the British left. A few companies of sepoys and two guns sent forward by Coote soon drove these in rear of their own army, and as the forces still continued approaching, by one o'clock the roar of musketry became general along both lines from flank to flank, and that broad plain on which a cloudless sun was shining became shrouded in snow-white smoke.

Undaunted by the cowardice of his cavalry, the hot-blooded Lally now threw himself into the line of his infantry, and at the head of the Regiment of Lorraine fell impetuously upon the British. Colonel Coote was on foot and at the head of his own regiment to receive them.

After giving and receiving two discharges of musketry, the Regiment de Lorraine rushed on with a fury that threatened to sweep all before it. Lally was in front, sword in hand; the bayonets crossed—the *British line was broken;* but though a momentary confusion followed, it was not driven back. A series of bloody single combats ensued, with the charged bayonet and clubbed musket; but these were of brief duration; for in three minutes the Regiment of Lorraine was broken in turn, routed, and driven back in headlong confusion, over a field strewed with their own killed and wounded. The explosion of a tumbril in rear of the French line created an additional confusion, of which Coote lost not a moment in taking advantage.

He ordered Major Brereton to advance with the regiment of Colonel Draper (who had returned to Europe for the benefit of his health), and by wheeling to the right to fall on the French left, and seize a fortified post which they were on the point of abandoning.

This service was performed with the utmost bravery; the French left was routed and driven pell-mell upon their centre. Draper's regiment was the 79th, not the present *Cameron Highlanders,* but a corps which was disbanded in 1763. All had now become confusion among the enemy, but the gallant and accomplished Brereton fell mortally wounded.

"Follow—follow!" he exclaimed to some soldiers who loitered near him; "follow and leave me to my fate!"

He soon expired; led by Major Monsoon, the regiment advanced impetuously on, and after a vain and desperate attempt, made by the Chevalier de Bussy, with Lally's regiment, to repel it, the French and their allies were completely routed in every direction by two o'clock in the afternoon. The Regiment de Lally was almost cut to pieces; the horse of Brigadier-General M. de Bussy was shot under him, and he was taken prisoner by Major Monsoon, to whom he surrendered his sword.

Lally having brought up his fugitive cavalry, formed them in rear of his infantry, and enabled these to make a secure though precipitate retreat, leaving on the field a thousand men killed and wounded, with fifty prisoners, including the Marquis de Bussy, Quartermaster-General le Chevalier de Gadville, Lieutenant-Colonel Murphy, three captains, five lieutenants, many other officers, and twenty-two pieces of cannon.

Coote lost 260 killed and wounded. Among the former was the gallant Brereton. Maréchal Charles Grant, Vicomte de Vaux, affirms that the losses were equal on both sides.

Covering the foot by the cavalry, Lally conducted his routed forces with considerable skill and good order to Pondicherry, while Coote lost not a moment in pursuing the advantage he had gained. Dispatching the Baron Vasserot towards that place with 1000 horse and 300 sepoys, and with orders to ravage and lay waste all the French territory in and around it, he advanced in person against Chittipett, a small town and fort in the Carnatic, which, after a defence of two days, was surrendered on the 29th January, 1760, by the Chevalier de Tillie, who with his garrison remained prisoners of war.

On the 2nd February he reduced the fort of Timmary on the Coromandel coast, and pushing on to Arcot, the capital, opened his batteries and dug his approaches within sixty yards of the glacis. The garrison, which consisted of 250 French with 300 sepoys, defended the place until the 10th, when they surrendered as prisoners of war, delivering up twenty-two pieces of cannon and a large store of warlike munition.

THE COUNT DE LALLY.

Thus the campaign ended gloriously for Britain by the conquest of Arcot, and by hemming up the indefatigable but most unfortunate Lally in the fortifications of Pondicherry, the capital of French India, which was soon fated to become the last scene of his valour and achievement.

Surat, a place of great consequence on the coast of Malabar, was taken by a Bombay detachment, which destroyed the French factory. The English had obtained a settlement there from King Jehan Jeer in the year 1020 of the Hijerah. By sea the operations had been carried on with equal vigour. On the 4th September, 1759, an engagement had taken place between the fleets of Count d'Aché and Admiral Pocock, who obliged the former to sheer off with great loss. In April, the fortress of Karical had fallen, and by that time Admirals Pocock and Cornish had united their fleets in the roads of Pondicherry, within the gates of which nearly all that remained of the French forces in India were shut up, or encamped four leagues in front of it, under the command of the Count de Lally, barring the way by which he knew the British would march to an attack.

In Karical 174 pieces of cannon were taken, and to add to the disasters of the French, one of their 64-gun ships (the *Haerlem*) was burned in the roads of Pondicherry by the British cruisers.

Encouraged by his long career of success, and by the pecuniary and political embarrassments of his enemy, Colonel Coote resolved on investing Pondicherry. The approach of the rainy season, together with the well-known reputation for skill, bravery, and resolution enjoyed by the general of the now almost ruined French India Company, caused a regular siege to be considered impracticable; "it was therefore determined," says the Sieur Charles Grant, "to block up the place by sea and land."

Lally had only 1500 Frenchmen with him; these were the remnants of nine different corps of the King's and India Company's Service; the cavalry, artillery, and invalids of the latter; the Creole volunteers of the Isle de

Bourbon; the king's artillery; the Regiments of Lally, Lorraine, Mazinis, and the battalion of India.

The British armaments on the coast were now much more considerable. On the land were four battalions of the line, and by sea were seventeen sail of the line, carrying 1038 pieces of cannon, the smallest being three 50-gun ships.

As the fortress of Pondicherry was as impregnable as nature and art could make it, Coote was perfectly aware that it could only be reduced by the most severe famine. It was also his opinion that with such an antagonist as Arthur Lally, a formal siege with regular approaches would prove perfectly futile with any force he could assemble; for, in addition to his French comrades, Lally had a strong force of armed sepoys, and a vast store of warlike munition, including nearly 700 pieces of cannon, and many millions of ball cartridges, all made up for service. The ramparts bore 508 pieces (independent of mortars), the walls were five miles in circumference, and had a deep broad moat before them. There were six gates and thirteen bastions. The cavalry of the French India Company openly deserted in great numbers, and were received with rewards by Colonel Coote. This exasperated Lally so much, that he erected gibbets all round Pondicherry in order to deter others from leaving the town or the lines before it.

To victual the place completely for the inhabitants and his garrison was the first care of Lally; for the town was large, and possessed an overplus of population, which gave him infinite cause for trouble and anxiety.

Pondicherry was surrounded by a number of forts, the defence of which, in all former sieges, had occasioned the inhabitants the utmost difficulty; but these were rapidly reduced, as all the adjacent country was in the hands of the British. The fleet of Sir Samuel Cornish came to anchor on the 17th March, and while Coote approached nearer by land, Lally, in order to retard him, retired from position to position, bravely disputing every inch of ground, until, in front of Pondicherry, he formed his famous lines, which he defended for three months with admirable skill and valour, thereby gaining sufficient time to have victualled the town for the half of a year. While thus holding the foe in check, he concluded a treaty with the Rajah of Mysore, who pledged himself to supply Pondicherry with provisions; but failed to perform his promise, and departed with his people. A short time afterwards, Lally resolved to attempt a *sortie*, and on the night of the 2nd September, 1760, he made a furious attack on Coote's advanced posts, but was repulsed with great loss, and had seventeen pieces of cannon taken. Coote lost but a few privates

The last of the fortified boundary, or chain of redoubts, was carried by storm on the 10th September; the French were driven in, and Coote had forty killed and seventy wounded; Major Monsoon had one of his legs torn off by a cannon-shot.

A body of Scottish Highlanders, who had just been landed from the *Sandwich* East Indiaman, behaved with their accustomed valour in this affair. Passing Draper's grenadiers in their eagerness to get at the enemy, they threw down their muskets, and with their bonnets in one hand, and their claymores in the other, hewed a passage through a jungle hedge, fell with a wild cheer upon the soldiers of Lally, and cut a whole company to pieces. Only five Highlanders and two grenadiers were shot. The Highlanders were fifty in number, and were commanded by a Captain Morrison. They belonged to the 89th Highland Regiment, which had been raised among the Gordon clan in the preceding year.

After that night, the operations of Lally were confined to the walls of Pondicherry.

Of the guns taken by the Highlanders, seven were found to be 18-pounders, loaded to the muzzle with square bars of iron six inches long, jagged pieces of metal, stones and bottles. They were on Lally's strongest battery, which was formed before a thick wood, one mile in front of Pondicherry, which could no longer have any succour from the seaward, as the Chef d'Escadre had sailed for Brest, where he arrived in April, 1761. Thus a 54-gun ship, a 36-gun frigate, and four Indiamen were left behind, and hopelessly shut up in the roadstead.

In the month of October, Admiral Stevens, who had

relieved Admiral Cornish, sailed with his portion of the fleet for Trincomalee to refit, leaving five sail of the line, under Captain Haldane, to blockade Pondicherry, while Colonel Coote pressed on the investment by land. By their dispositions and vigilance, the dense population became distressed for provisions even before a siege was formally begun, and while the incessant rains rendered a closer conflict impracticable. The blockade was supported by a number of batteries judiciously posted; by these the garrison was harassed on one hand, while their supplies were cut off on the other; and these posts were gradually pushed nearer and nearer to the town, notwithstanding the deluge of rain, which had swollen the broad currents of the Chonenbar and the Gingi, two rivers that unite near it, and roll their tides together to the sea.

On the 26th November, the rains abated, and Colonel Coote directed his engineers to erect batteries in other places; from whence, without being exposed, they could enfilade the works of the garrison, which was strictly closed in, and by the failure of the Mysorean rajah to fulfil his promise, was now enduring the utmost privations from scarcity of food. Lally was compelled to turn out of the town a vast multitude of native women and children; but Coote drove them back again, and, as the batteries were firing at the time, a great number of these poor wretches were slain or severely wounded.

During these operations, Captain Sir Charles Chalmers of Cults, a gallant Scottish baronet who served in Coote's artillery, died of fatigue. He possessed only the honours of his family, their estates having been forfeited for adherence to the house of Stuart about fifteen years before.

On the night of the 7th October, the armed boats of the British fleet were pulled with muffled oars into the harbour, and two ships were cut out, under the very muzzles of Lally's cannon; but not before he had killed and wounded thirty officers and men. The prizes were the *Balcine* and *Hermione*, a frigate and a valuable Indiaman. In this affair Lieutenant Owen, of H. B. M. ship *Sunderland*, lost an arm.

THE COUNT DE LALLY.

To encourage the British, the Nabob of Arcot promised to divide among them fifty lacs of rupees on the day Pondicherry should surrender, and, as each lac was valued at 12,600*l.* sterling, the greatest enthusiasm prevailed among the officers, soldiers, and seamen: moreover, as all the French colonists who fled from other places had stored up their effects in Pondicherry, the treasure there was reputed to be enormous.

On the 26th September, Coote's forces had been mustered at 3500 English and Scottish Highlanders, with 7000 sepoys, all of whom were strongly intrenched, having taken Arcupong, Villa Nova, and every French outpost, while fifteen sail of the line and three frigates swept the ocean to the seaward, cutting of all succour; indeed, none was ever afforded to the unfortunate Lally save by the Dutch settlers, who sent two unpretending boats; but even these were observed, and on being seized were found to contain 20,000*l.* in cash and many valuable stores. Every day provisions were becoming more and more scarce, and notwithstanding the weakness of his garrison, Lally was compelled to select 200 French and 300 black soldiers, whom he contrived to despatch towards Gingi for succour; but they were all cut off, and thus he found himself worse than before.

The scarcity increased, and now gaunt starvation and death met the eye on every hand; a thousand scenes of horror and distress occurred daily within the walls of Pondicherry. The soldiers of Lally and the citizens were compelled to eat the flesh of elephants, camels, and troop-horses; after which dogs, cats, and even rats were devoured. The count was frequently implored to surrender, but having now become sullen, revengeful, and determined, his lofty pride made him resolve to perish among the ruins of the French Indian capital, but never *capitulate.*

Twenty-four rupees were given for a small dog, and in some instances as many half-crowns.

On the 5th November, Lally dispatched a 54-gun ship, *La Compagnie des Indes*, to Trincomalee, a Danish settlement, for provisions; but after eluding the watchful blockading fleet, she was taken at sea by H. M. ships *Medway* and *Newcastle*, and with her loss all hopes of succour died away.

On the 9th November, Colonel Coote erected a *ricochet* battery for four pieces of cannon, at 1400 yards from the glacis (for the information of unmilitary readers, we may mention that *ricochet firing* means when cannon or mortars are loaded with small charges, elevated from five to twelve degrees, so that when discharged from the parapet, the shot may *roll* along the opposite rampart); this was more with a view to harass the French than damage their works; but meanwhile four other batteries were erecting in different places to rake and batter them.

One for four guns, called *the Prince of Wales' Battery*, was formed near the sea-beach, on the north, to enfilade the great street which intersects the White Town.

A second, for four guns and two mortars, was formed to enfilade the counterguard, before the north-west bastion, at a thousand yards' distance, and in honour of the "Butcher of Culloden," was called the *Duke of Cumberland's Battery*.

A third, called *Prince Edward's*, for two guns, faced the southern works at 1200 yards' distance, to enfilade the streets from south to north, and cross the fire of the northern battery.

A fourth, on the south-west, at 1100 yards' distance, and called *Prince William's Battery*, was mounted with two guns and one mortar, to destroy the cannon on the redoubt of San Thomé.

Lally beheld all these preparations with calmness, and by inspiring his soldiers with something of his own fierce ardour, laboured to retard the work of the besiegers, whose batteries commenced a simultaneous fire at midnight on the 8th December. Lally's cannoniers replied with the utmost vigour; they slew a master gunner, a subahdar of sepoys, and wounded a great many more.

On the 1st of January, a violent tempest of wind, accompanied by torrents of rain, had almost ruined the works of Coote, and blown the fleet off the coast. The French became elated by the delay this occasioned, and the consequent prospect of relief; but the sudden reappearance of

Admiral Stevens with his vessels caused their hopes to fade away; and once more this little band of starving and desperate men betook them to their muskets and lintstocks; for, still pressing on, Coote, on the 29th, formed a fifth battery, called *the Hanover*, at only 450 yards' distance, for ten cannon and three mortars, which opened a fire of shot and shell against the counter-guard and curtain.

At last, being driven frantic by their sufferings, the soldiers and citizens demanded that the place should be surrendered. Lally was immovable, but yet feeling keenly for what they endured, dissatisfied with the state of the French Indian affairs, and greatly exasperated by the disorderly conduct of his troops, and the baseness of their commissaries, he frequently burst into passionate exclamations which showed the keenness of his agitation.

"Hell has spewed me into this country of wickedness," he said on one occasion, "and like Jonas I wait until the whale shall receive me into its belly!"

"I will go among the Caffres, rather than remain longer in this Sodom," he exclaimed on another occasion.

But, nevertheless, he still defended the town like a good soldier, and on the disappearance of the British fleet during the storm, wrote the following letter to M. de Raymond, the Resident at Pullicot:—

"M. Raymond, the English squadron is no more! Out of twelve ships they had in our roads seven are lost, crews and all; four others are dismasted, and it appears that only one frigate has escaped, therefore lose not an instant to send us chelingoes upon chelingoes loaded with rice. The Dutch have nothing to fear now; besides —according to the law of nations—they are only to send us no provisions *themselves*, and we are no longer blocked up by sea.

"The saving of Pondicherry has once already been in your power. If you miss the present, it will be entirely your own fault. Don't forget some small chelingoes— offer great rewards. I expect 17,000 Mahrattas in four days; in short, risk all! attempt! force all! but send us some rice, should it be but a half garse at a time.

"LALLY.

"Pondicherry, 2nd January, 1761."

The British fleet suffered considerably; many vessels which had to cut their cables, were totally dismasted, and the *Queensberry, Newcastle*, and *Protector* were driven on shore; while *Le Duc d'Acquitaine* of sixty-four guns (French prize), commanded by Sir William Hewitt, Bart., and the *Sunderland* of sixty guns, commanded by the Hon. James Colville, both foundered, and all on board perished. Captain Colville was the son of Lord Colville, of Culross, a Scottish peer, who died on the Carthagena expedition in 1740, and brother of Alexander Lord Colville, who in 1764 was Commodore in North America.

On the reappearance of Admiral Cornish with more of the fleet, the hope of the French sank again, and Lally, enraged at what he considered the mutinous repining of his soldiers, met their remonstrances with turbulence and contempt, and by an unwise, and perhaps overstrained exercise of authority, at this fatal and desperate crisis, most unfortunately contrived to render himself unpopular with the Governor, the Council, and the proud chevaliers of old France, who officered his little band of troops.

Still, however, the siege was pressed, and still the defence went on.

On the 5th January, Coote attacked the redoubt of San Thomé, sword in hand, at the head of a body of Scottish Highlanders and English grenadiers, and won it, thus silencing four 28-pounders; but two days afterwards, Lally retook it by 300 grenadiers, from the sepoys who were left in charge of it.

On the 13th Coote sent 700 Europeans, 400 Lascars, and a company of pioneers under a major, to erect another battery of eleven guns and three mortars. Under the clear splendour of an Oriental moon, these works were carried on within 500 yards of the walls; and this *Batterie Royale* was permitted to be erected without molestation, for in their sullen despair the garrison never fired a shot at it. On the 14th the *Hanover Battery* ruined the north-west bastion, and on the following day the *Batterie Royale* beat down the ravelin at the Madras gate; thus by the 15th of January a great and practicable breach was effected, and the cannon of the gallant Lally were silenced or dismounted.

In the evening a parley was beat, and four envoys came from the ruined walls towards the British trenches. These were Colonel Duré (Durie?) of the French Royal Artillery, Father Lavacer, Superior of the Jesuits, and two civilians. These were unprovided by "any authority from the Governor," says Vicomte de Vaux; but Colonel Coote, in his dispatch to Mr. Pitt, affirms that they came direct from Lally with proposals for delivering up the garrison. In the town, at that moment, there were only three days provisions of the wretched kind described; thus the extremity of famine would admit of no hesitation. Rendered ungovernable by what they had endured, Lally's officers declared the defence to be frantic obstinacy, and murmuring aloud, also averred that illness, pride, and the climate had disordered his imagination; and that it was criminal rather than valiant to defend an untenable fortress.

The following were the proposals of Lally, presented by Colonel Duré to Colonel Coote:—

"The troops of the king and Company, by want of provisions, will surrender themselves prisoners of war to his Britannic Majesty, on terms of the cartel, which I claim equally for all the inhabitants of Pondicherry, as well as for the exercise of the Roman religion, the religious houses, hospitals, chaplains, surgeons, serjeants, reserving and referring myself to the decision of our two Courts, in proportion to the violation of a treaty so solemn. (He refers to the treacherous capture of Chandernagore.)

"Accordingly M. Coote may take possession of the Villenour Gate at eight o'clock to-morrow morning; and after to-morrow, at the same hour, that of Fort St. Lewis

"I demand, merely from a principle of justice and humanity, that the mother and sisters of Raza Sahib may be permitted to seek an asylum where they please, or that they remain prisoners among the English, and not be delivered into the hands of Mohammed Ali Khan, which are still red with the blood of the husband and father, which he has spilt, to the shame of those who gave them up to him; but not less to the shame of the commander of the English army, who should not have allowed such a piece of barbarity to be committed in his camp.

"As I am tied up by the cartel, in the declaration which I make to M. Coote, I consent that the Council of Pondicherry may make their own representations to him with regard to what may concern their own private interests as well as the interests of the inhabitants of the colony.

"Done at Fort Lewis, Pondicherry, 15th day of January, 1761.   LALLY."

To these the Colonel replied briefly by stating that the capture of Chandernagore was beyond his cognizance, and had no relation to Pondicherry; that he merely required the soldiers of its garrison to yield as prisoners of war, promising that they should be treated with every honour and humanity; that he would send the grenadiers of his own regiment to receive possession of the Villenour Gate, and that of Fort St. Lewis; and that according to the kind and humane request of M. Lally, the mother and sisters of Raza Sahib should be escorted to Madras, and on no account be permitted to fall into the hands of their enemy, the Nabob Mohammed Ali Khan.

To eight articles proposed by Father Lavacer, Superior of the Jesuits, requiring that the inhabitants should be treated in every respect like subjects of his Britannic Majesty; that they should have full liberty to exercise the Catholic religion; that the churches should be respected; that all public papers should be sent to France; and that forty-one soldiers of the Volunteers of Bourbon should be permitted to return to their homes—Colonel Coote declined to make any reply.

At eight o'clock on the morning of the 16th July, Lally with a bitter heart ordered the standard of France to be hauled down on Fort St. Lewis, and at that houi Coote's grenadiers received the Villenour Gate from the Regiment de Lally, while those of the 79th Regiment took possession of the citadel.* Thus fell Pondicherry after a blockade and siege which Lally's skill and valour had protracted under a thousand difficulties for the long period of eight months, against forces treble in number to those he commanded.

Notwithstanding his fallen condition and the severe effects of a long illness, aggravated by the sultry climate, by bodily sufferings and anxiety, Lally marched out of the citadel with the air of a conqueror. " He is now as proud and haughty as ever," says an officer (who beheld him) in a letter to a periodical of the time ; " but his great share of wit, sense, and martial ability are obscured by a savage ferocity, and an undisguised contempt for every person below the rank of general." This writer was ignorant of the high qualities of Lally, and the difficulties with which he had contended, or he would never have written thus.

According to the "*exact state of the troops of his most Christian Majesty, under the command of Lieutenant-General Arthur Count de Lally, when he surrendered at discretion on the* 16*th of January,* 1761," he marched out with the following — a miserable and famished band, hollow-eyed and gaunt—the few survivors of the Indian war :—

  Artillery of Louis XV., officers and men . 83
  The Regiment de Lorraine, ditto . . . 327
  The Regiment de Lally, ditto (of the Irish
    Brigade) 230
  The Regiment of the Marine, ditto . . . 295

* The 79th, or Draper's Regiment, lost in this siege, and encounters before it, thirty-four officers, whose names were inscribed on a beautiful cenotaph, erected on Clifton Downs by Colonel Sir W. Draper and which he dedicated as,
  " Sacred to the Memory of those departed Warriors,
    Of the Seventy-ninth Regiment,
  By whose Valour, Discipline, and Perseverance
The French land Forces in Asia were first withstood and repulsed.

Artillery of the French India Company	94
Cavalry of ditto	15
Volunteers of Bourbon	40
The Battalion d'India	192
Invalides	124

In all there were only 1400. One of their first acts was to cut their commissary to pieces. Among the officers of the king's artillery was Jean Baptiste Louis Romée de l'Isle, the celebrated crystallographer, who was then secretary to a corps of engineers. The quantity of military stores delivered over by Lally to Coote is almost incredible.

There were 671 brass and iron cannon and mortars; 438 mortar-beds and carriages; 84,041 shot and shell, round, double-headed, and grape; 230,580 lbs. of powder; 538,137 rounds of cartridge for arquebuses, muskets, carbines, pistols, and gingals; 910 pairs of pistols; 12,580 other firearms; 4895 swords, bayonets and sabres; 1200 poleaxes, and every other warlike munition in proportion. Tidings of the fall of Pondicherry occasioned the utmost joy in Britain; and on Sunday, the 2nd August, there were prayers and thanksgiving in all the English churches.

On that day Lally arrived at Fort St. George a prisoner of parole. He had begged to be sent to Cudalore that he might have the attendance of French as well as British surgeons; but the Governor of Madras insisted upon his removal to that place, whither he conveyed him in his own palanquin.

A regiment of Highlanders garrisoned Pondicherry, and as Lally had destroyed many of the British fortifications, Colonel—afterwards Sir Eyre—Coote retaliated by blowing up the works and hurling the glacis into the ditch. The plunder acquired amounted to 2,000,000*l.* sterling. The quantity of lead discovered in the stores was immense. Lally found means to convey his own cash and valuables (200,000 pagodas of eight shillings each) out of the garrison, but he was deprived of it by Coote's orders.

The plunder of the magnificent palace was a subject for regret to the officers who beheld it. It had been built by M. Dupleix, a former resident, at the cost of one million. On the same day that Lally surrendered, his Scottish compatriot, M. Law, on whose assistance he had for a time mainly relied, was defeated by Major Carnac.

M. Law was a nephew of the famous financial projector, John Law, of Lauriston, near Edinburgh, who, in 1720, was Premier of France, and Comptroller-General of Finance—the same whose desperate schemes brought the kingdom to the verge of bankruptcy. M. Law had made himself useful to the Schah Zaddah, son of the late Mogul, in supporting the young prince's hereditary claims, and enforcing his authority on the provinces of the empire. With 200 Frenchmen (principally fugitives from Lally's outposts) he persuaded the schah to turn his arms against Bengal; and accordingly the young and rash prince entered that rich and fertile province at the head of 80,000 Indians, whose operations were directed by Law, and certain chevaliers his friends. In the eye of the British (who had then become the arbiters of Oriental thrones), the presence of the Scottish refugee and his followers was more prejudicial to the title of Zaddah than any other objection, and they joined the Subah of Bengal to oppose his progress. A battle ensued at Guya, when Major Carnac, with 500 British, 2500 sepoys, and 20,000 blacks, cut the vast force of the young prince to pieces, and took prisoner M. Law, with sixty French officers.

Soon after the fall of Pondicherry, the French settlement of Mahé, on the coast of Malabar, was reduced by Major Hector Munro, of the 89th Highlanders, who captured there 200 pieces of cannon, and thus the whole commerce of the mighty peninsula of India, from the point of the Carnatic to the banks of the Ganges, fell under the dominion of Britain, together with the extensive trade of the vast and wealthy provinces of Bengal, Behar, and Orixa.

On the 3rd February, the nabob made his triumphal entry into Pondicherry, seated in a wooden castle on the back of a gigantic elephant, accompanied by twelve of his wives, escorted by British troops and by his own guards armed with lances, bows, and matchlocks.

Ultimately Lally received back his property, to the amount of 100,000*l*. in cash, and being brought to Britain a prisoner of war in H. M. S. *Onslow*, landed in September, 1761. He was confined for a time to a certain limit in Nottinghamshire; and on obtaining leave of George III. to depart, most unfortunately for himself, turned his steps towards France, the land of his father's adoption.

Having given his parole of honour to return whenever the British Government should require his presence, the count, on the 14th October, " after having discharged all his debts to tradesmen and servants" (as the London papers of the time state), sailed for France.

Notwithstanding the long and gallant defence he had maintained at Pondicherry, thus affording the highest proofs of firmness and fidelity, bravery and activity, he was arrested soon after his return, and committed to that prison of so many terrible memories—the Bastille—accused of many grievous things by the Government, which now instituted a severe inquiry into the conduct of the civil and military officials who had commanded in Canada, the Carnatic, and other possessions taken by Britain.

Among the charges brought against Lally were, betraying the interests of King Louis and of the French East India Company; abusing the high authority with which he had been invested; unwarrantable exactions from the subjects of his most Christian Majesty, and from foreigners resident in Pondicherry; for *permitting* that place to fall into the hands of the British; and generally for mismanaging the public affairs committed to his care.

In vain did this brave and unfortunate officer urge his many services, his many wounds, his grey hairs, his health broken by toil, by anxiety, and by a torrid clime, in the cause of France. In vain did he urge the numerous remonstrances he had sent to Paris, and Count d'Aché's detention of M. de Lequille's military chest; that at Madras he had resigned a desperate command, which the Chevalier des Soupirs declined to accept; in vain was the *protest* signed in the hall of Fort St. Lewis adduced to show how his efforts had been baffled, and rendered more than futile, by the insubordination of Count d'Aché; in vain did he explain how the Marquis de Bussy had loitered in Arcot; that he had long and frequently been without pay and without provision for his troops; how the Rajah of Mysore had failed in his promises; how his soldiers had deserted, and how famine in the streets of Pondicherry was a source of deadlier fear than the British cannon-shot; how his detachment sent to Gingi had been cut off to a man; how Chandernagore had been taken by treachery, contrary to the faith of treaties and that neutrality which had subsisted between the French and British in India, and immediately after the former had rendered the latter a signal service in not taking part with the Nabob of Bengal. The weak Government of Louis XV. required a victim to satisfy the people; thus his defence was useless. Brigadier-General the Marquis de Bussy and Admiral Count d'Aché, whose honour and safety were chiefly interested in his condemnation, were the principal witnesses examined against him. He was detained for four years in a close prison, and, according to the cruel and barbarous laws then existing in France, "the bequest of ages of violence and anarchy," was *repeatedly tortured*. Though his infamous judges were convinced of his perfect innocence, yet it was stated that, in consequence of the severe conclusions of the Procureur-General against the Count de Lally, on the night of Sunday, the 4th May, 1763, he was removed from the Bastille to the prison of the Conciergerie, which adjoined the Court of Parliament.

"Though it was but one o'clock in the morning when he arrived at the Conciergerie (to quote the report of his condemnation), he refused to go to bed; and about seven he appeared before his judges. They ordered him to be divested of his red riband and cross, to which he submitted with the most perfect indifference; and he was then placed on the stool to undergo a new course of interrogation."

At that crisis a pang of bitterness shot through his heart; clasping his hands, and raising his eyes—

"My God!" he exclaimed; "oh, my God! is *this the reward* of forty years faithful service as a soldier?"

The interrogatory lasted six hours, and D'Aché and De Bussy were successively examined against him. By nine in the evening the examination was over, and the count was re-conducted to the Bastille, surrounded by guards and several companies of the watch of Paris.

At six o'clock next morning the judges delivered their opinions, which were so various, that the clock of the Conciergerie struck four in the afternoon before they came to a conclusion and pronounced their *arrêt* or decree, which contained a brief recital of the charges against De Lally, without specifying the facts on which they were respectively founded; but for the reparation of which it was declared that he should be stripped of all his civil titles, his military rank, and dignities; that all his property should be confiscated to the king; and that his head should be struck from his body on the public scaffold.

Without emotion the count had heard their sentence, and with the utmost resolution prepared to die; yet he was detained, hovering as it were between life and death, until the morning of the 9th May, 1766, when he was drawn on a hurdle to the *Place de Grève*, and hastily, almost privately, beheaded, with his mouth filled by a wooden gag, to prevent him addressing the people—thus adding another to the many barbarous judicial murders which disgrace the annals of France.

His son, Trophine Gerard, who had been kept at the College of Harcourt in entire ignorance of his birth and of the proceedings against his father, only learned all these secrets when the public interest and commiseration became too great to conceal them longer. On the 9th the poor boy learned that the great General Lally, who was to die, *was his father*. He rushed, as he tells us, to the place of execution to bid this father, so recently found, "an eternal adieu—to let him hear the voice of a son amid the voices of his executioners, and embrace him on the scaffold when he was about to perish;" but he arrived only in time to see the axe descending and his father's blood pouring from a dismembered trunk upon a sanded

EXECUTION OF COUNT DE LALLY.

scaffold. Overcome with horror, Trophine—afterwards the great Count Lally Tollendal—swooned in the street, and was borne away insensible to the College of Harcourt.

Thus in his sixty-fourth year terminated the eventful career of Count Lally, the victim surrendered by a weak and tyrannical ministry to popular clamour, affording by his fate a memorable instance of the injustice, ingratitude, and barbarity of the Court of Versailles.

John Cameron, of Fassifern,
K.T.S.,

COLONEL OF THE GORDON HIGHLANDERS; SLAIN AT QUATRE-BRAS, 1815.

FROM among the many distinguished Scottish officers who served under Wellington, if we could select one for the delineation of his career, it would be John Cameron of the House of Fassifern and Locheil.

This brave soldier was the eldest of the seven children of Ewen Cameron, Laird of Fassifern (*i.e.* the Point of Alders), and his wife, Lucy Campbell, of Barcaldine, whose father succeeded to the estate of Glenure on the death of her uncle, Colin Campbell, who was shot at the Ferry of Ballachulish, in Appin, by Allan Breac Stewart, otherwise known as *Vic Ian, Vic Alaster*,—a crime for which the Laird of Ardsheil was judicially murdered by the Duke of Argyle at the Castle of Inverary.

Ewen Cameron was the son of John *the Tanister*, a younger brother of the great Locheil, who commenced the insurrection of 1745; and it is said that this powerful chief, on being summoned by Prince Charles to attend his memorable landing in Moidart on the 25th July, was predisposed to warn him against the projected rising of the clans.

"If such be your intention, Donald," said John of Fassifern, "*write* your opinion to the Prince, but do not trust yourself within the fascination of his presence. I know you better than you know yourself, and foresee that you will be unable to refuse compliance."

But Locheil preferred an interview with the Prince, and the event proved the truth of Fassifern's prophecy. He joined him immediately with all the clan Cameron, and the gallant revolt of the clans immediately followed. Fassifern was taken prisoner after Culloden, and was long detained in the Castle of Edinburgh; there he was kept so close that the year 1752 arrived, yet he heard nothing of the barbarous execution of his brother, the amiable and unfortunate Dr. Archibald Cameron, until one evening a soldier brought him a kettle with hot water. He took off a paper which was twisted round the handle, and found it to be the "last speech and dying confession, &c., of the traitor Archibald Cameron." He immediately ordered a suit of the deepest mourning, and on appearing in it before the authorities was brutally upbraided by the Lord Justice Clerk for putting on mourning for a traitor.

"Alas!" said Cameron, "that traitor was my dear brother!"

"A rebel!" retorted the judge, scornfully. He was exiled, but afterwards returned to die at Fassifern.

Colonel John Cameron, the grand-nephew of the Jacobite chief, was born in Argyleshire, at the farm of Inverscaddle (a house which belonged to his family before the acquisition of Fassifern), on the 16th of August, 1771, only twenty-five years after the battle of Culloden, and while those inhuman butcheries, for which the name of Cumberland is still abhorred in Scotland, were fresh in the memory of the people. According to the old custom, common to Scotland and Ireland, he was assigned to the care of a foster-mother named M'Millan, who dwelt in Glendescherie, on the shore of Locharkaig. Thus, born and bred among the Gael, while the clans were unchanged and uncorrupted, and when the glens were full of that gallant race, with all their old traditions and historic memories, their military pride, and peculiar prejudices, Cameron was reared as thorough a chieftain as if had lived in the days of James IV. Educated among his native mountains, sharing in the athletic sports of the people, and those in which his foster-brother, Ewan M'Millan, who was a fox-hunter in Croydart, and a year his elder, excelled, young Cameron grew up a handsome and hardy Highlander, and early became distinguished by that proud, fiery, and courageous temperament for which he was so well known among the troops of Lord Hill's division, and which sometimes caused him to set the rules of discipline, and the aristocratic coldness of Wellington, alike at defiance, if they interfered with his native ideas of rank and self-esteem.

In the "Romance of War," a work which has made his name familiar to the reading public, a faithful description of him will be found. He was above the middle height, had a pleasing, open countenance, curly brown hair, and bright blue eyes, which, when he was excited, filled with a dusky fire.

Arms were then the only occupation for a Highland gentleman; and thus in his twenty-second year, on the 8th of February, 1793, he obtained an ensigncy in the 26th, or Cameronian Regiment, commanded by Sir William Erskine. He never joined that corps; but on raising a sufficient number of men in Locheil, procured a lieutenantcy in an independent Highland company then being formed by Capt. A. Campbell, of Ard-chattan. He was gazetted on the 3rd of April; but this company was either disbanded or incorporated with the old 93rd Regiment, to which he was appointed lieutenant on the 30th of October in the same year. He did not join this regiment either, but busied himself in raising a company to procure the rank of captain in a corps of Highlanders, which, in obedience to a *letter of service*, dated 10th February, 1794, the Duke of Gordon was raising for his son, the young Marquis of Huntly, then a captain in the Scottish Regiment of Guards. This battalion was to consist of 46 officers, 64 staff, and 1000 rank and file, to be raised among the clan of Gordon.

From the lands of Fassifern and Locheil Cameron drew a company, principally of his own name and kindred, all hardy and handsome young Highlanders, among whom were his foster-brother, Ewen M'Millan, who never left him; three Camerons, Ewen, Alaster, and Angus, whom he made sergeants; Ewen Kennedy, for whom he procured an ensigncy, and another, who died a lieutenant. With these, all clad in their native tartans, he marched from the Braes of Lochaber to Castle Gordon, in Strath-

spey, where he was introduced to Alexander, Duke of
Gordon, the *Cock o' the North*, by his uncle, the Rev. Dr
Ross, of Kilmanivaig, the worthy author of the statistical
account of that parish. He at once received a company
in the duke's own regiment, to which he was appointed
on the 13th of February, 1794, and with which he attended the grand muster of the whole at Aberdeen on the
24th of June, when the corps was named the *Gordon
Highlanders*, or 100th Regiment, afterwards and now the
92nd. The uniform coats and vests were scarlet, faced
with yellow, and laced with silver to suit the epaulettes.
The kilts and plaids were in one piece, each containing
twelve yards of Gordon tartan; the claymores, dirks,
buckles, and sporrans were mounted with silver; the
bonnets were plumed with black ostrich feathers, and encircled by the old fess checque of the House of Stuart.
The men were all Highlanders; scarcely one of them, and
but very few of the officers, could speak English; the
enthusiasm was so great in Badenoch that, in some
instances, fathers and sons joined its ranks together.

At that time, when the French Revolution menaced
Europe with anarchy, and the Convention declared war
against Britain and Holland, the number of Highlanders
in our service is almost incredible. During a period of
fifty years the clans furnished *eighty-six* battalions of
infantry, some of which were twelve hundred strong.*

How many could the Highlands raise now? Centralization, corruption, and local tyranny of the most infamous
description have turned their beautiful glens into a silent
wilderness, and the very place where Cameron raised his
company of soldiers is now desolate and bare. "I can
point," says the author of a letter to the Marquis of
Breadalbane, on his late ruthless *clearings*, "to a place
where thirty recruits that manned the 92nd in Egypt

* As an example of the number of *officers* belonging to the clans,
who served during the war and escaped its slaughter, we may state
that there were on full and half-pay commissions, in 1816, 22 Buchanans; 67 Camerons; 22 Drummonds; 26 Fergusons; 41 Forbeses;
49 Grahames; 90 Frazers; 96 Grants; 144 M'Leans and M'Kenzies; 248 Campbells; and other names in the same proportion.

came from—men before whom Napoleon's Invincibles bit the dust—and now only *two* families reside there together. I was lately informed by a grazier that on his farm a hundred swordsmen could be gathered at their country's call, and now there are only himself and *two* shepherds."
The brave Gael, who crowded in tens of thousands to the British ranks, saw not the reward that was coming; evictions and wholesale clearings of the Scottish poor were then unknown. God gave the land to the people—they believed it was theirs; but the feudal charters have decided otherwise, and the clans have been swept from Lochness to Locheil, and from Locheil to the shores of Lochlomond. The hills and the valleys are there, but the tribes have departed, and who can restore them?

Cameron of Fassifern embarked with his regiment at Fort George, in Ardersier, for Southampton, where, as kilted corps were unusual then in England, its arrival created a great sensation. From thence the battalion sailed for Gibraltar, under the command of Huntly, its colonel commandant, and disembarked at the Rock on the 27th of October. It was on this occasion that Mrs. Grant, of Laggan, composed her now popular song, "The Blue Bells of Scotland."

At Gibraltar a coolness ensued between Cameron and the marquis, and from that hour they never were friends. The former having had a dispute at the mess with a Captain M'Pherson on some point of Highland etiquette, high words and a duel followed. Captain, afterwards Colonel Mitchel, C.B., and Knight of St. Anne of Russia, was Cameron's second. Happily nothing serious resulted; and next day at the mess Lord Huntly drank wine with them all, begging that in future no more such quarrels might occur, and concluded by saying—

"I may be pardoned in requiring this, as, I believe, all the gentlemen here are the tenants of my father."

"No, marquis," said Fassifern, loftily; "by Heaven, here is one who is no tenant of the house of Gordon."

The young marquis frowned; he did not reply, but never forgot the haughty retort.

In sentiments and character, even in manner, Fassifern

belonged to a past age—to a period of time beyond our
own; for the stern pride, the Spartan spirit of clanship,
with all the wild associations of the Gael, deeply imbued
his mind, and gave a decision to his manner and a freshness to his enthusiasm. Proud and fiery, like all his
race, he had the defect of being quick and hasty in his
speech; but he never called aloud the name of an officer
on parade, though more than one was reprehended by
him in terms of severity, which, when the gust of passion
was past, his generous spirit told him had been too great.
He was a rigid disciplinarian, strict even to a fault, and
yet withal he possessed a charm which won him the
affection and respect of all his regiment. To English
officers who did not understand him, to Wellington in
particular, his pride seemed perhaps mere petulance, and
his Highland chivalry (the result of his education) eccen-
tricity : but of these more anon.

After receiving its colours on Windmill Hill, the regiment embarked for Corsica, and on the 11th of July,
1795, landed at Bastia, where, under the influence of
Paoli, the allies had landed in the preceding year, and
united the birthplace of Bonaparte to the British dominions. After suppressing a rebellion in Corte, a town
in the centre of the isle, and forming the secret expedition
under their major, Alexander Napier, of Blackstone, to
reduce Porto Ferrajo in Elba, the Highlanders returned
to Gibraltar, where General de Burgh publicly testified
his approbation of their conduct.

Cameron who was now, by the death of Major Donald
M'Donald, of Boisdale, senior captain, accompanied the
regiment to Portsmouth, where it landed in May, and
from whence it went to Dublin in June, 1798. Here he
became attached to a young lady possessed of great personal attractions, and announced to his father his intention
of marrying. But old Ewen Cameron had imbibed some
curious prejudices against the Irish, for a false rumour
had gained credence in the Highlands that Prince Charles
had been betrayed at Culloden by his two Irish followers,
Sullivan and Sheridan. There was great consternation in
Fassifern and the Braes of Lochaber when it was au-

nounced that the young laird was about to wed a stranger; and however absurd this prejudice may appear, old Fassifern set all his wits to work, and contrived to have the engagement broken off completely. A quarrel ensued between the lovers ; rumour speaks of another duel with some one ; but from that time to the hour of his death, Cameron was never known to form another serious attachment.

At this time the Irish were in arms ; Vinegar Hill was valiantly fought and lost by them ; the Highlanders were kept incessantly on the march, and their belts were never off. During these operations, when encamped near Moat, they were re-numbered as the 92nd Regiment of the line.

After being quartered in Athlone, on the 15th June, 1799, Cameron embarked with the regiment for the camp at Barham Downs, where the troops destined for the expedition to Holland were assembling under Lieutenant-General Sir Ralph Abercrombie. The Gordon Highlanders were brigaded with the 1st Royal Scots, 25th, or Scots Borderers ; the 49th and Cameron Highlanders, under Brigadier Sir John Moore. The troops sailed from Ramsgate, landed near the Helder, and on that evening the Gordon Highlanders, after having fifteen men drowned, fought bravely at the battle of the Sandhills. Here they and Cameron first saw the French, for whom he felt an hereditary abhorrence, having been reared to believe, like every Highlander, that they had trifled, forty years before, with the best interests of Scotland, and betrayed Prince Charles and the clans to England.

He served at the head of his company in all the operations under the gallant Moore—during the advance to Oude Sluys, the action at Crabhenden, where Captain Ramsay of Dalhousie was wounded ; the engagement with General Brune ; the attack on Alkmaar ; the retreat to Zuype ; and the battle of Egmont-op-Zee, where it is probable that his French antipathy received an additional incentive, by the infliction of a severe wound. In that decisive charge, by which twenty pieces of cannon were *retaken* from the enemy, a ball struck one of his knees ;

and as he was falling, the arm of the faithful M'Millan was the first to support him. Here the Marquis of Huntly was wounded in the shoulder; and neither he nor Cameron ever fully recovered the effect of these bullets. In this affair the Highlanders had 288 officers and men killed and wounded.

Among the latter was the henchman Ewen, who lost an ear. Rendered furious by the wound, regardless of Cameron's orders, he rushed among the French, and drove his bayonet, with a ball at the same moment, through the body of the soldier who had wounded him. Returning to his company, he said in Gaelic, to Cameron—

"You see what yonder son of the devil has done to me," and pointed to his ear, which was dripping with blood.

"He served you rightly," said Cameron, in the same language; "why did you skirmish so far in front?"

"*Dioul!*" muttered Ewen; "he won't take my other ear."

Here Sir John Moore was severely wounded, and Cameron desired two Highlanders to carry him to the rear. Moore afterwards offered 20*l.* to the soldiers who carried him off. The reward was proffered to the regiment on parade, and it is a noble trait of it, that *no man* ever stepped forward to claim the fee. On being created a K.B., and requiring supporters for his arms, Moore addressed the following interesting letter to Lieutenant-Colonel Napier, then commanding the regiment:—

"Richmond, 17th Nov. 1804.

"MY DEAR NAPIER,—I have been for some days on leave in London, and received your letters there. I am here with my mother for a day, and return this night to Sandgate. My reason for troubling you for a drawing is, that, as a Knight of the Bath, I am entitled to supporters. I have chosen a light-infantry soldier for one, being colonel of the 1st Light Infantry regiment; and a Highland soldier for the other, in gratitude to, and in commemoration of, two soldiers of the 92nd, who, in the action of the 2nd October, raised me from the ground, when I was lying on my face, wounded and stunned (they must have thought me *dead*), and helped me out of the field. As my senses were returning, I heard one of them say, '*Here is the general; let us take him away,*' upon which they stooped and raised me by the arm. I never could discover who they were, and therefore concluded they must have been *killed*. I hope the 92nd will not have any objection (as I have commanded them, and as they rendered me such a service) to my taking one of the corps as a supporter. I do not care for the drawing being elegant; all I want is the correct uniform and appointments. Any person who can draw a figure tolerably, but will dress him correctly, with arms, accoutrements, and in parade order, will answer every purpose, as I want it for a model only, from which a painter may draw another. If you are at a loss for a person to do this, I dare say Lieutenant-Colonel Birch would do it, or get one of the officers of the department to do so, if you sent a man properly dressed to Colchester; but I think your own quarters will produce some one sufficiently expert. I received your letter by Captain (Peter) Grant, before I left Sandgate: he seems a very gentlemanly young man. I do not think I can recommend a proper adjutant to you at present. Remember me kindly to my friends of the 92nd, and believe me, my dear Napier, sincerely, &c.,

"JOHN MOORE.*

"Lieut.-Col. Napier, of Blackstone."

After the convention at Alkmaar, and the cessation of hostilities, the regiment embarked near the Helder, and landed at Yarmouth on the 29th October. Though still suffering from his wound, Cameron obtained the temporary command of a light infantry corps under Lord Hopeton. This provisional battalion was exercised on Barham Downs, where he won the reputation of a zealous and able officer. He came home on leave to his native glen, kindly bringing with him Ewen M'Millan, who had a craving to visit his old mother by the shore of Locharkaig.

They rejoined the Highlanders soon after, and the next

* MS. Records, 92nd Highlanders.

scene of Cameron's service was in Egypt. Before embarking, his regiment was supplied with *yellow* knapsacks, having a red thistle painted on the backs of them.

Fassifern accompanied his regiment on General Maitland's futile expedition to the Isle de Houat, from whence, with other regiments destined for the Mediterranean, they embarked under Lord Dalhousie's orders; and after touching at Port-Mahon in Minorca, passed on to the attack of Cadiz, which was abandoned, in consequence of a pestilence that infected the coast. The expedition then sailed for Malta; and from thence to the Bay of Marmora, on the coast of Asiatic Turkey, where Abercrombie had concentrated 15,000 men to expel the French from Egypt. He had six regiments of dragoons, and forty battalions of infantry, seven of which were foreign.

Fassifern served with distinction in all the operations of the Egyptian campaign, including the landing effected under a desperate cannonade on the shore of Aboukir; the bloody contest round the Tower of Mandora, where his company occupied a conspicuous position in front of the line, as skirmishers, and where his colonel, Erskine of Cardross, received a mortal wound, and of his comrades there were 109 officers and men killed and wounded. The intrepid conduct of his regiment was particularly mentioned in the dispatches of Abercrombie, whose guard of honour was daily furnished from its ranks. Cameron was at the battle of Alexandria, where, on the 21st March, 1801, he received a wound under the left eye, and saw the brave Abercrombie receive his death shot.

The troops then advanced to Rosetta; and by the time when the Gordon Highlanders entered Grand Cairo—"the Queen of Cities"—the capital of Moaz El Kehira, their shoes were completely worn away. Quarter-master Wallace was ordered to procure an immediate supply; but there was one gigantic grenadier from Speyside, for whom a suitable pair of brogues could not be found in all Grand Cairo.

For his services in Egypt, Cameron received a gold medal from the Grand Seignior; and on the promotion of Major Napier to the lieutenant-colonelcy, he obtained the majority on the 5th April, 1801 ; and seven months afterwards, on the conclusion of that convention, by which Grand Cairo was surrendered, the Highlanders were ordered home to Scotland, and were quartered in Glasgow.

About this time a dispute occurred among the officers. Some of them, who were Lowlanders, insisted that the Gaelic, which was generally spoken at the mess, should be abolished there. It was put to the vote, and by an overwhelming majority, the Celts secured its retention ; but in those days, there were in the regiment twelve gentlemen of the clan Donald, all kinsmen, who invariably voted together in everything, and could carry any point they pleased. These factions were known as the national and anti-national parties.

After the short peace of Amiens, war was declared again ; and when the army was increased, the Gordon Highlanders were strengthened by the addition of a second battalion, and Major Cameron marched with it to Weely in England, to join the force mustered to oppose the expected invasion by Napoleon. The invasion ended in smoke ; but the battalion remained cantoned in England until 1807, and in the preceding year lined the streets of London during the funeral of Nelson. Fassifern embarked with them at Harwich on the Danish expedition, under Lord Cathcart ; and, for the first time, served under Wellington—then Sir Arthur Wellesley—at the attack on Kioge, where Lieutenant-Colonel Napier, at the head of the Highlanders, charged the Danes, who were routed with the loss of their artillery.

After the bombardment of Copenhagen, and the return of the troops to Britain, Major Cameron, in consideration of his services, received a brevet lieutenant-colonelcy on the 25th April, 1808 ; a full lieutenant-colonelcy on the 23rd June following ; and was shortly afterwards ordered on the Swedish expedition under Sir John Moore, who led 10,000 men to assist Gustavus Adolphus IV., a gallant but fiery and intractable prince, against whom Russia and France had united their arms. The violent temper of the Swedish monarch rendered this undertaking completely futile, and, without achieving anything, the expedition returned to Britain.

As junior lieutenant-colonel, Cameron now remained with the second battalion at home; while the first, under Lieutenant-Colonel Napier, accompanied Sir John Moore a third time on that fatal service, from which he never returned. In 1809, the gallant Napier fell with his leader at Corunna, and then Fassifern obtained the command of the first battalion, committing the second, in February, to the care of Lieutenant-Colonel Lamond, of Lamond. Thus, at the early age of thirty-seven, and after only fifteen years' service, he found himself at the head of one of the finest Scottish regiments in the service of his country.

In July, with the right wing of the first battalion, he embarked on board H. M. S. *Superb*, 74, at Harwich, on the great expedition under the Earl of Chatham, in Sir William Erskine's brigade. He was at the landing on Breesand in Walcheren, and the occupation of Ter Goes on South Beveland. He landed with 998 Highlanders; but so fatal was the Dutch pestilence, that in October only 250 of them were on parade; and the grenadier company, which was entirely recruited from Aberdeenshire, was reduced to *two* sergeants and *three* privates. Cameron deeply regretted the loss of his men. The first who died was a fine young clansman, whom he had brought with him from Lochaber, and he attended his funeral in the churchyard of a neighbouring village. After addressing the soldiers on the merits of the deceased, "Cover him up with the greenest sods," said he, "for he was a brave lad, a good soldier, and true Highlander!"

On its return from this disastrous service, his battalion occupied Woodbridge Barracks in England. At this time an Englishman obtained an ensigncy in the corps, which Cameron considered an innovation; for while, on one hand, he disliked the French, from old associations, on the other, he was not, for the same reason, over partial to Englishmen, and was wont to affirm, "that a Southern in the kilt reminded him of a hog in armour." Unfortunately for himself, Ensign Mudge (for such was the name of the new acquisition) had no particular love for the kilt, at which he railed on all occasions, in very coarse terms, and once particularly at an Artillery ball in Woolwich, which so roused Cameron's Highland ire, that he vowed, "if such remarks were ever made again by Ensign Mudge, he would bring him to a general court-martial!" At this time, the officers of the 42nd wore the kilt constantly by their own desire.

Undeterred by Cameron's threat, Mudge wrote to the Commander-in-Chief, stating that his health would not permit him to wear a dress so unchristian and uncivilized. Sir David Dundas addressed an answer, not to him, but to Fassifern, stating that his Majesty had no further use for the services of poor Mr. Mudge, on whom this result, which Cameron and his Highlanders hailed with satisfaction, fell like a thunderclap.

While at Woodbridge, he invited to the mess Dr. Moore (the venerable father of the hero of Corunna), who afterwards addressed to him a letter, expressing his high sense "of the kind and social reception" he had met with from him and his officers. After this, in July, 1810, the battalion marched to Canterbury, previous to embarkation for Spain; Cameron obtained a short leave of absence, and so much had he become attached to the corps, that he wept when he left it even temporarily. On revisiting his native glen, his aged father, then in his seventieth year (the old laird was born in 1740), expressed great reluctance to part with him again, for, like a true Highlander, he had some dark forebodings of the future.

His three sisters were married: Mary, to M'Donald of Glencoe; Jean, to Roderick M'Neill of Barra; and Catherine, to Cluny M'Pherson; his eldest brother Duncan was practising as a writer to the signet, in the capital; and Peter, the second, was away to India in command of the Balcarras. The old laird was almost alone at Fassifern; he represented to the colonel, that, though he was only thirty-nine years of age, he had received two wounds, from one of which he still suffered; that he had been many times engaged with the enemy, and had seen

CAMERON'S HIGHLANDERS RECEIVING THE FRENCH.

enough of war. He urged him to settle at home and to marry; offering him his second estate of Arthurstone, in Angus; but the love of his profession was too strong in the heroic heart of Cameron, and he rejoined his battalion, then under the command of Major Archibald M'Donell (of the family of Keppoch), at the far-famed *Lines* of Torres Vedras.

To make his regiment as efficient as possible, he ordered that no officer who had been less than ten years in the service should ride on the march; this diminished the number of useless horses which every regiment then possessed; while to increase the number of bayonets, he turned the whole of the band into the ranks; thus, throughout the whole Peninsular War, he retained only the bagpipes, drums, and fifes. His regiment belonged to the 1st Brigade, or General Howard's, in the 2nd Division of Infantry, or Lord Hill's, with the 50th, under Colonel Stuart, and the 71st Highlanders, under Colonel Cadogan, with both of whom his fiery temper and jealousy on points of etiquette soon involved him in a coolness that lasted till they were both removed by death. The Highlanders entered Spain by the way of Albergaria, and their peculiar garb soon changed the constant cry of "*Live the English,*" to "*Viva los Escotos! Viva Don Juan Cameron, y sus valiante Escotos! Viva!*"

This was when following up the retreating Massena. Notwithstanding all efforts of that general to restore the barbarities of ancient warfare, much good feeling prevailed between the French and British when out of the field. Of this, one anecdote will suffice.

A French picket in front of Cameron's regiment, were about to slay a bullock for their dinner, when the animal broke loose, and dashed across the neutral ground, where a Highlander killed it by a single ball, and his comrades proceeded immediately to cut up their prize in view of the hungry and disappointed foe, who sent over two soldiers, waving white handkerchiefs. Under these extempore flags of truce, they brought a message from their officer, saying that he was "sure Scottish soldiers were too generous to deprive his men of the only provisions they had seen for some days." The Highlanders sent them back with half the beef, several loaves of bread, and a bottle of rum. After this, they became so familiar that some of our pickets went over and drank with those of the enemy, until Wellington's order forbade it as unsafe and improper.

Cameron distinguished himself by his activity, at the head of his gallant Highlanders, in all the arduous operations of that sanguinary war. He led his regiment at Fuentes d'Onor, where it was on the right, covering a brigade of nine pounders, when it endured a severe cannonade, and had thirty-seven officers and men killed and wounded. Major Peter Grant had his arm torn off by a cannon-shot, but he survived to die lately, at a good old age, amongst his kindred in Strathspey.

The regiment was then 897 strong. Cameron was at the second siege of Badajoz, and at the surprise of Gerard's division, on the 28th of October, 1811, when, on a dark, rainy morning, and under cover of a dense mist, Sir Rowland Hill's troops attacked the village of Arroya del Molinos, or the Mills-of-the-King. In this brilliant affair, Fassifern attacked the two retreating squares of the French with his Highlanders, and breaking through one, sword in hand, formed on the *other* side of the *Puebla*, and completed the overthrow of Marshal Gerard, who had all his artillery, baggage, money, officers, horses, and 1,400 men taken. In the charge through the village, Cameron received a wound in the sword hand, and Captain M'Pherson, with whom he fought the duel at Gibraltar, was shot by his side. On this occasion the Highlanders had a parody made on the old song of "Johnny Cope," for Gerard, until he heard the pipers of the 92nd playing that popular air, believed the attack to be a mere exchange of shots between his videttes and the guerillas. Cameron's wound was a narrow escape, and is thus mentioned by an eye-witness :*

"The captain of the grenadier company having been wounded early in the action, the senior lieutenant, on

---

* Lieutenant Hope, 92nd.

assuming the command of it, made a false movement; on perceiving which, the colonel, greatly irritated, repeated his former orders in a voice of thunder, and, as was his usual custom when displeased, struck his left breast with his right hand, which then grasped the hilt of his sword. The last syllable of his orders had just been delivered, when a bullet, despatched by one of the enemy's riflemen, struck the first joint of his middle finger, shattered the bone, passed through the handle of the sword, and struck his breast so violently, that he relinquished the command of the battalion to Major Mitchell, in the full conviction that the ball had passed into his body. On being undeceived, the gallant colonel instantly rejoined his battalion, and, with his middle finger dangling by a small piece of skin only, remained at the head of his Highlanders to the close of the engagement."

When the French were completely driven out, and when Hill's division was on the march for San Pedro, Cameron, who had lost much blood, was conducted by Ewen M'Millan to a house in Arroya, to have the wound dressed, and the finger, which yet dangled by a sinew, cut off. On entering, they found it occupied by a noisy and tipsy party of Spanish dragoons, who, notwithstanding the rank and wound of Fassifern, endeavoured to eject him. High words ensued, and a dragoon dared to aim a blow at his head with a sabre. Cameron instinctively raised his wounded hand for protection, and had his right arm cut to the bone. Rendered furious by the sight of his master's blood, M'Millan levelled his musket at the head of the insolent Spaniard, and would have shot him dead; but Cameron, who was aware that the Conde de Penne Villamur's dragoons occupied the whole village, exclaimed—

"Desist, Ewen, for God's sake do not fire!" and struck up his foster-brother's musket, the bullet from which pierced the ceiling. He never could discover the perpetrator of this severe wound, from the effects of which he suffered long.

During the harassing marches of Hill's division in the desolate Estramadura, his native hardihood never flinched, though the miseries endured by the troops were excessive in that naked district, where they were constantly in arrears of pay, bivouacking without tents or fires, or cantoned in roofless and ruined towns, marching day and night in the wet and chill of winter, or the heat of the summer solano, when the white dust blew down the mountain passes, and the air became thick with flies; when the soil of the vast plains cracked and rent; when the perspiration rose in hazy steam above the marching columns; when comrades fought like tigers around the wayside wells and casual pools, to fill their canteens at the puddle through which, perhaps, the advanced guard had passed an hour before; when years of hardship, danger, starvation, and rags were to be endured, Fassifern never had a day's illness or absence from parade; nor did his hardy Gordon Highlanders ever lose a man by fatigue, save upon two occasions.

These exceptions were Lieutenants Marshall and Hill, two fine young officers; the first of whom died in a wretched bullock car—died of sheer starvation, as he was being conveyed into Badajoz; and the second, unable to keep up with his men, perished of the same awful death among the mountains, between Talavera and Toledo. It is said that, on many occasions, Fassifern would have starved also, but for the vigorous efforts of his foster-brother and henchman, Ewen M'Millan, who, despite Lord Wellington's orders, plundered the Dons without mercy, when the comfort of his chieftain and master required him to do so.

After incessant skirmishes and daily marches along the banks of the Tagus, and after a desperate affair of outposts at La Nava, on the 18th May, 1812, Hill marched to destroy the forts erected by the French at the bridge of Almarez. The 50th, and a wing of the 71st Highlanders, formed one column, which was destined to attack Fort Napoleon; Cameron with his regiment, and the remainder of the 71st, had orders to support the attack, and storm the *tête-du-pont*. Both columns were amply provided with scaling-ladders. As the troops descended a **rut** of the sierra, in Indian file, about midnight, Mr.

Irvine, a gentleman volunteer, left his ranks to obtain a draught of water. This was contrary to express orders; and such was Cameron's strictness, that he dismissed him from the regiment on the instant, and the poor fellow was left alone among the mountains of Romangordo.

Being proud of his own regiment, Cameron had a great jealousy of the 71st Highlanders; and when the attack commenced, on some of their bullets, in the twilight and confusion, whistling over his own ranks, he called aloud—

"Seventy-first! what the devil are you about? Do you wish the ninety-second to return your fire?"

Fort Napoleon was stormed in gallant style. Captain Candler, of the 50th, was shot through the head; but the French were driven towards the *tête-du-pont*. Then Cameron entered it with them pell-mell, with bayonets charged, muskets clubbed, swords and sledge-hammers. But the commandant of Fort Ragusa, on the opposite side, cut the pontoon bridge, and thus the whole garrison of Fort Napoleon found the deep Tagus before them, and the foe behind.

Eager to capture Ragusa, many of Cameron's men flung themselves into the river, and daringly swam across. Privates Gall and Somerville were the first men who brought over the pontoon bridge. On gaining possession of the platforms, which were literally ankle-deep in brains and blood, the 1st brigade slued round the cannon upon the French, and blew their heads off in scores, as they crowded into the square of the little fortress, where the 71st Highlanders captured a standard of the *Corps Etranger*.

The dead, 436 in number, were thrown into the ditch; the ramparts, with eighteen cannon, were hurled over them; the stone towers were blown up; the barracks and storehouses burned down; and the whole place laid bare. In the general pillage which ensued, a Highlander became mutinous to Cameron, who raised his claymore to cut him down; but the descending blow was turned aside by a sergeant, named Taylor, who kindly interposed his pike between them. Even when the gust of passion passed away, Cameron could not forgive the affront of Taylor's interference before his men, and was headstrong enough to resent it in the following manner : When the sergeants drew lots for the command of a firing party to shoot a deserter at Coria, Taylor escaped this hateful ballot, but nevertheless Cameron ordered him to take charge of the execution. Taylor gave him a glance full of reproach, and burst into tears, yet he obeyed, and shot the culprit dead. Then Cameron repented the casual malevolence which is sometimes to be found even yet among the Celts, when an affront has been given them. At Merida, he was pall-bearer during the grand military funeral generously bestowed on the commandant of Almarez, who had been slain there by an officer of the 71st Highlanders, and who was buried with the honours due to a British officer of the same rank.

Cameron's native dislike to receive orders from seniors, his jealousy of the 71st, and *Old Half-hundred*, involved him in many quarrels with Colonels Cadogan and Stuart, and even in an angry correspondence with Wellington. It was then currently rumoured in the Highland regiments, that the great Duke had some dislike to their nation. The Gordon Highlanders added, that he viewed coldly old Sir William Stuart, Fassifern, and Major Mitchell, from whom they averred that he withheld many honours to which they were entitled. What amount of truth these rumours contained, it is *now* impossible to learn. High words ensued on one occasion between the colonel and his great leader, to whom he said :—

"My Lord Marquis, thank God! I am beholden to no man for my bread—not even to the service, for I have a comfortable home to retire to whenever I please."

The real source of this bitterness of feeling is unknown; but it continued during the whole war.

On one occasion his pride revolted at General Howard for keeping the regiment too long under arms before inspection! and he sent Lieutenant Grant to the Brigadier's billet with a brief message, " that the regiment awaited him."

On another occasion, it chanced that by mistake he

and a Spanish colonel were billeted on the same mansion, and as it was thought too small to accommodate both, he resolved to turn out the Don who was already in possession of the premises. On Cameron arriving with the colours, which were borne by his cousin, Ewen Ross, and another ensign, and were escorted by four sergeants with their pikes, the Spanish colonel appeared in the doorway with his Toledo drawn and pistols cocked. Fassifern drew his claymore. " Forward, gentlemen," said he ; " at all risks I command you to lodge the colours !"

The sergeants charged with their pikes, and we know not how the affair might have ended, had not Villamur's corps of Spanish horse turned the corner of the street; this forced the rash chieftain to parley with the cavalier, and share his quarters in peace.

After the night of blood at Almarez, Cameron and his Highlanders marched by Fuente del Maistre, Los Santos, the hill of Albuera, and many other places, bivouacking with their brigade wherever night found them, preparatory to the attack on the forts at Salamanca, and the battle there, which was fought, while Hill's division covered Lord Wellington's rear. After joining the grand army on these contested plains, the Highlanders were reviewed by their great general. Rations had been served out that morning ; the sheep-heads had been assigned to the 92nd, and when they marched past by open column of companies, every sixth man carried a sheep's head in his left hand.

When Wellington entered Madrid, the Highlanders of Cameron for one night occupied the Escuriel, in the chapel of which the remains of a king and queen of Scotland (Malcolm III. and St. Margaret) are said to lie, having been conveyed to Spain in 1560. After Cameron marched to Aranjuez, his cousin, Ewen Ross, had a narrow escape from a terrible death. Having been ordered to the rear with sick and wounded from the brigade, and having no less than twelve waggons-full of officers, he reached Badajoz, after encountering many difficulties, and there found that various outrages committed by the detachment of Lieutenant H———, of the 28th, were laid to the charge of his party, such as shooting and plundering the paisanos, robbing them of *burros*, wine, and provisions. Lack of Spanish prevented the gallant Highlander from explaining that he was not the guilty person; and the Marquis del Palacio, governor of Badajoz, illegally tried him by a Spanish court-martial, and unscrupulously sentenced him to death! Then fearing to carry this sentence into execution, he sent him, under an escort of Portuguese horse, to Elvas, where an English officer saved him from a rabble who were bent on his destruction, and he was enabled to rejoin Cameron in safety. On this march he saved from starvation Mr. Irvine, the poor volunteer, whom he found in a state of destitution near Truxillo.

Cameron and his Highlanders endured great misery on the disastrous retreat from Burgos. Deprivation of food reduced the poor men almost to skeletons; their uniform was worn to rags; many were barefooted, and shirtless. Undeterred by the cruel exhibition of a soldier hung *daily* at the head of the column (for of twenty men under sentence of death for plundering, one was thus sacrificed every day), the 92nd shot some wild pigs in a wood through which they passed. *Big* Dugald Campbell, one of their favourite officers, drove his long claymore through the body of a boar which he pursued through the thicket, and claimed from some cazadores. This prize he shared with Cameron and other officers; but the affair drew forth a most severe reprimand from head-quarters, and this was at a time when a *duro* was given for a handful of oats or nuts, and when some of the officers had no other food for six-and-thirty hours than a few mushrooms or acorns.

Fassifern's regiment formed part of the small force which was left with General Howard to secure Wellington's retreat, by defending the old ruined town of Alba at the passage of the rapid Tormes. There the 50th, 71st, and 92nd made a gallant stand on the 8th of November, 1812. After a long and fatiguing march, and just when about to receive a little ration of dry bread— the first food after three days of starvation—the appearance of the whole pursuing French army under Joseph

ESCAPE OF A FRENCH OFFICER.

Bonaparte, summoned the brigade to man the old and shattered walls of Alba—a relic of the Moorish wars—while the sappers undermined the bridge of the Tormes. Two green hills overlooked the town and river. Between these and the wall, within pistol-shot of the 92nd Highlanders, a French staff-officer, mounted on a white charger, had the temerity to ride leisurely reconnoitring, and followed by an orderly on foot. Twenty Highlanders levelled their muskets to shoot this daring fellow, but the chivalric Cameron cried aloud :

"Recover your arms there ! I will by no means permit an individual to be fired on !"

This officer who acted so boldly, and thus escaped so narrowly, proved to be no other than *Marshal Soult*, who, in ten minutes after, ordered eighteen pieces of cannon up to the heights, from whence they poured 1300 rounds of shot and shell on the brave brigade of Howard. This was endured until the 13th, by which time Cameron lost forty-two men killed and wounded. At daybreak, on the morning of the 14th, a despatch arrived from Wellington, directing Howard to abandon Alba, as the French cavalry, 3000 strong, had forded the river above the town and turned his flank. A Spanish garrison was left in the old castle of the *Castigador de Flamencos*—the walls were abandoned, and the bridge blown up. Lieutenant John Grant of the 92nd was the last officer who quitted the town, being left to bring off the sentinels, as the French entered, and he was struck by the stones as the mine under the bridge exploded, at the very heels of his party.

Wellington's admirable foresight saved Howard's brigade, which retired to winter quarters at Coria, in Leon, when, with many other officers and soldiers, Colonel Stewart of the 50th, as brave a Scot as ever drew a sword, expired of exhaustion and fatigue. A soldier of the 50th carved a rude stone to mark where this old officer was laid.

Refreshed by six months' rest in winter quarters at Banos, in a beautiful valley of Leon, overshadowed by high mountains, Cameron, after commanding the 1st brigade during General Foy's attack on Bejar, marched with his Highlanders, when the whole army advanced to turn the famous positions of Jourdan on the Ebro and Douro, and to meet him on the green plains of Vittoria, where, on the 21st of June, 1813, he again commanded the 1st brigade of Hill's division, and carried the heights of La Peubla, when the gallant Cadogan fell amid heaps, literally heaps, of his brave Highlanders.

Sir William Stuart having ordered Cameron to secure the heights, added, "yield them to none without a written order from Sir Rowland Hill or myself, and defend them while you have a man remaining." On this Fassifern ordered the pipers to strike up the "Camerons' Gathering," and the regiment advanced with great spirit and alacrity up the mountain side.

After this victory, the most decisive of the Spanish war, Cameron pushed on with his brigade towards the Pyrenees, beyond which the conqueror drove the French like a herd of sheep, and then garrisoned the heights by a chain of outposts, previous to besieging San Sebastian, and blockading Pampeluna. On this occasion the care of the important pass of Maya was entirely assigned to Cameron, with the 1st brigade, after it had crossed the Bidassoa, and skirmished with the routed French until darkness set in, on the 7th July.

Cameron commanded this great outpost until the 25th of that month, when the French advanced to storm the heights under the Duke of Dalmatia, who had assumed the command of Jourdan's discomfited host, and was directed to retrieve all its disasters by driving the British beyond the Ebro. Full of confidence and of hope, at least to relieve the two beleaguered fortresses, this brave marshal sent his legions against the various passes in the mountains which Wellington, who was then urging the siege of San Sebastian in person, had occupied by battalions and brigades.

Cameron's force was encamped in the centre of a lonely gorge, and his outposts were far down the hillside in advance; and these, on Sunday the 25th, descried the division of General Drouet, 15,000 strong, advancing on the road that led from Urdax. Coming on with great spirit,

they drove in the three light companies of the brigade
(which Cameron had dispatched as skirmishers in front),
and gained the high rock of Maya before the 2nd brigade
of infantry could come to his support. His little band
were thus left to defend that steep and narrow pass
against *five* times their number. On this fatal morning
the strength of the Gordon Highlanders was only fifty-
five staff, and 762 rank and file.

To deceive the foe as to his real strength, Cameron
skilfully divided his Highlanders into two wings, in open
columns of companies, thus giving the slender battalion
the aspect of *two* regiments; but this *ruse* was useless, as
the traitor-muleteers, who, for the few weeks preceding,
had been passing between the mountains and French outposts, had made Soult fully aware of the actual force left
to defend the Pyrenees at every point. The moment the
action commenced, Fassifern detached the 50th to the
right, where, after a desperate conflict, it was driven back
and forced to leave the ridge.

Under Major M'Pherson, Cameron then sent forward
first the right wing, and then the left, of his brave Highlanders. Then ensued one of the most appalling scenes of
carnage recorded in the annals of that protracted war.
The Highlanders stood like a rampart, in which, however,
frightful gaps were made by the bullets of the French,
who came on, in one vast mob, shouting and brandishing
their eagles. Separating the 1st and 2nd brigades, they
descended upon the pass of Maya from one flank, while a
fresh division poured upon its front from the Urdax road.
Cameron, who had repeatedly ordered a *charge*, which was
unheard amid the roar of the musketry, then made the
whole fall back gradually upon the rock of Maya; a movement which was slowly and desperately covered by the left
wings of the 71st Highland Light Infantry and of the Gordon
Highlanders, which, by relieving each other, drenched in
blood every inch of the ground; and there these gallant
men defended the rock for ten successive hours, until—
just when ammunition was falling short—the brigade of
General Barnes arrived to their succour, and Lieutenant-
General the Hon. Sir William Stuart, a fine old soldier

whom all the troops loved well, ordered Cameron's brigade *not* to charge ; but, exasperated by the slaughter they had endured, they rushed upon the French with the bayonet, and the Gordon Highlanders, "*for the first time disregarded orders, and not only charged, but led the charge,*" and recovered every foot of ground as far as the pass from which they had been driven. In this headlong advance the pipers played the " Haughs of Cromdale," and the line was led by Captain Seton of Pitmedden, bonnet and claymore in hand. But the slaughter in their ranks was terrible, for 19 officers and 324 rank and file were killed, wounded, and missing. Among the wounded were— Cameron, who was shot through the thigh, and forced to leave the field; Major Mitchel, who succeeded him; Captains Holmes, and Bevan, who died when his arm was taken out of the socket, and Ronald M'Donald of Coul ; Lieutenants Winchester, who commanded the light company; Donald M'Donald, Chisholm, Durie, M'Pherson, and Fife, who, after having one ball turned by a button, and another by his watch, was struck down at last ; Gordon, Kerr Ross, and John Grant, who was shot through the side. Among the ensigns were Thomas and George Mitchell, Ewen Kennedy (one of Cameron's Lochaber men), who bled to death on the field, and Alaster M'Donald of Dalchosnie, a youth of eighteen, who afterwards expired of a wound in the head, and was buried by four of his brother officers in a hole outside the towngate of Vittoria, where Holmes said a short prayer over his grave.

Sir William Napier, in his history, thus alludes to Fassifern and the two regiments of Highlanders: "And that officer (Lieutenant-Colonel Cameron), still holding the pass of Maya with the left wings of the 71st and 92nd Regiments, brought their right wings and the Portuguese guns into action, and thus maintained the fight; but so dreadful was the slaughter, that it is said the advancing enemy was actually stopped by the heaped-up mass of dead and dying. . . . . . The stern valour of the 92nd would have graced *Thermopylæ.*"

Strange to say, Lieutenant Gordon died at Edinburgh sixteen years after, under the hands of a surgeon who was extracting the ball received at Maya, and he lies now in the Calton burying-ground. Two balls grazed Cameron, but the third pierced the fleshy part of his right thigh. In great agony he called to M'Millan, who slung his musket, rushed to his side, and led his horse by the bridle out of the field. "The gallant Cameron, who has so frequently bled for his country," says the *Pilot* of 12th October, 1813, "received *three* shots in his person, his horse received three, and three more were found in his cloak, which was strapped before his saddle in the usual manner." He lost so much blood, that, being unable to reach Vittoria, which was a hundred miles distant, and to which all the wounded were ordered to repair, he remained at an intermediate village until the scar healed and he could rejoin the regiment at Roncesvalles, after it had been engaged between Lizasso and Eguaros, and o the heights of Donna Maria, having in both affairs 120 officers and men killed and wounded. Captain Seton brought the regiment out of the field: thus the Speaker of the House of Commons, on the 24th of June, might well say that the Spaniards of future times would point with pride to the places "where a Stuart made his stand, and where the best blood of Scotland was shed in their defence." For his bravery at the Pyrenees, his Majesty was pleased to permit Cameron to bear upon his shield the word *Maya*.

From this period he was incessantly engaged in all the operations along the French Pyrenees, in daily skirmishes, and the capture of entrenched camps. The country was now covered by snow, and the troops endured many privations, which Sir William Stuart (brother of Lord Galloway) did all in his power to alleviate, by issuing extra allowances of rum, which won him the cognomen of *Auld Grog Willie;* and his popularity was so great among all the troops, that his appearance was always hailed by a noisy cheer, and shouts of " God bless you, Sir William !" Lord Wellington disliked this, and compelled the general to refund to Government all those *extra* allowances of rum served out to the poor soldiers amid the snows of that severe winter on the Pyrenees.

Cameron, who had long remarked that those officers of his 1st Battalion who became by promotion members of the 2nd, and should consequently be at home, were always unfortunate if the corps were engaged, before the passage of the Nive ordered four of them to leave immediately for Britain, when the troops were about to cross the river.

"God bless you, gentlemen," said he, as they bade him adieu; "I am now tired of war, and may well wish I were going with you."

But, mounted on his charger, he was the first to cross the Nivelle, below Ainhoe, when his daring Highlanders were ordered to storm the strong redoubt in rear of the village, where they drove out the French and took possession of their huts. Here his favourite piper was killed by his side; and with his own hand he strove to raise him, exclaiming, "I would rather lose twenty men than have lost you!" He led them through the Nive at Cambo; and in the attack upon those heavy columns which occupied the ground between the entrenched camp at Bayonne and the road to St. Jean Pied-de-Port, he fought valiantly at the battle of St. Pierre. There (Napier relates), at one period of the day, the overwhelming cannonade and musketry drove the 92nd in rear of the hamlet; however, on being succoured by their old comrades, the 50th, and Ashworth's Caçadores, they re-formed behind St. Pierre, and "then their gallant colonel, Cameron, once more led them down the road, with colours flying and pipes playing, resolved to give the shock to whatever stood in their way. The 92nd was but a small clump compared to the heavy mass in front;" but Fassifern led them on as of old, and the *heavy mass* rolled before their bayonets like mist before the wind. Four times that day he led them to brilliant charges, and four times the foe was driven back. Cameron had 13 officers and 173 rank and file killed and wounded; but he obtained an honorary badge, inscribed with the word *Nive*.

After the attack on the enemy at Hellette, in the lower

Pyrenees, where General Harispe was driven out, and forced to retire to Meharin; and after that gallant conflict on the heights of Garris, where Cameron lost Seton of Pitmedden, and twelve other brave fellows, the scene of his next achievement was the pretty village of Arriverette, on the right bank of Gave de Mauleon, where the French endeavoured to destroy a wooden bridge, to prevent Wellington from following them; but a ford being discovered above it, Cameron boldly threw himself into the stream, at the head of his Highlanders, crossed under a fire of artillery, stormed the village, drove back the enemy, and, by securing the bridge, enabled the whole troops to pass. For this eminent service his Majesty granted to him, as an additional crest of honourable augmentation, a Highlander of the 92nd foot, "armed and accoutred, up to the middle in water, his dexter hand grasping a broadsword, in his sinister a banner, inscribed, '92nd,' within a wreath of laurel, all proper, and on an escroll above, the word *Arriverette*."* But Cameron had now a fresh cause of displeasure at his great leader; for, on applying to him, through Lieutenant-General Lord Niddry, for leave to inscribe *Arriverette* upon the regimental colours, Wellington declined, without affording any satisfactory reason. He acknowledged, in his reply, that "the 92nd forded the river, and took the village against a superior force of the enemy, in most gallant style;" but added that it was beneath their reputation to explain *why* they should not have Arriverette on their colours. This ambiguous reply Cameron considered another affront, and never forgot or forgave it.

He received an honorary badge for his conduct at the battle of Orthez; and on the 2nd March, 1814, distinguished himself at the capture of Aire so prominently, that George III. desired him to bear embattled in chief above the old cognizance of Lochiel (as the heraldic record above quoted has it), "a representation of the town of Aire, in allusion to his glorious services on the 2nd March last, when, after an arduous and sanguinary

* "Record:" Lyon Court, Edinburgh.

conflict, he succeeded in forcing a superior body of the enemy to abandon the said town, and subsequently had the honour to receive an address from the inhabitants, expressive of their gratitude for the maintenance of discipline, by which he had saved them from plunder and destruction." The address, which was so complimentary to his distinguished regiment, was signed by M. Codroy, the mayor, in the name of the people.

From thence he accompanied the troops in that hot and brilliant pursuit, which did not cease until the French evacuated Toulouse, and the white banner of Bourbon was displayed upon its walls. The seizure of Paris by the allies, the abdication of Bonaparte and proclamation of peace, the restoration of Louis XVIII., rapidly followed, and the Peninsular army was ordered home.

In the last skirmish near Toulouse, Cameron had his favourite horse shot under him; and, though there was a hot fire of musketry sweeping the place where it lay, M'Millan deliberately unbuckled the girths of the saddle, and brought it away with the cloak and holsters, saying, that "though the French were welcome to the dead carcase, they should not get the good accoutrements."

When encamped at Blanchefort, two miles from Bordeaux, Cameron obtained his brevet colonelcy on the 4th June, 1814 ;* and when cantoned at Pouillac, his Highlanders joyfully received the route for Scotland, and on the 17th July embarked on board H.M.S. *Norge*, which, however, by a change of destination, landed them at the Cove of Cork.

While his regiment, now reduced to one battalion, was in Ireland, Cameron returned, on leave, to his native glen at Fassifern.

Wellington had then won all the honours a subject could attain : patents of nobility, baronetcy, and knighthood were issued for generals of division and brigade ; Orders of the Garter, the Bath, and the Crescent were unsparingly lavished among the heroes of the war; but

---

* Note of his services furnished to author from Horse Guards.

the brave Cameron, notwithstanding all his services—though he had been almost riddled by musket-shot, and had served in Sweden, Denmark, Holland, Spain, Portugal, Egypt, and France, at home and abroad, for twenty-one years—found that the Duke of Wellington had *omitted* his name in the list of officers recommended for honorary distinctions. He visited London, and complained to the Duke of York, who offered to have him gazetted as an additional Cross of the Bath.

"I beg your highness will excuse me," said he, "for as my name has been omitted, I will not accept of it now."

"Sir," replied the duke, "do you know to whom you are speaking?"

"A prince of that royal blood for which I have too often shed my own; but am yet willing to do so again. And I have the honour to wish your Highness good morning."

In this haughty fashion he quitted the Horse Guards, but was afterwards prevailed upon to write to Wellington.

Justly indignant, he wrote a fiery remonstrance to the duke, who was then at Vienna, and who, in one of his letters to Earl Bathurst, dated 5th February, mentions it as a *somewhat imprudent production;* but his Grace replied to the following effect :—

"Vienna, 5th February, 1815.

"SIR,—I received your letter of the 8th January, this morning, and I have transmitted it to the Secretary of State, with my recommendation of you.

"The Government fixed the occasions on which medals should be granted to the army, and framed the rules, according to which I was bound to make the lists of those to whom they were to be granted; and not having received their orders to recommend for medals, for the service at Arroya del Molinos, Alba de Tormes, Bejar, Aire, or at Arriverette, it was impossible for me to recommend you for a medal at Fuentes d'Onoro, or in the Pyrenees, according to the rules by which I was bound to make out the lists of those I recommended. I have not an accurate recollection of the lists for Bayonne, the

Nivelle, Orthez, and Toulouse; but of this I am very certain, *that I have never failed to do your services justice,* as it was my earnest desire to render it to every officer and soldier I had the honour of commanding.

"I have nothing to say about the selection of the officers recently appointed Knights Commanders of the Order of the Bath. I did not know their names till I saw the list of them in the *Gazette*. If you had known these facts, I hope that the same spirit of justice by which I have always been animated, would have induced you to spare me the pain of reading the *reproaches and charges of injustice* contained in your letter; and that you would have defended me in the 92nd Regiment; and would have shown them that the regulation, and not I, deprived you of those marks of honour which they wished to see you obtain. As these facts are in the knowledge of everybody, it is scarcely possible to believe that you were not aware of them, and I attribute the harshness of your letter solely to the irritation which you naturally feel in considering your own case. However, the expression of this irritation, however unjust towards me, and unpleasant to my feelings, has not made me forget the services which you and your brave corps rendered upon every occasion on which you were called upon; and, although I am afraid it is *too late*, I have recommended you in the strongest terms to the Secretary of State; and have the honour to be, &c., WELLINGTON.

"To Lieut.-Colonel Cameron, 92nd Regiment."

Cameron saw there was something at least generous in the tone of this letter, and he sent a memorial for the Order of the Bath; for the medal which had been given to officers engaged at Fuentes d'Onoro, and also for the Order of the Tower and Sword. Wellington replied as follows:—

"Vienna, February, 1815.

"SIR,—I have received your letter of the 13th January, and the copy of your memorial; in answer to which I can only inform you, that I had no concern whatever in the selection of the officers of the army lately under my com-

mand to be Knights Commanders of the Order of the Bath; and as I see that the number limited is filled, I am quite certain that no application I can make will answer any purpose. I will inquire about your claim to a medal for Fuentes d'Onoro. I have recommended you for the Portuguese Order of the Tower and Sword; and have the honour, &c.,   WELLINGTON.
"To Lieut.-Colonel Cameron, 92nd Regiment."

Fassifern received the Portuguese order, but he was too much of a Highlander to forget the first unmerited affront, of being omitted or forgotten; and now we can but hope that this omission of the great duke was, at least, an unwitting one.

Like every Highlander of the old school, and like many of the present day, Cameron believed in the Taisch, or Second Sight; he had one other fancy, a dread of being on the water, or at sea; thus he who would face without flinching a shower of grape or hedge of bayonets, has been known to grow pale at the rocking of a small boat.

When at home, on leave, in 1815, he visited Mor'ar, in Lochaber, the seat of Colonel Simon M'Donald, a retired officer who had joined the 92nd at their first muster in 1793. One day when passing along a corridor together, and about to enter the dining-room, M'Donald started back, with his eyes fixed in their sockets, his face pale as death, and his limbs trembling.

"In God's name, what is the matter Mor'ar?" asked Cameron.

"Nothing," replied M'Donald, after a pause, and greatly agitated; "nothing."

"You *have* seen something, Simon," continued Cameron, impressively, for he knew, or believed, that the gift of the Taisch was hereditary in the family of Mor'ar.

"Well, then, I have seen something, Fassifern," said M'Donald, passing a hand over his eyes with a troubled expression; "but do not ask me what it was."

Mor'ar was thoughtful and sad for a long time after, and it was currently believed that he had seen some vision of his old friend's approaching end; for the day-dreams of the Highland seers are always fraught with death and sorrow. Immediately after this, war broke out again; Bonaparte quitted Elba, returned to Paris, and resumed the reins of government, while Louis XVIII. withdrew to Ghent.

Wellington once more took the field, and the 92nd Highlanders were ordered to Flanders, with the other forces under his command. Cameron hastened to rejoin, in Ireland, where the regiment was still stationed. Its second battalion, under Lamond of that ilk, had been disbanded at Edinburgh, all save twelve sergeants and 174 soldiers, who, with five officers, marched to Portpatrick to join the head-quarters; and on this route an interesting episode occurred.

As the Highlanders, with pipes playing, marched past a little wayside cottage, an old and white-haired man came out to see them, and was immediately recognised as their brave and favourite general in Spain, Sir William Stuart, who, neglected by the Government, had retired there to brood over his unrequited services. A hearty cheer welcomed *"Auld Grog Willie."* Then the brave Stuart burst into tears, and wept like a child. The detachment was formed into line, and inspected by him; perhaps the last military duty he ever performed, for rumour says that he died soon after of a broken heart.

Cameron embarked with his Highlanders at Cork, for Ostend, from whence, with eight battalions under his command, viz., the third battalion of the Royal Scots; the 28th, 32nd, 42nd, 44th, 79th, 92nd, and third battalion of the 95th Rifle corps, he marched, *via* Ghent and Bruges, to Brussels, where, on the 3rd June, 1815, his Highlanders, with the brigade to which they belonged—the 5th or Sir Denis Pack's—were reviewed by Wellington, then a field-marshal. In the 5th corps were also the 1st Royal Scots, the 42nd Highlanders, and 44th Regiment.

When Pack's brigade was under arms in the Park of Brussels, the Duchess of Richmond, who had been Lady Charlotte Gordon, passed in an open carriage along the line. Colonel MacQuarrie, of the 42nd, gallantly made

his Highlanders *present arms* to her, as the Duke of
Gordon's daughter, while the pipes played a salute ; but
on her approaching the 92nd, Cameron, still true to his
old feud with her brother the marquis, gave the order—
" Gordon Highlanders, order arms—stand at ease !" and
thus coldly was the fair duchess received by the clan
regiment of her father.

On the 12th June, Napoleon left Paris at the head of
his brave army, and the British poured from Brussels.
" The 42nd and 92nd Highlanders marched through the
Place Royale and the Parc," says the " Circumstantial
Detail ;" " one could not but admire their fine appearance, their steady, military demeanour, with their pipes
playing before them, and the beams of the rising sun
shining upon their glittering arms. On many a highland
hill and in many a lowland valley will the deeds of these
brave men be remembered. It was impossible to witness
such a scene unmoved."

It was at four o'clock, on a bright midsummer morning, when the Highlanders of Pack's brigade marched
through the Namur gate, and, mounted on a black Spanish
horse, Fassifern was at the head of the 92nd. Gallant
MacQuarrie led the Royal Highlanders. They were in
the division of Sir Thomas Picton, and, about two o'clock
in the day, came within range of the French artillery in
front of Gemappe, near a farm-house, now immortalised
as *Les Quatre Bras*, where the main road from Charleroi
to Brussels is crossed by that which leads from Nivelle to
Namur. This was doomed to be, as his friend Mor'ar
had, perhaps, too surely foreseen, the scene of Cameron's
last achievement.

The 92nd were ordered to line a ditch in front of the
Namur road, on the left flank of the farmhouse ; Wellington took his station near, and a hot cannonade swept
over them. The proud and fiery Cameron, still pursuing
his feud with the duke, never deigned to take the
slightest notice of him, but allowed him to pass and
repass his post without according either salute or recognising. At four in the afternoon the Black Brunswick
which failed in a charge in front of this position, and

78 THE CAVALIERS OF FORTUNE.

their brave prince fell by a mortal wound. Inspired with new ardour, a body of French cavalry, which had taken the colours of the 69th, or South Lincolnshire Regiment, swept forward, and then the 92nd, the moment the Brunswickers were past, poured an oblique but deadly volley upon the foe, piling men and horses breast high before the roadway. Attended by one soldier, his servant, M. Bourgoyne, an officer of these horse chasseurs, clad in light green uniform, tried to escape round the flank of the 92nd. His brass helmet had fallen off, and displayed his curly black hair; he was a handsome young man, and waved his sabre, repeatedly shouting " *Vive l'Empereur.*" Cameron evinced no disposition to molest this gallant Frenchman, but Wellington exclaimed, " 92nd, d—n it, do not let that fellow escape." Fifty or sixty men then fired at him; but, such was the speed of his horse, the smoke, confusion, and inutility of firing with fixed bayonets, that he escaped all their shots, and caracoled his horse along the whole line of the 92nd. Then private Harold Chisholm, and a corporal of the 42nd Highlanders (who had lost his regiment and joined Cameron), unfixed their bayonets, knelt down, fired, and the chasseur fell to the earth, while his charger limped away on three legs. M. Bourgoyne had been shot through both ankles. Several Hanoverians now rushed forward to bayonet him, but he was rescued by Lieutenants Chisholm and Ewen Ross, who had him borne to the rear. Lieutenant Hector Innes encountered his servant, who was run through from behind by a Belgian lancer and slain. M. Bourgoyne was afterwards sent to Brussels; and his family in Paris expressed to Lieutenant Winchester, and other Highland officers, their deep gratitude for his preservation.

Again the chasseurs charged, and again they were repulsed; while a fire of cannon and musket-shot was thinning fast the ranks of Cameron. Forming under cover of these attacks, the French infantry, flanked by artillery, possessed themselves of a two-storied house, and in heavy column advanced beyond it with great spirit. At that moment,

"92nd!" exclaimed the Duke of Wellington, waving his cocked hat, "prepare to charge."

Fassifern raised his bonnet, set spurs to his horse, the whole regiment sprang over the ditch which bounded the road, and with bayonets charged, dashed through the smoke upon the enemy, and routed them. Officers and men fell fast on every side; but on went the 92nd until the gable of the two-storied house at the corner of the Charleroi road broke the centre of their line. Then they formed up in two wings, rank entire, with the house in the centre; and Cameron sent forward his cousin Ewen Ross, with the light company, into a wood of olives to skirmish, where he received a severe wound in the groin. At that time the grape-shot of the French artillery was sweeping the corn-field between the wood and the farm-house, and shredding away the ripe ears like flakes of snow in the wind. A body of French, who occupied the upper story, were firing briskly from the windows; and others who lined a thick thorn hedge, defended the avenues to the building.

Here it was that the brave Cameron, of Fassifern, fell; but the accounts of his death, as related by Siborne and others, are not strictly correct in detail. He had led his Highlanders close to the hedge, when a shot from the house passed through his belly, entering on the left side, and passing out on the right, tearing the intestines, and inflicting a mortal wound. At the same moment his horse sank under him, pierced by four musket balls.

The regiment gave a wild cheer, burst in the gates of the garden, and fearfully was he avenged by the charged bayonet and clubbed musket; but ere this Captain William Grant, Lieutenants Chisholm, Becher, and M'Pherson were killed, and soon after were barbarously stripped by the French. Nineteen officers of the 92nd were wounded, and 280 rank and file killed and wounded. The aged mother of Chisholm received a widow's pension from the Government, and Campbell, the adjutant, brought his claymore and watch home to her in Strathglass, as mementos of that dark day at Les Quatre Bras.

"The warlike and lamented Colonel Cameron," says his

cousin Lieutenant Ewen Ross (92nd), who was wounded on that day by his side, and whose letter is now before me, "Cameron, than whom there was not a braver or better officer in the best or bravest of armies, was left to the chance care of his orderly sergeant, William Grant, who with a private of the 4th company led him carefully and slowly to a square of office houses at Quatre Bras. His horse being perforated by four musket balls, could carry him no further, and was then shot. The colonel was then carried in a blanket to Gemappe by Sergeant Grant, Colin Mackenzie the drum-major, two drummers named MacLean, and three MacRaes belonging to the band."

Ewen M'Millan and another Highlander carried Cameron into what the soldiers not inaptly named the *bloody hospital* at Gemappe, where his wound was at once pronounced to be mortal. On the position being abandoned, in his hereditary hatred and horror of the French, he expressed great dread of being left to die in their hands; and by nine in the evening his faithful and sorrowing foster-brother procured a common cart, the only vehicle to be had, and placed him in it with Ensign Angus M'Donald, who was also severely wounded, and conveyed them towards Brussels. On the way Cameron asked if the enemy had been defeated? M'Millan answered " yes," though such was not the case, but the poor fellow's heart was ready to burst.

" Defeated—then I die happy !" said Cameron ; " but, oh ! I hope my dear native country will believe that I have served her faithfully."

After this the power of language failed him ; but Angus M'Donald (who afterwards died from the effect of his own wound) related that he heard him praying fervently in Gaelic, and in whispers. He was sinking fast. As the cart passed near where his cousin Ross lay wounded, the latter sent his servant, Angus Sutherland, to inquire how he was; but Cameron's speech was gone—he could only shake his head mournfully, without replying ; and just as the cart entered the village of Waterloo, he laid his head on the breast of the brave and good M'Millan, on whose arm he had reclined, and expired without a sigh.

His faithful follower conveyed the body in by the Namur gate, through which Cameron had that morning ridden forth at the head of his Highlanders, and took it straight to the billet they had occupied in Brussels. As he was obliged to rejoin the regiment without delay for the coming conflict at Waterloo, he made a rough deal coffin, and in this placed the body of his master, brother, and friend—for Cameron had been all these three to the poor Highland private; and thus he interred him, still in his full uniform, by the side of the King's Avenue, on the Ghent road, the Allée Verte. This was on the evening of Saturday, the 17th of June. The body was conveyed to its hastily-made tomb, in a common cart, for poor Ewen could afford nothing better; and the only persons who accompanied him were the landlord of the billet, an honest Belgian, and three wounded Highlanders, who, with their open scars, had tottered out of Brussels to pay the last tribute to him they loved so well, and had followed so long.

"Your lordships will see in the enclosed lists," says Wellington, in a dispatch to the Treasury, dated Orville, 25th June, "the names of some most valuable officers lost to His Majesty's service. Among them, I cannot avoid to mention Colonel Cameron, of the 92nd Regiment, and Colonel Sir H. Ellis of the 23rd, to whose conduct I have frequently called your lordships' attention, and who at last fell, distinguishing themselves at the head of the brave troops which they commanded. Notwithstanding the glory of the occasion, it is impossible not to lament such men, both on account of the public and as friends."

Such was the eulogium of Wellington!

When Cameron was lying dead in the hospital of Gemappe, there was found in the pocket of his Highland regimentals a touching memento, illustrative of his character, and more honourable even than the trophies of battle which he bore on his breast; viz, a pocket-book, containing the names of all the Highland soldiers who had come with him from his father's lands and from Lochaber; marking those whom he had promoted, and those who were dead ; for he counted many of them as his clansmen and kindred, and had ever looked after the interests and welfare of them all as if they had been the children of his own hearth, and he had carried this list with him in all his battles, for it was dated at Alexandria, in Egypt, 24th September, 1801.

A captain of an English regiment was buried near him; and there in that lonely place the graves lay undisturbed until the month of April, 1816. In that year the colonel's brother, Captain Peter Cameron, of the Balcarris, came to Brussels, accompanied by Ewen M'Millan, who led him to the well-remembered place, where the graves lay, near three trees at a corner of the Allée Verte. The colonel's remains were exhumed, placed within another coffin, and brought to Leith ; from whence a king's ship conveyed them to his native Lochaber, where a grand Highland funeral was prepared.

From Fassifern the remains of the colonel were borne for five miles, on the shoulders of his friends and clansmen, to the old kirkyard of Kilmalie, where, in presence of 3000 Highlanders, his aged father, then verging on his eightieth year, laid his head in the grave a second time, while the pipes played a lament ; and now he sleeps in his native earth by the tomb of the MacLauchlans, the *Leine Chrios* of Locheil. Donald Cameron, his chief, was in attendance, with Barra, Barcaldine, and Glencoe, and seventy gentlemen of the clans dined in honour of the occasion, at the Inn of Maryburgh.

Old Highlanders yet tell how sadly and how solemnly on that day the march of *Gille Chriosd* rang in the great glen of Caledonia, and yet remember the dirge composed on that occasion by *Ailean Dall*, or "Blind Allan," the bard of the chieftain of Glengarry—perhaps the last of the family bards in the Scottish Highlands.

In consideration of his son's brilliant services, the venerable Ewen of Fassifern received a baronetcy, and in Kilmalie a monument has been raised above the grave of the hero of Arriverette. Its epitaph is from the pen of Sir Walter Scott, and is remarkable for the elegance of its expression :—

"Sacred to the memory of Colonel John Cameron, eldest son of Ewen Cameron of Fassifern, Bart., whose mortal remains, transported from the field of glory where he died, rest here with those of his forefathers. During twenty years of active military service, with a spirit which knew no fear, and shunned no danger, he accompanied or led, in marches, sieges, and battles, the 92nd Regiment of Scottish Highlanders, always to honour and always to victory; and at length, in the 42nd year of his age, upon the memorable 16th June, 1815, was slain in command of that corps, while actively contributing to achieve the decisive victory of Waterloo, which gave peace to Europe. Thus closing his military career with the long and eventful struggle, in which his services had been so often distinguished; he *died*, lamented by that unrivalled general, to whose long train of success he had so often contributed; by his country, from which he had repeatedly received marks of the highest consideration, and by his sovereign, who graced his surviving family with those marks of honour which could not follow, to this place, him whom they were designed to commemorate. *Reader, call not his fate untimely, who, thus honoured and lamented, closed a life of fame by a death of glory!*"

Few of Cameron's old comrades now survive. I know of only three officers and four privates living of the regiment which, between the 27th August, 1799, and the 18th June, 1815, had lost, in killed and wounded, 117 officers and 1634 men. After being discharged, Ewen M'Millan (who could never learn one word of English) died, in 1840, at Callart, the seat of Cameron's brother, and he now sleeps by his old master's side at Kilmalie. He it is whose memory Scott has embalmed in his "*Dance of Death*," and—

> "Who for many a day
> Had followed stout and stern,
> Where through battles, rout, and reel,
> Storm of shot and hedge of steel,
> Led the grandson of Lochiel,
>   Valiant Fassifern!
>
> Though steel and shot he leads no more,
> Low laid 'mid friends' and foemen's gore

> But long his native lake's wild shore,
> And Suinart rough, and high Ardgower,
>   And Morven long and tell;
>
> And proud Bennevis hear with awe,
> How, upon Bloody Quatré Bras,
> Brave Cameron heard the wild hurrah
>   Of conquest, as he fell!"

Riddled with wounds, Colonel Donald M'Donald of Inch, Knight of St. Vladimir, died in 1830, and is interred at Edinburgh; Lieutenant Winchester died there in 1846. Captain Campbell died, by leaping over a window, with a pistol in each hand, to chastise a person who had insulted him; some have died as emigrants among the wilds of the far West; many more are lying near Uppark, in Jamaica, where the close-ranked headstones show where 1300 of the Gordon Highlanders are sleeping far from their native hills; and now Paymaster Gordon, and Lieutenants Ewen Ross, John Grant, and Alexander Gordon alone survive to wear the *war decoration*.

Sir Samuel Greig.

SIR SAMUEL GREIG, Governor of Cronstadt, Admiral of all the Russias, and commonly called *the Father of the Russian Navy*, was a Scotsman of humble but respectable parentage, and was born at the ancient seaport town of Inverkeithing, in Fifeshire, on the 30th of November, 1735.* He was educated by the parochial schoolmaster. who lived long to boast of his pupil, for the Dominic would seem to have been still alive when the old statistical account of Scotland was published in 1794.

When very young, Samuel Greig entered the British navy, and at an early age obtained the rank of lieutenant. In 1759 he served with the fleet of Admiral Sir Edward Hawke, C.B. (afterwards Lord Hawke), when blockading the harbour of Brest, where a fine French fleet lay, under the pennant of the Marquis de Conflans. At that time a double invasion of Britain (one by the way of Scotland, the other on the coast of England) was threatened; but Commodore Boys blocked up Dunkirk, and Rodney bombarded Havre-de-Grace, while the French transports and flat-bottomed boats lay inactive in Brest, with the fleet of M. de Conflans; till a violent storm in autumn, having driven the ships of Sir Edward Hawke into Torbay, the marquis put to sea with twenty-one sail of the line and four frigates, and threw all England into consternation.

With twenty sail of the line, Hawke left Torbay, and came up with the French fleet between Belleisle and

---

* His father was a seafaring man. In the *Edinburgh Courant*, 24th June, 1761, was the following notice: "The *Thistle*, Capt. Charles Greig, of Inverkeithing, bound for St. Petersburg, passed the Sound on the 6th instant." In Russia, the admiral bore the name of Samuel *Carlovitch* Greig (*i.e.* the son of Charles).

Cape Quiberon, close in on the coast of France, and in the desperate conflict which ensued, "young Greig," though a subaltern, is said to "have eminently distinguished himself." The battle began at two o'clock, P.M., on the 20th of November.

Sir Edward, in the *Royal George*, 110, lay alongside De Conflans in the *Soleil Royale*, 80, which was soon driven on shore and burned. He then lay alongside the *Thesée*, and sent her to the bottom by one broadside. *La Superbe* shared the same fate; the *Juste* was sunk off the mouth of the Loire; the *Hero* was burned; and thus M. de Conflans was totally defeated. Nothing saved the rest of his fleet from irretrievable ruin but the shadow of a tempestuous night, in which two British ships of the line were lost. Lieutenant Greig served with the fleet in all its operations, during the long cruise off the coast of Bretagne, and the blockade of the river Vilaine, to prevent seven French ships which lay there from joining Conflans, whose battered squadron had reached Rochefort; but so dangerous were the storms, and so incessantly tempestuous the weather, that the fear of invasion passed away. Sir Edward Hawke was at length recalled, and the thanks of Parliament and a pension were awarded to him. In this war the British destroyed, or took twenty-seven French ships of the line and thirty-one frigates. Six of their vessels perished. Thus, in all they lost sixty-four sail, while Britain, by every casualty, lost only seven line-of-battle ships and five frigates.

The next scene of Greig's service was at the capture of several of the West India Islands.

War having been declared against the Spaniards, an attack on their settlements in the West Indies was arranged, and Martinico, St. Lucia, St. Vincent, and Grenada were taken. Then Cuba was assailed. Greig was with the fleet, consisting of nineteen sail of the line, eighteen frigates, and 150 transports, which had 10,000 soldiers on board, and sailed for Cuba under Admiral Sir George Pocoke, K.B., whose commodore was the Hon. Augustus Keppel, raised to the peerage in 1782.

The energy and exertions of Lieutenant Greig, during

that tremendous cannonading which preceded the siege and capture of the Moro Castle, elicited the praise of his commander; but no promotion followed, for the time was unfavourable for either Scotsmen or Irishmen rising in the British service. After incredible exertions, difficulties, danger, and slaughter, Havannah was captured, with 180 miles of coast; the Puntal Castle, the ships in the harbour, three millions sterling of booty, and an immense quantity of arms, artillery, and stores were surrendered to the British. Greig's share of this enormous prize-money was very small, being somewhere about 80*l*.

Lieutenant Greig served in many other engagements during that successful war and his bravery, activity, and skill as a seaman had so frequently elicited particular attention, that after the treaty of peace which was signed at Paris in February, 1763, under Lord Bute's administration, when the Court of St. Petersburg requested that a few British officers of distinguished ability might be sent to improve the Russian fleet, Greig was one of the *five* who were first selected, and his rank as lieutenant in the navy of Russia was confirmed by the Empress Catherine II., in 1764. The only stipulation he and the others made was, that they were to have the power of returning to the British service whenever they chose.

Russia, since the beginning of the seventeenth century, has ever been an excellent field for Scottish talent and valour. Thus Greig, by his superior skill in naval affairs, his intelligence and diligent discharge of the duties entrusted to him, soon attracted the special notice of the Imperial Government, and the Empress appointed him a captain in her fleet. He drew many other Scotsmen around him, and, with these, he was at incredible pains to teach the half-barbarous and wholly unlettered Russians the science of seamanship and the art of gunnery, in all of which they were very deficient, "and he rapidly raised the Russian naval service to a degree of respectability and importance which it never before had attained."

In 1769, when he was in his thirty-fourth year, a war broke out between Russia and Turkey, consequent on the civil strife which religious intolerance had kindled in Poland. The Czarina marched in her troops; and while pretending that her sole object was to rescue one body of Polish citizens from the tyranny of the other, she secretly sought to enslave them all, and render their country a province of the Russian empire.

The growing greatness of the latter had alarmed its old hereditary enemy, the Grand Seignior, who required Catherine immediately to withdraw her troops from the Polish republic. Evasions were given, and conflicts began between the Russian and Turkish outposts, on the borders of the Ottoman empire, until the sack of Balta, in Lesser Tartary, and a general massacre of its inhabitants, by the soldiers of the Czarina, procured the committal of her ambassador to the Castle of the Seven Towers, in October, 1769; and hostilities, which were only suspended by the rigour of the season, began early in the spring of the ensuing year.

Captain Greig was appointed commodore of the fleet which was to sail for the Mediterranean, under Alexis Count Orloff; and in that ample arena of service he had an opportunity of displaying his zeal and intrepidity in such a manner as led to his immediate promotion to the rank of flag-officer.

A partial breaking up of the ice in the Baltic enabled some of the fleet to sail; and so early as the 14th of January, 1770, one part of the armament, under the Scottish admiral Elphinstone, consisting of one 70-gun ship, two of sixty guns each, and five others, arrived at Spithead, *en route* for the Archipelago.

The other division, of twenty-two sail of the line, reached Port Mahon, in Minorca, so early as the 4th of January; and by the 6th of March appeared off Cephalonia, the largest of the Ionian Isles, and, with a fair wind, bore away directly for the Morea. At Minorca they left some vessels to wait for Elphinstone, who left Spithead on the 14th of April, passed Gibraltar on the 4th of May, and before the end of July had twice defeated the Turkish fleet—on one occasion encountering three times his force, and destroying eight ships; on the second occasion, with nineteen ships, encountering Giafar Bey, with twenty-three. Giafar's largest ships were destroyed, and his fleet dispersed.

In the great battle of the 6th of July, Greig, Mackenzie, and other officers in the Russian fleet, had an opportunity of eminently rendering good and gallant service; and by their energy and skill the world now saw a naval force, which, as Cormick says, had issued from the foot of the Baltic, able " to shake the remotest parts of the Mediterranean, to intercept the trade of the Levant, to excite and support the insurrection of the Greek Christians, and to leave nothing of the vast empire of their enemies free from alarm and confusion."

The united squadron of the Admirals Count Orloff, Elphinstone, Spiritoff, and Commodore Greig, followed the Turkish fleet, which consisted of fifteen sail of the line, twelve frigates, &c., into the Channel of Scio, which divides the island from Anadoli, or the Lesser Asia; there the Turks were at anchor in a most advantageous position, at the foot of the Gulf of Liberno, where their rear and flanks were protected by rocks.

Early in the morning of the 5th, Commodore Greig was sent to reconnoitre the roads between Scio and the main; and in the afternoon he signalled *the enemy in sight*, consisting of *thirty sail in all*. Orloff, the admiral-general, held a council of war, at which Greig's opinion was specially asked, and his advice followed.

On the 6th, at ten in the morning, Orloff signalled to form line, and the Russian fleet approached the Turks. Orloff was in the centre, with three *Birnates;* Commodore Greig led one division, and Elphinstone the other—in all, ten sail of the line, and five frigates; and they each bore down with ensigns flying, all their ports open, and decks cleared for action. There were many French officers on board of the Turkish fleet, which had been joined by about thirty lieutenants, who had received the permission of King Louis to enter the Sultan's service. A terrible scene of carnage ensued, and the whole conflict is admirably detailed in a letter published in the *Scots' Magazine* for that year, by a Lieutenant Mackenzie, who served on board of her Imperial Majesty's ship the *Switostoff*.

At eleven o'clock the battle began. Admiral Spiritoff ranged up alongside of the Turkish admiral, who was in the *Sultana*, of ninety brass guns, and thus they fought yard-arm and yard-arm together, pouring in and receiving cannon-shot, chain-shot, hand-grenades and musketry. Spiritoff's topmasts were shot away, his bulwarks battered down, and blood ran from his scuppers into the sea. He led his sailors in an attempt to board the *Sultana*, and tore the banner of the Crescent from her stern; but the boarders were repulsed, and obliged to sheer off, for the Turk took fire, and his burning mainmast fell on board of Spiritoff's ship, which also became wrapped in flames; and in ten minutes both ships blew up. "I leave you to judge," says Mackenzie, "of the dreadful scene of seeing so many hundreds of poor souls blown into the air, while the rest were hotly engaged." Spiritoff and twenty-four officers saved themselves in the barge.

The remainder of the Turkish fleet, after being severely mauled by Elphinstone and Greig (Orloff was little of a seaman), cut their cables, and ran into the harbour of Chismeh, a small town in the Sanjak of Siglah, at the bottom of a bay one mile broad, and two miles long. Across the mouth of this bay the fleet, under Orloff, Elphinstone, and the Commodore, lay for the whole night, firing round shot, and throwing in bombs. The fire of Greig's ship was particularly destructive; but on the Turks getting batteries established on the height between Scio and the coast of Anadoli, he and the two admirals were obliged to haul off. Two fireships were prepared on the 7th, under the direction of Elphinstone and Greig; and a council of war was held by the principal officers in the cabin of Count Orloff. It was there suggested by the Commodore, and resolved upon, that at midnight four ships of the line, two frigates, and the bomb-ketch, should enter the harbour, and while attacking the enemy, send the fireships on their errand of destruction; but volunteers were required to lead, and three officers, all Scotsmen, at once stepped forward. These were, Commodore Greig, Lieutenant Mackenzie, of the *Switostoff*, and Captain-Lieutenant Drysdale (or Dugdale, for this officer is called alternately by both names in many accounts of these wars), and they made every preparation for the desperate duty before them. At half-past twelve at night the signal was made to weigh anchor, and bear into the little bay ; Drysdale and Mackenzie had the fireships ; Greig led the ships of the line and the two frigates, which, at four hundred yards' distance, cannonaded the Turks, while the bomb-ketch plied its mortars. Greig signalled the fireships to bear down ; Drysdale and Mackenzie answered it, and, favoured by the wind, ran right into the teeth of the Turks, whose centre ship was at that moment set on fire by a fortunate shot from the Commodore.

Drysdale's crew unfortunately left his ship before the proper time. Indeed, the Russians were so overcome with terror by the darkness of the night, the boom of the Turkish shot, and by the fireships, of which they were unable to comprehend the use, that it was only by dint of his sword and pistols that Drysdale kept them to their duty ; but when near the enemy the helmsman abandoned the rudder, the whole crew sprang into their boat, and abandoned the brave Scotsman on board of the fireship !

In this terrible situation his native courage never deserted him ; he lashed the helm, and (though a boat full of armed Turks was pulling alongside) held the ship on her course till, with his own unaided hands, he hooked the grapnel-irons to the anchor-cable of the nearest ship, which proved to be a large caravella. He then fired the train by discharging a pistol, and in doing so was severely scorched by the explosion. At the moment the Turks boarded him on one side he sprang into the sea from the other, and swam from the blazing ship. Many a shot was fired after him, but he escaped, and was saved with difficulty by the boats of Greig.

The fireships blew up with the most admirable effect, and the result was, beyond Greig's utmost expectations, decisive and disastrous, for in five hours the whole Turkish fleet was burned to the water-edge and totally

destroyed—all, save one ship, Giafar Bey's, of seventy
guns, four row-galleys, and some gilt barges of twenty-four
oars. The morning sun, as he shone upon the Isle of
Scio and Anadolian shore, saw a scene of unexampled
devastation—every Turkish mast had vanished from the
bay, and pieces of charred and floating wreck alone remained! The following were the ships destroyed by
Greig:—

Capitan Alebi, 84 guns.	Achmet, 86 guns.
Bashaw, 90 guns.	Hamisi, 60 guns.
Patrona Ayckrece, 80 guns.	Ali Randioto, 60 guns.
Reala Mustapha, 96 guns.	Melehin, 80 guns.
Mulensi Achmet, 84 guns.	Rapislan Bashaw, 64 guns.
Emir Mustapha, 84 guns.	Zefirbe, 84 guns.

La Barbarocine, 64 guns, was towed out of the harbour
by his boats. Two other large ships (names unknown)
were burned, with four frigates, eight 40-gun ships, eight
galleys, and several row-boats. He rescued 400 Christian
slaves, hauled close in shore, bombarded the town, blew
up the castle, and reduced the whole place to a heap of
rubbish before nine o'clock in the morning, by which time
more than 6000 Turks had been shot, burned, or
drowned.

For this brilliant service Greig was at once made a
rear-admiral by Count Orloff, while Lieutenants Drysdale
and Mackenzie received the rank of captain, all of which
appointments the Empress was pleased to confirm.
Though the unfortunate Capitan Pacha, who commanded,
was severely wounded, the Sultan ordered his head to
be struck off, and appointed Giafar Bey admiral in his
place. As rear-admiral Greig's pay amounted to 2160
roubles per annum. Immediately after this victory Admiral Elphinstone sailed with his squadron for the Isle of
Tenedos, to block up the Dardanelles, where he captured
forty vessels destined for Constantinople, forced most of
the Isles of the Archipelago to declare for Russia, and
levied contributions everywhere, taxing Mitylene in
150,000 piastres. Greig accompanied Count Orloff to the
siege of the Castle of Lemnos, which proceeded slowly,
the only troops they had being revolted Greeks, who were

afterwards cut to pieces by Hassan Bey, and then the Russians bent all their efforts to force the passage of the Dardanelles ; but so strongly was it fortified by the Chevalier Tott, and other Frenchmen, that every attempt proved futile.

In the winter of 1770 Greig's commission was further confirmed by a letter from the Empress, and in his ship, the *Three Primates*, he brought the nominal commander-in-chief, Count Orloff, to Leghorn on the 7th of December, as the fleet was leaving the Archipelago for want of men, and the batteries of the Dardanelles were daily becoming stronger under the skilful eye of Tott, to whom the grateful Sultan paid 100 scudi daily, as the saviour of his capital.

At Leghorn the Sieur Rutherford, Commissary of the Russian Court, sold all the prizes taken by the fleet. Having secret views of his own concerning the unfortunate Princess Tarakanoff, the Count Orloff, who is styled minister plenipotentiary, general of the Russian troops, and admiral-general, proposed to spend the winter partly at Pisa, and partly at Leghorn, " in order to take care of the Russian squadron," as peace was expected. Greig is said to have demurred ; Admiral Elphinstone expressed dissatisfaction, and when ordered to sail on "a secret expedition" he bluntly declined. An altercation ensued between him and the count. He was put under arrest, and reported to the Empress, who recalled him, and he retired from her service in disgust. On his presentation to Catherine he appeared in the blue uniform of the British navy, on which she turned coldly away, saying to one of her favourites, " It is high time this Scot was out of my service, when he has laid aside my uniform !"

Meanwhile the fleet was not inactive, for Mackenzie, Brodie, and other officers, who served under Spiritoff, were very zealous. Thus, by the 20th January, 1771, they had destroyed nineteen Dulcignotte tartans, and exacted from the Isles of the Archipelago the same tribute which they yearly paid the Sultan. At the same time the Russian troops had taken the city of Sinope, on the Black Sea, the fortress of Giurgievo, and other places in the

Turkish provinces. A squadron, commanded by the Knights of Malta, joined Orloff's flag; Scio was again ravaged by the Russians, a large dulcignotte destroyed, and the fighting among the fertile and beautiful isles of Greece was incessant; Greig was constantly employed, and daily added to his reputation as a brave and skilful officer.

He had assisted in the destruction of all the magazines which had been formed to supply the Turkish capital; at the bombardment of Negropont, the capital of the ancient Eubœa, where the troops were landed to destroy the stores of corn and flour; he had cruised along the shore of Macedonia; been at the bombardment of Cavalla in Romelia, and the destruction of the storehouses at Salonica; and in the Gulf of Kassanderah, while Count Theodore, the brother of Count Alexis Orloff, scoured all the shores of Anadoli, and cannonaded Rhodez. The united Russian fleet, under the three admirals, Orloff, Spiritoff, and Greig, made sixty-six sail in all on the 1st of November.

While the Russian army by land was making daily successful attacks on the Turks, and had crossed the Danube under General Romanzow, and twice besieged Silistria, pushing the war round the shores of the Black Sea, and into the Crimea, the naval squadrons had many desperate encounters in the Archipelago, and one very sharp action off the Isle of Scio, when seven Russian ships of the line and two frigates engaged ten Turkish ships and six large galleys, on the 10th of October, 1773, and after fighting from ten in the morning until long past mid-day, entirely defeated them, taking five sail, sinking two, and putting the rest to flight. In one of these encounters a ball struck Admiral Greig, and bent one of the points of his cross of St. George, carrying away a piece of the enamel. Every captain of the Russian navy then wore the military order of St. George, the badge of which is a knight and dragon, attached to a black ribbon.

A descent was made upon the Isle of Cyprus; another on Candia, and elsewhere; but the Russians were repulsed, and four sacks filled with their *scalps* were sent from Stanchio as a proof of the reception they had met with in that island.

In the end of 1773 Greig returned to St. Petersburg, and, with Admiral Sir Charles Knowles, made every exertion to have a better and more efficient squadron dispatched to the Dardanelles. With this under his command he sailed again from Cronstadt, and after touching at Portsmouth, bore on for the Mediterranean on the 17th of February, 1774. With his flag flying as vice-admiral, he reached Leghorn, where, for purposes of his own, Alexis Orloff was again loitering. On this expedition Greig was accompanied by his wife, for whom every accommodation had been made in his ship, the *Issidorum;* but being of course unwilling that she should risk the dangers of the Turkish war, he landed her at Leghorn, where the house of the Russian consul was assigned to her as a residence. The ships composing his fleet were—

The Issidorum, 74 guns . . .	Captain Surminoff.
The Mironfitz, 74 guns . . .	Captain Mouskin Pouskin.
St. Alexander Newski, 64 guns	Captain Voronari.
Demetrius Douski, 64 guns . .	Captain Pajaskoff.
St. Paulus, 30 guns	Captain Palovski.

During Greig's brief sojourn at Leghorn there occurred one of those atrocities which so frequently blackened the reign of Catherine II.

Alexis Count Orloff, a man of the most inhuman character and brutal propensities, had conceived a passion for the young and beautiful Princess Tarakanoff, daughter of the late Empress Elizabeth, by her clandestine marriage with the Grand Veneur. This princess had been conveyed to Rome by the artful Prince Radzivil, beyond the reach of Catherine's intrigues and tyranny. But Orloff had been ordered to *decoy her back* to St. Petersburg on the first opportunity. Accordingly, during one of his visits to Leghorn, he laid a snare for her, by sending an Italian, named Signor Ribas, afterwards a Knight of Malta, to visit her. This vile person, who found the poor princess in a mean lodging, told her that he "had come to pay homage to her beauty and misfortunes, and to deplore the destitution in which he found her." He then offered her money, adding that he "was commissioned by Alexis Orloff to promise her the throne her mother had filled, and at the same time his sincere love, if she would honour him with her hand." After some hesitation she was overcome by the apparent sincerity and brilliance of the proposal, which seemed the more splendid by her destitute condition, and accepted the offer of Orloff He visited her repeatedly; a feigned marriage was performed by two Russian officers, disguised as Catholic priests; villainy completed the imposture: for a time—two or three months—he placed her in a magnificent palace at Pisa, and then brought her to Leghorn. It was at this crisis that Admiral Greig entered the port, and his wife* is mentioned as being among the first to visit the young princess, who was far from suspecting the terrible snare laid for her—a snare of which the *English* consul is said to have been cognizant. Deluded by the caresses and feigned love of Orloff, she begged to be "shown the large and beautiful ships of the Russian fleet," which was ordered to prepare for her reception.

On her arriving at the beach, she was placed by Orloff in a handsome boat, screened by a silken awning; the second barge conveyed the vice-admiral and other British officers, who for many years after were all unconscious of the villainy of Orloff. Music, huzzas, and salutes of artillery welcomed the unhappy daughter of the Empress Elizabeth on board the nearest ship; and the moment she stood upon its deck, she was *handcuffed* with heavy irons, and thrust into one of the lowest cabins. She threw herself at the feet of Orloff, and implored pity as *his wife;* but was answered by laughter and mockery, while the anchor was weighed, and the ship sailed for St. Petersburg, where she was shut up in a fortress on the Neva, and was *never heard of again!*

Rumour adds a darker tinge to this tale of Russian cruelty, by asserting that, two years afterwards, when the

---

* Tooke states that Mrs. Greig was not at Leghorn; but the French authorities affirm that she *was*, and place this event in 1774 waters of the Neva rose ten feet by an inundation, they filled the horrid vault in which she was confined, and drowned her. Her body was then flung into the stream, and swept by its current into the Gulf of Finland.

But to return. As the wind continued fair, Greig bore away for Paros, a beautiful isle of the central Cyclades, which was the rendezvous of the fleet under Spiritoff, and where a great many small vessels of an entirely new construction, were prepared for the purpose of embarking and landing troops.

Here the Russians had seized and sold a number of Venetian ships, consequently the senate ordered all their vessels of war to be prepared to resist the new armament of Greig, and in March rigged two ships of 84 guns each, and two more of 75: these ultimately came to blows with the Turks, and defeated them off the Isle of Candia.

On the 10th of March, tidings having come to Paros that the Turkish fleet were about to surprise the Russian garrison at Sciros, a 50-gun ship and four frigates were despatched to oppose the attempt, but signally failed— for they were all burned or taken but one. The general head-quarters of the Czarina's forces were at the Isle of Paros; and there, during the spring of 1774, the Admirals Spiritoff and Greig anchored their armaments at Port Naussa, on the northern shore—one of the finest harbours in the Archipelago, and in the channel between Paros and the bold and lofty coast of Naxos. Their regular troops occupied Marmora and Zimbido, while their Albanian allies were at Bachia. Greig and Spiritoff made every effort to refit the old ships, and prepare them for hostilities in summer, and when their cruisers joined them from Patmos and Tasso; but before anything of importance was achieved, the Empress concluded a peace with the Turks—a peace, says Frederick the Great, "resplendent with glory, by the success which her arms had met with against her enemies during the war;" and by this peace, the treaty of Kutchuk-Kainardgi, Catherine stipulated that the Crimea, which had hitherto been under the subjection of the Turks, should be, in all time coming, an independent sovereignty under its own khans, thus lessening the power of the Porte.

Admiral Greig now returned to Russia with the fleet, and for many years devoted himself entirely to the improvement of the Russian marine, and the development of the naval resources of the Empire—remodelling its code of discipline, relaxing its barbarity, civilizing and educating its officers and men, by training the marine cadets on board of two frigates or floating academies, and thus justly earning for himself the honourable and endearing sobriquet of the *Father of the Russian Navy.* For these and other valuable services the grateful Empress bestowed upon him the government of Cronstadt, and a commission as High Admiral of all the Russias, at the same time decorating him with the Orders of St. Andrew, St. George of the second class, St. Vladimir, which she instituted on the 22nd September, 1782 (her twentieth coronation day). and St. Anne of Holstein, which is always the gift of the Grand Duke. His great assistant was Mr. Gordon, director-general of the ship-building, who at one time had building, under his own immediate care, two ships of 100 guns each, three of 90 guns each, six of 70 guns each, and ten of 40 guns each—all of which, for their skilful construction, strength, swiftness, and beauty of mould, had never been equalled by any previous effort of Russian naval architecture.

The admiral's pay was now 7000 roubles per annum.

In accordance with the custom of the Russian nobility, who add the Christian name of their father to their own, with the termination *owitch,* which signifies *the son of,* we find the Scottish admiral signing and designating himself "Samuel Carlovitch Greig." He was ever treated with the greatest consideration and honour by the Empress, who, in the year 1776, paid him the compliment of a visit—then esteemed an unparalleled act of condescension for the crowned head of Russia, who, among many absurd and hyperbolical titles, had (and perhaps still retains) the blasphemous one of "Chamberlain to Almighty God."

On the 18th of July the Empress, attended by all the

great officers of her state and household, went in a magnificent barge from Oranienbaum to Admiral Greig's ship, the yards of which he had manned. As soon as he had handed her on board, the Imperial standard was hoisted, and the whole fleet fired a salute, which was responded to by *nine hundred* pieces of cannon in Cronstadt. Dinner was set in Greig's cabin for the Empress and a hundred guests, who were the principal officers of her marine and other departments. The whole fleet then weighed anchor, and Catherine, accompanied by the infamous Orloff, Field-Marshal Count Galitzin, and Count Bruce, the adjutant on duty, was rowed in her barge along the line amid another salute of cannon. Before returning to Oranienbaum she placed on Greig's breast the golden and eight-pointed star of St. Alexander Newski, with the red ribbon, which is worn over the left shoulder.

During the peace, Greig was unremitting in his efforts to draw British officers into the service, and the number who offered their swords and valour to the Czarina soon conduced, by their skill and talent, to render her navy for the first time respectable and formidable in Europe.*

Thus it was that, in 1799, in Lord Duncan's line of battle, August 24th, at the Texel, we find among the Russian ships of war, the *Ratisvan*, commanded by Captain Greig; and in September, under the same gallant admiral, the Scottish captains Scott, Dunn, Boyle, Maclagan, Ogilvie, and Rose, commanding the Russian ships *Alexander Newski*, 74; *Neptune*, 54; *Rafaill*, 44; *Revel*, 44; *Minerva*, 38; and *St. Nicholas*, 38, embarking the Russian troops at Revel; and thus it was, that when Russia, fifteen years before, projected a new war against

---

* In the battle with the Swedes in 1790, four Russian ships were commanded by Scottish captains, viz., Denniston, whose head was shot off; Marshal, who was drowned when leading his boarders; Miller and Aikin, who each lost a leg. The latter died under the torture of his wound. Six Russian admirals, all Scotchmen, Mackenzie, Ogilvie, Mercer, Mason, and the two Greigs, have hoisted their flags in the Black Sea. Mackenzie was the first naval chief at Sebastopol.—See SLADE'S *Travels*, vol. ii.

the Turks, in consequence of their interference with the affairs of the independent Crimea, the Empress found her fleet to consist of upwards of ninety sail at Cronstadt, Revel, and in the Sea of Asoph.

By the 11th of October, 1783, Admiral Greig had ready a fleet for the Mediterranean consisting of twelve sail of the line—viz., one of 76 guns, two of 74, three of 70, four of 64, two of 60, four frigates, a sloop, three storeships, two fireships, two bomb-ketches, and two galleys. The vice-admiral of this fine armament was his old brother-officer, who had shared with him the glory of that night's desperate work in the Bay of Chismeh. All these ships were in the best condition, and British officers were judiciously distributed among them; but the poor Khan of the Crimea, Sahim Gueray—the last of the lineal descendants of the far-famed Ghengiz Khan—abdicated his power, which he transferred to the Czarina, and his valuable territory on the Black Sea was quietly confirmed to her by a treaty with the Sultan in 1784. Since then it has formed a part of the Russian Empire, together with part of the Kuban and all the land between the Boog, the Dneister, and the Black Sea.

The next scene of Admiral Greig's active service was against the Swedes, who became implicated in the dispute which ensued between the Porte and the Czarina, against whom they rashly declared war. Hostilities ensued; the Swedish troops advanced into Finland, and recaptured several towns.

"Alexis Count Orloff, appointed to command the Mediterranean fleet, has declined that honour, and left the court," says the *Gentleman's Magazine* for April, 1788; "and Admiral Greig, on whom it in course devolved, has pleaded the necessity of a journey to his native country, to be excused from that service." The armament offered Greig by the Empress was on a magnificent scale; it consisted of twenty-eight ships of the line, three of them carrying 100 guns and 800 officers and seamen each; six of 90 guns, with 650 seamen each; four of 80 guns, with 600 seamen each; eleven of 74 guns, with 500 men each; two of 64 guns, with 400 men each; two hundred and forty-eight sail of frigates, sloops, and transports, containing eleven battalions of infantry; two carracques, with 1000 horse, and seven of marines; twenty-five victual and hospital ships, mounting in all 1194 pieces of cannon, and having 28,000 men on board.

But the admiral does not seem either to have visited Scotland or sailed with this armament to the Mediterranean, as he assumed command of the Imperial Baltic fleet, destined to oppose the Duke of Sudermania, brother of the King of Sweden, who put to sea with twenty-one sail, consisting of the *Gustavus*, 111, *Sophia, Magdalena*, and *Prins Gustaf*, of 70 guns each; nine 60-gun ships, six 40-gun frigates, and three smaller vessels.

Count Wachdmeister led the van, Captain Linderstedt the rear. Sweden made incredible exertions in this war, the object of which was to retake Finland and Carelia; four 40-gun frigates were fitting out at Gottenberg, and nine ships of the line at Carlscrona. The news of these and other armaments filled St. Petersburg with something very like consternation; but Greig prepared for sea with all the vessels he could collect, and the utmost activity prevailed at Riga, where Count Brown, a veteran Irish general, was governor. Greig declared, however, to the Empress, that if the United Kingdoms of Great Britain engaged in this war antagonistic to Russia, he would feel himself under the painful necessity of resigning his high rank, and returning to his former position of lieutenant in the Royal Navy; "that he would always exert himself to the utmost against any other power who might be in alliance with the enemy, but that he would never fire a shot in the face of his native country." He ordered the calibre of the ship guns to be altered, directing that all from 24-pounders downwards should be of less weight with a larger bore.

In May, 1788, while war and preparations were pending, a dispute ensued between the Empress and upwards of sixty British officers of her fleet, on occasion of a rumour being spread abroad, that she meant to receive into her service Paul Jones, the celebrated Scottish renegade. These gentlemen nearly all of whom were Scotsmen, waited on the President of the Admiralty, and resigned their commissions, delivering, at the same time, a manifesto, "whereby they not only refused to serve under, but even *with* that officer." The French officers who were paid by the Czarina displayed the same repugnance to have this famous privateersman for a comrade; and by this dispute, which, however, was soon arranged, ten sail of the line were for a time completely unofficered. To the satisfaction of Admiral Greig and his compatriots, it was arranged, that "Mr. Jones should never be appointed to command in that part of the ocean where they were employed." In the meantime, a scandalous adventure of the Chevalier Paul with a girl of loose character, ended his hope of employment *even* under Catherine II.

Greig now received from the Emperor of Germany a present of 10,000 roubles and a valuable estate in Livonia. This was just before he sailed from Cronstadt with the fleet, which consisted of one three-decker, eight 74-gun ships, eight 66-gun ships, and seven frigates, to oppose the formidable force of the Duke of Sudermania, whom he overtook between the island of Schten Seaker and the Bay of Cabo de Grund.

The Duke of Sudermania states, that with thirty-one sail he was cruising in the Narrows of Kalkboden and Elkhomen in a dense fog, with an easterly wind, when, early on the morning of the 17th of July, the report of alarm guns ahead summoned his crews hurriedly to quarters, and almost before order of battle could be assumed, amid the dangers of a lee shore, enveloped in the morning mist, the fleet of the Scoto-Russian Admiral, consisting then of thirty-three sail, all in close order, were within gunshot, his van being close to the prince's centre. After considerable manœuvring, in which the skill of Greig is praised by the prince in his dispatch, they were within musket-shot by five P.M., when the battle began in all its fury, and sixty-four ships, twenty-nine of which were sail of the line, engaged in all the carnage of a yard-arm conflict; and so thickly did the smoke of the Russian fleet settle down upon the Swedes, "that it was impossible to make or answer signals," says the Duke of Sudermania, "or even to distinguish our own line."

The duke was in the *Charles Gustavus*, a three-decker; Greig fought his own ship, the *Rotislaw* of 100 guns; and the operations of the day are thus detailed by him in his dispatch to the Empress:—

"I most humbly beg to inform your Imperial Majesty, that on the 17th of July, about noon, we fell in with the Swedish fleet, consisting of fifteen ships of the line, carrying from sixty to seventy guns; eight large frigates (carrying 24-pounders), which were brought into the line owing to their weight of metal; five smaller frigates, and three tenders, commanded by the Prince of Sudermania, with an admiral's flag, and having under his command one vice and two rear admirals. I immediately signalled to make sail towards the enemy; they formed line and awaited us—our fleet, as it came up, formed also. The weather was clear, with a light breeze from the south-east. We bore right down on the enemy's line, and my flagship, the *Rotislaw*, engaged the Swedish admiral about five P.M.

"The engagement was very hot on both sides, and lasted without intermission till six. Twice the Swedes attempted to retreat, but as it fell quite calm during the contest, and the ships would not answer their helms, the two fleets fell into some confusion, but the fire was kept up on both sides till dark, and then the Swedes, assisted by their boats, got to a distance from our ships. In this action we have taken the *Prince Gustavus*, of 70 guns, which carried the vice-admiral's flag.

"She was defended with great bravery for more than an hour against the *Rotislaw*, and we had above 200 men killed and wounded on board before she struck. On board of her was the Count Wachdmeister, A.D.C. General to the King of Sweden, who commanded the van of the Swedish fleet. He came on board of my ship with an officer whom I sent to take possession, and delivered to me his flag and sword. In consideration of his gallant defence, I restored to him the latter.

"I am sorry to inform your Majesty, that in the night, and *after* the battle had ceased, the *Wadislaw* dropped astern of our line and fell among the Swedish fleet, by whom she was taken, as the darkness of the night and the thickness of the smoke concealed her from us. I received notice of this disaster about midnight from a petty officer, who was dispatched to me before the enemy took possession. In this engagement several of your Majesty's ships have received considerable damage, and the whole fleet so much in masts and rigging, that I was not in a condition to pursue the enemy, who, favoured by the wind, crowded all the sail they could to reach the coast of Finland, to the east of Cabo de Grund, and we lost sight of them steering north-east. This action began between the island of Schten Seaker and the Bay of Cabo de Grund, the former bearing SSE. distant three German miles, and the latter NWW. about the same distance, seven and a half miles east of Hohlang. I subjoin a list of the killed and wounded. The whole fleet are now repairing sails and rigging.

"I must say, on this occasion, that I never saw a battle maintained with more spirit and courage on both sides; and we have nothing to boast of but the capture of the commander of the vanguard, and that the enemy left *us in possession* of the field of battle. All the flag officers, and the greater portion of the captains gave proofs of the utmost courage and firmness; and the bravery of the subaltern officers in general is entitled to every praise; BUT it is with grief, that I am obliged to declare myself very much dissatisfied with the conduct of certain captains, whom I shall be under the necessity of superseding This will be done after a more particular inquiry, the account of which I shall transmit to your Majesty. If they had done their duty like good officers and faithful subjects, this action would have been more completely decisive, and have produced consequences equally satisfactory to your Majesty and your glorious empire.

must not fail, at the same time, to make a special report of those who, on this occasion, personally distinguished themselves by their courage and conduct. (Here follow the lists.)

"SAM. CARLOVITCH GREIG.

"H. I. M. Ship *Rotislaw*, July 18th, 1788."

The duke says that his fleet was swept round by the current, and every ship was thus raked fore and aft by those of Greig; that after a lull in the conflict, it was renewed at 8 P.M., when, after another desperate encounter, the Swedish fleet, with lights at the mast-heads, bore away for Helsingfors with all sail set, leaving the *Prins Gustaf*, of seventy guns, lying disabled and without a flag; that many of the Russian ships were severely mauled, but the Swedes were riddled; for masts, spars, and even the rudders of some were knocked to pieces, while most of them had received perilous shots between wind and water.

The *Wadislaw*, which they took, was a copper-bottomed seventy-four, carrying 32 and 42-pounders, with 738 men. It was ten at night before the last shot was fired. The Russians remained masters of the channel, with all their colours flying; but had the officers all done their duty, the Swedes would not have escaped so easily, if at all. Greig had 6000 troops on board; their presence in close action greatly increased his list of casualties, for he had 319 killed and 666 wounded, whereas the Swedes had only eight officers struck, and the number of seamen is not known.

Admiral Greig was soon after reinforced by four ships of the line; but as the Duke of Sudermania received six more of seventy guns each, the fleets remained of nearly equal strength.

Count Wachdmiester had yielded his sword to Greig, who returned it to him, saying, "I will never be the man to deprive so brave and worthy an officer of his sword—I beseech you to receive it."

After making a suitable reply, the count sheathed it, and said, "that neither he nor any other person in Sweden believed that the Russian fleet was in so admirable a condition as he found it."

The Russian seamen had fought with incredible ardour and bravery; when the wadding ran short, many of them tore off their clothing to clean and charge home the cannon; but *all* the officers were by no means partners in their glory; for Greig found himself under the painful necessity of placing under arrest two captains, two captain-lieutenants, and thirteen other officers, all Russians, and sending them to St. Petersburg in the frigate *La Kergopolte*, of twenty-four guns, charged with having "abandoned Rear-Admiral Bergen when he was surrounded by four Swedish ships, and defending himself against them for two hours with the greatest bravery, till he was compelled to strike, when his ship, the *Wadislaw*, was completely shattered."

Sir Samuel Greig added, that he had repeatedly signalled to those officers "to advance and support the commander of their division, but that either from not understanding the said signals, or from some other reason, they remained where they were, and saw him taken." Concerning their misconduct, and the battle of the 17th July, the Empress immediately wrote, with her own hand, the following characteristic letter to her gallant Admiral:—

"TO THE MOST WORTHY AND BRAVE, &c.

"We should be wanting in that gratitude and politeness which should ever distinguish sovereigns, did we not with the utmost speed convey to you our approbation of your exemplary conduct; and the obligations which we owe you for your intrepid conduct in your engagement with the fleet of our enemy, the Swedish king. To the constant exertion of *your abilities*, and *your zeal* for the glory of the common cause of ourselves and the whole Russian Empire, may, under God, be attributed the very signal victory you have gained; and we have not the smallest doubt, but that every part of our dominions, to which this event shall be transmitted, will behold it in its proper view. It is with grief we read the record of these poltroons, who, unable to catch fire from the spirited exertions of their brother-warriors, have so signalized themselves in the annals of treasonable cowardice! and to that cowardice the Swede has to boast that any ship of their fleet escaped when so encountered.

"It is our pleasure that the delinquents mentioned in your despatch be immediately brought to Cronstadt, to await our further displeasure. We sincerely wish *you*, and all with you, health, and the most signal assistance of the Almighty God, whose aid we have invoked, and of whose assistance we cannot doubt in a cause so just.

"Your services will live perpetually in our remembrance; and the annals of our Empire must convey your name to posterity with reverence and with love!

"So saying, we recommend you to God's keeping ever. Done at St. Petersburg, the 23rd of July, in the year of grace 1788.

"CATHERINE."

The punishment of the seventeen unfortunates was peculiarly Russian in its barbarity; for they were placed in chains, with iron collars around their necks, and doomed to perpetual slavery in the hulks at Cronstadt, though many were cadets of the noblest Muscovite families.

In 1789, Professor Schloeger, of Gottingen, published in his political magazine the orders issued by the Czarina to the admiral before leaving Cronstadt; and by these it appears, that he "was to attack, and, if possible, to carry away the Swedish admiral-general, even at the total loss of the whole fleet of Russia."

For nearly a fortnight Greig busied himself in thoroughly refitting his fleet; on the 6th of August he signalled to weigh anchor at dawn, and on the 7th arrived off Sveaborg, where he found four Swedish ships at anchor in the roads; but they cut their cables, and, under a press of sail, retired into port in confusion. Greig followed them boldly, and just as his leading ship came within musket-shot of the sternmost Swede, the latter struck upon a sunken rock; her mainmast went by the board, and after maintaining a short cannonade with Admiral Roslainow, she struck her colours. The other three escaped into shallow water. Greig's boats took possession of the bilged ship, which proved to be the *Gustavus Adolphus*, of 64 guns, commanded by *Colonel* Christierne, who was taken prisoner with thirteen officers and 530 men, after which Greig ordered her to be blown up. He next seized a ship laden with cables, sails, medicine, &c., for the Swedish fleet.

Meanwhile the Duke of Sudermania remained a quiet spectator in Sveaborg, where he was completely blocked up by Greig, although he had under his command sixteen ships of the line and eight frigates.

Till the 9th Greig remained off Sveaborg, which is strongly fortified by nature and art, and then, in the hope that the duke would come out, as the wind was favourable for his doing so, he sailed slowly across the Gulf of Finland towards the opposite coast of Revel, and on his approaching the isle of Margen, placed his cruisers towards the west, so as completely to cut off the Swedish fleet from all succour by way of Carlscrona, and to prevent them forming a junction with five ships laden with stores, of which they were in the greatest need.

Here Greig was joined by two 64-gun ships; and on the 14th of August he was off Revel in Esthonia. Meanwhile the Swedish and Russian troops had many fierce encounters in Finland; but the former were unsuccessful, and this expedition ended in defeat and disaster.

The indefatigable Greig continued to cruise in the gulf until the month of October; and, though suffering from a severe illness, he completely blocked up the Swedes in Sveaborg, cut them off from succour, and saved St. Petersburg from alarm.

On the 2nd October, the weather became exceedingly stormy, and the Russian fleet were all dispersed. Then the Duke of Sudermania thought he might essay something against Greig; but, though sick and infirm, the latter soon collected all his ships, and the blockade was resumed more strictly than ever ; but, unhappily, his illness terminated in a violent fever, and, on the 26th of that month the brave admiral expired, in the fifty-third year of his age, on board of his flag-ship the *Rotislaw*, to the great sorrow of every officer and seaman in the fleet, where, by his bravery, justice, generosity, and goodness of heart, he had indeed won for himself the honourable title of the *Father of the Russian Navy*.

The tidings of his death were the signal for a general mourning at St. Petersburg ; and, while Admiral Spiritoff assumed the command of the fleet, the Empress ordered the interment of her favourite officer to be conducted with a pomp, solemnity, and magnificence never before witnessed in Russia.

The funeral took place on the 5th of December. Some days before it, the body lay on a state bed in the hall of the Admiralty, which was hung with black cloth, while the doors were festooned with white crape, and the vast apartment was lighted by silver lustres. Under a canopy of crape the body was placed on three small arches, dressed in full uniform, the head being encircled by a wreath of laurel. At its foot stood an urn, adorned with silver anchors and streamers, inscribed—

"S. G. nat. d. 30 Nov. 1735—obit d. 15 Oct. 1788."

The coffin stood on six feet of massy silver. It was covered with black velvet, lined with white satin ; the handles and fringes were of pure silver, and the pillows of blonde lace. On three tabourettes of crimson and gold lay his five orders of knighthood—one of them, the St. George's Cross, mutilated by a shot in the Archipelago ; and around were twelve pedestals, covered with crape and flowers, bearing twelve gigantic candles. At the head of the bed hung all his flags ; and two staff officers and six marine captains were constantly beside it until the day of interment, when Lieutenant the Baron Vanden Pahlen pronounced a high eulogy in honour of the brave deceased.

The cannon of the ramparts and fleet fired minute-guns during the procession from the Admiralty to the Cathedral of St. Catherine, through streets lined by the troops. The funeral pageant was very magnificent and impressive.

Swartzenhoup's dragoons, with standards lowered; the grenadiers of the Empress, with arms reversed; the public schools of the capital; the clergy of the Greek Church; General Lehman, of the marine artillery, and two marshals bearing Greig's admiral's staff and five orders of knighthood; eighteen staff officers, and three bearing naval standards, preceded the body, which was borne on a bier drawn by six horses, led by six bombardiers, and attended by twelve captains of ships, followed by their coxswains. Then came General Wrangel, governor of the city, with the nobles, citizens, the marshals with their staves, and a regiment of infantry with arms reversed, and its band playing one of those grand deadmarches which are peculiar to Russia. So, with a band of choristers preceding it, and amid the tolling of bells, the remains of Admiral Greig were conveyed to the great cathedral, and there lowered into their last resting-place, amid three discharges of cannon and musketry from the ramparts, the troops, and the fleet, where he was so well beloved and so much lamented.

Every officer who attended had a gold ring presented to him by Catherine II., with the admiral's name and the day of his death engraved upon it; and a magnificent monument has since been erected to mark the place where he lies—a man " no less illustrious for courage and naval skill, than for piety, benevolence, and every private virtue."

His estate in Livonia is still in possession of his descendants.

His son John died in China in 1793. Another son became Sir Alexis Greig, Admiral of the Russian fleet, and Knight of all the Imperial orders. In 1783 he studied at the High School of Edinburgh; he served as a volunteer on board the *Culloden* under Admiral Trowbridge, and commanded the Russian fleets at the sieges of Varna and Anapa in 1828 ; though in 1801 he had been exiled to Siberia for remonstrating with the Emperor Paul for his severity to certain British sailors. His son Woronzow Greig (also educated, I believe, at the High School of Edinburgh) was A.D.C. to Prince Menschicoff, and bore a flag of truce from Sebastopol to Lord Raglan. He died of a mortal wound on the desperate field of Inkermann.

Field-Marshal Count Brown.

ULYSSES MAXIMILIAN BROWN, Field-Marshal of the armies of the Empress Maria Theresa, Governor of Prague, and Knight of the Golden Fleece, was born on the 24th of October, 1705.

His father, Ulysses Baron de Brown and Camus, the representative and descendant of one of the most ancient families in Ireland, was then a Colonel of Cuirassiers in the service of Joseph I., Emperor of Austria, and was one of the many brave Irish gentlemen who, after the unfortunate battle of Aughrim, the surrender of Galway, and capitulation of King James's army under St. Ruth, at Limerick, were forced to feed themselves by the blades of their swords in the service of foreign countries. When Marshal Catinat and the Duke of Savoy laid siege to Valenza in 1696, they had no less than six battalions of Irish exiles in their army. Baron Brown had served under the Emperor Leopold I., who died in 1703; and by the Emperor Charles VI. had been created Count of the Holy Roman Empire; while his brother George received the same exalted rank, being at the same time a distinguished general of infantry, colonel of a regiment of musketeers, and councillor of war.

In his childhood Ulysses Maximilian was sent to the city of Limerick by his father, and there, for a few years, he pursued his studies at a public school, until his uncle, Count George Brown, sent for him, when only *ten* years of age, to join his regiment of infantry, which was then with the army marching into Hungary, under the famous and gallant Prince Eugene of Savoy, against the Turks, who had invaded the Imperial frontier. With this army the great Count Saxe was serving as a subaltern officer.

The Turks had broken the peace of Carlovitz in 1715, conquered the Morea, declared war against Venice, besieged Corfu, and spread a general alarm among the courts of Europe. The Emperor's mediation was rejected with disdain by Achmet III., the imperious Porte, whose army, 150,000 strong, hovered on the right bank of the Danube; but Prince Eugene, with a small, well disciplined force, having passed the river in sight of the inactive Osmanli, encamped at Peterwaradin, on the confines of Sclavonia. Ulysses Maximilian Brown was with this army in the regiment of his uncle.

A battle ensued on the 5th August, 1716, near Carlovitz, and the Turks were totally routed, with the loss of their Grand Vizier Ali, and 30,000 slain; while fifty standards, 250 pieces of cannon, and all their baggage, were taken. Other, but minor victories followed, and in the month of June the brave Prince Eugene invested Belgrade, the key of the Ottoman dominions on the Hungarian frontier. For two months it was vigorously defended by 30,000 men, while the Turkish army, under the new Grand Vizier, was intrenched close by, in a semicircle which stretched from the Danube to the Save, thus inclosing the troops of Eugene in the marshes between those rapid rivers.

By war and disease the Imperialists suffered fearfully; fighting of the most desperate kind ensued daily; and there, while yet a child, the little Irish boy was taught to handle his espontoon, and became a witness of, if not an actor in, those military barbarities which have always blackened a war along the Ottoman frontier.

It was apparent to Eugene that the Turks, by destroying the bridge of the Save, might obstruct his retreat, surprise a body of his Austrians at Semlin, or cut off his artillery, which were bombarding the lower town of Belgrade, while sickness and scarcity pressed severely upon his slender force; thus it became evident that nothing but a decisive victory would save him from gradual destruction. Already the Turks, 200,000 strong, were within musket-shot, and would soon storm his lines, which were defended by only 40,000 men, exclusive of the 20,000 who were blocking up Belgrade.

On a dark midnight—the 16th of August—after uniting his forces by firing three bombs, he attacked the mighty host of the Sultan Achmet—the most complete that Turkey had ever equipped for battle. Favoured by a thick fog, the Austrians broke through the slow and heavy Osmanli, stormed all their intrenchments at the point of the bayonet, turned their *own* guns upon them, and grape-shotted the turbaned fugitives, whose unwieldy army was totally routed, and fled, leaving every cannon and baggage-waggon behind. The surrender of Belgrade, two days after, was the immediate consequence of this brilliant victory, and the Peace of Passarovitz, which, under the mediation of Great Britain, was signed in July, 1718, succeeded in establishing a twenty-five years' truce, and securing to Austria the western part of Wallachia, Servia, Belgrade, and part of Bosnia.

After this battle, Ulysses Brown, then in his twelfth year, was sent to Rome, where he continued his studies at the Clementine College, for the period of four years.

In 1721 he went to Prague, and in two years completed himself in the study of civil law.

He then entered the Austrian army, and in 1723 became a captain in the regiment of infantry commanded by his uncle, Count George Brown; and such was his ardour and such his knowledge in the art of war, that only two years after, in 1725, we find him appointed to the lieutenant-colonelcy of the same corps.

On the 15th of August in the following year he married Maria Philippina, Countess of Martinitz, the beautiful Bohemian heiress, and the last of an ancient and noble line.

In 1730 he served in the expedition to Corsica, and by his bravery and example contributed greatly to secure the capture of Callansara, where he was severely wounded in the thigh. This successful expedition caused a rumour that the island was to be erected into a kingdom for the Chevalier de St. George—James VIII. of the Scottish

Jacobites; and George II., on being bribed by the Genoese, prohibited his English subjects from furnishing any assistance to the troops or inhabitants.

In 1732, Count Brown was made Chamberlain of the Austrian Empire; and in 1734 was appointed full colonel of infantry, and Italy was the next scene of his service.

France had resolved on humbling the overweening power of the House of Hapsburg; the venerable Marshal Villars crossed the Alps, and with a combined army of French and Spaniards, burst into Milan, overran Austrian Lombardy, and carrying victory wherever he marched, in two months' time left only Mantua under the flag of Charles VI. The latter made strenuous efforts to protect himself—to secure the passage of the Rhine against the Marshal Duke of Berwick on one hand, and to recover his power in Italy from Villars on the other. The Diet voted him 120,000 men; the Count de Merci marched 6000 of these to protect the important fortress of Mantua; and with a force increased to 60,000 soldiers, drew towards the head of the Oglio and Po.

Leaving his young wife at the court of Vienna, Count Brown accompanied this force with his regiment of German infantry; and it was among the first of those brave battalions which effected the arduous passage of the Po near Santo Benedetto, where the Count de Merci so boldly and skilfully surprised the French troops, and drove them back at the bayonet's point, with the loss of all their ammunition, baggage, and the cities of Guastalla, Novella, and Mirandola, of which he immediately took possession.

During this campaign Count Brown distinguished himself on every occasion, but most particularly at the great battle of Parma, on the 29th of June, 1734. There a desperate hand-to-hand conflict ensued in front of the city, on the high road which leads to Piacenza; and after a struggle as deadly as Italy ever saw, the Austrians remained masters of the field; but the Count de Merci, their general, was mortally wounded by a musket-ball, and Count Brown and the Prince of Wirtemberg, the lieutenant-general, had their horses shot under them. The

French made their most desperate stand at a farmhouse from the walls of which " they mowed down whole companies of the Imperialists by grape and musket-shot. This dreadful conflict lasted for ten hours without intermission, when the enemy retired in good order towards the walls of Parma." On the field lay ten thousand corpses; of the Imperialists there fell the commander-in-chief, seven generals, and three hundred and forty officers were killed and wounded. Thus ended an attack which the Count de Merci risked in direct opposition to the *advice* of Count Brown and other officers of experience. The Imperial army now fell back upon Guastalla, where it was the good fortune of Count Brown to save it and the cause of Charles VI. from total destruction.

The Austrians, under the Prince of Wirtemberg, were posted between the Crostolo and the Po, near some strong redoubts at the head of one of their bridges; and there, on the 19th of September, they were attacked by the French, when after a hard conflict of eight hours, during which Brown, then in his twenty-ninth year, charged repeatedly at the head of his regiment, the Austrians were driven back, with the loss of four standards, while the gallant Prince of Wirtemberg, old General Colmenaro, the Prince of Saxe Gotha, and many other brave men, were slain.

Count Brown made incredible exertions to preserve discipline, and with his own regiment to cover the rear of the discomfited Imperialists, who were thus enabled to fall back in good order to a new and stronger position on the northward of the Po, where they kept the field until January in the ensuing year, when the wearied French and Spaniards retired into winter quarters. One of the most brilliant feats of the campaign was the destruction of the bridge which the Marshal Duke de Noailles had thrown over the Adige. At the head of his regiment the brave Irish soldier of fortune achieved this arduous task in sight of the whole French army, under a heavy discharge of cannon and musketry. Thus terminated the Lombardo campaign, in which Austria, if she did not lose her honour, won but little glory, though in the two battles of Parma and Guastalla she lost ten thousand soldiers.

The French strengthened their forces, and a cruel edict was issued at Paris, ordaining all British subjects in France between the ages of fifteen and fifty to enlist in the Irish Brigade, or go to the galleys—an edict which was enforced with such rigour, that in fifteen days all the Parisian prisons were crowded with British residents, chiefly poor Scottish Jacobites; but France soon found other and more worthy means of reinforcing her armies in Italy and on the Rhine, than by resorting to such inhospitable tyranny.

For his services in the Italian war, Count Brown received a general's commission in 1736 from the Emperor Charles VI., who, discouraged by his reverses, signified a desire for peace; but it was scarcely negotiated, before he became involved in a new war that broke out on the confines of Europe and Asia. The rapid progress of the Russians against the Turks, and their capture of the Crimea, excited the ambition of Charles, who, by the treaty of 1726, was bound to assist Russia against the Porte; and now that prophecy, so often propagated, was in every one's mouth, that THE PERIOD FATAL TO THE CRESCENT WAS ARRIVED!

Again the Osmanli turned their arms against Hungary; and to protect that ancient kingdom rather than to assist the Czarina (who demanded of Austria 10,000 horse and 20,000 foot), Charles sent 8000 Saxon infantry, under Field-Marshal Seckendorf and General Count Brown, with whom the Duke of Lorraine went as a volunteer. By the peculation of the commissaries and contractors, these forces suffered incredible hardships, and their leaders found Gradisca, Bioc, even Belgrade, and all the Hungarian frontier fortresses dilapidated, and incapable of being defended. More troops and 600,000 florins were promised to them from Vienna, but neither came. Thus Seckendorf and Brown found themselves before the Turks with a small army of recruits, destitute of horses, caissons, and all the munitions of war. On receiving 10,000 florins, they raised 26,000 infantry, 15,000 horse, and

4000 irregulars; but the indecision of the Emperor, who interfered with all their arrangements, the nature of their forces, clamours among their soldiers, cabals among their officers, the severities they encountered, and the pressing ardour of the Osmanli, gave to the Imperial arms but a succession of humiliating defeats; and though Brown's fiery energy captured many small fortresses, others of greater importance were lost by Seckendorf, and at last Belgrade, the scene of our hero's earlier service, was besieged.

Banjaluca, a strongly fortified town, which has two castles to defend it, and which stands on the frontier of Bosnia, at the confluence of the Verbas with the Save, was skilfully invested by the Austrians under the Prince of Hildburghausen, but he was compelled to raise the siege, and after a bloody conflict, was driven towards the Save by the Turks.

Charles, alarmed for the safety of Austria, ordered Seckendorf and Brown to march through Servia, and form a junction with the prince, which they immediately did, after dispatching a reinforcement to Marshal Kevenhüller. With only 20,000 men they fought a way through Servia, and made themselves masters of Utzitza, after a short siege, and would have taken Zwornick, but for an inundation of the Drina. On the 16th of October they encamped on the southern bank of the Save. Thus, they arrived in time to share some of the fighting near Banjaluca, and on the retreat from thence the Austrian baggage, sick, and wounded, were only saved from the barbarous Mussulmans by the personal exertions of Count Brown, who secured that movement by his valour and example.

Discouraged by the misfortunes of his army, Charles VI. resolved to end a strife in which his troops gathered nothing but disgrace; and, leaving the quarrel to the mediation of France, he bequeathed to the Czarina the whole brunt of the war. The ill-success of the Austrians was attributed to the unfortunate Seckendorf, the victim of circumstances and the cabals of the Jesuits; thus he was committed, for an unlimited time, to the gloomy Castle of Glatz, an old fortress on the mountains of

Silesia. On the peace of Belgrade being signed, Marshal Wallace was also sent prisoner to Zigieth, and Count Neuperg was placed in the Castle of Holitz; and as these three generals were ordered to remain captive during the lifetime of the Emperor, no part of the stigma of their ill-success fell on their Irish compatriot, Brown, who, on his return to Vienna, in 1739, was created Field Marshal-lieutenant, and a member of the Aulic Council of War.

In the following year, his friend and master, Charles VI. (having unfortunately surfeited himself with mushrooms), died. He was the *last* prince of the ancient House of Hapsburg, sixteenth Emperor of Germany, and eleventh King of Bohemia; and the grave had scarcely closed over him, ere the disputed succession to his hereditary dominions kindled another war in Europe.

By the Pragmatic Sanction his ancient possessions were guaranteed to his daughter, the Archduchess Maria Theresa (Queen of Hungary and Bohemia, and wife of Francis Stephen, Duke of Tuscany), by Britain, Russia, Holland, France, Spain, and Prussia; but the three last-named powers fell—as an old writer says—"upon the poor distressed orphan queen, like three wolves, without mercy or equity;" and in defiance of their solemn league, the Bavarian Elector laid claim to Bohemia; the sovereigns of France, Poland, and Saxony demanded all the vast inheritance of Austria each for themselves; and all prepared for open war, while Maria Theresa quietly took possession of her father's throne.

At this startling crisis Count Brown was in command at Breslau. The first blow of this new and general contest was struck by Frederick III. of Prussia, who, having at his disposal all the immense treasure which had been accumulated by the rigid economy of his politic father, together with 76,000 idle troops, for whom he had been left to find employment, now revived an ancient claim to Silesia, based upon such pretensions as the English kings of old advanced to the thrones of Scotland and France; and suddenly marching twenty battalions of infantry and thirty-six squadrons of horse into the duchy, he took possession of Breslau, its capital, from which Count

Brown was forced to retire, having only 3000 men, with whom he retreated towards Moravia, leaving small garrisons in Glogau and Breig, which Frederick blockaded with six battalions. This was in the January of 1741.

Frederick now offered to supply the Queen of Hungary (as Maria Theresa was styled) with money and troops to support her claims against *the other* violaters of the Pragmatic Sanction, provided she would cede to him the Silesian province. Aware of the danger of yielding to one pretender, she sent Count Neuperg (who, since the Peace of Belgrade, had been a captive) with an army to the assistance of the faithful Brown, who, after disputing every inch of Frederick's progress, had maintained the contest with him single-handed for two months.

The King of Prussia sent a detachment of infantry across the Oder to attack Brown's garrison of 300 men in Namslau, where they surrendered in a fortnight. Leaving one regiment in Breslau, he marched against Brown's next garrison, consisting of 400 men, in Ohlau, under Colonel Formentini, who finding the place ruinous, and the Prussians overwhelming, capitulated. Then General Kleist invested Breig with five battalions and four squadrons.

Count Neuperg, one of Austria's best generals, being a senior officer, assumed the command of the whole force, which he had first assembled in the environs of Olmutz, and sent General Lentulus to occupy the narrow defiles of Glatz in Silesia, and thus protect Bohemia. Neuperg, meanwhile, meditated operations on the Neiss, and his hussars cut off the King of Prussia's convoys and outposts in every direction. The skirmishes around Neiss were incessant, and in one cavalry encounter Frederick was nearly taken prisoner—a stroke which would have ended the war at once. After many manœuvres and encounters, the armies of Neuperg and Frederick drew near each other, on the 10th of April, 1741, at Molowitz, a village in the neighbourhood of Neiss, where a desperate battle was fought.

On this inauspicious day—inauspicious for the Austrian cause—General Count Brown (or *Braün*, as the King of

FIELD-MARSHAL COUNT BROWN.

Prussia names him in his works) commanded the infantry. The scene of the encounter was within a league of the river Neiss, and the ground was mantled with snow to the depth of two feet. The Prussian army consisted of twenty-seven battalions of infantry, twenty-nine squadrons of cavalry, and three of hussars.

The Prussian infantry were, at that time, says Frederick, who had brought their discipline to perfection, "walking batteries! The rapidity of loading tripled their fire, and made a Prussian equal to three adversaries." They came on with such ardour, that Marshal Neuperg had to form his troops in order of battle under a cannonade from Frederick's artillery; but the right wing of his cavalry (thirty squadrons), under Rœmer, fell headlong on the Prussian left, and drove back their blue-coated dragoons. On they continued to press, with swords uplifted, until the steady fire of two grenadier battalions routed them, and slew the brave Rœmer as he led them to the charge for the third time.

At this critical moment, the infantry under Brown rushed on, and, though unsupported by cavalry, made incredible efforts to break through Frederick's serried ranks; and in this struggle the first battalion of his guards lost half its officers, and no less than 800 men. For five hours the firing continued; and, as ammunition failed, the dead were all turned on their faces, and their pouches emptied, to carry on the strife, which was only ended by Marshal Schwerin making a motion with his left, which threatened the Austrian flank. "This," says Frederick, in the *History of his Own Times*, "was the signal of victory, and the Austrian defeat—their rout was total." This was at six, P.M.

Count Brown was severely wounded, and Maria Theresa had 180 officers, 7000 horse and foot, killed, and three standards, seven cannon, and 1200 prisoners taken, with 3000 wounded. Brown, though faint with loss of blood, never left his saddle; but, by his efforts at the head of the infantry, covered the retreat of the whole army, which Neuperg, who was also wounded, ordered to retire under the cannon of Neiss, leaving Frederick victorious on the field, where he remained for three weeks.

Availing himself of this success, the victor, after a short siege, took Breig, removed his head-quarters to Strehlen, and, on driving 4000 Austrian hussars from the important pass of Fryewalde, began to recruit his army among the conquered Silesians. Re-establishing himself in Breslau, on being joined by the Duke of Holstein, his army, consisting of forty-three battalions and seventy squadrons, would soon have cut off all communication between the troops of Neuperg and his supplies; and moreover, would have formed a junction with the armies of France and Bavaria, which had now taken the field in his favour—the former under the famous marshal, Duke de Belleisle, and the latter under their Elector. The outposts of their allied enemies were now within eight German miles of Vienna, and the cause of the young and beautiful Maria Theresa seemed almost desperate. She retired to Presburg, where her appearance before the assembled Palatines, with an infant son in her arms, kindled such an enthusiasm that, as one man, they drew their sabres, exclaiming "We will die for our sovereign, Maria Theresa!"

She sent for Count Brown in 1743, to be present at her coronation, and, as a reward for his past services, made him a privy councillor of the kingdom of Bohemia.

The brave Hungarian nobles now rose in arms, and old Count Palfy marched at the head of 30,000 men to relieve Vienna, the Governor of which, Marshal Kevenhüller, had only 12,000 men to resist the three armies of France, Prussia, and Bavaria, while the Marshals Neuperg and Brown covered the roads to Bohemia with 20,000 men, as a protection against the kingdom of Bavaria. In all the operations of the Austrians, during the many encounters and severe campaigns of 1742-3, Count Brown commanded the vanguard or first division, and always with honour.

Prince Charles of Lorraine having succeeded Marshal Neuperg in command of the army, encountered the enemy near Braunau, and a desperate, but drawn battle (in which his forces suffered most) was fought, while

Prince Lobcowitz, on marching from Bohemia, drove the French from all their posts and garrisons in the Upper Palatinate Then the combined forces of the Prince, Brown, and Lobcowitz, forced those of Marshal Broglio to abandon their strongly intrenched camp at Pladling, on the Danube, and to fall back in confusion on the Rhine, while the irregular horse, Croats, Pandours, and Foot Talpaches, harassed their rear-guard, and exterminated the stragglers.

In this expedition Count Brown seized Deckendorf at the head of the vanguard, captured a vast quantity of baggage, and obliged the French, after immense slaughter, to abandon the banks of the Danube, which the whole Austrian army, under the Prince of Lorraine, passed in security on the 6th of June.

On this spot a pillar was afterwards erected, bearing, in the following inscription, an honourable testimony to the valour of the Irish hero:—

> "Theresiæ Austriacæ Augustæ Duce Exercitus,
> Carlo Alexandro Lothairingico,
> Septemdecim, superatis hostilibus villis,
> Captoque Deckendorfio, renitendibus undis,
> Resistentibus, Gallis,
> Duce exercitus Ludovico Borbonio Contio
> Transivit hic Danubium,
> Ulysses Maximilianus Brown, Campi Marashalus,
> Die 5° Junii," A.D. 1743.

When Marshal Broglio reached Donawert, in the Swabian circle, he was joined by 12,000 men, under the warlike Maurice Count de Saxe, afterwards Marshal General of France and Duke of Courland; but finding his main body almost destroyed, instead of hazarding a battle, he retreated before Prince Charles and Brown to Heilbron, and there abandoning to them his artillery and baggage, retired with greater precipitation to Prague.

Lorraine followed, and encamped in sight of them, along the hills of Girisnitz. The French marshals offered to surrender Prague, Egra, and all their captures in Bohemia, provided they were permitted to march home with the honours of war These offers were rejected with disdain; Prague was invested on all sides, and though the Marshal de Maillebois marched to its relief, he achieved nothing, for the Austrians possessed all the passes of the mountains, and he was compelled to retreat as a fugitive, harassed and galled by the troops of Prince Charles, who left Prince Lobcowitz to watch the motions of the Dukes of Belleisle and Broglio in the beleaguered city.

The latter of these marshals fled from his command in the disguise of a courier; the former abandoned the city in a dark and cold December night, and, with 14,000 men and 30 guns, made his way towards Alsace, enduring unheard-of miseries; 900 men whom he left behind him surrendered at discretion; and thus again the ancient capital of Bohemia reverted to the House of Austria, which, however, lost the Duchy of Silesia by the treaty of Breslau, which ceded it for ever to the kingdom of Prussia.

In the year 1743 Count Brown was sent by his Imperial Mistress to Worms as her plenipotentiary to George II. of Great Britain, with whose ministers he spared no pains to arrange the important alliance between the Courts of London, Vienna, and Turin. On this service he acquitted himself with an ability no way inferior to the courage he had displayed in so many fields.

The arena of his next service was again in Italy, where the Austrian forces were still fighting against the Spaniards, and pursuing the old war between the houses of Bourbon and Hapsburg.

The Count Gages, who commanded the Spaniards in Bologna, having received instructions from his imperious queen to fight the enemy within *three* days, or resign, and to fight whether he was prepared or not, passed the Parano in the beginning of February, and, on the 18th, attacked the Austrians under Count Traun, at Campo Santo, a town of Modena, where another *drawn* battle was fought, and both sides claimed the victory. Count Gages found himself obliged to repass the river, and retire into Romagna, where he intrenched himself, and remained undisturbed till October, when Prince Lobcowitz, having assumed command of the Austrian army, boldly advanced.

and drove him back on Fano. It was at this crisis that Count Brown was sent by Maria Theresa to join her Austrians, whose ultimate object was the conquest of the Bourbonic kingdom of Naples, to punish its king for violating a *forced* neutrality, and having joined Count Gages with 25,000 men.

At this time the Empress-Queen engaged to maintain 30,000 men in Italy, provided the King of Sardinia would pay another force of 45,000, while Britain was to send a naval squadron to co-operate by sea. Lobcowitz and Count Brown had established their head-quarters at Monte Rotondo, near Rome, when their final orders arrived to invade the kingdom of Naples. Breaking up the camp, and marching towards Viletri, the prince dispatched Count Brown, with a division of German infantry and another of Hungarian hussars, to pursue the Spaniards (who began to retreat) as far as the river Tronto, with the double purpose of harassing them and endeavouring to excite an insurrection among the wild mountaineers of the Abruzzo. In fulfilment of his orders, Brown distributed everywhere manifestos in the name of Maria Theresa, urging them to throw off the Spanish yoke, and place themselves under her protection, promising, at the same time, to banish for ever the obnoxious Jews from Naples; but these proclamations were unheeded by the Abruzzesi, who evinced no inclination to revolt.

Meanwhile his commander, Prince Lobcowitz, had halted in the marquisate of Ancona, being somewhat uncertain in which direction to march. Pushing on, Count Brown crossed the Tronto, which separates the kingdom of Naples from the Papal territory. Entering, he gave all to fire and sword as he advanced. His route lay along the shore of the Adriatic by the high road to Naples, which crosses the river Potenza near its mouth, and lies on the confines of Ascoli. He laid most of the small towns in the Abruzzo under contribution. Some were fined in money—others in a certain quantity of barley bread; but his necessary severity was greatly tempered by mercy. His advanced guard of hussars had daily skirmishes with the Spanish cavalry.

The passes being deep with snow, so as to be almost impassable for artillery and baggage, Lobcowitz gave up all thought of entering Naples by the coast road, which was the only clear one, and very unwisely recalled Count Brown with his forces; and as soon as they joined, began his march by the way of Umbria and the Campagna di Roma, with 6000 horse and 20,000 foot. Among the former were 2000 hussars; among the latter were some irregulars, or free companies of what Buonamici, in his *Commentaries,* styles "Condemned persons and deserters, who, despairing of pardon, and urged by the prospect of plunder, panted for an opportunity of coming to blows with the enemy." This small army advanced in three columns, two days' march apart, that the people might not be oppressed. Brown commanded the first. Advancing by Spoleto, Terni, and Narni, they reached Castellana, and held a council of war, at which Brown, the Cardinal Alessandro Albani, and the Bishop of Gurck assisted. A stormy debate ensued, and nothing was decided upon.

Meanwhile the alarmed King of Naples, with the combined armies of Naples and Spain, was encamped on the hill of Anagni, in the Campagna di Roma. The Spaniards under Count Gages consisted of eleven battalions of infantry, three regiments of cavalry, under the Duke of Atri, five hundred horse-archers, and three hundred of the Duke of Modena's archer-guards (archers, of course, but by name); with the *Irish Brigade,* and a regiment of hussar deserters. The Neapolitan army consisted of eighteen battalions of foot and five regiments of horse. The vanguard was composed of light-armed mountaineers. The artillery was commanded by the veteran Conte di Gazola.

Lobcowitz and Brown now began their march towards Rome; crossed the Tiber at Teverone, and halted at Marino, where of old stood the villa of Caius Marius. After a great deal of severe marching, counter-marching, and skirmishing, the prince resolved on assailing the chiefs of the allies in their head-quarters, which they had established in Viletri ; and this daring enterprise he committed to Brown, his most active and able general.

In Viletri, the King of Naples and the Duke of Modena, with most of the nobles and officers of their troops, had quartered themselves, and taken every measure to secure and fortify the town, which is situated upon a high mountain, surrounded by deep valleys, all difficult of access, but beautifully planted with vineyards and groves of olive-trees. It had several gates, a Minorite convent, and a town-house, which crowned the summit of the hill. Charles of Naples occupied the noble palace of the Ginnetti family ; adjacent to which were spacious gardens, a lane, and a bridge, all guarded by soldiers, and barricaded, and planted with brass cannon. The gardens communicated with the Valmonte road, and thereon were posted two battalions of the Walloon Guard. The custody of the Roman gate was committed to the Royal Regiment of Horse, and the Duke of Modena's Life Guards, while at the foot of the eminence, to sweep all approaches, the most of the artillery were posted near the Capuchin convent. The right flank of the town was occupied by Spanish and Italian infantry ; the left by the cavalry, the Irish Brigade, and four battalions of the Walloon Guard.

The Austrians had intrenched themselves on a hill, only a mile distant ; and there, by means of spies and deserters, Count Brown had accurately informed himself of all the arrangements which had been made in Viletri ; but, brave as he was, on Prince Lobcowitz first proposing this hazardous duty to him, he was struck by the too evident desperation of the service.

"The Austrian forces," said he, "are insufficient for attempting so daring an enterprise ; it is impossible to reach the Neapolitan cantonment undiscovered, and I do not think we could force it without imminent danger, and a warm reception. In my opinion, the easier and the safer way would be to make a general attack with all our strength upon the enemy's works."

Brown afterwards adopted the general's opinion, that a

night attack was best; and the time and manner he proposed met with the consent of all who were present at their conference.

Selecting 6000 men, he chose the 10th of August for this desperate expedition; and Lobcowitz, to conceal all knowledge of the route chosen by the count in attacking Viletri, threw a chain of picquets and videttes over a vast extent of country. In silence, and without the sound of drum or bugle, he marched from the camp; and none of his troops, save the Marquis de Novati, his second in command, were informed of the object until they reached a valley at the foot of the mountain, near a church dedicated to St. Mary. The darkness of the night (says Castruccio Buonamici) was rendered more dense by the shade of the overhanging vines.

At this moment, during a temporary halt, it was reported to the count that a soldier had deserted, and perhaps to the enemy. The Marquis de Novati fearing they were betrayed, urged a retreat, but Brown exclaimed:—

"No; I am determined to advance. The die of war has been thrown!"

And promising his soldiers ample rewards, he exhorted them to behave like brave men. Pushing on with ardour, the attack was commenced just as day began to break, by the cavalry outposts being cut to pieces, and the left flank of Viletri being furiously assailed, the infantry pushing on through walls and vineyards, and the Hungarian horsemen with lance and sabre hewing a passage to the streets. A regiment of Italian dragoons were put to flight. The brave Irish Brigade attacked the advancing Austrians with such fury, as to hold them in check for half-an-hour, but in the end were nearly cut to pieces at the Neapolitan Gate. Marsiglia of Sienna, a Knight of Malta, defended a cottage with fifty dismounted dragoons, and displayed incredible bravery. The Walloon Guards were unable to assist the Irish until they were nearly all slain. Colonel Macdonel, eleven captains, thirty subalterns, and a heap of Irish dead, blocked up the gate they had defended. The fury, the firing, and the slaughter on all sides of the hill were frightful. The King of Naples put himself at the head of his guards, crying, "Remember your king and your ancient valour." But his efforts were vain; the gates were all forced, his troops driven out, and nine of their standards taken. The street which led to the Ginnetti palace was set in flames; the Duke of Atri was nearly burned alive, and General Count Mariano was captured in bed. Brown's second in command, the Marquis de Novati, was taken prisoner, and finding his troops, who were busy plundering, about to be surrounded by those of Count Gages, he ordered his drums to beat a retreat, and retired to the intrenched camp of Lobcowitz. In this expedition he killed and captured 3000 men, hamstrung 800 horses, and brought off 500 more laden with plunder; one general, one hundred other officers, twelve standards, and three small colours. His own loss was only 500.

Disheartened by the partial failure of this affair—for the King of Naples had escaped them—destitute of forage for their cavalry and artillery, and encumbered with many sick and wounded men, Lobcowitz and Brown finding themselves unable to hazard a general engagement, and that autumn was at hand, became desirous of retreating; and after pillaging Valmonte and cutting the Duke of Portocarrara's Italian corps to pieces, transporting their baggage and sick by sea to Tuscany, they threw a pontoon bridge across the Tiber beside the Ponte Molle, and commenced a retreat in the night, demolishing all bridges as they left them behind, to bar pursuit.

The count was named "the right hand" of Lobcowitz during the arduous operations which ensued; and, by his usual activity and bravery, he frequently repulsed the pursuing Spaniards on the retreat from Viletri, during the fortification of the Austrian camp at Viterbo, the retreat from thence through the forests of Orvietto, with a force now diminished to 13,000 men; the assault upon Nocera, where Count Soro and 900 Italian deserters fell into the hands of Count Gages, who sent them in chains to San Giovanni, where every fifth man was shot—and many other similar affairs, until the Imperialists reached their winter quarters at Rimini, Cesano, and Forli, on which the Spaniards and Neapolitans retired to Pesero and Fano.

In the beginning of the following year, 1745, he was recalled from Italy by Maria Theresa, and sent into Bavaria at the head of a body of troops against the young Elector, who was in alliance with France. He took the town of Vilshosen by assault, and captured 3600 prisoners: 2000 were slain on both sides, and 6000 Hessians were forced to lay down their arms, and enter the British service for the campaign against the unfortunate Prince Charles Stuart. The count would have performed many other feats of equal brilliance, had the war against Bavaria not been terminated suddenly by the terrified Elector, who, at the same time that Vilshosen was taken, lost Pfarrkirchen, Landshut, and had all his magazines destroyed, which compelled him to sign the treaty of Fussen, and in April to conclude a peace with the Empress-Queen. In the same year Count Brown was appointed General of the Austrian Ordnance.

Though peace had been made with the Bavarian Elector, there was no rest for the soldier of fortune, who was immediately dispatched a *third* time to Italy, with 18,000 men, against the Spaniards, by Maria Theresa, whose husband had now been elected Emperor of Germany. He joined the Prince of Lichenstein, who was carrying on the war against the still-allied French and Spaniards under the Marshal de Maillebois; and one of his first essays in the new Italian campaign was to attempt the recovery of the Milanese, out of which, solely by his activity, the allies were ultimately driven.

He also formed a daring scheme to cut off the communication between the main body of the Spanish army and their forces under the Marquis de Castellar, by detaching General Nadasti along the left bank of the Po, with orders to amuse the enemy by countermarches, and by pretending to lay a pontoon bridge across the river at Casale-maggiore, a town in Lombardy. While the deceived Spaniards were busy watching these feigned motions, their guards, who occupied the right bank of the

Po, were surprised and utterly cut to pieces by the Austrian irregulars; and then Count Brown crossed the river at Borgoforte, near the strong Venetian castle, and pushing on from thence, captured Luzzara, a Parmese town four miles north of the scene of his services twelve years before—Guastalla, which he immediately invested, and took by assault, when Marshal Count Corasin surrendered, with 2000 prisoners. At this very time Castellar, with 7000 Spaniards, hovered on one flank of the count's little force, and Gages was advancing on the other; two movements by which his division must have been overwhelmed, had not the Prince of Lichenstein advanced to his support; and on uniting they took Parma.

At the battle of Piacenza Brown performed one of his most brilliant deeds, by destroying the right wing of the allies under the Marshal de Maillebois. This great encounter took place in front of the city, which stands on an extensive plain near the right bank of the Po; earthen ramparts surround, and a castle protects it. Count Gages' army abounded in cavalry; and besides its natural strength, his position was defended by the cannon of the city; so there was no hope of starving him out of his trenches—but battle was given on the 16th of June. The French, who had encamped without the Antonian gate, formed in three lines, and were the right wing of the enemy, with sixteen battalions of Spaniards under Lieutenant-General Aramburc; the centre consisted of nine battalions, the flower of the Spanish infantry; the left were the regiments of Naples and Genoa.

The battle began at daybreak, and the Spaniards charged with such fury that an Austrian battery, consisting of twenty-six pieces, was taken by Aramburc, who was dangerously wounded. Count Gages broke their left, when 250 gallant men of Prince Eugene's dragoons bore them back, and struck a panic into the French, amongst whom the Marshal de Maillebois was fighting on foot. These dragoons were led by Count Brown, and by their charge the Spanish and Walloon Guards were routed, trampled under hoof, and destroyed. The allies made a precipitate retreat. Two days after the battle they were reviewed, and found to have lost 3220 who were killed, 4460 wounded, and 915 prisoners. The Count de Brostel, General of the French artillery, the Chevalier de Tesse, two Spanish lieutenant-generals, and the commander of the Swiss, were among the slain. Ten pieces of cannon and thirty pairs of colours were left upon that sanguinary field, where the Austrians buried 3500 of their own dead. The King of Spain survived these tidings but a few days.

On the 9th of August the combined French, Spanish, and Neapolitan armies attempted to cross the Po at the Lombra and Tydone. Count Sabelloni, with 7000 Austrians, made a noble stand against them, from nine in the evening till ten the next morning, when General Botta and Count Brown hastened to his relief, and the conflict began again with renewed fury; and after a terrific crossfire of cannon and musketry, and a furious mêlée, in which Spaniard, Frenchman, Swiss, Italian, and Austrian soldiers were all mingled, with musket, sword and bayonet—no man valuing life or limb when compared with the glory of the day—the three allies were driven back, leaving 8000 killed, wounded, and prisoners, with nineteen guns and twenty standards, on the field.

The Austrians lost General Barenclau (whose courage was ever rash) with 4000 men. Counts Brown and Pallavicini were wounded. The Spaniards lost the flower of their officers, and among them the young and noble Colonel Don Julio Deodato of Lucca, an accomplished cavalier and scholar.

Marshal Maillebois and Count Gages retreated to Genoa, from thence to Nice, and from thence to Parma; abandoning Piacenza, of which the Austrians took immediate possession, and wherein they placed 9000 men, most of whom were suffering from wounds received in previous battles. Despite his wound, Brown remained at the head of his division and with the army which pursued the Bourbon allies towards Genoa, taking every place by storm or capitulation on their route, except Tortona and the mandamento or fortified town of Gavi.

On the Austrian vanguard under Count Brown (who

commanded during the absence of Count Botta, the new commander-in-chief) reaching Santo Pietro d'Arena, a suburb of Genoa, the city became filled with consternation, and the senators sent the Marshal di Campo Esceria to learn from him on what conditions he would receive the city. But for some private reason Brown declined to admit him to an audience. Raynerio Grimaldi and Augustino Lomellino were next sent to the Austrian camp and the count demanded the object of their visit.

"General," they replied, "the people of Genoa have made war on no one, and least of all upon the Empress-Queen of Hungary, for whom they have ever entertained a profound veneration. Had they been her enemies, would their ambassador have been at this very time in her city of Vienna? Hard necessity forced us to embrace an alliance with the Bourbons, and it was with no other view than to defend ourselves, for we would be the vilest of mankind to suffer our Fatherland to be taken tamely from us. There can be no reason now, noble general, to distress those who have only armed them in their own defence, or treat as enemies the Genoese, who have committed no act of hostility."

"Seigneurs," replied Count Brown, "you have acted the part of our most bitter enemies, for without your assistance what could the united armies of the Bourbons have effected? You sent them auxiliaries! you supplied them with provisions; and after six years' striving to cut a passage into Italy, it was *you* Genoese, alone, who opened up a path to them, enabling them to essay the ruin of the Austrians in Venice and in Lombardy. Begone! and without loss of time inform your senate to say no more of friendship for the present, but submit to us on those terms which my friend, General Gorani, will lay before you in writing."

Lest Brown should have the entire glory of reducing Genoa, General Botta hastened from Novi to resume the command, and he also required the immediate surrend. of the city.

The allies having left 4000 men to defend the pass of La Bochetta, in the northern Apennines, a gorge which has always been considered as the key of Italy on the side of Genoa, and which is well defended by several redoubts, Count Brown advanced against it, and stormed the ravine, though it is so narrow that in some places only three men could march abreast. He attacked and routed another party on his way to Ponte Decimo; and after this, the Genoese, finding themselves completely abandoned, gave up all their gates, posts, and arsenals, and paid 50,000 genovines to the victorious Austrian troops. After this, Count Brown was appointed the generalissimo in Italy; and all thought of invading Naples having been completely laid aside for the time, it was arranged by the British and Austrian ambassadors, in a conference which they held in Santo Pietro d'Arena, that without loss of time he should make an invasion of Provence, into which the allies had retired. In obedience to this desire, after detaching General Gorani (who soon after was unfortunately killed) to fall upon the enemy's rear, and leaving the Marquis de Botta at Genoa with 18,000 men, he embarked on board a squadron consisting of three ships and eight pinnaces, commanded by the Scottish Captain Forbes, and sailing from Santo Pietro d'Arena, had a quick passage to Villa Franca, from whence he walked on foot to Nice, a two days' journey. He was disguised, for in such a country, convulsed as it was by war, assassination, and disorder, every precaution was necessary for personal safety.

Having waited on the King of Sardinia, and settled their plan of future operations, he waited at Nice only until Captain Forbes brought over the Austrian artillery, &c., from Genoa, and until the forces collected for him by the Sardinians were reinforced by the troops from Piedmont, Milan, Genoa, and those which had been blocking up Tortona; and while they were collecting, at the head of a small force he reduced, by assault, Mont Albano, in the county of Nice.

In triumph, and in defiance of the French troops under the Marshal Duke de Belleisle, he passed the Var on the 9th of November, with a fine army, consisting of forty-five squadrons of horse, and sixty-three battalions of foot—in all, 50,000 men. Among these were twenty regiments of the Piedmontese. The wild Croats on their swift grey horses, and the dashing Hungarian Hussars, clad in their brown uniforms, formed his vanguard; and fell with such fury upon the French with their long lances and sharp sabres, that they swept all before them; while the British sailors, under Vice-Admiral Medley, drove the enemy from Fort Laurette, and thereby secured his left flank. Thus safely and victoriously he passed the Var, and entered Provence, the ancient patrimony of the House of Anjou.

With the assistance of a British bomb-ketch, he reduced and took 500 soldiers in the little isles of Saint Marguerite and Saint Honorat, on the south-east coast of France, opposite to Antibes, which he invested by land, while Admiral Medley cannonaded it by sea. Leaving Baron Roth with twenty-four battalions to press the siege against the Chevalier de Sade, he made himself master of Draguignan, with the loss of 2000 men, laid all the open country under contribution, and threw forward his outposts as far as the river Argens. During these arduous operations he was seized by a fever, which confined him to a camp-bed, but he soon relinquished it for his saddle.

The batteries opened against Antibes on the 20th of September. It was cannonaded for thirty-six days, and all its houses were demolished; but on collecting a numerous army, the Marshals De Belleisle and De Boufflers advanced to its relief, while other forces, amounting to *sixty* battalions, were hastening forward from Flanders. Meanwhile the Genoese, driven to despair by the extortions and severity of the Marquis de Botta, resolved to break their Austrian fetters or die in the attempt. The circumstance of a German officer striking an Italian who refused to drag a mortar to which he was harnessed, kindled a flame; and all the Genoese rushed to arms, and forced the arsenals. The city barriers were stormed, the Austrians driven out, and two regiments, who defended the gate of Santo Thomaso, were cut to pieces. All these circumstances combined, obliged Count

Brown to raise the siege of Antibes, abandon the projected expedition against Toulon, and repass the Var. This was executed on the 23rd January, 1747, but not without considerable loss, for his rearguard was furiously attacked. Ordering a column of horse and foot into Lombardy to join Count Schulemberg, he lined the southern bank of the Var with his main body, and kept the French under the great Belleisle completely in check, till the King of Sardinia secured all the mountain defiles, to prevent them from penetrating into Piedmont.

Brown still continued that masterly retreat which excited the admiration of all military men, and even of his enemy, the brave Belleisle, who followed him across the Var on the 25th May, and retook Mont Albano, Villa Franca, and Ventimiglia, from his garrisons, driving back forty-six Piedmontese battalions with terrible slaughter at the pass of Exilles, where the Chevalier de Belleisle (brother of the marshal), Knight of St. John of Jerusalem, fell, pierced with three wounds. Meanwhile Brown, with a force diminished to 28,000, continued his retreat towards Finale and Savona. The despatch, which was sent to him by Major-General Colloredo, detailing the affair at Exilles, was published in the *London Gazette*. In Lombardy he ordered two intrenched camps to be formed; one to hold 14,000 men, to guard the banks of the Tanaro; the other to hold 11,000, and guard the Po, near Pavia; but fatigue and want of food soon compelled all to seek quarters for the winter. The King of Sardinia marched to Turin; Brown established his head-quarters at Milan, after winning the praise of all Europe by his skilful operations in Provence. While here, by the severity of his remonstrance, he forced Marshal Schulemberg to abandon his important enterprise against Bisignano, and draw off his division to assist the King of Sardinia in covering Piedmont and Lombardy.

The remainder of that year he occupied by innumerable skirmishes and movements in defending the Italian States of Maria Theresa; among these (after the great review at Coni) was the march upon the Dermont, the assault by the French upon Maison Meau, the attack upon forty

three French battalions who were intrenched near Villa
Franca, and other affairs, until the peace so happily signed
in 1748, when he was sent by his mistress to Nice, where,
in conjunction with the Duke de Belleisle and the Marquis
de la Minas, he skilfully adjusted certain difficulties which
had arisen in fulfilling the treaty of Aix-la-Chapelle. In
reward for his many great and gallant services, the Empress-Queen now made him Governor of Transylvania
where he won the love and admiration of the people by
his justice, affability, and honourable bearing.

In 1752 he was made governor of the city of Prague,
and commander-in-chief of all the troops in the kingdom
of Bohemia; and in the following year the King of
Poland, as Elector of Saxony, honoured him with the
Order of the White Eagle, the collar of which is a gold
chain (to which a silver eagle is attached), and first worn
by Udislaus V. on his marriage with a daughter of the
Duke of Lithuania. In 1754 he was raised to the rank
of Marshal of the Empire.

After five years of peace the clouds of war again began
to gather on the Prussian frontier, and Marshal Brown
was summoned for the *last* time to the field. A quarrel
having ensued between the courts of Berlin and Vienna,
the warlike King of Prussia became alarmed by the
hostile preparations that were made along the Livonian
frontier, and resolving to anticipate the designs of his
enemies, in 1756 invaded Saxony, and made himself
master of Dresden. On the first tidings of this invasion,
Marshal Brown put himself at the head of the army of
Prague, and marched to relieve the Saxons; but this
movement was anticipated by Frederick, who left 40,000
men to continue the blockade of Pirna on the left bank of
the Elbe (where Augustus III. of Poland was shut up),
and penetrated into Bohemia at the head of 24,000
soldiers.

Brown encamped at Kolin, while his compatriot, Prince
Piccolomini, was posted at Konigingratz. From Kolin
he marched on the 23rd of September to the fine old city
of Budyn, which was surrounded by walls, and contains
the ancient fortress of Hassenberg. Here he endeavoured

to concert measures with the Saxons for securing their freedom; but Frederick, on being joined by another column of his army, under the great Scottish Marshal Keith, marched to encounter him.

Passing the Egra, Count Brown encamped at Lowositz, on the Elbe, and near the Saxon frontier, and there the King of Prussia came in sight of his army, in position, at daybreak on the 1st of October, with 65 squadrons, 26 battalions, 102 pieces of cannon, which formed in order of battle as they advanced, in that steady manner for which the Prussians had now become so famous. The infantry were formed in two lines, and the cavalry in three in their rear. Frederick's right wing occupied a village at the foot of the Radostitz, a wooded mountain; and on the Homolkaberg, in front of it, he had placed a battery of heavy guns; his left wing rested on the Loboschberg; and his centre occupied the fertile valley between.

The high and steep face of the Loboschberg was covered by vines, and intersected by many stone walls. Among these Marshal Brown advanced a large body of Croats, with several battalions of Hungarians to sustain them; a deep ravine and rugged rivulet lay between the army of Frederick and the Austrians, which consisted of 72 squadrons, 52 battalions, and 98 pieces of ordnance, being 70,000 men. Brown formed them in two lines, with his horsemen on the wings. He planted cannon in the village of Lowositz, and in redoubts on the level ground before it.

At seven in the morning, and during a dense fog, the battle began between the Prussian left and the Croats on the Loboschberg, who continued firing till noon, when Frederick, seeing that Brown's right was his weakest point, marched from the summit of the mountain and drove down the Croats and Hungarians from the vineyards into the plain and ravine below. The marshal, believing that the fortune of the day depended on the retention of Lowositz, threw his retiring right wing into the village, where it soon gave way. He then led forward his left, but the infantry fell into confusion at the village of Sulowitz, being exposed to a dreadful fire of shot and shell from redoubts and field-pieces, grape, canister, hand-grenades, and musketry, which mowed them down like grass, and drove them back in disorder; the marshal then ordered a retreat, which he conducted in so masterly a manner, that no effort was made to harass him. He fell back at three in the afternoon to a new position, so well chosen that Frederick dared not follow, but contented himself with keeping his line behind the ravine of Lowositz, though by sending forward a body of cavalry under the Prince of Bavern, he turned the marshal's left flank, a manœuvre which compelled him to re-pass the Egra, and again occupy his old camp at Budyn.

Such was the battle of Lowositz, where the marshal left 4000 of his men dead on the field, and in his retreat had to blow up his magazine, while the Prussians had only 653 killed and 800 wounded. Having failed to relieve the Saxons, he marched to Lichtendorf, near Schandau, to join the King of Poland, and made an attempt to force back the Prussians at the head of 8000 chosen soldiers; but the effort proved ineffectual, and Augustus III. was compelled to capitulate, and deliver 17,000 men and eighty pieces of cannon into the hands of Frederick—a mortification as bitter to the marshal as it was to the Polish monarch.

On the 14th he retired towards Bohemia. The Prussian hussars followed his rearguard, and put 300 Croats to the sword. For his services he now received the Collar of the Golden Fleece—one of the first of European knightly orders.

In 1757 a confederacy was completed to punish Frederick of Prussia for his invasion of Saxony. France sent 80,000 men to the Rhine, under the Marshal d'Estrees; 60,000 Russians threatened Livonia; the Swedes gathered on the Pomeranian frontier; and Maria Theresa mustered 150,000 soldiers, the most of whom were stationed in Prague, under Prince Charles of Lorraine and the Marshals Brown and Daun. The Austrians were then formed into four divisions—one under Marshal Brown, at Budyn; second under the Duke d'Aremberg, at Egra; a third under Count Konigsegg, at Richtenberg; a fourth under Marshal Daun, in Moravia. Undeterred by this vast array against him, Frederick in April marched straight upon Prague, and driving before him a column under Marshal Schwerin, attacked Brown at Budyn, before Daun's division could join him from Moravia. On finding his flank turned, Brown fell back upon the Bohemian capital, and Frederick, leaving one division of his army under Marshal Keith, followed him fast with the rest, and gave battle to the Austrians on the 6th of May, at dawn in the morning.

The Imperialists under Marshal Brown were 80,000 strong; his left wing rested on the Ziskberg towards Prague; his right on the hill of Sterboli. In the front were steep and craggy mountains, which no cavalry could climb or artillery traverse; but the deep vale at their foot was lined by hussars and hardy Hungarian infantry. The battle was commenced by Lieutenant-General the Prince of Schonaich assailing the Austrian right with sixty-five squadrons of cavalry; a movement which Brown skilfully repulsed by drawing off his cavalry from the left, and overwhelming the prince by the united rush of one hundred and four squadrons. Thus outflanked, they were repulsed, after two charges, until General Zeithen hurled the Austrians back upon their infantry by a magnificent charge of twenty squadrons of hussars.

The battalions of Prussian grenadiers were routed by a discharge of twelve-pounders loaded with musket-shot, and the noble Marshal Schwerin, who, seizing the colours, placed himself on foot at their head, was shot through the heart; but his officers rallied the troops, and assailed the Austrian right, at the same moment that Frederick broke through their centre, and drove it towards Prague. A desperate struggle with the bayonet now ensued between the Austrian left and the Prussian right under Prince Henry: and Marshal Brown, while in act of issuing orders to an aid-de-camp, received a deadly wound in the body; and as he could ill brook the double mortification of a defeat and of resigning the command to Prince Charles of Lorraine, it became mortal. He was compelled to leave the field, from which his right wing fled to Maleschitz, while the left followed the centre in hopeless disorder to Prague, leaving the victory to the Prussians, who by their own account had 3000 killed and 6000 wounded (by another account, 18,000 killed), 397 officers fell, many of them high in rank; 8000 Austrians were slain, 9000 taken prisoners, and 50,000 were shut up in Prague, while all the cavalry fled to Beneschau, and joined Marshal Daun. Such was the terrible and disastrous battle of Prague, and seldom has the sun set upon such a scene of suffering or slaughter as the field presented, for there were more than *twenty thousand killed and wounded men lying upon it at six in the evening!*

Marshal Brown was conveyed by his soldiers into Prague, where he endured the greatest torture from his wound, which was aggravated by the bitterness of being disabled at such a critical time. Thus by the agitation and bitterness of his mind it became fatal, and fifty-one days after the battle he expired of mingled agony and chagrin, on the 26th of June, 1757, at the age of fifty-two.

Thus died Austria's most able general and diplomatist—and one of Ireland's greatest sons; one of whom she has every reason to be proud, for he was the military rival of Frederick of Prussia, and of France's most skilful marshals, and he filled all Europe with the fame of his exploits in the field and his talent in the cabinet.

A magnificent monument was erected to his memory, and his titles and estates were inherited by his sons, of whom he left two by his countess, Maria Philippina of Martinitz. One of these died at Vienna, on the 1st May, 1759, a major-general in the service of Austria: he expired in great torture, under wounds received in battle.

Memoirs of the Lacys.

IRELAND has given to the armies of Europe five brave soldiers, all kinsmen of the name of *Lacy*—viz., Marshal Lacy, who overran the Crimea in the service of Russia, and was the fellow-soldier of the great Count Munich; Marshal Count Lacy, his son, the friend of Leopold Daun, and, like him, a distinguished general in the Septennial War; Francis Anthony Count de Lacy, who died Captain-General of Catalonia; his brother Patrick Lacy, Major of the Ulster Regiment in the Spanish service; and his son, Louis Lacy, who fought with such bravery in the wars of the Peninsula, and was *Chef-du-Battailon* of the Irish in 1807.

All those Lacys were of the old Irish family of Bruree, and their native place originally was Athlacca, a parish in the county of Limerick, on the Maig. Many of this gallant race are buried there, in the ancient churchyard, where an old tomb is yet extant, inscribed—

"John, Thomas, and Edward Lacy, 1632."

The family followed to foreign wars the fortunes of the exiled James Fitz-James, Duke of Berwick, Commander of the first troop of Irish Horse Guards, and natural son of James II. of England and VII. of Scotland. He was married first to a daughter of the Earl of Clanricarde, by whom he had a son, the successor of his titles and estates in Spain, and who also became the friend of the Lacys.

The first of the family who rose to eminence was Marshal Peter Lacy, who entered the service of Russia, and commanded with such distinction and success against the Turks.

He served as a subaltern and regimental officer in the

armies of Peter the Great, and first learned the art of war in those sanguinary and desperate conflicts between the forces of the Czar and those of Charles XII. of Sweden, against whom Peter made an alliance with the Kings of Poland and Denmark in 1699, and with whom his general, the brave Prince Menschikoff, fought so many battles in the early part of the last century.

In the year 1736 Lacy had attained the rank of general in the Russian army, under Anne Ivanowna (niece of Peter I.), who at that time governed the vast and barbarous empire of the Muscovites. Count Munich, who, for her service, had left the army of the Elector of Saxony, was at the head of her troops. "He was the Prince Eugene of Muscovy," says Frederick the Great; "but he had the vices with the virtues of all great generals. *Lascy* (the younger), Keith, Lowendhal, and other able generals, were formed in his school." Sir Patrick Gordon, a Scottish soldier of fortune, had already disciplined the Russian army, and brought it from barbarism to an equality with others in Europe; and in the time of Lacy and Munich it consisted of 10,000 guards, 60,000 infantry of the line, 20,000 dragoons, 2000 cuirassiers, 30,000 militia, with Cossacks, Tartars, Calmucs, and other barbarians, in unnumbered hordes.

In the year 1736 the differences between the Czarina Anne and her hereditary enemy the Grand Seignior, came to a crisis; and she declared war, in consequence of the provoking outrages of the Tartars of the Crimea, and the neglect of the Sultan to her repeated remonstrances on that subject; and the Emperor of Austria concerted with her the plan of the new campaign against Turkey. It was agreed that a Russian army, under General Lacy (or *Lasci*, as it is often spelt), should march against the city of Azoph; that another Russian army, commanded by the Count de Munich, should penetrate to the Ukraine; while the Austrians, under Count Seckendorf, should prepare to assault Widin, in Servia; and all these armies marched accordingly.

The Khan of the Crimea was, in those days, a powerful prince, who paid tribute to the Sultan, though he was styled *Emperor* by his Tartar subjects, and, being descended of the Ottoman blood, had a claim to the Turkish throne, on the extinction of the race of Achmet III. The sultans had the power of deposing them, and, being jealous of their rank and authority, allowed few of them to die at liberty. Thus most of the Khans of the Crimea have ended their lives in chains in the dungeons of Rhodez. Among his own people the khan could then, at any time, command an army of eighty or a hundred thousand men; but darts, arrows, and spears, with a few muskets, were their weapons, with wooden saddles and stirrups. His revenues were, the tenth of all captives, a *black mail* paid by the Poles and Muscovites, and twenty cart-loads of honey from the Moldavians. He had vast flocks, coined copper money, and maintained a guard of Janissaries, who bore his green and purple standard. The Crimea then contained several great cities, and, besides many noble monuments of the Genoese, was covered by the ruins of the Grecian age and power.

Lacy came in sight of Azoph in March, 1736. It stands on the left bank of the most southern branch of the Don, in a district full of dangerous swamps, and on an eminence, the only spot capable of bearing buildings in that bleak and barren district. The city was then of a square form, situated at the foot of an acclivity, and having a castle of great strength. Lacy attacked both town and castle with great vigour; and though assailed by incessant showers of bullets, arrows, darts, stones, and other missiles, shot by its strong garrison of Tartars and Turks, he took it by storm, after a twelve days' siege, and completely reduced it.

Field-Marshal Count Munich, with 100,000 men, was equally successful elsewhere.

Lacy next forced the far-famed lines of Perekop, which, till then, had been considered impregnable. They extended across the Isthmus, from the Euxine to the Palus Mæotis, and had been the labour of 5000 men for many years. The great ditch (from whence we have the name of *Perecopz*) was seventy-two feet broad by forty-two feet deep, and the rampart was seventy feet in height, from its base to the cope of the parapet. The town was defended by a castle, the residence of the Aga of the Guards upon the Don and Dnieper, and by six great towers mounted with cannon; but the whole of these ample fortifications were manned by an army which made the most pitiful resistance; for this Irish soldier of fortune forced them, sword in hand, at the head of his troops, cut to pieces all who resisted, and hewed a passage into the peninsula.

He took Bakhtchissari, which lies within twenty-two miles of Sebastopol. It then contained about 4000 houses, a mosque with a fine palace, and many stately tombs where the khans were buried. Around it were baths, gardens, and orchards; and near it, in the narrow valley, there still stands the now deserted mausoleum of a famous Georgian beauty, who was the chief wife of the Khan Khareem Gheraee.

While Munich was marching towards Bessarabia, Lacy overran the whole Crimea, and ravaged the country with fire and sword, up to the northern slopes of the Tauric mountains; but being foiled before Kaffa (on the sea shore), which was defended by strong walls, two castles, and a garrison under a bashaw, he was compelled, by the approach of winter, to retreat, after subjugating the whole country, and defeating more than 20,000 Tartars in one pitched battle.

"General Lacy," says Smollett," routed the Tartars of the Crimea; but they returned in greater numbers, and harassed his Muscovites in such a manner, by intercepting their provisions and destroying the country, that he was obliged to abandon the lines of Perekop." The great Field-Marshal, Baron Loudon (descended from an Ayrshire family), served in this war, under Lacy, as a subaltern officer. Among the Scottish volunteers who also served there, were Colonel Johnstone; the gallant General Leslie, who, with all his soldiers, was destroyed on the Steppe by the Tartars; and General Balmaine, who stormed Kaffa.

After these triumphant operations, Lacy entered the

Ukraine, joined Marshal Munich, and together, in 1737, they laid siege to Oczakow, at the mouth of the Borysthenes.

Oczakow, or *Dziar Cremenda*, had then about 5000 houses, a mosque, a palace, with a number of tombs of the Crimean khans, which stood among their gardens and orchards. It had a castle, built by Vitolaus, Duke of Lithuania, and therein a Turkish garrison had been established since 1644. Munich and Lacy assailed the town and castle on the landward side; but towards the sea they were attacked by the cannon of eighteen galleys. The Muscovites carried all their approaches with such impetuosity and perseverance, that, in a few days, the Turks and Tartars became filled with terror.

Among those who distinguished themselves particularly in this service were, General the Honourable James Keith (brother of the exiled Earl Marischal of Scotland), who was dangerously wounded in the thigh, and another Jacobite exile, Colonel Count Brown, a brave Irishman—"A Catholic," says Tooke, "who was compelled to seek his fortune in foreign countries, by the exertion of those talents which he would willingly have dedicated to the service of his *own*."

The garrison, which consisted of 3000 Janissaries and 7000 Bosniacs, stoutly defended themselves; but Oczakow was carried by assault. A bomb set fire to the town, and blew up its magazine; Lacy and Munich seized this opportunity to lead on their stormers, and, pressed by the foe before them and the flames behind, the Mussulmans were nearly all cut to pieces; but not before they had slain 11,000 regular troops and 5000 Cossacks by bayonet and scimitar.

The rapid success of these two generals against the Crim Tartars awakened the restless ambition of Austria; and the Emperor believing that, if he assailed the Porte by the Hungarian frontier while the Czarina pressed her victorious arms along the shores of the Black Sea, the Empire of the Osmanlies would be finally subverted, declared war, and to co-operate with his troops, the Count

Brown* left Lacy and Munich, and marched into Hungary at the head of a Russian column. But the hopes of the Emperor were frustrated! The Turks turned all their vengeance against him, defeated his generals, and besieged Belgrade. The Austrian Field-Marshal Wallace was defeated at Crotska, and the gallant Earl of Crawford who served under him as a volunteer, received a wound from which he never recovered. The troops of Brown were also routed, and he was taken prisoner. The barbarous Osmanlies stripped him quite naked, and bound him back to back with another prisoner for forty-eight hours. He was four times exposed for sale as a slave in the common market-place, and four times was bought by different masters, who treated him with the greatest cruelty.

He gave out that he was a captain to lessen the price of his ransom, and in this deplorable condition was discovered by an Irish gentleman, who communicated his story to M. de Villeneuve, the French ambassador at Constantinople, by whom he was generously ransomed for three hundred ducats, and sent back to Russia, where he died a general and governor of Riga, in 1789, in his eighty-eighth year.

The reverses on the side of Hungary overbalanced the success of Lacy against the Crim Tartars; the Emperor lost heart, and the Czarina, though victorious again at Choczim in Bessarabia, where, on the 31st August, 1739, the forces of Munich defeated the Turks and swept the right bank of the Dneister, fearing that she was about to lose her ally, concluded a treaty of peace, by which Austria ceded to the Porte, Belgrade, Sabatz, the island and fortress of Orsova, with Servia and Wallachia, while the Danube and the Saave were to be the boundaries of their empires; but the Czarina retained Azoph, the important conquest of Marshal Lacy, who, in obedience to her orders, demolished the walls and fortifications of the

* This is *not* the same Irish officer of whom a memoir is given elsewhere.

city. To commemorate the exploits of him and Munich, she ordered a medal to be struck, having direct reference to the war in the Crimea, which was thenceforward to be an independent state. On one side of this medal was the legend—

"ANNÆ IVANOWNA, D.G., RUSSIÆ IMPECUTRIX."

On the other was an eagle, with the words—

"PACE EUROPÆ PROMOTA, TARTARIS, VICTIS, TANAI LIBERATO, ANNO 1736."

Marshal Lacy ended his days in honour, and a noble monument was erected to his memory; but his less fortunate compatriot, Marshal Munich, incurred the displeasure of their capricious mistress, and was banished for twenty years to the most northern confines of Siberia. Recalled in his old age by the Czar Peter III., he was made Governor of Esthonia and Livonia; but died at Riga almost immediately after receiving that appointment, in his eighty-fifth year.

JOSEPH FRANCIS MAURICE COUNT LACY, one of the great captains of the Seven Years' War, was the son of the preceding.

He was born at St. Petersburg, in the year 1718, and learned the art of soldiering under the eye of his father, and in the camp of Marshal Munich, in the service of the Czarina Anne, during her Crimean and Bessarabian campaigns.

At the age of twenty he was a captain, and to his knowledge and love of the art of war united a polished education, gained under the best masters in Germany.

In 1740, on the accession of Maria Theresa to the Austrian throne, he entered her service, with the permission of the Czarina, and there, by his talents, courage, and gentle bearing won the esteem of his soldiers; thus he soon attained a majority, and then the rank of colonel. He served in the Italian campaign as aide-de-camp to Count Brown, and at Viletri, had three horses shot under him. He distinguished himself still more at the siege of Maestricht, and obtained command of a regiment.

In the war of the Hungarian Succession, after the cowardice and extraordinary mismanagement of the Duke of Cumberland had covered the British army with disgrace in the Low Countries, by allowing it to be outflanked at Khloster Seven, by failing to defend the position at Maestricht, and forcing it shamefully to capitulate, on the 8th of September, 1757, and thus abandon our ally, Frederick the Great of Prussia, that warlike monarch only pushed on the war with greater vigour. In this disastrous contest the activity and vigilance of Count Lacy soon recommended him to the notice of Leopold Count Daun, a native of Bohemia, and son of Philip Lorenzo, Prince of Tiano, the pupil of Kevenhuller; and he improved the good opinion of that great soldier by his fascinating manner and courtier-like behaviour. The friendship of Daun soon won him the rank of major-general; and as such he commanded a brigade in his division, when, in 1757, conformable to the defensive system taken by Russia, Austria, and Sweden, the army of the Empress-Queen was broken into four great columns, to prosecute the war against the Prussians, French, and Bavarians, the violators of the famous Pragmatic Sanction.

One column, under the Duke d'Aremberg, was posted at Egra; a second, under Marshal Count Brown, was posted at Budyn; a third, under Count Konigsegg, held Reichenburg; a fourth, under Marshal Daun, occupied Moravia.

In his column were the brigades of Lacy and Lowenstein, whom Frederick of Prussia styles "two young officers who ardently sought to distinguish themselves." Lacy was then in his thirty-eighth year.

In Lusatia, during the winter of 1756 and the spring of 1757, these officers had given infinite trouble to the troops of Frederick. They had frequently attacked, sword in hand, his post at Ostritz, a Saxon town on the Queiss; at other times, his intrenchments at Hirschfelde, a manufacturing town on the left bank of the Neisse, and also at Marienthiel. Hirschfelde, which was garrisoned by one battalion of Prussians, they assailed at four o'clock one morning, with 6000 men; two redoubts, which stood without the gates, each defended by two pieces of cannon, were repeatedly taken and retaken; but after losing 500 men, Lacy and his brother-brigadier retired, bringing off the Prussian guns as a trophy. These assaults were ineffectual, and many men were slain. Among others fell Major Blumenthal, of the Prince Henry's regiment—a brave officer. The Prussian corps of Lestwitz at Zittace, and of the Prince of Bavern at Gorlitz were harassed by perpetual alarms; and such was the activity of young Lacy and Lowenstein, that they kept them continually under arms, if not in action, during the winter months.

As a brigadier, Lacy bore a distinguished part in the battles of Reichenberg and of Prague, and in all the operations consequent to the invasion of Bohemia by Frederick the Great, whose policy it was ever to keep the scene of his wars as far as possible from his own territory; thus his army entered the Bohemian frontier in four columns, from Saxony, Misnia, Lusatia, and Silesia, under himself and Marshal Keith; Prince Maurice, of Anhalt Dessau; Prince Ferdinand, of Brunswick-Bavern; and the aged Marshal Schwerin. The division of the latter entered in five brigades, at five different places, and won the dangerous defile of Gulder Oelse from the Pandours, at the point of the bayonet.

Everywhere the Austrians were driven back before this sudden torrent of Prussian soldiers, who advanced against the position of Count Konigsegg at Reichenberg, where 28,000 men were formed in order of battle, under cover of strong redoubts, and among steep mountains covered with dense forests. But the lines were stormed and the Austrians defeated, with the loss of 1000 killed, among whom were two counts, a prince, and a general, while twenty officers, four hundred soldiers, and three standards were taken as an augury of greater victories. On hearing of this defeat, Leopold Daun marched with all speed from Moravia to reinforce the main body of the Austrians, which, when joined by the regiments of Prague and Bavern, mustered 100,000 men. Making a feint towards Egra (which drew off 20,000 Austrians in *that* direction), the King of Prussia and Marshal Keith marched against the other troops of the Empress-Queen ; and, crossing the Moldau on the 5th May, turned the flank of the Imperialists, under the famous Ulysses Count Brown, whose steady defence made the Prussians waver and fall back. On this the venerable Marshal Schwerin, then in his eighty-second year, stung by the unmerited reproaches of the king, who urged him to advance, dismounted in the marshy ground, and taking an infantry standard in his hand, cried, "Let all brave Prussians follow *me* !"

But at that moment an Austrian bullet pierced his breast ; and falling thus, covered with years and glory, he closed a long career of faithful military service ; but the Prussian foot pressed furiously on, and after three charges totally routed the Austrians, whose general, Count Brown, also received his mortal wound, as already related.

Finding the day irreparably lost, Count Lacy, Prince Charles of Lorraine, the Princes of Saxony and Modena, and the Duke d'Aremberg, with the remnant of their infantry, in all 50,000 men, took refuge in Prague, where the gallant Brown expired of his wound, on the 6th May. Meanwhile 16,000 cavalry fled to Marshal Daun, who had encamped at Bohmishbrodt the night before the battle.

The Prussians followed up their victory with ardour ; Prague, with 100,000 souls within its walls, was invested closely ; Frederick pushed the blockade on one side, and Marshal Keith on the other. In four days they had it completely surrounded, and cut off every means of supply, agreeably to the last words of Marshal Brown, who, when dying, said : "Tell Prince Charles of Lorraine instantly to march out and attack Marshal Keith, or all is lost."

Lacy and others proposed to assail the Prussians in the night, with 12,000 Austrians, who were to be sustained by all the Pandours and Hungarian Grenadiers ; and thus to hew a passage, sword in hand, through Frederick's lines, and relieve Prague of the multitude of soldiers who were rapidly consuming the provisions of the people. An infamous deserter informed the Prussians of this gallant design, and thus they were all on the alert, when about two o'clock, in the darkness of a misty morning, a fiery tide of armed men rolled out of Prague, and assailing Marshal Keith at the bayonet's point, pressed desperately on towards the Moldau; but, after a fierce and desultory conflict, in which Prince Henry (Frederick's youngest son) had a horse shot under him, the Austrians were routed, and Lacy and other brave leaders were forced to fall back into Prague, with the loss of many killed and wounded.

After this the Prussian batteries opened, and in twenty-four hours threw 300 bombs, besides many fire-balls into the town; its streets were soon sheeted with fire, and men, women, and horses, with the sick and wounded, perished in vast numbers. The city burned for three days; flames and starvation drove the citizens to despair. Seeing their loved Bohemian capital on the verge of destruction, they besought Lacy, d'Aremberg, and other commanders, in the most moving terms, to surrender; but war had hardened their hearts, and instead of complying, they drove out 12,000 persons who were considered as a mere incumberance. These unfortunates were hurled back by the Prussians to the walls of Prague, and thus the Austrians were soon reduced to eat their troop and artillery horses, forty of which were shot daily, and cut up for rations, or sold at four pence per pound to the wretched people, who still perished hourly by fire, shot, and famine.

Two other sallies were made, and the Prussian camp was kept in a state of perpetual alarm. In this defence, so disastrous to the city, Lacy was of incalculable service in harassing the Prussian trenches, by his vigilance and restless bravery. Contrary to the advice of Keith, the king, on the 13th of June, left a small force before Prague, and, drawing off his main body, marched against Daun, who defeated him in battle at Kolin, and forced him to leave Bohemia—a movement by which the blockade of Prague was abandoned; and the imprisoned Austrians received their deliverer with inexpressible joy. Lacy and other generals issued out, with their breasts full of ardour and vengeance, and followed the retreating Prussians over the Saxon frontier, sabring all stragglers who fell into their power.

To narrate all the military operations in which Count Lacy bore a part, would be to rehearse the history of the Seven Years' War. He owed his elevation and high consideration as much to his own bravery and skill as to the patronage and friendship of Daun, who consulted him on every occasion, and employed him in the execution of the most delicate measures.

Though by his vigour and decision he frequently urged Marshal Daun on many a bold enterprise, he was possessed of great coolness and presence of mind. "His ardour," says the historian of the House of Hapsburg, "never exceeded the bounds of prudence, or hurried him into attempts which might incur the censure of his patron." He was of great service in drilling and training the Austrian forces to perform those new and difficult manœuvres of which Daun was the inventor; he was a strict disciplinarian, a friend to order, and by his precept and example succeeded in introducing a degree of economy into every branch of the Austrian military service.

In 1758 the King of Prussia commenced the new campaign, and entering Moravia, invested Olmutz. General Lacy was then of great service in protecting the roads which led to Upper Silesia; and, when posted at Gibau with a large body of Austrians, he sent a detachment of grenadiers to Krenau, where they harassed the Prussian rear-guard, till they were driven back by Wied. When Frederick retired from Konigsgratz, Lacy and St. Ignan followed him with 15,000 men, and had many severe encounters with the Putkammer hussars, who formed the rear-guard of the Prussians.

He served valiantly at the great battle of Hochkirchen, when the good old Marshal Keith, Knight of the Black Eagle, and Governor of Berlin, a general second to none in the Seven Years' War, was slain that day, when fighting on foot at the head of the Prussian infantry; and here ensued an affecting incident. After the battle, his body was shamefully abandoned by the routed Prussians, and stripped by Austrian stragglers. Thus it lay long on the field, undistinguished from the thousands of others which covered it. In this degrading situation it was found by Lacy, who was riding over the ground, and with whose father (old Marshal Lacy) the venerable Keith had served in Russia, and by whose side he had been wounded in the Crimea. The count recognised the body, says Dr. Smollett, by the large scar of a dangerous wound which General Keith had received *in his thigh* at the siege of Oczakow, and could not refrain from tears on seeing his father's honoured friend lying thus at his feet, a naked, lifeless, and deserted corpse; and it must have been an interesting scene to witness these two exiles—the young Irish Jacobite weeping over the old Scottish Cavalier—on that sanguinary field. Lacy had the body immediately covered, and interred with the honours of war, in the adjacent churchyard, from whence it was afterwards removed to Berlin.

Lacy, with Daun and Loudon, bore a conspicuous part in the campaign of 1760, particularly in those manœuvres by which the King of Prussia, notwithstanding all his skill and cunning, was frustrated in his Silesian operations.

Proposing to invade the Duchy again, he crossed the Elbe, on the 15th June, and was joined by the Prince of Holstein. On this, Lacy, who had been watching them, drew in his outposts, and retired to Zehaila. On his march Frederick passed very close to Lacy's camp, with his infantry covered by only four regiments of Saxon horse. These drove in Lacy's pickets; on which he shifted his ground to a position at the foot of the hills of Bockerdorf and Reichenberg. Frederick made preparations to assail them on the morrow, and only waited for reinforcements under General Hulsen; but Daun, who had crossed the Elbe at Dresden, and was hastening to the assistance of his friend, dispatched an officer to him, with orders "to shift his ground;" and together they took up a new position at Lausa, while Frederick occupied the place which Lacy had left by three regiments of hussars, two of dragoons, and two free corps, which were attacked, but unsuccessfully, by Lacy in the night.

Both armies, Prussian and Imperialist, began their march for Silesia on the same day, each eager to anticipate and shut the other out. The former marched by the way of Crackau: the latter marched through Bischofswerder; and *en route* Daun detached Lacy to Keulenburg, to cover his left flank; but Frederick attacked the young brigadier unexpectedly, and captured 200 of his rearguard. The heat was so excessive at this time that eighty men dropped dead on the march. Lacy continued to harass the Prussian rear, till at Salzforstien Frederick turned and attacked his Uhlans with four regiments of horse, who in the first charge shot and sabred 400 men. At that time Lacy's whole cavalry were encamped at Rothen Nauslitz; but he brought them up by successive troops—for here again he was taken by surprise—and a desultory and destructive skirmish ensued, after which both parties separated. Frederick now decided it was necessary either to follow Daun, who had already reached Silesia, or to rid himself at once of the resolute Lacy, who hung like a wolf upon his skirts, and encumbered every movement. Thus, on the evening of the 8th of July, after making a feigned movement towards Gorlitz, he suddenly broke into Lacy's camp, and drove him beyond the defiles of Horta, where his Prussians passed the night, while the Austrians occupied the mountain of the White Stag. From this Lacy's small force was driven next day, and had to recross the Elbe at Dresden, from whence he marched to a position at Gros Seidlitz, while lines of circumvallation were drawn round the city. A letter written by Daun to Lacy, containing all his plans of the campaign, was intercepted here, and brought to Frederick, to whom it proved of great service.

On the 10th of August, Lacy lost his tents and baggage when escaping an attack meditated by Frederick, who was baffled by the timely arrival of Daun at Hennersdorf. Marshal Loudon invested Breslau, but raised the siege on Prince Henry of Prussia marching to its relief. Frederick then made his memorable march to prevent the Russians from forming a junction with Daun and Lacy; he passed five rivers, the Elbe, the Spree, the Neiss, the Quiess, and the Bober, though trammelled by 2000 caissons and a ponderous train of artillery; but he was unable to bring Loudon to action before that general was joined by Lacy and Daun. The three leaders then encompassed his camp at Lignitz, and his affairs seemed desperate; for Daun, after a reconnoisance, announced to Lacy and Loudon his resolution of storming the Prussian position by a night attack; but the subtle Frederick eluded them all, by suddenly and secretly passing the Elbe, and hastening into Saxony, whither Daun and Lacy followed him, at the head of 80,000 men. Then Cunnersdorf, the bloodiest battle of the Seven Years' War, was fought and lost by Frederick. In that field he had 20,000 of his soldiers slain, and all his generals killed or wounded. He made incredible exertions to retrieve the day, and his uniform was riddled by musket-balls.

The Russians passed the Oder, and pushed a strong column into Brandenburg, under Count Czernichew, who was joined by a large body of Austrians under Lacy, and together they made themselves masters of Berlin, the capital, about the end of October. They levied a severe contribution upon the citizens, destroyed all the magazines, arsenals, and foundries, pillaged the royal palaces, and ravaged all the adjacent country, burning a vast amount of property and military stores; but they retired by different routes on hearing that the mortified Frederick was advancing to the relief of his plundered capital. And soon after he had his revenge at the battle fought near Toorgau, on the 23rd of November. There Lacy commanded the reserve of 20,000 men, who covered the causeway and several ponds which lay at the extremity of Daun's position, and on which his left flank rested; Lacy endured a severe cannonade at the beginning of the action. General Count O'Donnel commanded the cavalry. When Daun gave way, Lacy brought up his reserve, and twice with the bayonet he strove desperately and heroically to regain the day, but was twice driven back by the Prussians; nor did he abandon that disastrous field until half-past nine in the dark November evening. By that time Daun, after receiving a shot in the thigh, had been borne away wounded, and O'Donnel had assumed the command of the broken and discomfited army.

"Although I have been in twenty-eight battles," says a Swiss officer, whose letter appears in a Scottish newspaper of the time,* " I never saw anything more dreadful than the field presented. It was near six o'clock, a most obscure night—to use the words of Harlequin, *a night of ink*—the only light we had was the infernal fire of the artillery and musketry, the horrid noise of the combatants rendered more dreadful by the night; the melancholy cries of the wounded, mixed with the sound of drums and trumpets, filled the soul with horror. *Kill! Kill!* was cried out everywhere. In a word, I never saw anything that better corresponded with the melancholy idea given us of hell itself!"

The Austrians, despite their 200 pieces of cannon, were routed and driven over the Elbe; 10,000 of them lay slain on the field, and four generals, 200 other officers, and 8000 men were taken, with twenty-seven stand of colours, and fifty guns, for of all Frederick's victories this was the most successful and glorious. He recovered all Saxony except Dresden, in the neighbourhood of which an Austrian division, under General MacGuire, another Irish soldier of fortune, was hovering. The troops of the Empress-Queen evacuated Silesia, while the Russians abandoned Colberg and retired into Poland; and thus closed the year 1760.

Leaving Lacy to watch the Prussian general Zeithen, Leopold Daun, accompanied by his countess, repaired to Vienna, and so soon recovered, that in the spring of the following year he was able to assist at the councils of war. Fifty thousand men were now prisoners on both sides. In February, 1761, Lacy, now a field-marshal, meant to have visited Finland (where his father had received extensive estates), to settle certain family disputes which had arisen; but the preparations for another campaign, and

* *Edinburgh Courant.* 8th January, 1761.

the knowledge that his old friend Daun was about to resume the command, made him defer this journey for a time.

On the 21st of March, Marshal Daun departed from Vienna to join the army, and all the generals repaired to the head of their different brigades and divisions, for it was intended that the greatest efforts should now be made to crush the warlike King of Prussia. Daun took the command in Saxony; Marshal Count Loudon in Silesia, where he was to be supported by the Russians under Marshal Butterlin, whose train of artillery was tremendous. It consisted of no less than eight ninety-six-pounders, twenty-two forty-eight-pounders, seventy twenty-four-pounders, eighty-three twelve-pounders, eighty-six eight-pounders, and 106 lighter field pieces, drawn by 13,834 horses.

O'Donnel marched with 16,000 men to Zittau, from whence he was to assist the armies of Saxony or Silesia, as occasion might require, and he pushed one division as far as Dresden.

In June, Lacy's corps took post on the right bank of the Elbe, to preserve a communication with the division of his countryman. Several other Irishmen had high rank in the Austrian service about this time, and we may particularly note Nicholas Count Taaffe, who died a colonel-commandant in 1770, aged ninety-two, and was succeeded in his title and regiment by his son, Count Francis; and Count O'Rourke,* Knight of St. Louis, descended from an ancient family in the county of Leitrim, whose ancestors Cromwell is said to have stripped of an estate worth 70,000*l.* per annum.

On the Prussians, under Prince Henry, passing the Elbe in July, Daun reinforced Lacy with six battalions and some regiments of horse. In spite of their utmost efforts, Frederick, after fighting the Imperialists on the heights of Buckersdorf, where an Irish officer named O'Kelly ably defended their redoubts with only 4000 men, recovered the city of Schweidnitz on the 22nd July,

---

* Count O'Rourke died at Lincoln's Inn, London, in 1785.

though defended by 9000 men, under *another* Irish general named Butler. He then turned his eyes towards Saxony, and proposed to besiege Dresden.

After Loudon entered Silesia in August, some severe fighting ensued, especially at Munsterberg, and on the hills of Labedau. Lacy was then hovering with his troops near Grossenhayn, and encamping at Gros-dobritz, from whence he advanced his videttes as far as Strehlen along the Elbe—for Count O'Donnel still occupied Dresden or its neighbourhood.

In September, Lacy was sent with his brigade, 15,000 strong, by Daun, to join the Russians at Brandenburg, with orders to ravage all the electorate, which, while covered by the army of Soltikoff, he did so effectually as to compel Frederick either to shift his camp from Buntzelwitz, on which he had 466 guns with 182 mines, or to weaken his army by sending out detachments to protect the burning country. In doing the latter some of Prince Henry's cavalry were severely cut up by Lacy's dragoons in a forest near Reisa; and to avoid such unpleasant surprises in future, the Prussians cut down all the magnificent timber that surrounded the old castle of Hubertsbourg; but on Lacy's nearer approach they retired to Potsdam and Spandau. In October, Prince Henry of Prussia and Marshal Daun were both encamped—one under the walls of Dresden, and the other under the ramparts of Meissen, while their hussars and light troops fought together hourly, and Lacy hovered in the neighbourhood of Lusace, watching some large detachments of Prussians.

In December he again terrified the inhabitants of the capital by appearing suddenly within seven miles of Berlin; but on an overwhelming force under General Bandemer being sent against him by Prince Henry, he recrossed the Elbe and retreated.

Fortunately in 1762 there was concluded with the Court of Vienna a cessation of hostilities for the provinces of Saxony and Silesia. This partial truce induced the Princes of the Empire to sign a treaty of neutrality to save their petty dominions from the ravages of Frederick;

and as Sweden and Russia, on the accession of the Czar Peter III., had concluded a truce with him, the Septennial War was thus left to be finished by the two powers which began it—Prussia and Austria.

In that year the Khan of the Crimea proposed to join the former, and indeed marched 5000 men towards the frontier of Poland for that purpose; but the death of the Czarina Elizabeth, and the consequent revolution in Russia, had so bewildered the poor Tartar, that not knowing what side to take, he timidly retreated to Perekop. On this Frederick recalled the Prince of Bavern from Moravia, with his troops, that together they might make doubly sure of Schweidnitz.

They joined forces, and the prince encamped on the heights of Peilau. Scarcely had this junction been effected before the Austrians, under Daun, Lacy, and O'Donnel, entered among the mountains on the 16th of August, 1762, and after a skirmish at Langan Bielau, encamped with forty battalions and forty squadrons close by; while General Beck, another Imperialist, occupied the Kletchberg with twelve battalions and twenty squadrons. All night the Prussians were under arms; their cavalry bitted and saddled, their muskets loaded, and port-fires lit; every trooper slept beside his horse, and each gunner by his cannon. Daun assailed the Prince of Bavern in his position with great impetuosity. Lacy passed the village of Peilau with six battalions, which he skilfully kept concealed behind a hill whereon his artillery were posted. To cover his left flank, O'Donnel marched forty squadrons directly from Peilau, and three times his Imperial cuirassiers were repulsed from the valley, and by a volley of grape from fifteen six-pounders his confusion was completed. O'Donnel, with the loss of 1500 dragoons, fell back, and thus exposed the left flank of Lacy, who, after making great efforts to storm the heights occupied by the foe, was compelled to retreat; and next day Daun retired by Wartha and Glatz to Scharfneck, where he remained till the close of the campaign.

This was the last military service of importance performed by Marshal Count Lacy at that time; for soon after, the war came to a close, by the treaty of peace, signed in February, 1763, by which it was agreed that a mutual restitution of conquests and oblivion of injuries should take place ; and that Prussia and Austria should be put in the same position as when the hostilities began ; and thus happily ended this truly atrocious strife, in which nearly NINE HUNDRED THOUSAND SOLDIERS PERISHED. Prussia fought ten pitched battles, and lost 180,000 men ; Russia, four great battles, and lost 120,000 men ; Austria, ten battles, with the loss of 140,000 men ; France lost 200,000 ; Britain, 165,000 ; Sweden, 25,000 ; and the Circles 28,000 ; while Austria found herself encumbered by one hundred millions of crowns of debt !

For fourteen years Lacy led a life of peace, devoting himself to the development of discipline in the Austrian army, till the death of the Bavarian Elector, on the 30th December, 1777, opened up a new prospect of aggrandizement to the Imperial Government, and again lighted the torch of war in Germany. The Elector Palatine, the Elector of Saxony and Duke of Mechlenburg-Schwerin laid claim to the vacant Electoral hat ; but their voices were lost when the formidable and covetous House of Hapsburg also put forth a demand, and the Emperor Joseph and Marshal Lacy appeared with 100,000 men, and an immense train of artillery, at the celebrated position of Konigsgratz, above the confluence of the Adler and the Rhine.

The Prussians and Saxons broke into Bohemia, and compelled Loudon to retreat, and a year of the old manœuvring war and devastation followed, till the Congress of Teschen, by which Charles Theodore, Elector Palatine of the House of Neuberg, obtained the Bavarian hat, on the 13th May, 1779. The Emperor was compelled to relinquish his unjust claims, and tranquillity was restored to Germany, enabling Count Lacy, then in his sixty-first year, once more to sheath the sword ; and this command which he held in the Bavarian dispute was the last act of importance performed by him in the service of Austria.

He had now the rank of Field-Marshal. which at the

age of thirty-six he had declined, on the plea that his achievements were unworthy of it. He had the Grand Cross of Maria Theresa; he was a member of the Aulic Council, Chief of the Staff, and General of the Ordnance.

During his command-in-chief of the Austrian army, the following romantic incident occurred.

A young Neapolitan noble, who, by war or gambling, had been reduced to poverty, became anxious to obtain military employment in the service of Austria; and on being furnished with a letter of introduction to Lacy from another soldier of fortune who served in the army of Ferdinand IV., he travelled on foot towards Vienna. He reached the Austrian territories almost penniless, and one evening found himself at a poor way-side inn, not far from the capital. In the drinking room he met three officers who were also travelling towards Vienna; and they, with the frankness of German soldiers, invited the stranger to sup with them, and in the course of the evening he told them what were his views and wishes, and that all his hopes depended upon Lacy.

"I regret to say that your plan is a bad one," said one of the Austrian officers who wore the cross of Maria Theresa; "we have had a long peace, and so many of our young nobility are crowding to Vienna in search of military employment, that I fear there is little likelihood of Marshal Lacy being able to befriend a stranger."

Undeterred by this, the young Italian said that he was resolved to persevere; and he added an account of himself, of his family, their past importance and services in war, of his present necessity and circumstances; and all this was related with a candour and modesty which so pleased him who appeared the senior officer, that he said,—

"Well, sir, since you are resolved to try your fortune at Vienna, I will give you a letter to the Marshal Lacy; it may prove of use to you, for he knows me well."

Furnished with this additional credential, the Italian reached Vienna. He waited on Lacy and presented his papers; all, at least, save the Austrian officer's letter, which unfortunately he had mislaid. Lacy read them, and frankly told him that to grant what he wished was impossible. Crushed by this, the Italian retired in desperation, for the state of his funds could ill brook delay. Three days elapsed, until chancing to find the letter he had obtained so peculiarly at the inn, he again presented himself at the levée of Lacy and delivered it. The marshal opened it, and on reading the contents, his face expressed the utmost astonishment.

"How comes it. sir," said he, with severity, "that you did not deliver this letter to me sooner?"

"Because it was mislaid; and from the casual manner in which it was received, I deemed it of little value."

"Do you know from whom it comes?"

"No," replied the Italian; "but the writer wore the gold cross of Maria Theresa."

"That officer with the gold cross was *the Emperor—* Joseph II. You ask me for a subaltern's commission, and he desires me to give you the rank of captain in a newly-raised regiment, and I have much pleasure in obeying his orders."

This young volunteer died a colonel of Hussars, and fell in battle against Custine, on the Upper Rhine, in 1792.

Lacy's plans of military reform won him a high renown in the Empire, to which he extended the mode of defence previously employed with such success upon the frontiers of Bohemia. He established the great fortress of Koningsgratz, and strengthened the defences of Theresienstadt and Josephstadt, which are still the admiration of all engineers. He regulated the war finance by a system of economy, still remembered with gratitude in Austria. True and faithful to the land he served, he was ever ready to sacrifice his personal interests and feelings for the good of the State. Of this he gave a prominent example in 1788, when Joseph II., having experienced only reverses in his contest with the Porte, was recommended by Lacy to entrust all to Baron Loudon (with whom he had ever been on terms of coldness), as being the *only general* capable of repairing the misfortunes of the war.

Finding his health failing, he visited the Spa at Baden

and on his return to Vienna died, full of years and honours, on the 28th November, 1801.

He bequeathed to the Archduke Charles an extensive park in the environs, with a request that the people should have free use of it.

He had enjoyed the trust and confidence of Maria Theresa, of Francis I., and of Joseph II., to the full ; and until he became enfeebled by time and wounds, he had more State patronage than any other subject in the empire. Frederick the Great had the highest esteem for his character as a soldier, and pronounced him the first tactician of the age, and assuredly the King of Prussia was no mean authority. They had often met in the field. With his characteristic acuteness, Frederick thus spoke of the two greatest generals against whom he led the Prussian armies.

"I *admire* the dispositions of Lacy, but I *tremble* at the onset of Loudon!"

Loudon, his companion and rival—of whom elsewhere —ended his career victoriously, after defeating the Turks and capturing Belgrade with the same soldiers whom Lacy had led to many a battle-field.

FRANCIS ANTHONY COUNT DE LACY, the celebrated Spanish general and diplomatist, was the next member of this Irish family who attained an eminent position in the history of Europe.

He was born in Spain, whither his father had followed the Duke of Berwick, in 1731, and after receiving the usual rudiments of education, commenced his military career at the early age of sixteen, in the brave old Irish regiment of Ulster infantry, then in the service of his Most Catholic Majesty Ferdinand VI., who had succeeded his father, Philip Duke of Anjou, on the Spanish throne, in the preceding year, 1746.

Francis Anthony Lacy served with this regiment in the Italian campaign of 1747, which was undertaken to advance the claims of the Spanish Bourbons to the crowns of Naples and Sicily, and to the Duchy of Milan, which had been claimed by Philip V., as successor to the House of Austria ; while he also demanded Parma, Placentia, and Tuscany, in right of his queen, though he had been obliged to relinquish them *all* by the solemn treaty of Utrecht ; but such is the faith kept by princes.

The Irish regiment of the young Count Lacy was with the army of the Count de Gages, the Spanish commander-in-chief, who had then under his orders the combined armies of Spain and Naples. Genoa had revolted against the Austrians ; Marshal Boufflers had entered it at the head of 4500 Frenchmen, and thus encouraged, the Genoese resolved to die, rather than submit to the tyranny of the House of Hapsburg, whose armies made incredible exertions to recover it. Then ensued the passage of the Var by the Marshal Duke de Belleisle ; the storming of Montalbano and other places ; the investment of Genoa by the Austrians and Piedmontese, and other operations of that extensive campaign, in which *le Régiment Irlandais d'Ultonie Infanterie* bore a most prominent part, more so, perhaps, than their enemies relished, till the naval victories of the British Admirals Anson and Warren in the East Indian Ocean, and those of Fox and Hawke elsewhere, forced Louis XV. and his allies to listen to those proposals by which peace was secured to Europe by the treaty of Aix-la-Chapelle, on the 7th October, 1748.

Passing through all the successive grades with honour to himself, Count Lacy, in his thirty-first year, obtained the colonelcy of the Ulster regiment, and, at its head, served in the war against Portugal in 1762, when Charles III. of Spain added to the calamities of his unfortunate neighbour Don Joseph, by invading his small dominions with a powerful army, which threatened with still further destruction his hapless city of Lisbon—then recently ruined by the great earthquake. One Spanish column, under the Marquis de Sarria, entered Portugal on the north ; a second, under the Count O'Reilly, took Chaves ; a third entered by Beira and spread along the Tagus. This wanton invasion was suggested to Spain by France, as a means of insulting an ally of their common foe—Britain—and also of extending by conquest the power of the Houses of Bourbon

Britain supplied Portugal with arms, ammunition, and 10,000 men, under Brigadier General Burgoyne, who skilfully co-operated with the Count de la Lippe, a German, and with General Forbes, a Scot, who commanded the army of Don Joseph. Two regiments of Catholics were raised in Ireland especially for this service, and these are still existing in the British line.

In all the operations of this war Lacy acquitted himself with the greatest honour.

In 1780, he was appointed Commandant of the Spanish Artillery, and as such was employed at the famous Siege of Gibraltar, and was present with the army which, under the Duke de Crillon (the conqueror of Minorca), made "the last desperate and unparalleled efforts" to restore the key of the Mediterranean to the hands of King Charles III.

General Elliot of Stobs, in Midlothian, with 7000 men, valiantly defended the rock against 40,000 soldiers who assailed it by land with 200 pieces of cannon : and against the combined fleets of France and Spain, forty-seven sail of the line, seven three-deckers (the strongest that had ever been built), eighty gun-boats, and a swarm of frigates and smaller vessels, which opened a shower of shot from 400 pieces of cannon against him.

The first shot was fired on the 12th January, 1780, and it killed a woman in Gibraltar. The Spanish camp was crowded by French *noblesse* and Spanish hidalgos, who had all hastened there to behold the *fall* of this great fortress.

Under Lacy, the Spanish artillerists fired with great precision and effect ; but the determined old General Elliot defended Gibraltar with the most obstinate bravery ; and General Boyd (his countryman) recommended, for the first time, a discharge of red-hot balls, which had the most disastrous effect upon the Spaniards by land and sea ; for at least 1500 of them perished. The British fired 716 barrels of powder and 8300 rounds of cannon-balls (more than half of which were *red hot*) between the time of firing the first cannon and the *last*, on the 2nd February, 783, when the French and Spaniards were completely discomfited, and a peace was signed, which ceded the fortress to Britain for ever.

For his services Lacy obtained the Grand Cross of Charles III., and the rank of Commander of the Cross of San Iago, an old Spanish order of chivalry instituted by King Ramiro, in commemoration of a victory over the Moors in 1030—their badge is a red cross in the form of a sword. He was also made Titular of the rich Commanderie of *Las Cazas Buenas*, at Merida, in Estramadura.

After the peace between Spain and Britain was firmly established, he was sent successively as plenipotentiary to Gustavus III. of Sweden, and to the Empress Catherine II. of Russia (widow of the Czar Peter III.); and the success he obtained in his embassies proved that he had secured for himself and his royal master the love and esteem of the courts of Stockholm and St. Petersburg.

Immediately on his return fresh honours were heaped upon him; he was named, *par interim*, Commandant General of the Coast of Granada and Member of the Supreme Council of War; then Lieutenant-General of the Spanish Army, Commandant of the Corps of Royal Artillery, and sole Inspector-General of that branch of the service. He was also made Inspector-General of the manufactories of arms, cannon, and all the munitions of war throughout Spain and the two Indies.

In consequence of an unlooked-for *émeute* in Barcelona the governor of which had not fulfilled his trust, in March, 1789, Lacy was appointed to the important and arduous office of Governor and Captain-General of the Province of Catalonia. The Catalonians, who had long resisted the authority of the kings of Spain, and had frequently risen in arms to assert their independence and choose princes of their own, were still liable to partial insurrections against the viceroys, to whose yoke they submitted with sullen apathy, while they treated their monarchs with hatred and contempt, till the conciliatory visit of Charles IV. But Lacy contrived to win the love and esteem even of those sullen and jealous provincials, and in every step of his career gave constant proofs of disinterestedness, skill, and devotion to the king and country of his adoption.

He seconded with great energy the measures taken by the Spanish Government to prevent the principles of the French revolutionists from crossing the Pyrenees. " Et fut reconduire sur la frontière le consul de France, qui avoit tenu des propos indiscrets à Barcelone. Par le même motif," adds a French writer, " Lacy retenait dans catalogue les emigrés Francois."

The pupils of the Royal School of Artillery at Segovia obtained from Count Lacy the amelioration of their severe system of discipline, an augmentation of the number of their scholars and cadets, and the increase of certain branches of knowledge relating to their branch of the military profession, by the establishment of the schools of chemistry, of mineralogy, and of pyrotechny, of all of which he urged the creation.

Some have supposed that Count Lacy was more admirable for his lofty spirit, his sparkling wit, and tall and handsome figure—which approached the gigantic—than for his talents as a soldier; but his amiable and conciliatory character have never been denied, while his benevolence, his Christian virtues, and patriotism were extolled even by his enemies; for he stood too high in the favour of the Spanish King to have friends *alone*. Such was Francis Anthony Lacy.

He died at Barcelona, in the time of Charles IV., on the 31st December, 1792, in the sixty-first year of his age.

On that occasion the most universal regrets were manifested at his funeral, which was conducted with great splendour and solemnity; and the officers and cadets of the Spanish artillery, by whom he was sincerely beloved, celebrated him in high eulogies, which were published in all the journals of Madrid and Catalonia.

Don Antonio Ricardo Carillo, of Albornoz, succeeded him as Captain-general of Catalonia.

PATRICK LACY, the brother of Count Anthony Francis, was major of the Ulster Regiment of Irish Infantry in the service of Spain, and died early in life, leaving a son named Louis, who was justly celebrated for his bravery, his misfortunes, and romantic history.

Louis Lacy was born on the 11th January, 1775, at San Roque, a judicial partido and town of Andalusia, six miles distant from Gibraltar, after the capture of which it was founded, in 1704. His father, Major Lacy, dying while he was yet an infant, his mother married an officer of the Brussels Regiment of infantry in the service of Charles III. Young Louis, at the early age of nine years, entered this corps as a cadet, with his stepfather, and accompanied it to Puerto Rico, one of the Spanish West India islands, which was used then as a penal colony; it had been so for two centuries before. Thus a strong garrison was maintained at the capital, San Juan de Puerto Rico.

As he grew older, Lacy showed so decided a vocation for the life of a soldier, that on his return to Spain, in 1789, Charles IV. removed him into the Ulster Regiment, among the gallant Irishmen of which his family name was held in high veneration; and in that battalion of exiles he obtained a company in 1794.

In that year, when the French Republican forces invaded Spain, and commenced those operations which ended in the capture of Fontarabia and San Sebastian, Lacy was, with the regiment of Ulster, attached to the army of Catalonia, and fighting against them. The French were 40,000 strong, the Spaniards only 20,000.

In Catalonia their progress was small; but in Guipuzcoa many places of importance fell into their hands; for the Court, languid and slow in all its warlike operations, opposed to them forces of inferior strength, and unhappily more accustomed to defeat than victory. Bellegarde was besieged by the French, who defeated the Spaniards before it; yet its commandant, the Marquis de Vallesantero, held out bravely. On the shores of the Bay of Biscay the arms of the invaders were successful; they made themselves masters of Passages, and the strong old castle of San Sebastian; they penetrated as far as Tolosa, assaulted Placentia, and besieged Pampeluna

Lacy is recorded as having personally and particularly signalized himself in battle against the French on the 5th of February, and the 5th, 16th, and 25th days ot June, 1794; and to these circumstances their own military historians bear honourable testimony.

Driven to extremities, Bellegarde surrendered on the 17th of September; and the brave Conde de la Union, after making a desperate and futile attempt to save it. fell in battle for his country, on the heights of Figueras, where 9000 Spaniards and 171 pieces of cannon were taken. The fall of Rosas followed, and the Court of Madrid trembled for the safety of the Catalonian coast. But the war was ended in the following year by the peace of Basle; and up to that period Lacy served, with the Regiment of Ulster, with honourable distinction, and attained great experience in the art of war—that arduous profession to which all the exiles of his family had so successfully and especially dedicated their lives.

In December, 1795, he embarked with his regiment for the Canary Islands. While there he unfortunately had a love intrigue with a young Spanish lady, of great personal attractions; and in gaining her favour, won, also, the enmity of the governor and captain-general of the colony, who, by ill-luck, proved to be his rival. Enraged by the success of the handsome Lacy, the proud and revengeful Spaniard was so weak and unjust as to exile him from his regiment and the society of his companions in arms, by banishing him to Ferro, one of the smallest and most westerly of the Canary Islands. An arid and barren place, it is a mere mountain pass, composed of dark grey land, dotted here and there by sombre bushes.

Indignant at such arbitrary treatment, Louis **Lacy** wrote bitter and fiery letters to the captain-general, who made him a prisoner, and brought him before a *Consijo de Guerra*, or court-martial, by sentence of which he was condemned to imprisonment as one labouring under mental alienation, and, after all his gallant services, was deprived of his commission.

After a time he was permitted to return to Spain, and was sent to Cadiz *en retrait*.

At that time Spain, having made peace with France, was at war with John VI. of Portugal. This contest was productive of no important event, and was terminated in 1801. Lacy arrived in Europe just as the last campaign was opened against the Portuguese; and hearing of it, he vainly solicited from the government of Charles IV. the honour of being permitted to serve in the Spanish army as a simple grenadier; but the mal-influence of his enemy, the Governor of the Canaries, still followed him, and this humble request was refused him. Poor Lacy, in bitterness of spirit and almost without a coin in his purse, resolved to push his fortunes elsewhere. He wandered on foot through the Peninsula, crossed the Pyrenees, and, like an humble wayfaring pedestrian, passed through France, and arrived at the town of Boulogne-sur-mer in October, 1803, when Bonaparte was assembling his great army for the invasion of Britain.

Finding himself destitute, and without resources, Lacy enlisted in the 6th Regiment of light infantry of the French line, as a private soldier; but his previous military knowledge, which was soon discovered by his comrades and officers, obtained for him, in one month, the rank of sergeant. About the same time General Clarke (who was afterwards, in 1809, created Duc de Feltre) having heard of him, related the history of Lacy, of his father and uncle, to the Emperor Napoleon. Struck by a narrative so singular, Napoleon sent for the sergeant, and being charmed by his manner and bearing, in virtue of the rank he had previously held, generously gave him the commission of captain in the Irish Legion, which was then being organized at Morlaix, under Arthur O'Connor, for the service of France. General Clarke, Minister of War under Napoleon, being of Irish descent, had the idea of gaining over some of the old Irish aristocracy; and Nadgett, another Irishman in the Foreign Office, had a scheme for enlisting Irish prisoners in the French prisons; a scheme which proved, however, unsuccessful. Arthur O'Connor had been M.P. for Philipstown, but rebelled in 1798, and after being imprisoned at Dublin, and tried for high treason at Maidstone, he was acquitted. In France he became a general, married the daughter of the Marquis de Condorcet, and died at Bignon in 1852.

From Morlaix Lacy marched with his regiment to Quimper-Corentin, an old manufacturing town in the departement of Finisterre; and while there became acquainted with a pretty French girl, Mademoiselle Guermer, to whom he became attached, and whom he married, in June, 1806, although her parents—old royalists probably—were bitterly opposed to her espousing a soldier of fortune in the Legion of Exiles.

Lacy was then in his thirty-first year.

Three days afterwards the Irish Legion marched for Antwerp, and he took his wife with him. From Antwerp the Irish went to the pestilential Isle of Walcheren; there also his young wife accompanied him, and he obtained a majority.

In 1807, he was appointed *Chef-du-Battailon* of the Irish attached to the army which Murat, Grand Duke of Berg, was to command in Spain, for the purpose of accomplishing Bonaparte's unjustifiable scheme of usurpation and conquest.

Lacy's generous mind became deeply agitated at the prospect of being obliged to serve against that nation among whom his exiled family had found a home; and, notwithstanding the bitterness yet rankling in his mind against those who had treated him so ill in Spain, and who had dismissed him from the Regiment of Ulster, he determined not to draw a sword against the country of his father's adoption, and with sorrow sent his young wife, with their infant son, back to her family at Quimper, there to await the settlement of the Peninsular affairs. As *Chef-du-Battailon*, he still remained with the army which crossed the Pyrenees, in virtue of the base conspiracy of the Escurial, and which marched unmolested through the barrier-towns of San Sebastian, Figueras, Pampeluna, and Barcelona, in the spring of 1808; and in the summer of that year he found himself with the French army at Madrid.

The events of the 2nd of May—the decoying of the

Royal Family to Bayonne by Bonaparte—their compulsory renunciation of the Spanish crown—and other dark transactions, decided the noble Lacy on the course he should pursue. He relinquished his command of the Irish, and quietly quitting the capital, surrendered himself a prisoner of war to the venerable Spanish general, Don Gregorio de la Cuesta, who, in his seventieth year, still held the command of the forces to which Ferdinand VII. had appointed him, as Captain-General of Castile and Leon.

Struck with the story and magnanimity of Lacy, and revering his character, Cuesta, the last of the old Spanish cavaliers, appointed him at once Lieutenant-Colonel-Commandant of the Battalion of Ledesma, which had been raised in the small province of that name, near Salamanca; and he gave all his energy and talent to discipline this regiment. For now Spain had risen bravely against the invaders, and the sturdy Asturians and Galicians, under Don Joachim Blake, a young officer of Irish parentage, had commenced the War of Independence. In all the operations of the Spaniards Lacy fought gallantly, at the head of his new regiment; but more particularly at Logrono, in Old Castile, and on the retreat to the Ebro, at Guadalaxara, thirty-two miles from Madrid; after the betrayal of which, the Spanish vanguard, which, under Venegas, had saved the army at Buvierca, by so bravely defending the pass, entered the city on the night of the 4th of December, 1809. The battalions (*tercios*) "of Ledesma and Salamanca, under Don Louis Lacy and Don Alexandro de Hore," skirmished for three hours with the French that night, on the banks of the Henares; but after a desperate encounter, the flower of the Spanish troops had to retire before them.

He was now appointed Colonel of the Burgos Regiment of Infantry; and in the same year defended several defiles of the Sierra Morena—that long, steep chain of mountains which the novel of Cervantes (more even than the valour of his countrymen) has made famous in Europe, and which divides Andalusia from New Castile. At

Toralva he surprised and captured 3000 French cavalry, and afterwards took command of the Spanish advanced guard, with the rank of Brigadier-General.

He distinguished himself again at Cuesta della Reyna, and at the beautiful old town of Aranjuez. While Venegas occupied it, he despatched Lacy with a division to drive the enemy, 2000 strong, out of Toledo, which (as he did not wish to destroy the houses from whence they fired upon him, as it was a Spanish town) did not succeed. He next occupied Puente Larga on the Zarama, which was crossed by the foe; and the Spanish general, fearing his retreat would be cut off, ordered Lacy to destroy the Queen's Bridge, and rejoin him, which he skilfully achieved; but not before the enemy's cavalry from Cuesta della Reyna had attacked him, and driven his troops to some heights above the river, the passage of which he left Don Luis Riguelmo to defend, with three battalions and four field-pieces. He was present, also, at the engagements at Almonacid de Zoreta, on the left bank of the Tagus, where, for nine consecutive hours, he remained under fire at the head of his brigade, and where 4000 Spaniards fell; and again he met the French at the pass of Despina Perros, and in the unfortunate battle of Ocana, where Venegas, in his chivalric attempt to save his friends, the people of La Mancha, rushed, with his cavalry only, on a force consisting of 5000 foot and 800 horse, and was defeated with great loss on the 19th November, 1809.

The repeated reverses of the Spaniards after the battles of Ocana and Medellin (which was lost solely by the indecision of Don Francisco de Eguia), forced Brigadier Lacy to retire into Cadiz, where, as a reward for his services, he was named successively, Sub-Inspector, Major-General, *Mariscial de Campo*, and Commander of the Isle de Leon, which is a triangular tract of ground separated from the mainland by the river of San Pedro. The river side was strongly fortified, and the channel flanked by batteries; the whole position, as it contained 50,000 inhabitants, was one of great trust and importance. Here he directed the increase of the fortifications, and commanded in many of those desperate and sanguinary sorties which were made against the enemy, who boasted that the *Insurrection* was confined to this small corner of conquered Spain. And now ensued the long blockade, which was not raised until the British won the battle of Salamanca, in 1812.

On the 5th of May, 1811, Lacy took an active part in the battle of Chiclana, which was fought on the eastern bank of the channel of San Pedro, and immediately opposite the Isle de Leon. The brave defence at Cadiz greatly encouraged the Spaniards elsewhere.

In June he was appointed Commandant-General of Catalonia; but, unfortunately, was unable to prevent the ancient seaport of Tarragona from falling into the hands of the French. Indefatigable and unwearying, he rallied the remains of the Spanish forces, and, with the Guerillas, organized a new army, at the head of which, for a year and eight months, he maintained a constant, an obstinate, and unequal struggle with the troops of Napoleon. His glorious courage and undying perseverance gained for him, in 1812, the chief command of the army in Gallicia, about 10,000 strong. This force joined Lord Wellington; but, after active operations ceased, marched back into the province from which it was named, and went into winter-quarters. On the new campaign being opened, he appeared at the head of the brave *Gallegos*, and continued to display the highest military talent against the enemy, until they were driven over the Pyrenees by the British; after which, the battles of Orthes and Toulouse, and the capture of Paris by the allies, by securing the peace of 1814, restored tranquillity to ravaged Europe, and Ferdinand VII. to the throne of Spain.

Strange to say, this event, for which he had struggled so hard, was unfortunate for Lacy, who, in consequence of his known attachment to the constitution of the Cortes, was deprived of all his offices—a base return for his many noble services—and he was coldly permitted to retire in obscurity, with his family, to Vinaroz, in the province of Valencia, where he spent two years in peace, though brooding over his wrongs, and planning means of redress.

In 1816, fatally for himself, he returned to active life; for, since the death of Parlier, and other brave men, who had fallen in attempting to secure to Spain that independence for which they had struggled against France, the eyes of all the Liberalists were turned on Louis Lacy, and in him their hopes reposed.

Having gone to Calvetes, in Catalonia, to drink the mineral waters, it chanced that he met there an old companion in arms, General Milano, and his brother, Don Raphael Milano, with two other Spanish gentlemen, whose political sentiments coincided with his own; and, after several secret meetings, they boldly resolved on re-establishing the Cortes at the point of the sword; for Lacy, relying on the sympathy of several regiments, and the regard they paid to his name and achievements, hoped to make them revolt in his favour, on the 5th April, 1817, and proclaim the Constitution.

Denounced by two traitors, the whole enterprise fell to pieces, and the four projectors failed to save themselves.

Abandoned nearly by all on whom he had relied, the unfortunate Lacy was arrested, with a few faithful friends, and conveyed, under care of a strong guard of soldiers, to a prison at Barcelona, where he was hastily tried by a subservient military commission, and sentenced *to death*— a doom which he heard with a calmness that staggered even the stern and partial judge who pronounced it.

As a rising of the Catalonians in his favour was feared and expected, the officials of the arbitrary Government at Barcelona secretly embarked him on board of a small vessel, at midnight, on the 20th June; and, resolving not to be cheated of their victim, sailed for the island of Majorca; and there he was quite as secretly landed on a solitary part of the coast, and conducted, on the night of the 4th July, to the Castle of Belver, which was garrisoned by a regiment of Neapolitan soldiers.

At four o'clock next morning he was suddenly brought

out of the fortress, just as day was breaking, and conducted to the deep fosse before the gates; there he was barbarously shot by a platoon of Italians, pursuant to the orders of those who had conveyed him from Barcelona.

Louis Lacy had already faced death too often to receive it otherwise than with the hereditary courage and coolness which had distinguished him through his eventful life, and h efell with his face to his destroyers.

His body was deposited in the old cathedral church of San Dominic, at Palma, the capital of the island; but there it was exhumed, in 1820, and conveyed, with much religious pomp and solemnity, to Barcelona, and interred near the remains of his uncle, the Captain-General Count Francis Anthony; while the newly-established Cortes, vainly to honour the memory of one who had died for them, named his son *the first grenadier of the Spanish army.*

Thus perished Louis Lacy, in his forty-second year, one who, more even than Riego, had secured, by his patriotism, the Revolution of 1820.

"*Lacy,*" says a French writer, "etait doué d'une forte constitution, et d'une âme ardent, energique et généreuse. Habile général, intrepide dans les dangers, *il s'était distingué par des faits d'armes, et par un patriotisme dignes des Grecs et des Romains!*"

Colonel Walter Butler,

OF THE IRISH MUSKETEERS.

IN the army of Ferdinand II., Emperor of Austria (who succeeded his brother Matthias in 1619), then commanded by Albrecht, Count of Wallenstein and Duke of Friedland, were two brave Irish soldiers of fortune—James Butler, who commanded a regiment of Irish dragoons; and his younger brother, Walter, who was colonel of a regiment of Irish musketeers.

These gentlemen were nearly related to James, then Earl of Ormond, and were driven to seek service in foreign wars by the result of a quarrel between their family and King James VI. of Scotland and I. of England, who had unjustly wrested from the Butlers their valuable estates, and bestowed them upon his Scottish favourite, Sir Richard Preston, Laird of Craigmillar (near Edinburgh), and Knight of the Bath. This gentleman, who was afterwards created Lord Dingwall in the peerage of Scotland, and Earl of Desmond in that of Ireland, 6th June, 1614, claimed Ormond in right of his wife, Lady Elizabeth Butler, who was the only daughter of Thomas, Earl of Ormond, and widow of Theobald, Viscount of Theophelim. Such was the undue partiality of James for his countryman, the Viscount Dingwall, that in 1614, when Sir Walter, eldest son of Sir John Butler, third brother of the old Earl of Ormond, inherited that title, the Ormond estates (which in ancient times were an Irish principality on the left bank of the middle Shannon, in the northern part of Munster) were bestowed upon the stranger; and the king, to enforce his claim, wrote a very peremptory letter to the Irish Privy Council. Sir

Arthur Chichester, Baron of Belfast, was at that time Lord Deputy and Chief Governor of Ireland. Finding the Council averse to this injustice, James, who was notorious for entertaining the most absurd ideas of his prerogative, took the matter into his own hands, and, charging the Earl of Ormond with "non-compliance,' threw him into the Fleet prison, where he remained for eight years, enduring great want and misery, while all his old hereditary possessions were seized and confiscated, by which his family were reduced and ruined.

Preston, Lord Dingwall, was drowned in June, 1621 when on his way from Dublin to Scotland. He left an only daughter, Lady Elizabeth Preston, through whom his titles and Irish estates went afterwards to the Earls of Ossory.

The trouble in which the family became involved, and the wandering spirit which possessed the Irish, like the Scots of those days, led the earl's two cousins, James and Walter, into the Imperial service, where they soon obtained the command of regiments, and served under John de Tscerclai, the Count Tilly, and the great Wallenstein, in most of the battles of the Thirty Years' War.

In 1631, Walter Butler, with his battalion of Irish musketeers, formed part of the Imperial garrison which defended the town of Frankfort-on-the-Oder against the victorious army of Gustavus Adolphus.

Frankfort was even then a large town, and being capital of the middle mark of Brandenburg, was remarkable for its fairs and university. As it stood only forty-eight miles from Berlin, the imperial generals were anxious about its safety. Hannibal Count de Schomberg, the successor of old Torquato Conti, commanded the garrison, which consisted of ten thousand horse and foot. The town was surrounded by strong ramparts and gates, but was divided in two by the Oder.

At the head of eighteen thousand men, with two hundred pieces of cannon, and a pontoon bridge one hundred and eighty feet long, the warlike King of Sweden marched along the banks of the river, and appeared near the town on the 1st day of April. No troops ever presented a finer aspect than the Swedish, as they marched in several columns to the investment of Frankfort, the attack on which was planned by Sir John Hepburn, of Athelstaneford (afterwards a maréchal de camp in France), who then commanded the green brigade of Scots in the service of Gustavus. In the army of the latter were no less than fifteen thousand Scots at this time.

There is an old rhyme, which says—

> " He who lyes before Frankfort a year and a daye,
> Is lord of the empire for ever and aye."

But, knowing well that the fiery King of Sweden would not remain a week if he could help it, Count Schomberg, the commander-in-chief; the Count de Montecuculi, an Italian; Campmaster-General Teiffenbach, and Colonel Herbertstein, made the most vigorous preparations to defend the place; and to *Walter Butler* and his Irish musketeers assigned a post of the greatest danger.

"Take him in every respect," says the historian of Gustavus, " he was one of the bravest officers in the Emperor's service; but as the Imperialists envied this gallant foreigner, care was taken to place him in *the weakest part* of the fortification; or, to speak more to the purpose, in a part that scarcely deserved to be called a fortification." In no way either daunted or disheartened, Butler resolved to make the best of it, and ordered his Irishmen to dig a trench and form a breastwork in rear of it; and thus, after incredible labour, they formed a solid rampart in one day; but that evening he went to Count Schomberg, and represented " that the post assigned to him was almost incapable of being defended, and that unless a sally was made that very night, to prevent the Swedes and Scots from coming nearer his indifferent parapet, the place would be taken."

But Schomberg heard him without interest or attention.

" Give me but five troops of cuirassiers, Count Hannibal," said he, "and five of dragoons, and at the peril of life and reputation, I will undertake to make the Swedes raise the siege."

Envious of the honour already won by the stranger, the Imperialist declined alike the offer and advice, though secretly he dispatched, on the very service coveted by Walter Butler, a certain German commander, whose cuirassiers failed to perform the duty required, for they were driven in by the Scottish Highlanders of Gustavus, and their leader was shot, while Major Sinclair, of Sir John Hepburn's Scots musketeers, followed them almost into the town.

Covered by the Rhinegrave's cuirassiers, under Colonel Hume, of Carrolsidebrae, Hepburn's brigade of Scots intrenched themselves before the great gate of the town; the yellow brigade occupied the Custrin road; and the white brigade of Swedes was spread throughout the suburbs. After a smart cannonade, on Palm Sunday, the 3rd of April, the King of Sweden ordered a general assault.

"The Swedish soldiers wanting ladders for the scaling of the walls, runne to certaines Boores' houses hard bye, whence they bring away the racks in the stables, and those others without, upon which the Boores used to lay their cowes' meat. With these and some store of hatchets they had gotten, to a mightie strong palisadoe of the enemies' neere the walls they goe, which they fell to hewing downe. The enemies labouring to defend the stocket or palisadoe, to it on both sides they fall; the bullets darkening the very aire with a showre of lead. The Imperialists being at length, by main force, beaten off, retire through a sally-port into the towne. Being entered within the outer port, there stay they and shoote amaine. The King calling Sir John Hebron and Colonel Lumsden unto him—'*Now, my brave Scotts*' (snies he), '*remember your countrymen slain at New Brandenburg!*'"*

The Scottish infantry advanced with their pikes in the front rank and their musketeers firing over their heads; thus a terrible slaughter was soon made of the Imperial-

---

* *Swedish Intelligencer*, 1632.

ists. "One Scottish man," continues the quaint record of the Swedish war, "killed eighteen men with his own hand. Here did Lumsden take eighteen colours; yea, such testimony showed he of his valour, that the king after the battle bade him aske what he wolde, and he wolde give it to him." This brave officer was Colonel Sir James Lumsden, of Invergellie, in Fifeshire, afterwards made Governor of Newcastle by the Scottish Parliament, and a major-general in the army which invaded England in 1640.

Meanwhile Gustavus was pressing with his own brigade upon the quarter occupied by Butler and his Irish musketeers, who defended themselves with incredible resolution; so much so, that when one of them was dragged over the rampart, he was asked by the Swedish king, "what soldiers these were who fought so valiantly?" "Colonel Butler's Irish regiment," replied the prisoner. This was at half-past one in the day, and Gustavus, on hearing it (according to Harte), drew off his brigade, and in despair of forcing a passage through the Irish, assailed the strong Gueben gate, and about four in the afternoon broke into the town through the Germans.

The Governor, Schomberg, Campmaster-General Tieffenbach, the Count de Montecuculi, Colonels Behem and Herbertstein, with most of the Imperialists, fled out of the city with great baseness, leaving the faithful Butler to fight single-handed against the tides of Swedes and Scots who surrounded his almost indefensible post. Already three Irish lieutenant-colonels, O'Neil, Patrick, and Macarthy were slain, with Captain-Lieutenants Grace and Brown, and Ensign Butler, all Irish, and many of their men. At last Walter Butler was pierced by a bullet, and had his sword-arm broken by a musket-ball, and when he fell the remnant of his gallant soldiers surrendered, and resistance was at an end.

Meanwhile the fugitive generals fled towards Silesia, and everywhere gave out that Butler and the Irish had betrayed Frankfort, by permitting the enemy to enter by *their* quarter, as it was the weakest; and had it not been for a providential accident, adds an historian, Butler might have been beheaded and degraded, in spi.. of all his gallant services ; but next day, says one of the stormers, the Scottish Colonel Munro, in his history, "It was to be seen where *the best service was done ;* and truly had all the rest (of the Imperialists) stood to it as well as the *Irish did*, we had returned with great loss, and without victory." He adds, there were taken fifty standards, one colonel, five lieutenant-colonels, "and one Irish cavalier, Butler who behaved himself honourably and well." Hundreds of Imperialists were drowned in the Oder, and a vast quantity of plunder was taken. That night the King of Sweden gave a banquet to his principal officers and colonels, Sir John Hepburn, Munro, Lumsden, Sir John Banier, and others ; and when they were assembling, " Cavaliers," said he, " I will not eat a morsel until I have seen this brave Irishman of whom we hear so much ; and yet," he added, to Colonel Hume, " I have that to say to him which he may not be pleased to hear."

Butler's wounds rendered him incapable of exertion ; but on a litter of pikes being formed, he was conveyed into the presence of Gustavus, who gazed at him sternly, and asked with anger—

" Sir, art thou the elder or the younger Butler ?"

" May it please your Majesty," replied the wounded man, " I am but the younger."

" God be praised !" said Gustavus Adolphus. " Thou art a brave fellow. Hadst thou been the elder, I meant to have run my sword through thy body ; but now my own physicians shall attend thee, and nothing shall be omitted that may procure thee happiness and ease."

The action by which James Butler had kindled so much indignation in the breast of the usually placid Gustavus is now unknown ; but it must have been something very remarkable to excite such angry bitterness. Had Walter Butler been a Protestant, the king would, no doubt, have endeavoured to lure him into the Swedish service ; but the wounded Imperialist was as famous for his strict adherence to the duties of the Roman Catholic church as for his gallantry in the field.

While lying thus helplessly at Frankfort, he was deeply stung and mortified by the rumour so wickedly and so industriously spread by the Imperial generals, that he had occasioned the loss of the town ; and he cast his honour under the protection of the generous Gustavus.

" Sir," said the latter, " it is in my power to do your character ample justice, and in such a manner that it can never be controverted. I will bear full testimony to your faith and valour under my own hand and royal seal."

Assuming a pen, he drew up a certificate, which set forth the heroism displayed by Butler in the strongest terms, and added, " that if the Imperial generals, instead of acting like poltroons, had performed but a fifth part of what this gallant Irishman had done, he (Gustavus) should never have been master of Frankfort, but after an obstinate siege alone."

"This, sir," said the king, " is no more than is due to a brave and injured man ; so every general in the room will take a pride in signing this paper with me." This was accordingly done by Sir John Banier, the Scottish colonels, and others.

James Butler, who was then at the court of Ferdinand II., at Vienna, was stung to the soul by the tidings that his brother had betrayed a post, and he wrote to Walter a letter full of the bitterest reproaches. " You have tarnished the lustre of the Imperial arms, as well as the name of Butler," he wrote ; and Cæsar's court-martial will make your name a bye-word of reproach."

Walter Butler was grieved by this insolence and unkindness, and hastened to show the letter to the King of Sweden.

" Heed it not, Colonel Butler," said he ; " send our testimonial to the Emperor, and trouble yourself no more about it."

Thirty thousand pounds' worth of plunder, and ten baggage waggons, with all the plate of the fugitives, were taken, and all their munitions of war ; however, they had buried in the earth a great quantity of arms. In 1850, a labourer, when digging a trench in a field near the outworks of old Frankfort, came upon a depôt of old weapons, decaying, and covered with rust. Among them were 2000 matchlocks, being part of the munition concealed by the garrison of Count Schomberg. As soon as his wounds permitted him to travel, Walter Butler left Frankfort, for Gustavus was too generous to detain as a prisoner one whose gallant spirit was writhing under unmerited reproaches. He travelled towards Silesia, and sought out a Colonel Behem, who had commanded a regiment of German infantry at the defence of Frankfort, and to whom he was fortunate enough in tracing the first of the slanderous reports, and challenged him to single combat on horse or foot, with sword and pistol; but, awed by the justice of Butler's cause, his known skill and courage, and by the formidable testimonial of Gustavus Adolphus, he signed a full retractation and apology.

Butler then went into Poland, and at his own expense raised a fine regiment of cavalry, all clad in buff coats, with back and breast pieces, and triple-barred helmets. While recruiting there he daily ran the risk of being murdered by the Polish peasantry, who were averse to the Imperial service; but he marched as soon as his new levy was completed, and on his return to the Emperor's army took possession of Prague, the capital of Bohemia. This made him more than ever a favourite of the great Wallenstein.

Soon after this exploit he married the Countess of Fondowna.

He was at Prague when the ambitious Wallenstein became false to the interests of the Empire, and fell into the deadly snare prepared for him at Egra by Colonel James Butler and others, on whose unscrupulous fidelity the Imperial court could rely. Had Walter not been a rigidly honourable man, he might have realized a large fortune by the death of his leader, who, being always fond of foreign troops, wished him to return to Ireland for the purpose of raising a body of infantry to cope with the Scottish brigades of Gustavus. For this purpose he offered him money to the amount of 32,000*l.* sterling by bills of exchange at Hamburg, and ready cash, which was lying useless at his palace of Sagan, on the bank of the Bober, in Prussian Silesia. But he declined the service with these remarkable words—"Poor old Ireland has been drained too much of her men already." This anecdote, says Walter Harte in his history, I learned at Vienna.

The wild schemes and daring ambition of Wallenstein now made him indulge in the hope of dismembering the great conquests of the Empire, and seating himself upon a new throne, to be erected by the sword in northern Europe. This hope was crushed in 1634, when the great duke was spending the holidays of Christmas in the old castle of Egra in Bohemia. The garrison in this fortress was commanded by John Gordon, a Presbyterian, a native of Aberdeenshire, who was colonel of Tzertzski's regiment, and had once been a private soldier. Wallenstein's personal escort consisted of 250 men of James Butler's Irish regiment, commanded by that officer in person.

James Butler (without communicating the matter to his brother Walter), John Gordon, and Major Walter Lesley, son of the Laird of Balquhan in the Garioch, on receiving private instructions from Vienna, resolved, without scruple or remorse, on removing the ambitious general from the path of the emperor for ever. Butler prepared a grand banquet, to which he invited the generalissimo's attendants. Previous to the latter, Butler, who, felt some distrust of Lesley and Gordon, who were both Scots and Presbyterians, while he was a Catholic, made some remarks expressive of admiration for the duke.

"You may do as you please, gentlemen, in the matter at issue," said Gordon; "but death itself shall never alienate me from the duty and affection I bear his majesty the emperor."

Thus encouraged, Butler produced a letter from Mathias Count Galas (who, after the siege of Mantua, obtained the supreme command of the Imperial army), wherein Ferdinand II. authorized them and all his officers to withdraw "their allegiance" from Wallenstein, for all the troops had taken an oath of obedience to *him* by the emperor's express order. Fully empowered by this document to do what they pleased, the three mercenaries resolved on his immediate destruction. One proposed to poison him; another suggested that he should be sent a prisoner to Vienna; a third, that he should be slain after *disposing* of his friends at the *banquet*. The last was at once adopted, and several were invited, among whom were Wallenstein's brother-in-law, Colonel Tzertzski; Colonels Illo, William Kinski, and the secretary, Colonel Niemann. The castle was filled with soldiers on whom Gordon and Butler could rely. As the fatal evening drew on, Captain Walter Devereaux, Watchmaster Robert Geraldine, and fifteen other Irishmen, entered the keep, and took possession of a postern; while to Captain Edmund Bourke, with one hundred more, was assigned the duty of keeping the streets quiet; for Tzertzski's dragoons occupied the town, which is the capital of its circle, and was then surrounded by a triple rampart, washed on one side by the Egra.

The banquet was protracted so long that at half-past ten the dessert was still on the table, when Colonel Gordon filled up a goblet of wine, and proposed the health of the shy and cunning John George, Elector of Saxony, the enemy of the emperor.

Butler affected astonishment, and said "he would drink to no man's prosperity who was the enemy of *Cæsar*."

Pretended high words ensued, and while the unsuspecting friends of Wallenstein gazed about them in wonder and perplexity, the doors were flung open, and Geraldine and Devereaux, with their soldiers armed with drawn swords or partizans, rushed in.

"Long live Ferdinand the Second!" cried Devereaux.

"God prosper the house of Austria," added Geraldine; while Butler, Gordon, and Lesley, snatched up the candles, held them aloft, and drew their swords. Wallenstein's friends saw that they were betrayed; they sprang to their weapons, all flushed with wine and with fury at this treachery; the tables were dashed over, and a deadly combat began. Colonel Illo was rushing to his sword, which was hanging on the wall, when an Irishman ran him through the heart. Tzertzski placed himself in a corner, and slew three; for the assailants, believing him to be proof to mortal weapons, were afraid of him.

"Leave me, leave me for a moment," he continued to cry, while fighting with all the energy of despair; "leave me to deal with Lesley and Gordon—I will fight them both hand to hand—after that you may kill me; but, O, Gordon, what a supper is this for your friends."

At that instant he pierced the young Duke de Lerida by a mortal wound, but was almost immediately overpowered by ten strokes, and, with Kinski and Tzertzski, nearly hewn to pieces. Unglutted yet with blood, Captain Devereaux, finding his rapier broken, snatched up a partizan, and, followed by thirty soldiers, rushed to the apartments of Wallenstein; who, having heard the uproar in the hall, had double-bolted his door within; and they assailed it with noise and great fury, while Butler stood, with his sword drawn, on the staircase below. Even the bold heart of Wallenstein was appalled by the unusual uproar—he leaped from his bed, and threw on a dressing-gown. He raised the window of the room; but the wall of the tower was too high for escape, and he cried aloud—

"Will none here assist me? Alas! is no one here my friend?"

Upon this Devereaux knocked again, and commanded his soldiers to burst open the door. Five times their united strength failed before it, till he applied his own shoulder to it; and, being a man of great power, he broke it to fragments, and then they beheld before them the formidable Wallenstein, Duke of Friedland and Prince of the Vandal Isles, standing near a table, in his shirt, pale and composed, but defenceless—for he had neither sword nor pistols; for Schiller asserts that he was disturbed in the study of astrology.

"Art thou not the betrayer of Ferdinand and the Empire?" cried Captain Devereaux, as he charged his partizan; "if so, now thou must die."

DEATH OF WALLENSTEIN.

Wallenstein made no reply, but opened his arms, as if still more to expose his naked breast, into which the Irish captain thrust his weapon, and he expired without a groan, while all the soldiers shrunk back, as if appalled by the act; yet his naked body, and the bodies of the Colonels Niemann, Tzertzski, Illo, and Kinski were carried in a cart through the streets of Egra, and tossed into a ditch. So perished the magnificent Wallenstein, the dictator of Germany!

James Butler and Devereaux hastened to Vienna, where the Emperor Ferdinand II. fastened round the neck of the former a valuable chain, giving, at the same time, his Imperial benison and a gold medal, saying, "Wear this, Colonel Butler, in memory of an emperor you have saved from ruin." He then created him a Count of the Holy Roman Empire, and gave him the gold key of the bedchamber, with extensive estates in the kingdom of Bohemia; and, to crown all, by an act of abominable hypocrisy, he ordered three thousand masses to be said for repose of the murdered general's soul. Devereaux also received a gold chain with the gold key and a colonelcy; but he left the Imperial service, and returned home to Ireland in 1638.

Colonel Gordon was created a marquis of the Empire, Colonel-General of the Imperial army, and High Chamberlain of Austria. Major Walter Lesley, who was then a captain of the Body Guard, was created Count Lesley, and Lord of Newstadt, an estate worth two hundred thousand florins. He died Field-Marshal, Governor of Sclavonia, and Knight of the Golden Fleece.

James Butler enjoyed his countship only one year; for he died at Wirtemberg in the early part of the year 1634, leaving a very ample fortune, and money to found a college of Irish Franciscans, which still exists in the Bohemian capital. To Laurmayne, confessor to the emperor, he left a memorial worth twenty pounds by his will. To the Scottish and Irish colleges at Prague he bequeathed 3300*l.*; to the Irish students at Prague, 500*l.* among them equally; to his sister, 1000*l.*; to Walter

Devereaux whose partizan slew Wallenstein, 150*l*. His widow, whom he left in easy circumstances, conveyed his body into Bohemia, escorted by a troop of lancers and cuirassiers, and there she interred him near his own estates, with great pomp and splendour. In 1638, Thomas Carve, an Irish priest, chaplain of Butler's regiment, and author of a minute account of these affairs,* obtained a commission as chaplain-general " to all the Scottish and Irish forces in the Imperial service."

During the development and *denouement* of this daring conspiracy against the great Imperialist, his friend, Walter Butler, was in command at Prague, about seventy miles distant from the castle of Egra; and he was filled with horror and dismay at the part played by his brother in the dark and terrible tragedy. It was, moreover, an unfortunate event for *him*, as he never obtained any place at court, any military order, or rose one rank higher in the army from thenceforward—for, as a favourite of Wallenstein, he was an object of distrust to the emperor.

In the same year his brother died. Walter served with distinguished bravery at Nordlingen in Swabia, where, on the 26th of August, 1634, a general engagement was the result of Field-Marshal Gustaf Horne's attempt to relieve the town, then besieged by the Imperialists, who obtained a complete victory; for the Swedish army was defeated with great loss, and had 4000 baggage-waggons, 80 pieces of cannon, and 300 stand of colours taken. The Scottish brigades suffered severely. In particular the Highland regiment of Colonel Robert Munro, which by the slaughter of that fatal day was reduced to *one* company.

By his valour and example Walter Butler, at the head of his regiment, "decided the victory in favour of the Imperialists." To quote Harte—" He stood firm, without losing one inch of ground, for three-and-twenty hours, during a continual fire, and though 16,000 soldiers were killed in that engagement."

Soon after this great battle he died of a severe illness. The descendants of his brother distinguished themselves

* Thomas Carve (Tipperariensis), *Itinerarium*, 12mo. 1639-1641.

repeatedly in the future wars of the grasping House of
Austria, particularly in those waged against Frederick
the Great, King of Prussia; and there is now living in
Bohemia an old nobleman named Baron Bütler, who
boasts of being the fourth in descent from James Butler
of Ormond, one of the slayers of the great Duke of Friedland.

Marshal Clarke,

GOVERNOR OF VIENNA AND BERLIN.

HENRY JAMES WILLIAM CLARKE, Duc de Feltre, Minister of War under the Emperor Napoleon Bonaparte, and afterwards under the Bourbons, was born on the 17th October, 1765, at Landrecies, a town of France, situate on the Sambre, westward of Maubeuge, and about one hundred miles from Paris.

His father belonged to one of the many exiled Irish families who followed to France the abdicated James VII. of Scotland, and II. of England; and after serving King Louis as a subaltern officer, died at an early age on obtaining the rank of colonel, leaving his son, the future general, an orphan, to the care of his uncle, Colonel Shee, who was then "Sécretaire des Commandement du Duc d'Orléans," and afterwards Prefect of Strasbourg, and a peer of France. It is strange how well fortune favoured all these Irish exiles in the various lands of their adoption.

By Colonel Shee, Henry Clarke was well and carefully reared, as he intended him for the service of Louis XVI. Thus, on the 17th of September, 1781, he entered the Military School at Paris as a cadet; and after going through a brief curriculum, left it on the 11th of November, 1782, to join the regiment of the Duc de Berwick as a sub-lieutenant. Wishing to join the cavalry, on the 5th of September, 1784, he was appointed cornet of hussars, with the rank of captain in the regiment of the colonel-general of this branch of the service.

On the 11th of July, 1790, he obtained a captaincy of dragoons, and in the same year received leave of absence to visit Great Britain, as a gentleman in the suite of the ambassador.

It was to the friendship and patronage of the Duke of Orleans that Clarke owed these favours, and generally, his rapid advancement in the army; and it was to this prince that the hussar regiment of the colonel-general belonged, according to a custom of the old *régime*.

On his return to France, Clarke applied immediately for active service, and on the 5th of February, 1792, was appointed a captain of the first class, and soon after he attained the rank of lieutenant-colonel of cavalry.

He remained in command of his regiment during all the horrors of the Revolution; and, at its head, served in the two campaigns which followed the attack on the Tuileries, the deposition of the king, and the murders of 1792. In September he assisted very materially at the capture of Spire, the *ci-devant* capital of a bishopric in the palatinate of the Rhine, along the upper circle of which Custine had spread his brilliant conquests.

The French attacked the Austrians, who were in order of battle in front of the city. They were outflanked, and driven back; the gates were cut down by axes, or blown to pieces by cannon, and the republicans stormed the place, taking 3000 prisoners, with a vast train of cannon and mortars. Clarke bore a conspicuous part as an active cavalry officer in all the subsequent operations of the French army, including the capture of Worms, with all its stores, and of Mentz, before which the army arrived on the 19th of October, after forced marches, performed amid torrents of rain; and the taking of Frankfort, which was ransomed from destruction and pillage on the payment of 500,000 florins.

On the 17th of March, after the rout of Bingen, he defended the passage of the Nahe, a German stream, which falls into the Rhine near the former place, and there he was of signal service to the retreating troops. He was present at the affair of Horcheim, which was afterwards annexed to France, and the capture of Landau, on the 17th of May. His distinguished bravery on these occasions obtained him the rank of General of Brigade, provisionally, the commission of which he received on the field of battle. He then received the command of three regiments of dragoons, which formed the advanced guard of the army of the Rhine.

Soon afterwards we find him exercising in this army the functions of *Chef d'Etat-Major Général;* but on the 12th of October, 1793, the Commissioners of the National Convention, in virtue of a most unjust decree of that tyrannical assembly, deprived him of his rank, as he happened to be at that time on their secret list of the *suspected.*

He received intelligence of this on the very evening before the Austrians stormed the French lines at Weissembourg, on the Lower Rhine, and he retired at once to Alsace, where he was confined on a species of parole; nor did he recover his military rank and position until after the downfall and death of the cruel and infamous Robespierre.

Under the protection of M. Carnot, who was then Minister of Public Safety, Clarke was placed at the head of a committee of military topography; and in this service he exhibited the greatest talent as a director and instructor, and spared no pains to fulfil the duties imposed upon him. The restless and suspicious Directory, in thus maintaining M. Carnot at the head of their affairs as minister, caused also the retention of Clarke, whose importance seemed to increase with that of his patron.

He was confirmed a General of Brigade in March, 1795; and on his appointment to the rank of General of Division, on the 17th of September, in the same year, our Irish exile could scarcely believe that fate had higher or more brilliant destinies in store for him; but now his talents as a diplomatist were about to be put in requisition. This was when the astonishing successes of Napoleon in Italy had alarmed the Directory, who dispatched Clarke to Vienna, entrusting to him the difficult mission of preparing the terms of the projected peace between Republican France and the Imperial Court; but, as he was adverse to the wishes of the Directory, and inimical to the task, his arrangements proved unfortunately disadvantageous to the French.

After this he visited the army of Italy, the General-in-Chief of which, being influenced by the Directory, placed him in a subordinate position, alike repugnant to his love of freedom and authority. As simple plenipotentiary, Clarke, after traversing Germany, showed himself at Vienna to be the political confidant of the powerful Directory, and, above all, of M. Carnot.

In the minute instructions given to General Clarke by the French Government we are enabled to trace him in his route, which lay through Piedmont, Milan, Medina. Bologna, and Venice; and by the Directory he—more than all their other diplomatic agents—was specially recommended to observe narrowly the secret purposes of the different great personages who held important positions at the court of Vienna.

"Your journey, M. Clarke," said the minister De la Croix, in a letter written on the 17th November, 1796, "will be sufficiently useful when you have no longer anything to know or to discover for the profit of the Republic or the cause of humanity." But it was generally believed —nay, it was openly asserted in Paris—that the mission of Clarke to Vienna was all a *ruse*, and was meant merely to conceal some artful plot woven by the Directory against Napoleon Bonaparte, before whose power and popularity they were beginning to tremble.

However, the Directory really wished a peace, and provisionally demanded an armistice; but Bonaparte, who had no desire to see a general peace in Europe, and, least of all, one formed by any person save himself, by his formidable interference and potent influence, caused the negotiations entirely to fail. We are enabled to perceive how the Directory, in their overtures for peace, above everything else counted on those territories which they could offer in exchange for Luxembourg and other provinces which they had annexed to France. This system of compensation admitted of alterations, which their envoy could vary at his pleasure, on perceiving the effect produced by each offer on the various members of the Austrian cabinet.

In the armistice extended to the two armies they wished the terms to be similar to those given by their general, Napoleon Bonaparte, when besieging Mantua. viz.:—That they should be supplied daily with ammunition and provisions, according to their numerical strength. But Bonaparte declared these terms absurd; and explained to them that the suspension of arms alone gave to France the prospect of greater advantages than could accrue from terms based on those framed at Mantua. But the commands of the Directory were imperative; and the cabinet of Vienna, on receiving their overtures, had already sent the Baron Vincent to Vicenza, to confer with General Clarke, who repelled with all his energy the advice and interference of Bonaparte; but the latter, on being supported by Barras against him, as one trusted by Carnot, said plainly to Clarke, " Si vous êtes venu ici pour faire ma volonté, je vous verrai avec plaisir; si c'est le contraire vous pouvez retourner d'où vous êtes venu."

By this language he made Clarke feel that his patron, Carnot, was not secure in office, and that he must prepare other supporters for himself. Indeed, some rumour of this nature had reached him before. The result of these disagreements between Clarke and Napoleon caused the former to omit all praise of the latter in public communications to the government at Paris; but, in the first report of Clarke to the minister De la Croix, dated 7th December, 1796, we find him exculpating Bonaparte of all blame for the awful ravages and atrocities committed by his troops in Italy.

Bonaparte succeeded in postponing the conferences at Vicenza until the 3rd January, 1797; and so many despatches passed to and fro between the Directory, Carnot, and Clarke, that the Baron Vincent lost patience, and declared, that if France had any further communications to make, they must in future be addressed, not to him, but to Gherardini, the Austrian minister at Turin. Bonaparte took care that this resolution of the baron should be effectual. Clarke was several times at Turin and Lombardy, negotiating; and after happily completing a friendly arrangement with his general, was left without other duties to fulfil, than to complete, with the Piedmontese court, those amicable treaties which were terminated by an alliance with France on the 5th April, 1797.

After this, he brought before the Directory a series of complaints against certain generals and commissaries of the French army in Italy. With the substance of the charges against these officers he had been furnished by Bonaparte; and the result was, that many of them were displaced and recalled to France.

The complaints or charges furnished to Clarke were sometimes far from correct; but Bonaparte, by means of the envoy, wished to rid his army of those devastators and peculators, without drawing upon himself their lasting and personal hostility. To the honour of Clarke, it must be confessed that his dislike for those who had been guilty of mal-demeanour in Italy was at least sincere; and in this he proved himself worthy to be the friend of Carnot.

He found himself again at Turin during the discussion which ensued concerning the preliminaries of Leoben. Bonaparte, who had neither desire nor authority to conclude anything that resembled a peace, affected to wish much for the presence of Clarke as a plenipotentiary, while he secretly contrived such means to delay his journey, that it was impossible he could arrive in time. Thus ten days passed, and on the 17th of April Clarke had not appeared, so Bonaparte signed the articles *alone*; and on the 6th of the following month, the Directory invested them both with full power to sign the final treaty.

Two negotiators, the Marquis di Gallo and Meerfeldt, had been appointed by Austria to meet them; but at the very commencement of their proceedings the proud and haughty spirits of Bonaparte and Gallo domineered over their colleagues so completely, that they became as mere machines in their hands. Clarke had, nevertheless, occasionally sole charge of the negotiations at Udina, a town in Friuli, where they had many meetings concerning the entangled affairs of France and Austria; but this was only when the tergiversations of the latter, who wished to recommence the war, were embarrassing the conferences, which, according to the caustic expression of Bonaparte, " were nothing more than a series of pleasantries."

In the midst of these incertitudes and delays, a new revolution took place at Paris, on the 4th September, 1797, when the legislative was entirely absorbed by the executive power, and when the famous pamphlet of Bailleul, which provoked such a violent debate in the Council of Five Hundred, was the tocsin of alarm. On this day—the 18th *Fructidor*—Clarke was declared a " creature of Carnot ;" and, as such, was deprived of all power. Thus Bonaparte was left sole plenipotentiary of the Republic, and had the honour of signing alone the famous treaty of Campo Formio, which secured a peace between France and the Emperor Francis II., and which took its name from the place of meeting—a castle of maritime Austria, situated on a hill in the province of Friuli. It was signed on the 17th October, and was undoubtedly more glorious for France than the treaty which General Clarke had prepared for the same purpose in November, 1796. But Bonaparte behaved with great generosity towards his fallen colleague : he defended him against the virulence of the Parisian pamphleteers and journalists, protected him while in Italy, and employed him about his staff and person in many ways. " Could he do less to the star which he had so completely made his satellite ?" exclaims a French writer.

The brilliant reception which awaited Bonaparte on his triumphant return to France, and still more, the high enthusiasm kindled by his departure for Egypt, threw Clarke completely into the shade ; and he was almost forgotten by the volatile Parisians during two years that he lived in retirement.

M. Xavier Audoin, son-in-law of Pache, succeeded Clarke as chief of the Bureau Topographique et Militaire at the Directory. The Parisian journals accused the general of having enjoyed the confidence of Carnot too much, and to be too deeply attached to the House of

Orleans, to which he and his family were indebted for much of their good fortune in France.

The *Dublin Journal* of the 7th October, 1797, contains a paragraph to the effect that it was known that Clarke had been "for forty hours, during the last week," in that city, "that he had held conferences with the leaders of the United Irishmen, and having obtained his information and given his directions, had embarked in a fishing smack from Killinbay, on Sunday morning last. That he could have no other purpose than the arrangement of a French invasion we have no doubt," adds the editor, "and when our readers have learned that there is strong ground to believe that he has been for some time past in the north of Ireland, they will naturally join in our opinion. Our readers will recollect that this General Clarke was announced in the French papers to have left the Italian army some time since on his way to Vienna to negotiate with the emperor—there has been *no* negotiation at Vienna—the treaty is under discussion at Udina—so that this journey has obviously been fabricated to *conceal* his real destination."

But, notwithstanding all these details, there is no solid proof for believing that General Clarke ever visited the land of his forefathers on this secret duty.

He ought, perhaps, to have followed Napoleon, even as a volunteer, to the banks of the Nile; but being of a proud and jealous spirit, he was unfortunately without this feeling of devotion to his new protector. Bonaparte appeared to feel this; for on his return from his distant and dangerous expedition, and finding himself master of the government, by the 18th *Brumaire* (9th November, 1799), he seemed to look coldly on the general at times.

Clarke now neglected nothing that might serve to reinstate him in the good graces of the First Consul, who, in September, 1800, intrusted him finally with the charge of the negotiations at Luneville, and soon after with the military command of that large city, which lies in the departement of the Meurthe. But Clarke felt that these two posts were alike insignificant and unworthy one of his talent and enterprise; for the recent victories in Germany and Italy had greatly simplified his duties as a negotiator, and the little that remained Bonaparte directed in Paris. When the arrangements were completed, to the infinite annoyance of Clarke, he sent his brother Joseph to sign them.

Clarke had meanwhile been preparing for the departure of a body of Russian officers who were prisoners of war at Lisle; and the kindness with which he did so, caused the Emperor Paul I. to present him with a magnificent sword, and other marks of his approbation.

Such is the weakness of the human heart, that these honours inflated Clarke so much, that for a time he appeared to feel himself equal to the First Consul, and indeed he was rash enough, and unwise enough, to say so.

Coming early one evening to the opera, he entered the box usually appropriated to Napoleon, and assumed that august person's place in the front seat. When the First Consul came, Clarke had the bad taste to sit still during the performance, and leave to his master the second place!

These mistakes of temper, united to his punctilious spirit, in affairs of state, and love of diplomatic work, caused the French government to give him the office of minister of France at Florence, that he might be away from Paris and near the young Duke of Parma, who wished to be named King of all Italy; but this post, say the *Memoirs of St. Helena*, proved exceedingly distasteful to him.

Clarke's talent—a most useful, if not brilliant one—consisted in an amazing facility for keeping on the best possible terms with all the parties among whom he was cast. The secret of his influence with Bonaparte appears to have been, a sentiment of profound gratitude in the latter for the high praise bestowed by Clarke in his "Secret Report" to the Directory on the conduct of the young general in Italy. This document afterwards fell into the hands of the First Consul, who never forgot its contents.

Clarke, tired of his residence in Florence, wrote letter after letter, demanding his recal to Paris, terming his embassy a species of exile ; and Bonaparte, believing that his punishment was sufficiently severe, at last gave him leave to return ; but desired him to travel by the way of Lisle (a fortified city in the departement of the north), to the camp at Boulogne. In Belgium he gave him the title of Councillor of State, and created for him two places in the cabinet—one as secretary for the marine, and the other for the war.

Arrived at the camp of Boulogne, one of the earliest matters entrusted to the general was the proposed establishment of Irish brigades, to co-operate in the projected invasion of Britain ; and these corps Clarke believed might be recruited among the Irishmen who were prisoners of war in France. While this project was on the *tapis*, he had many interviews with the famous Theobald Wolfe Tone, who had been appointed by the Directory chef-de-brigade, and afterwards adjutant-general; and with Lazarus Hoche, a frank, resolute, and zealous republican, who, from being a stable-boy and private of the French guards, raised himself to one of the highest positions in the army of France. In 1792, he was a corporal; in 1793, he was a *general*, commanding the army of the Moselle ; and in the two subsequent years he subdued La Vendée.

Tone was introduced to Hoche by Clarke, and in his *Memoirs* he details the questions they asked him concerning the state of Ireland ; where a landing might be effected ; where provisions might be relied on, particularly bread ; whether French auxiliaries might count on being able to form an Irish Provisional Government, either of the Catholic Committee, or of the chiefs of the Irish patriots? On these subjects Tone had many a long and anxious conference with his countryman Clarke, and with Hoche.

After a long interview with Hoche, in the cabinet of Fleury one day, Wolfe Tone was asked, what form of government the Irish would adopt, in the event of their successfully encountering the British troops?

"I was going to answer him with great earnestness," says Tone, in his interesting *Memoirs*, "when General Clarke entered, to request that we would come to dinner with Citizen Carnot. We accordingly adjourned the conversation to the apartment of the President, where we found Carnot, and one or two more. Hoche, after some time, took me aside, and repeated his question. I replied, '*Most decidedly a republic.*' He asked again, 'Are you sure?' I said, 'As sure as I can be of anything. I know nobody in Ireland who thinks of any other system——.' Carnot joined us here, with a pocket-map of Ireland, and the conversation between Clarke, Hoche, and him became pretty general, every one else having left the room. I said scarcely anything, as I wished to listen. Hoche related to Carnot the substance of what passed between him and me. When he mentioned his anxiety as to bread, Carnot laughed and said, 'There is plenty of beef in Ireland—if you cannot get bread, you must eat beef.' I told him I hoped they would find both; adding, that within twenty years Ireland had become a great corn country, so that at present it made a considerable article in her exports."—Vol. ii. pp. 14–18.

The patience of Wolfe Tone was sorely tried by many and unnecessary delays; and, after all, the hopes of the Irish exiles ended only in mustering a regiment of their countrymen, which, instead of embarking for Ireland, marched to the invasion of Spain, under the unfortunate Colonel Lewis Lacy, the son of a race of hereditary Irish soldiers, as related elsewhere.

In the year following his double appointment as minister for the war and marine, Clarke made the German campaign on the staff of Bonaparte, and was present at the capture of the free city of Ulm, in the Swabian circle, on the 17th October, 1805, and at other operations, which drove the army of the Archduke Ferdinand across the Danube; and, on the capture of Vienna by the corps of the brave Murat and Lannes, he was named governor of the city and also of Upper and Lower Austria, Carinthia, Styria, Friuli, Trieste, &c. His moderation and justice in this high command elevated him among the victors, and won him the love and esteem of the vanquished. He also received the cordon of Grand Officer of the Legion of Honour, and soon after was ordered to define the line of demarcation between Brisgau, in the kingdom of Wirtemberg, and the Grand Duchy of Baden.

Two months were spent by him in conferences and diplomacy. From the 9th to the 20th of July, 1806, he was engaged with the Russian plenipotentiary, and their interviews were terminated by the wonderful treaty which opened and ceded to France, Cattaro, a Venetian territory in Dalmatia, with its capital, harbour, and citadel; and which maintained Gustavus IV. in possession of the ancient Duchy of Pomerania, and left to be achieved, at an early period, the junction of Sicily to the kingdom of Murat—the whole being arranged by them, without condescending to ask the advice of Great Britain, which was then the faithful ally of Prussia. This treaty was never ratified by the Emperor Alexander. The other conferences took place between Clarke and Lord Yarmouth, to whom Charles Fox added the Scottish Earl of Lauderdale ; while, to assist Clarke, the French government added Jean Baptiste Champagny, the Duc de Cadore, who was only a spectator of the negotiations, which were without result, and are of no consequence to the reader; but Clarke, who had displayed his usual acuteness, tact, and skill in all his meetings with the Lords Yarmouth and Lauderdale, was not a little proud of having prevailed upon M. D'Oubril to sign certain clauses he submitted to him.

Russia, however, was in no haste to evacuate Cattaro, and the Emperor Alexander began to augment his army; so from September, 1806, it became evident that if France declared war against Prussia, she would have to encounter Russia also. In the first meeting concerning these affairs Clarke said, "that the convention recently concluded with Russia was for France equivalent to a victory; and that henceforward his master, the Emperor Napoleon, nad the right of proposing articles more advantageous than those he had lately made." He qualified the terms of the treaty which he wished them to adopt, and in particular *l'uti possedetis;* of vague conversations on the politics of Rome, he said that Bonaparte had never adopted this *uti possedetis* for a basis, without which Moravia, Styria, and Carniola would have remained still in his hands.

Similar language, encumbered by diplomatic technicalities, was applied to the two envoys of Fox, but failed to succeed with them, as they were resolved not to depart in a single instance from the basis of the position taken before by the envoy of Prince Talleyrand. The death of Charles Fox put an end to all the hopes of peace, although Lauderdale and Champagny did not despair of procuring it until the 6th of October; but by this time Clarke had set out for Germany, having accompanied Napoleon to the Prussian campaign. After the two battles of the 14th October, he was named Governor of Erfurt, a fortified city on the Gera, and capital of the Elector of Mentz. It was then crowded with Prussian prisoners, and with sick and wounded Frenchmen.

For having been more in the palaces than in the camps of Bonaparte, and being, moreover, of foreign blood, Clarke was reproached with being more of a diplomatist than a soldier by those who were envious of the favour shown him by the Emperor. While at Erfurt he caused the Saxon grenadiers of Hündt to take arms, and supplied them with ammunition, colours, and several pieces of cannon.

On the 27th Napoleon summoned him to Berlin, and appointed him governor, saying :—

"I wish that in the *same year* you should have under your orders the capitals of two monarchies we have conquered—Prussia and Austria."

"Thus Clarke, the inevitable Clarke, was appointed Governor of Berlin," says De Bourienne, "and under his administration the wretched inhabitants, who could not flee, were overwhelmed by every species of impost and oppression. As in the execution of every measure there operated the most servile compliance with the orders of Napoleon, so the name of Clarke is held in detestation throughout Prussia."

The measures of Clarke, as Governor of Berlin, were doubtless mortifying, ruinous, and often sanguinary; but then it must be remembered that he was compelled to enforce the iron will, and obey the stern orders, of his inflexible master; though it must be acknowledged that it would have been more noble in him to have softened them to the vanquished Prussians. The military contributions were rigorously levied, and those were not the least of the severities exercised upon the people of Berlin. Offences were uselessly created, and then barbarously judged of by a military commission.

The punishment of the unfortunate Burgomaster of Ciritz is forgotten amid the many barbarous executions of which Prussia became the theatre, and against which her people dared not protest. When the king, Frederick William, found himself seated with Clarke at the table of Louis XVIII. in 1815, he could not refrain from bitterly reproaching Clarke with what he termed "the useless murder of the father of a family."

"Sire," responded Clarke, "it was an unfortunate error."

"An error, monsieur?" reiterated the king, striking his hand upon the table; "an error—it was a crime!"

Withal, it must be acknowledged that Clarke, in the high place he occupied, fulfilled, in every way, the trust reposed in him by Napoleon; and that during his command at Berlin, which occupied a year, he gave ample proof of his inflexible probity; and we may perhaps believe, that many of the accusations made against him were the echoes of those complaints which are naturally raised by the vanquished against the troops of the victor. Doubtless he would have received greater praise had he striven to please others more, and his master less. By the official collections of Schœll, we are informed that Vendomme one day wished to appropriate to himself the magnificent furniture in the palace of Potsdam, where he resided; but that Clarke, by his determined intervention, forced him to relinquish the idea.

Clarke was again named minister of war, *vice* Marshal Berthier, Duke of Neufchatel and Prince of Wagram

He acquitted himself with great credit during his administration, which was prolonged without interruption for several years; but it was marked by two remarkable episodes—the descent upon Walcheren in 1809, and the conspiracy of Mallet in 1812. But we ought previously to have mentioned that in 1808 Clarke had been ennobled by the title of Count Hunebourg, and in 1809 he was created Duc de Feltre, from a town in Venetian Lombardy.

The descent of the British upon Walcheren took Clarke by surprise; but seconded by Bernadotte and Fouche he collected, in less than five weeks, an army of 100,000 men, near the mouths of the Scheldt, to watch their operations; but the swamps of South Beveland, and the Walcheren fever, proved more deadly to the British troops than the bayonets of France.

When Napoleon was absent on his disastrous Russian campaign, the unfortunate disturbance, or rather wild enterprise of the republican General Mallet, with his compatriots Guidal and Lahoire, placed Paris for some hours in the hands of an armed mob. The coolness and presence of mind exhibited by Clarke during this momentous crisis is above all common praise. Mallet forged an account of Bonaparte's death; and on obtaining twelve hundred men from the 10th cohort of the National Guard, made prisoners M. Pasquer and Savary, the Duke of Rovigo, and assailing General Hullin, Commandant of Paris, in his quarters, shot him through the head by a pistol-ball. Mallet led his party to seize Clarke as minister of war; but the plot was soon discovered, and Mallet was captured and disarmed. This finished his proposed reassertion of the Republic, and fourteen of his followers were put to death, while Clarke ordered the arrest of many others upon very slight suspicions. He then dispatched to Bonaparte a report, which displayed his own vigilance and acuteness in escaping the snare into which General Hullin, Colonel Soulier, Savary, and Pasquer had fallen so easily.

The excessive zeal of Clarke began to relax about the end of 1813, although his language always continued the same; thus, when Napoleon, acting under the pressure of his disasters in Russia, proposed to make a peace, and yield up some of his conquests, the Duc de Feltre, knowing how to touch one of the sensitive chords in his breast. said, "that he would consider the Emperor dishonoured if he consented to abandon the smallest village which had been united to the Empire by a senatorial decree!"

"What a fine thing it is to talk!" added old Bourienne.

Clarke's opinion, however, prevailed with Napoleon, and the war, so fatal to him, continued; though without doubt, in his secret soul, he had begun to see the exact and perilous position of the Emperor. Before the startling events of March, 1814, when the allies advanced upon Paris, and before the communications of Joseph had forced the determination of the Assembly, the acute Clarke had advised, very decidedly, the departure of Maria Louisa, who set out at once for Blois. The ostentatious language with which he accompanied this advice failed to deceive any one; but in spite of his efforts it was singularly cold and discouraging.

He commenced his oration by a vivid picture of the conflicting state of parties, and of the state of Paris and its environs; and his enemies accused him not only of exaggerating the dangers which menaced the capital, but of concealing its actual resources; but one fact is evident, Clarke was clearly and honestly of opinion that Paris was indefensible, and that to resist would be to destroy it! It is said that Bonaparte had a contrary opinion, though it was not then publicly avowed.

When once Maria Louisa had left Paris, Clarke, foreseeing its certain capitulation, did not take the necessary measures either to defend it or to check the progress of the allies. For three days he did not open the arsenals to the Parisians, nor would he allow them to transport the cannon from the Hôtel des Invalides, and the Ecole Militaire to the heights about the city; finally he clubbed all the troops of the line about Montmartre. "Posterity," says a recent writer, "will decide if these measures were correct."

Then followed the battle of Paris; Marshal Marmont's return within its walls; the nights of the 30th and 31st of March; the capitulation; the entry of the allies, and the strange enthusiasm with which the vacillating population received them. Napoleon was dethroned by a decree of the Senate, and a Provisional Government was formed; and changing, like many others, in that time of change, to this new government, Clarke sent in his formal adhesion on the 8th of April, about *one week* after Paris was taken.

On the 4th of the following June he was created, by Louis XVIII., a peer of France.

When Marshal Soult retired from office, King Louis appointed Clarke Minister of War—the same post he had held under the Emperor, who was then maturing plans of new operations in the little isle of Elba.

It was tauntingly said of Clarke that it was his destiny and misfortune to see the affairs of both Bonaparte and the Bourbons go to wreck, while entrusted to his care.

The *Memoirs of St. Helena* assure us that Clarke, during the events of the Hundred Days, wished to *retake* service under the Emperor Napoleon! If so, how different was his conduct from the faith that characterized Ney. Cambronne, and Macdonald! A rumour of this, in 1815, led to the immediate departure of Clarke for Ghent, where, at the fugitive court of Louis XVIII., he exercised his functions as Minister of War; and from thence, some time after, he travelled to London, charged with a mission from the king to the Prince Regent, afterwards George IV.

During the time the allied armies occupied Paris, Clarke had a remarkable interview with the King of Prussia. On this occasion he was accompanied by M. de Bourienne and Marshal Berthier. They remained for some time in the saloon, before his Prussian Majesty appeared from his closet, and when he did so, the embarrassment of his manner, and the cloudy severity of his countenance, was apparent to the three visitors.

"Marshal," said he to Berthier, "I should have preferred receiving you as a peaceful visitor at Berlin; but war has its successes, as well as its reverses. Your troops are brave and ably led; but you cannot oppose numbers, and Europe is armed against the Emperor; patience has its limits. You have passed no little time, marshal, in making war on Germany, and I have great pleasure in saying to you that I shall never forget your conduct, your justice, and moderation in those seasons of misfortune.

Marshal Berthier, who deserved this eulogium, made a suitable reply; after which the King of Prussia turned sternly to the Duc de Feltre, saying,—

"As for *you*, General Clarke, I cannot say the same of your conduct as of the marshal's. The inhabitants of Berlin will long remenber your government. You abused victory strangely, and carried to an extreme measures of rigour and vexation. If I have an advice to give you, it is—*never show your face in Prussia.*"

"Clarke was so overwhelmed by this reception from a crowned head," says M. de Bourienne, "that Berthier and myself, each taking an arm, were absolutely obliged to support him down the grand stair."

On returning to King Louis, at Ghent, he resumed his duties of Minister for the War Department; and assuredly his task was both a severe and a difficult one.

He had to arrange the disbanding of the Imperial and the re-organization of a Royal army; he had to examine and decide upon the various claims presented by hundreds of soldiers; he had to satisfy the demands of two thousand officers who adhered to the king, and to send them into the interior; he had to classify nine thousand officers of the disbanded army; to arrange for the pay of six thousand others who were *reformed*—that is, continued on pay, but without being regimented; he had to examine six thousand claims for arrears of pay and pensions, claims that could admit of no delay, and which amounted to forty-six millions of francs; he had to organize the Royal Garde du Corp; to reconstitute the gendarmerie; to provide for the maintenance of the allied armies of occupation; and all this he had to do, amid obstacles, disorders, and complexities without example.

Such was the mighty mass of labour submitted to the care of Clarke; and of this herculean task he nobly and ably acquitted himself in less than two years.

All impartial writers unite in exculpating him from the angry and unjust accusation of peculating with the enormous sums which were required and absorbed by the reorganization of the French army. But he was severely handled by military men for instituting those tribunals styled *Les Cours Prévotales*.

In June, 1815, Clarke was with Louis XVIII. at Arnouville, and while there saved his friend, François Marquis de Lagrange, a lieutenant-general who in 1813 commanded the 3rd Regiment of Gardes d'Honneur, from great danger, if not from death. The marquis had been accused of offering his services to Napoleon, and hastily arrived at Arnouville with his son, on the 30th June. As he was about to wait upon Louis he was assailed by several soldiers, in whose hearts the love of Napoleon was strong. They called him *a traitor*, and tore away his sword, cross, and epaulettes. On becoming aware of these outrages, Clarke sent two influential officers to repress the tumult, and himself led the marquis to Louis XVIII., who appointed him captain of the Black Musketeers.

The zeal which Clarke now employed in the cause of the house of Bourbon was ultimately the means of his downfall. Louis XVIII., who each day conceded more and more to the enemies of his dynasty, after bestowing upon Clarke the bâton of a Marshal of France, displaced him from office, and appointed Gouvin St. Cyr in his room.

We know that after his dismissal all was changed in the department of the Minister of War.

The position in which Clarke found himself during the last years of his stirring, active, and useful life was very painful and humiliating, especially to one of so proud a spirit as his. Some of the more favoured personages who crowded the court of Louis XVIII., could not behold with a favourable eye this foreigner, who had been the War Minister of the great Napoleon, a confidant of his, and his co-operator in a thousand schemes of conquest; on the other hand, his old comrades of the Imperial army affected to see in Clarke a deserter, a transferer of his allegiance, and, indeed, all but a traitor. Those whose base extortions he had repressed in other times now joined their clamours against him, and the Royalists cared not to say a word in his defence.

Thus, at the end of his career, he was unjustly despised alike for his talents and virtues, as for his mistakes and weaknesses—for the good he had done as well as for evil. Clarke now found himself isolated and abandoned, and the conviction of this, together with the coldness with which he was treated, sank deeply into his proud and sensitive heart.

It aggravated an illness which preyed upon him, and he died on the 28th of October, 1818, in his fifty-third year.

Such was the career of the Duc de Feltre, one of the most famous of the Irish exiles.

Clarke was master of many languages. He wrote with ease, with elegance, and with correctness; his style was often brilliant, and he knew thoroughly all that appertained to the details of a war administration. The state of complete disorganization in which he found the French service after March, 1814, proves the admirable tact and skill with which he could bring order out of disorder.

Many of the old Imperialists, his enemies, coarsely accused him of treason and treachery, but Napoleon takes care partly to exculpate him from charges so severe. On being asked at St. Helena if he believed that Clarke had been true to him, the fallen Emperor said, with a sigh—

"True to me—yes, when I was in my strength;" and after a time he added—"I cannot boast of him being more constant to me than Fortune."

This lessens the alleged crime of Clarke, while, at the same time, it lessens his nobility of conduct; though it must be acknowledged that he did not leave Napoleon until he could no longer be of service to him. The Emperor was not easily deceived as to the fidelity of a follower.

From Bourienne we know that, in 1796 and 1797, after all that passed between Napoleon and Clarke, the former still trusted in the latter, and never attempted to interrupt his despatches to the Directory or to the Chevalier de la Croix; and nothing was ever found in them displeasing to the Commander-in-chief.

Two great traits in the character of Clarke were, first, his hatred of all peculation and political knavery; the other was his mania for office, and the despatches and details connected therewith. So poor was he during the earlier years of his career, that Napoleon had to portion one of his daughters; and no instance of profusion or luxury has been cited against him.

Inflated by his patent of nobility, he wished to make his genealogy great and lofty, and one day he believed that he had discovered his descent, by the female side, from the Plantagenets—an idea which exceedingly amused Napoleon, who once said to him in a numerous company, about the time of his projected invasion of Britain,—

"Clarke, you have not yet spoken of your claims to the English throne—you ought *now* to make them good!"*

* *Biographie Universelle, &c.*

General Kilmaine,

COMMANDANT OF LOMBARDY AND GENERAL OF THE ARMÉE D'ANGLETERRE.

CHARLES JENNINGS KILMAINE, a gallant and celebrated general in the French army, was born in Dublin in the year 1750, and was descended from an ancient Irish family which had always been strongly attached to the Roman Catholic religion, and opposed to the interests of England. So deep was the animosity of his father to the church and government as established in Ireland, that in 1765 he took Charles to France, and there recommended him, when only in his fifteenth year, to enlist as a private hussar in the Regiment de Lauzun, a distinguished cavalry corps of the old French service, raised originally in the departement of the Garonne. He accompanied this corps to America, where he served in the War of Independence under the celebrated Marquis de Lafayette, Grand Provost of the kingdom of France, and was present in most of those battles in which Washington and his generals so signally discomfited the troops of Great Britain. Association with officers of the United States army, added to those impressions made upon him during his youth in Ireland and the teachings of his father, caused Kilmaine to imbibe strongly the sentiments of a revolutionist.

He repeatedly distinguished himself in action; and his colonel, the gallant Biron, after passing him through the more subordinate ranks, appointed him sous-lieutenant of a troop.

On the conclusion of the war, the Irish hussar returned with his regiment to France, full of those ideas of liberty and insurrection which he had seen so signally triumphant in the New World; and nearly all his brother officers had imbibed the same opinions. Thus it was with ill-concealed joy that the young Kilmaine and his comrades, the Hussars de Lauzun, in 1789, saw a Revolution which seemed destined to achieve results like those they had witnessed in America, break forth in old monarchical France.

In 1789 he was appointed captain of his troop, and continued to serve with the hussars, who became so much attached to him, that during the tumults of 1794 he contributed greatly, by his influence, presence and example, to retain under their colours nearly the whole of the regiment, which like the regiment of Royal Germans and the Hussars de Saxe, seemed disposed to desert *en masse*. Thanks to the patriotic zeal displayed by Kilmaine in the cause of his adopted country, the officers of noble family who chose to become emigrants were alone lost to the service; but this proved to him a new source of advancement, and he was soon appointed a *chef d'escadre*, which in the French army is equal to the rank of a general officer, being commander of a division; and about this time he enjoyed the friendship of his countryman, the Comte O'Kelly, who was ambassador of France at Mayence, with an income of 30,000 livres per annum.

As a chef d'escadre Kilmaine served throughout the first campaigns of the Revolution, and under Dumourier and Lafayette commanded a corps of that army which burst into the Netherlands and annexed that territory to republican France.

He fought with remarkable bravery at the great battle of Gemappes, on the 6th November, 1792, and with his hussars repeatedly charged the Austrians, driving them *sabre à la main* along the road that leads from Mons to Valenciennes; and so pleased was his general, the unfortunate Dumourier, that in the moment of victory he named him colonel; but this nomination was not confirmed by the minister of war. However, he was soon after gratified by a brevet of maréchal de camp, which made him, in rank, second only to a lieutenant-general.

He continued to serve with this army, and to be one of its most active and able officers, during all the sufferings which succeeded the victory at Gemappes. It consisted of forty-eight battalions of infantry, and three thousand two hundred cavalry. In December, by the neglect of the Revolutionary Government, these troops were shirtless, shoeless, starving and in rags; fifteen hundred men deserted; the cavalry of Kilmaine were soon destitute of boots, saddles, carbines, pistols and even sabres; the military chest was empty, and six thousand troop and baggage horses died at Lisle and Tongres, for want of forage. "To such a state," says Dumourier, "was the victorious army of Gemappes reduced after the conquest of Belgia!"

Honourable testimony has been given to the unceasing efforts of Kilmaine to preserve order among his soldiers amid these horrors; and with other staff-officers, he frequently endeavoured by private contribution to make out a day's subsistence for their men, who roved about in bands, robbing the villages around their cantonments at Aix-la-Chapelle, and in revenge many were murdered by the peasants when found straggling alone beyond their out-posts.

After the defection and flight of General Dumourier, Kilmaine adhered to the National Convention, and by that body was appointed a general of division; and now he redoubled his energies to restore order in the army, which by the defection of its leader was almost disbanded; thus, in one month after General Dampierre took command, so ably was he seconded by Kilmaine, the discipline was completely established.

He commanded the advance-guard of Dampierre in the new campaign against the allied powers, on the failure of the congress at Antwerp on the 8th of April, 1793; and his leader bears the highest testimony to the gallantry and noble conduct of Kilmaine, in the "murderous affairs of the 1st and 2nd May;" in which, according to the official report, he had two chargers shot under him.

Six days of incessant skirmishing succeeded, during which Kilmaine never had his boots off, nor returned his sabre once to the scabbard; and he displayed the most reckless valour on the 8th of May, in that battle fought by Dampierre to deliver Condé.

The French were routed with great loss; Dampierre was slain; and on Kilmaine as an active cavalry officer devolved the task of covering the retreat of the infuriated and disorderly army, which fell back from Condé-sur-l'Escaut, which is a barrier town, and was then the nominal lordship of the unfortunate Duke d'Enghien.

On General la Marche succeeding Dampierre, he sent Kilmaine with his division to the great forest of Ardennes, which formed a part of the theatre of war, on the invasion of France by the allies; but he remained there only a short time, and rejoined the main army, which he found in the most critical circumstances.

The fall of Dampierre and the arrestment of Custine acted fatally on the army of the North, which was now reduced to about thirty thousand rank and file, and these remained in a disorderly state, without a proper chief, and without aim or object—its manœuvres committed to chance or directed by ignorance; for, with the exception of Kilmaine, its leaders were destitute of skill, experience, and energy. Quitting the camp of Cæsar, they returned to their fortified position at Famars, three miles distant from Valenciennes, the approach to which it covered. Here they were attacked on the 23rd of May, driven back, and obliged to abandon the city to its own garrison under General Ferrand; a success which enabled the allies under the Duke of York to lay immediate siege to Condé and to Valenciennes, the two most important barrier towns upon the northern frontier. While the army of the North continued in full retreat towards the Scheldt, the British commander-in-chief briskly attacked Valenciennes, which General Ferrand first laid in ashes, and then delivered up; his garrison, as the reward of their obstinate defence, being permitted to march out by the gate of Cambray, on the 28th of July, with all *the honours of war*. Condé had already fallen on the 10th of the same month.

General Custine, who in the two preceding campaigns had rendered such essential services to the faithless Convention, was meanwhile brought to trial on the charge of corresponding with the enemy, and fell a sacrifice to the malice of his accusers.

It was on the banks of the Scheldt that Kilmaine rejoined the army early in August, with his division from Ardennes; and now his position became almost desperate. In presence of the scaffold erected by the ferocious mutineers for all the vanquished generals, and in a camp where no suspected person dared to assume the precarious office of leader, when pressed upon him, he accepted the bâton provisionally, and in the meantime said to the representatives who were sent from Paris to manage affairs and act as spies upon the army, "that he wished another more skilful than himself should take the great responsibility of leading the troops of the Republic."

His presence for a time appeased the tumults in the army. Though upon the banks of the Scheldt, and having before him both the Duke of York and the Prince of Coburg, Kilmaine, with only twenty-four thousand ill-appointed troops, dared not attempt to attack them; for if he fought and lost the day, he could thereafter assume no position of sufficient strength to prevent the allies from penetrating to Paris and crushing the power of the Convention. After so many levies and enrolments, that body had no longer a battalion to spare, and had around it only the frothy orators of armed clubs, and the refuse of prisons; thus it dared not abandon the capital or retire beyond the Loire, for now the men of Poitou, Bretagne, and La Vendée were in arms under the white banner, and elsewhere the tides of war and politics were setting in against them. At this crisis Mayence had capitulated, after a three months' bombardment. Toulon was under the cannon of the British; the Spaniards had invaded Roussillon; the Austro-Sardinians menaced Provence, the ancient patrimony of the House of Anjou; and on the Alps their troops hung over Dauphine and Vienne; finally, after the revolution of the 31st of May, which had assured the triumph of Robespierre, Lyons, Marseilles, and all the departments of the south, with those of the west, were roused against the pride, power, and oppression of the Convention.

If it was really true that the allied monarchs wished to re-establish the fallen throne of Louis XVI.,—if, as they had so proudly announced in their manifestos, it was to restore order to bleeding and desolated France and to repress the Republic and its horrors,—they had displayed their standards in the Netherlands, never were circumstances more favourable to them than after the retreat of Kilmaine towards the Scheldt: but the secret measures of wily diplomatists had more influence then, on events, than the arms of the allied kings.

It appears that, in the second campaign, when the allies were masters of Condé and Valenciennes, and saw that the road to Paris was almost open to them, the Austrians wished to take their revenge locally for the cruel deeds of which they had been spectators in the Camp de la Lune; and were more intent upon gratifying this sentiment than advancing into the heart of France.

The Prince of Coburg had shown himself from the first frank, loyal, and gallant; he had promised to Dumourier to concur in his daring project for re-establishing the monarchy, and for that purpose had engaged to form an auxiliary force to aid him, while solemnly renouncing all projects of aggrandizement for the crown of Austria. But for these engagements he had not received from his cabinet either instructions or authority. When Thugut was supreme director of the Austrian affairs, it was to these rash promises of the prince his consent was required; he disapproved of them so strongly, that they were cancelled by the Emperor of Austria, and a congress met at Antwerp, where, in concert with Britain, it was decided that in the result of the war the allies ought to find indemnities for the past, and guarantees for the future peace of Europe.

These were the expressions of the protocol which the members of the congress comprehended without difficulty; but French diplomatists loudly declared that a projected dismemberment of France was clearly announced in its phraseology.

One thing is certain : not a reference was made therein to the House of Bourbon, or to the throne of Louis— that throne of which Dumourier, in concert with the

Prince of Coburg, had so boldly promised the restoration in his manifesto of the 5th April; and not a measure was taken for the advantage or safety of the beautifu and unhappy Marie Antoinette, then languishing in prison at Paris, and over whose devoted head hung the blade of the guillotine, and whom a simple menace from her nephew the Emperor, threatening the advance of his armies, might perhaps have saved.

At all events, it seemed sufficiently evident to the jealous and excitable French that the allies were no longer true to the interests of the fallen Bourbons; and equally so that it was not to restore them the Austrians at least made war. It was in *his own name*—not that of Louis XVII., king of France and Navarre—their emperor took possession of those fortified places and provinces which his armies overran; and after he became master of Condé and Valenciennes, he no longer cared to define or form a frontier for those districts of the Netherlands which once he proposed to cede to the Prussians; but which Thugut now wished to preserve to the descendants of Rudolph of Hapsburg.

At the same time the Duke of York, who from his own cabinet had received orders and instructions similar to those given to the Prince of Coburg, in the name of George III., resolved to seize upon Dunkerque, which the English had coveted of old; but he did not wait for the departure of a British fleet prepared for this object. The naval squadron was delayed, and in the meantime the duke deliberated with the Austrian general under the ramparts of Valenciennes, to learn if, before engaging in new sieges, they might not give to the French army a final blow which would deprive Kilmaine of all power of interrupting their combined operations.

This was a very simple question, yet they were fourteen days in coming to a conclusion. Though Valenciennes, as already stated, had capitulated on the 28th of July, it was not until the 8th of August that the Austro-British army was in motion, and its advance guard beheld the camp of Cæsar; this on the very day after

Kilmaine had wisely evacuated the fortifications and retreated southwards.

It is said that he fully anticipated the march of the combined armies; and this was sufficiently probable, for we know that the committees of the National Convention had mysterious means of procuring secret intelligence, not only from the cabinets of the allies, but from the staff officers of the German troops!

Kilmaine in retiring only obeyed the dictates of wisdom and necessity, and quitted a position which he could not defend, as his army was reduced by defeat and desertion, mutinous, or as the French style it, *demoralized*.

If the allies had wished to follow and engage him upon the Scarpe or the Somme, a last effort could easily have been made to disperse his troops completely, and then seize upon Paris, where they might have torn the Revolution from its very basis. But such was not the intention of the allied generals. "Their aim on this occasion," says a French writer, "was to profit by our disorders and revolutions to make themselves masters of our places and provinces after assuring themselves of indemnities and guarantees, and to leave the volcano to consume itself, as a Prussian prince said, not long ago: it must be admitted, that never had this policy shown itself more evidently in its shameful nudity!" But the reader must bear in mind that these are the opinions of a Frenchman and a sympathizer with the Convention.

Such was the state of matters when Kilmaine, having abandoned the untenable camp of Cæsar, and fallen back beyond the Scarpe, a navigable river of French Flanders (but still a narrower barrier than the Scheldt) prepared again for retreat, and marched towards the Somme, another river which falls into the British Channel between Crotoy and Sainte Valori. This was his last position—his last asylum; and now the chiefs of the allies, instead of pushing on in pursuit of his retiring bands to complete the triumphs so well begun, faced about, and wheeled off to seize Dunkerque and Quesnay.

It was in autumn that the Royal Duke appeared before the former; and there his troops received a check which proved but the commencement of a long series of disasters; the latter was stormed by the Austrians, and retaken by the French in the following year.

But what must astonish us, even at this epoch of deception and duplicity, political insanity and revenge, is the startling fact that the brave Kilmaine, who had rendered such gallant services to that new and most faithless Republic—he who by a judicious retreat (executed *against* the advice of the meddling and presumptuous representatives of the people, and in consequence thereof perilled his life) had preserved to shattered France her most important army, was precisely for that reason denounced to the Convention, arrested by its orders, and flung into a loathsome prisons at Paris, where he passed a year; being but too happy, in the obscurity of his dungeon, that he had not perished on the scaffold like the gallant Custine, his predecessor in the command; like his old colonel and protector Biron, and like Houchard, who for the brief period of fifteen days had been his successor, and who, after winning a signal and decided victory over the Duke of York—a victory alike honourable to himself and to the arms of France, expiated by a cruel death the grave fault of having forgotten for a moment the powers of a bullying representative of the people!

Kilmaine only recovered his liberty after the fall of Robespierre; but he still remained for some time in Paris, without military employment, though he eagerly and anxiously sought it. He found himself there at the epoch of the insurrection of the 22nd May, 1795, and with much zeal and valour he seconded General Pichegru in the struggle made by that officer to defend the National Convention against the excited mobs of the Parisian fauxbourgs. Amid a thousand dangers Kilmaine continued to fight for the Convention until the 13th Vendemaire of the year following, actively co-operating with Bonaparte and the revolutionary party.

Being appointed to the command of a division in the army of Italy, he marched with Napoleon across the Alps to the invasion of that country, and shared in the glory of his first victories, and in that brilliant campaign in which the French destroyed two armies, took two hundred and eighty pieces of cannon, and forty-nine stand of colours from the Austrians, who were commanded by the veteran Wurmser, the bravest of all brave men.

At the head of his division Kilmaine fought with remarkable courage at Castiglione delle Stiviere, a fortified town in Lombardy, where, in the beginning of August, 1796, several severe engagements took place between the French and Austrians, which resulted in the discomfiture of the latter. Mantua was the next scene of Kilmaine's achievements; and in July that ancient city, after fifty years of peace, beheld the army of Napoleon before its walls, while all the country on the right bank of the Po was laid under contribution.

The whole direction and charge of the siege of Mantua was committed to Kilmaine by Bonaparte in September, when Wurmser, after being successful against General Massena, was overthrown by Augereau and our Irish soldier, and after a six days' contest shut himself up in the city on the 12th, after which the siege was pressed with great vigour. Twice after this did an Austrian army under Alvinzi attempt its relief, and twice were they baffled by the besiegers; on the last occasion an advancing corps of seven thousand men were compelled to surrender to Bonaparte and Kilmaine within gunshot of the walls, and the position of the aged Wurmser, his garrison, and the Mantuans, became desperate in the extreme.

In an action before Mantua in October, Kilmaine had his horse killed under him, and a rumour was spread through France and Britain that he was killed. Wurmser made several furious sallies, and on one occasion was severely routed by Bonaparte. In the *Courier du Bas Rhin*, we are told that the French repulsed him with the loss of eleven hundred men and five pieces of cannon, and that "their dispositions were made by General Kilmaine, commander of the siege of Mantua." Bonaparte, in his dispatch to the Directory, dated the first day of October, writes thus :—

GENERAL KILMAINE'S HORSE SHOT.

"On the 20th of September, the enemy advanced towards Castellocio, with a body of horse 12,000 strong. Pursuant to the orders they had received, our advanced posts fell back, but the enemy did not push forward any further. On the 23rd September, they proceeded to Governolo, along the right bank of the Mincio, but were repulsed, after a very brisk cannonade, with the loss of eleven hundred men and five pieces of cannon.

"*Le Général Kilmaine*, who commands the two divisions which press the siege of Mantua, remained on the 29th ultimo in his former position, and was still in hopes that the enemy would attempt a sortie to carry forage into the place; but instead they took up a position before the gate of Pradello, near the Carthusian convent and the chapel of Cerese. The brave General Kilmaine made his arrangements for an attack, and advanced in two columns against these two points; but he had scarcely begun to march when the enemy evacuated their camps, their rear having fired only a few musket-shots at him. The advanced posts of General Vaubois have come up with the Austrian division which defends the Tyrol, and made one hundred and ten prisoners."

In November a series of sanguinary actions were fought between the French and Austrians at Arcola, where the latter were completely overthrown; and there fell Citizen Elliot, a Scotsman, who was one of Bonaparte's principal aides-de-camp. During this time Kilmaine was at Vicenza with three thousand men; all the French cavalry were sent there to be under his orders; and though still commanding the operations against Mantua, he shared in the disastrous battle fought near Vicenza by the aged Alvinzi, who was advancing to raise the siege. Despairing to reach Mantua, the latter fell back upon the Vicenza road, and was routed after a bloody conflict of eight hours' duration.

Early in December, Wurmser led a sortie, sword in hand, against Kilmaine. The Imperialists sallied out of Mantua at seven in the morning, and almost in the dark, under a furious cannonade, which lasted all day; "but General Kilmaine," says Bonaparte, "made him return, as usual, faster than he came out, and took from him two hundred men, one howitzer, and two pieces of cannon. This is his third unsuccessful attempt." So energetic were the measures, and so able the precautions of Kilmaine, that Wurmser, seeing all hope of succour at an end, surrendered, after a long, desperate, and disastrous defence, at ten o'clock on the morning of the 3rd February, 1797, giving up his soldiers as prisoners of war. The following is a translation of Kilmaine's brief letter on this important acquisition :—

> "Kilmaine, Général de Division and Commandant of Lombardy, to the Minister of War. Milan, 17 Pluviose (Feb. 5), 1797.
>
> "Citizen Minister—I avail myself of a courier which General Bonaparte sends from Romagna (in order to announce to the Directory the defeat of the Papal troops), to acquaint you with the capture of Mantua, the news of which I received yesterday evening by a courier from Mantua itself. I thought it necessary to announce this circumstance, because General Bonaparte, who is occupied in Romagna annihilating the troops of his Holiness, may probably have been ignorant of this fact when *his* courier departed. The garrison are our prisoners of war, and are to be sent into Germany in order to be exchanged. I have not yet received the articles of capitulation; but the commander-in-chief will not fail to send them by the first courier. KILMAINE."

The capture of Mantua was celebrated in Paris by the firing of cannon and the erection of arches in honour of Bonaparte and the Irish Commandant of Lombardy, and a general joy was diffused through every heart in the city on the fall of what they styled the *Gibraltar* of Italy; while Bonaparte, loaded with the diamonds of the vanquished Pope, and the spoils of our Lady of Loretto, pushed on to seek fresh conquests and new laurels.

Kilmaine remained for some time in command at Mantua after its capitulation.

During the siege and other events, a revolutionary spirit had pervaded the Venetian States. Peschiera, a fortified town in the province of Verona, and Brescia, a large city in the beautiful plain on the Garza, had been both seized, garrisoned, and republicanized by the French. The people rose in arms, fired by new and absurd ideas of liberty and equality, and frightful scenes of bloodshed ensued when the more loyal and sensible inhabitants resisted these new patriots; but the latter, on being joined by fifteen hundred banditti from Bergamo, pressed the Venetian troops, who were driven out with great slaughter.

On hearing of these things, the politic Kilmaine wrote from Mantua to the French general commanding in Brescia, desiring him "*not* to interfere in behalf of these insurgents, lest by so doing he might infringe that strict neutrality which the generals of the French Republic were bound to observe."

In April, however, he was compelled, by the violent proceedings of the Italians against the French garrison in Verona, to unite his forces to those of Generals Victor and La Hotze, and march to the succour of General Ballaud, who was there assailed by forty-five thousand men, whose war-cry was *Viva San Marco!* who had cut to pieces six hundred Frenchmen, taken two thousand more after a four hours' contest, and driven the rest into the castle. From its ramparts Ballaud threatened to lay in ruins the unfortunate city, which had enjoyed profound peace for ages, until Bonaparte arrived on the banks of the Adige, and added it to the new kingdom of Italy.

On the 24th the insurgent Veronese capitulated, for on the approach of Kilmaine the governor, the two proveditori, and the Venetian general Stratico, fled with all their cavalry; on which he took as hostages the bishop, four of the principal nobles of the city, and several cavaliers of distinction, and peace was thus restored for a time. He disarmed all the insurgents, and seized three thousand slaves, whom he marched under an escort to Milan. In every way Kilmaine aided Napoleon most efficiently in these operations which preceded the capture and subjugation of Venice; and thus gave his great leader a thousand causes to admire and appreciate him during those campaigns which were so disastrous to Italy but so glorious to the arms of France. During his command in Lombardy he settled or compromised the contested question of the free navigation of the Lake of Lugano, in the south of Switzerland, which had occasioned many angry disputes between the jealous Switzers and the aggressive generals of the French army in Italy. By his intervention it was satisfactorily arranged that France should have the open navigation of the lake by boats of any size: but the cantons violated the treaty; on which Napoleon threatened to send a column of his troops among them, if they did not behave more amicably towards their faithful and ancient allies.

At this time General Sir John Acton, the favourite minister of Naples at Milan, was a soldier of fortune, and the intimate friend of Kilmaine. The story of Acton is rather a singular one.

He was the son of a Jacobite gentleman who had emigrated to France and settled at Besançon. An unsuccessful love adventure forced him to leave that city, at the college of which he was studying physic with every prospect of distinction. Repairing to Toulon, he enlisted in a battalion of French marines. From this corps he passed into the Neapolitan service, and distinguished himself at sea against a Barbary corsair; on which he received a commission in the marines of Naples, and rose to the rank of general, Counsellor of State, and Knight of San Gennaro and Saint Stephen. He possessed a high spirit, great courage, good address, and a handsome figure; and he soon became at the Court of Naples what the Prince of Peace was at Madrid—the favourite and lover of the Queen. He died in 1811. Another of Kilmaine's friends was the veteran general O'Cher, a *chef de brigade*, who had been upwards of forty years in the service of Louis XVI. and of the Republic, and held an important command in the army of Italy.

In the *Memoirs* published by General Count Montholon, and which were written by that faithful officer at St.

Helena, we have the following descriptive reference to the
Commandant of Lombardy:—

"Kilmaine, being an excellent cavalry officer, had coolness and foresight; he was well fitted to command a corps of observation, detached upon those arduous or delicate commissions which require spirit, discernment, and sound judgment. He rendered important services tt' the army, of which he was one of the principal generals, notwithstanding the delicacy of his health. He had a great knowledge of the Austrian troops: familiar with their *tactiques*, he did not allow himself to be imposed upon by those rumours which they were in the habit of spreading in the rear of an army, nor to be dismayed by those heads of columns which they were wont to display in every direction, to deceive as to the real strength of their forces. His political opinions were very moderate."

These are the words of a brother soldier, who must have known him well in the land of his adoption.

In the spring of 1798, the French Government was seriously employed in preparations for a descent upon the British Islands; and, in the February of that year, marched to the coast of the Channel forty demi-brigades of infantry, thirty-four regiments of cavalry, two regiments of horse artillery, two regiments of foot artillery, six companies of sappers and pioneers, six battalions of miners and pontooniers. These forces were led by eighteen distinguished generals of division, and forty-seven generals of brigade—the most brave and able in France. Among the former were Charles Kilmaine, Berthier, Marescat, Kleber, Massena, "the son of Rapine;" Macdonald, Ney, Victor, and others whose names were to become famous in future wars as the marshal dukes of the great military empire.

The brave but blustering Jean Baptist Kleber, who had originally been an architect of Strasbourg, commanded the right wing of this *Armée d'Angleterre*, which was to stretch from Calais to the mouth of the Scheldt, while another corps assembled at Flushing.

Kilmaine commanded the centre.

These forces were partly composed of troops returned from Italy, and were all experienced soldiers, the victors of Mantua, Lodi, and Arcola. Headed by bands of music, the *état-majors* marched through Paris, displaying black banners, indicative of a war of extermination, and inscribed, "*Descent upon England*—Live the Republic! May Britain perish," &c.

On St. Patrick's day, the 17th of the following month, Kilmaine, O'Cher, Colonel Shee, and all the Irishmen in Paris celebrated their ancient national and religious festival by a grand banquet, at which the notorious Thomas Paine—then a political fugitive—assisted. All the corresponding members of the Irish clubs and malcontent party at home were also present. Many fierce and stirring political toasts were drunk, amid vociferous enthusiasm ; and among these—one in particular—" Long live the Irish Republic !" and speeches were made expressive of the rapid progress which republicanism had made in their native country, and of the strong desire of the Catholics and Dissenters to throw off the yoke of England—that yoke which Kilmaine in his boyhood had been taught to abhor and to hate. Napper Tandy, a *general de brigade*, was in the chair ; on his left sat Tom Paine, and on his right sat Kilmaine, who, immediately after the banquet, left Paris to rejoin his column of the army on the coast.

Five hundred gunboats were ordered to be prepared, and three hundred sail of transports were collecting at Dunkirk, to be protected from the British fleet by a Dutch squadron then at the mouth of the Scheldt ; and all Britain was in arms on hearing of an armament so formidable.

The condition of France was then desperate ; assignats were at 6500 livres the louis ; she had to maintain a million of men in arms from an empty treasury ; the ruffian demagogues and savage soldiers of the Republic, men steeped to the lips in the blood of women and priests, nobles and aristocrats, hardened by the atrocities in La Vendée, and trained to the war in the campaigns of Austria and Italy, occupied every post and place under the unstable government; a rabble of brutal ministers occupied the palaces of the fallen line of St. Louis, armed with sabres and pistols, to which they resorted in every trivial dispute and on every difference of opinion, and while warring against all manner of title and form, appeared on the rostrum in cassocks and stockings of rose-coloured silk, with knots of scarlet ribands in their shoes; and, with that mixture of ferocity and tom-foolery which caused Paris to be characterized as a city of monkeys and tigers, debated on the cut of a coat and the massacre of a city.

In April, Kilmaine repaired to Paris, after having executed, by order of the government, a survey of the coasts of France and Holland, then reduced to a province of the former; and the chief command of this famous Armée d'Angleterre on which the eyes of all Europe were fixed, and the command of which had been given to the noble Dessaix, the hero of Marengo, was now bestowed upon him.

A French writer asserts that this expedition was destined, not for Britain, but for Egypt; and that Kilmaine received the command of it, not so much for his great military skill, as to deceive our ministry; supposing that the name of an Irishman would cause them to believe that the armament was destined for Ireland; and so they named him General in Chief of the Armée d'Angleterre, which never existed at all." Unfortunately for this writer, history affords abundant proof to the contrary. The number of transports was soon increased to a thousand, and all the naval and military resources of Holland were pressed into the French service.

Colonel Shee, Wolfe Tone, Generals Clarke and Kilmaine, were by this time well acquainted with the extent of the military organization of the United Irishmen, and knew that by the close of the preceding year the people were well provided with arms, and knew the use of them. In the beginning of 1797, great quantities were discovered and seized by the British Government, who, in Leinster and Ulster alone, captured 70,630 pikes, with 48,109 muskets. Had the Irish managed their projected rising with the vigour which has ever characterized the Scottish insurrections, we cannot for a moment doubt what would have been the result, had this formidable expedition once landed in Ireland, where no yeomanry were organized; where the militia were not to be depended upon; and where the king's troops, on whom the ministry mainly relied, were so little superior to the French in tact and skill, that Humbert, with less than a thousand men, was able to defeat double that number, and immediately after received into his ranks 250 of the drilled and attested Irish militiamen.

On the 12th April, Kilmaine, with General Bonaparte, had a long audience with the Directory at Paris, reporting on the state of their armaments. The appointment of the former to the chief command relieved Britain of the apprehension that the conqueror of Italy would cross the Channel in person, and great was the disappointment of the malcontents at home.

The duties of Kilmaine were alike harassing and arduous, as he had to superintend the equipment and organization of this vast force, composed of men of all arms and several nations; and he was repeatedly summoned to Paris, even in the middle of the night, by couriers who overtook him in his progresses; thus, though suffering under severe ill health, the Directory once brought him on the spur from Bruges early in July, and again from Brest about the end of the same month.

Citizen d'Arbois, an officer on the staff of Kilmaine, in a letter published in the Parisian papers of the 7th August, 1798, states that his general "is on his return," after having made a tour of the coast, from Port St. Malo to L'Orient; that he was well satisfied with the state of the French ports and armaments, and had enjoyed with delight the magnificent aspect of Brest, in the harbour of which he saw thirty sail of the line, with a fleet of frigates and transports. D'Arbois states that Kilmaine had been surveying Brittany, where all was then peaceful, by the "wise measures" of the constituted authorities. "The eagerness with which our troops, both by sea and land, await the moment when, under the brave Kilmaine, they will engage the English, is the best pledge of our approaching success, and the ruin of our enemies."

It is evident that Citizen d'Arbois had then no thought of fighting in Egypt.

But doubts hovered in the minds of the Directory, if there were none in the hearts of their generals, and long delays ensued. General Hoche, under whom the future Dukes of Rovigo and of Vicenza were serving as private soldiers, and who was the main spring of the projected movement in favour of Ireland, died in September, 1797; and Bonaparte, to whom Kilmaine, Tone, Shee, and others of the Irish patriots turned, had no sympathy with their cause, as all his views were now directed towards a warfare in the East. By the beginning of autumn the Directory began to break up their boasted Armée d'Angleterre, and withdrew their troops to reinforce their columns on the Rhine. Upon this, Kilmaine came anxiously and hastily to Paris to confer with the government and the Minister of Marine concerning the embarkation of the troops and departure of the fleet from Brest; but his questions were waived, or left unanswered, although the division of Bompard, consisting of the *Hoche* of 74 guns and eighteen frigates, filled with troops under General Hardy, destined for Ireland, remained with their cables hove short, and all ready for sea at a moment's notice.

Of the forces that really sailed for Ireland, and their fate, we need not inform the reader. For a time all Britain supposed they were led by the commander-in-chief in person; and all the press of England and Scotland teemed with blustering or scurrilous remarks on "Paddy Kilmaine and his followers;" but the general never embarked, though he certainly superintended the departure of a body of troops from Rochfort.

"We are assured," says a Brussels print, "that in case the French republicans shall be able to make a successful descent upon Ireland, the Belgic youth will be employed in that country under General Kilmaine, who, being a native of it, will there have the command of the united French and Irish forces." Citizen Macdonagh was to have a high command in the corps of Irish Marines. He held the rank of Lieutenant-Colonel in France.

By the end of 1798 the army of England and its expedition were alike dissolved, and the Directory wished to give Kilmaine command of the forces assembled for the war in Egypt; but for the present his career finished with the military examination of the coasts of France and Holland.

In 1799 the Directory appointed him generalissimo of the army of Helvetia, as they chose to designate Switzerland; thus reviving the ancient name of the people whom Julius Cæsar conquered. The French troops already occupied Lombardy on one side, and the Rhenish provinces on the other; thus they never doubted their ability to conquer the Swiss and remodel the Helvetic constitution. Kilmaine accepted the command with satisfaction, but his failing health compelled him to give up his bâton to Massena; and with a sorrow which he could not conceal, he saw that army march which penetrated into the heart of the Swiss mountains, and imposed on their hardy inhabitants a constitution in which Bonaparte, under the plausible title of Mediator, secured the co-operation of the valiant descendants of the Helvetii in his further schemes of conquest and ambition.

In a feeble condition Kilmaine returned to Paris, where his domestic sorrows and chagrins added to the poignancy of his bodily sufferings, for his constitution was now completely broken up.

Struck by a deadly malady, he died on the 15th of December, 1799, in the forty-ninth year of his age, at the very moment when the triumphant elevation of Bonaparte was opening up to his comrades a long and brilliant career of military glory. He was interred with all the honours due to his rank and bravery, and a noble monument was erected to his memory.

Counts O'Reilly, O'Donnel,
AND THE IRISH IN SPAIN.

IRELAND, says a popular Scottish writer, can boast not only of having transplanted more of her sons to the soil of Spain than either of the sister kingdoms, but of having acquired by the deeds of her exiles a degree of renown to which the others cannot aspire.

True it is, that in every land brave men find a home!

The deeds of the Irish regiments in the Spanish service, during the War of the Succession, like those of the O'Donnels in the war of the Peninsula, and the civil strife of more recent times, would fill volumes. Of the Spanish Lacys I have already given a memoir; and of many other brave Irish soldiers of fortune, who won distinction on the soil or in the service of Spain, I can here give but the names alone.

Owen Roe O'Neil, of Ulster, rose to high rank in the Spanish Imperial service and held an important post in Catalonia. He defended Arras against Louis XIII. in 1640, and when forced to surrender, he did so, says Carte, "upon honourable terms; yet his conduct in the defence was such as gave him great reputation, and procured him extraordinary respect even from the enemy;" and the brave O'Sullivan Bearra of Dunbuy, who fled in the days of James I., became Governor of Corunna under Philip IV.

Lieutenant-General Don Carlos Felix O'Neile (son of the celebrated Sir Neil O'Neile of Ulster, slain at the battle of the Boyne), was Governor of Havannah and favourite of Charles III. of Spain; he died at Madrid in 1791, after attaining the great age of one hundred and ten years.

In 1780, Colonel O'Moore commanded the Royal Walloon Guards of Charles III. In 1799, Field-Marshal Arthur O'Neil was Governor-General of Yucatan under the same monarch, and commanded the flotilla of thirty-one vessels which made an unsuccessful attack on the British settlements in the Bay of Honduras. In the same year, Don Gonzalo O'Farrel was the Spanish ambassador at the Court of Berlin, and in 1808 he was Minister of War for Spain. In 1797, O'Higgins was Viceroy of Peru, under Charles IV., one of whose best generals was the famous Alexander Count O'Reilly.

Don Pedro O'Daly was Governor of Rosas when it was besieged by Gouvion St. Cyr in 1809 ; and General John O'Donoughue was chief of Cuesta's staff, and one of the few able officers about the person of that indolent and obstinate old hidalgo, whose incapacity nearly caused the ruin of the Spanish affairs at the commencement of the Peninsula war. He died Viceroy of Mexico in 1816.

O'Higgins was Viceroy of Peru under Ferdinand VI. and the third and fourth Charles of Spain. He signalized himself with great bravery in the wars with the Araucanos, a nation on the coast of Chili, who were ultimately subdued by him and subjected to the Spanish rule. John Campbell, a midshipman who escaped from the wreck of the *Wager*, one of Commodore Anson's squadron which was lost on the large island of Tierra del Fuego, and who arrived, after inconceivable sufferings, at St. Jago de Chili, furnished O'Higgins with various notes and outlines of the coast, and other memoranda concerning the natives, all of which he had ingeniously written on the bark of trees. These observations, which were afterwards printed in England, were of the greatest value to O'Higgins, who was wont to affirm that by the knowledge they gave him of the barbarians under his government, "he owed the foundation of his good fortune to Campbell."

In 1765, he marched against the Araucanos with a battalion of Chilian infantry, and fifteen hundred horse named Maulinians. He was thrice brought to the ground by having three horses killed under him; but the Araucanos were routed, and the Spanish rule extended over all Peru, of which he died viceroy in the beginning of the present century, after fighting the battles of Rancagua and Talchuana, which secured the independence of Chili.

Few names bear a more prominent place in Spanish history than those of Blake, the Captain-General of the Coronilla, and O'Reilly, a soldier of fortune, who saved the life of Charles III. during the revolt at Madrid, and who reformed and disciplined anew the once noble army of Spain.

ALEXANDER COUNT O'REILLY was born in Ireland about 1735, of Roman Catholic parents, and when young entered the Spanish service as a sub-lieutenant in the Irish regiment with which he served in Italy during the war of the Spanish Succession, and received a wound from which he was rendered lame for the rest of his life. In 1751 he went to serve in Austria, and made two campaigns against the Prussians, under the orders of Marshal Count Lacy, his countryman. Then in 1759 he passed into the service of Louis XV., under whose colours was still that celebrated Irish Brigade whose native bravery so mainly contributed to win for France the glory of Fontenoy.

O'Reilly distinguished himself so much that the Marshal de Broglie recommended him to the King of Spain, with great warmth of expression, on his retiring to Madrid. The marshal's interest won him the rank of Lieutenant-Colonel, and as such he served in that war which conduced so little to the glory of Portugal, though favoured by the alliance of Britain. Nevertheless, O'Reilly found many opportunities for distinction at the head of the light troops which were confided to him, and soon won the proud reputation of being one of Spain's most gallant officers. He was now named Brigadier of the Armies of the King, with the post of *aide major de l'exercise*. In these capacities he drilled the Spanish infantry according to the best system of tactics and exercise then practised in the British service.

At the peace he was appointed Mariscal de Campo, and named Commandant en Seconde of Havannah, which was to be given up to Spain by the treaty of Fontainbleau. On arriving there, he restored and strengthened the fortifications of the colony, and soon after returned to Spain, where the king named him Inspector-General of Infantry, and desired him to assist in the manœuvres of a great camp, of which he gave him command. He then sent him to New Orleans, where the inhabitants had scarcely become accustomed to the Spanish yoke, and where the rigorous means employed by O'Reilly to subdue them gained him many enemies. The count returned again to Madrid, and was treated with every mark of favour by Charles III., who knew all his talents, capacity, and courage; and could never forget that it was to the strong hand and stout heart of O'Reilly he owed his life during the fiery sedition at Madrid in 1765, when the people rose in arms. Every honour Charles could bestow upon a foreigner was showered upon O'Reilly, who now gave the Spanish army (which was many years behind every other in Europe in the march of progression and improvement) a new spirit, vigour, and impulse. In this task he was assisted by his brother-in-law, Francisco Xavier Castanos, afterwards Duke of Baylen, Captain-General of Estremadura, Old Castile, and Galicia, whom he took with him to Prussia when he visited that country, like all the principal officers of Europe, to witness and examine the manœuvres practised by the troops of the Great Frederick.

In 1774, he obtained command of the expedition against Algiers. The great means of attack were entirely confided to him, and he sailed from the Spanish coast with a squadron of forty sail of the line and three hundred and fifty transports, carrying an army of thirty thousand men; but this immense armament failed to achieve its object, and O'Reilly was compelled to bear away for Spain, humiliated and mortified, and landed his discomfited troops at Barcelona, on the 24th of August in the same year.* Though this unfortunate result was much against his reputation as a general, it did not lessen his favour with the king, who placed him at the head of a military school which was established in Avila, at Puerto de Santa Maria, on the Adaga, in Old Castile.

Soon after this, O'Reilly was named Captain-General of Andaluzia and Governor of Cadiz. In these important posts he displayed the talents of a skilful soldier and able administrator; but he fell into complete disgrace on the death of Charles III., in 1788, and lived afterwards in a quiet retreat in Catalonia. Despite his many enemies at court, who rose into power with Charles IV., O'Reilly maintained his high military reputation in the Spanish army, and on the death of General Ricardos in 1794, the government knew of none so able as he to direct the war against the invasion of the French republican armies. He was accordingly named General of the Army of the Eastern Pyrenees, and was on his way to assume that high command when he was seized by a sudden illness, and died in his sixtieth year.

O'Reilly was fortunate, perhaps, in escaping thus the misery caused to Spain by the mistakes of the Conde de la Union, and the misfortunes consequent to reverse and defeat. His age would not have permitted him to sustain the fatigue of a war so active; and though he was the instructor of Blake and others who were esteemed the best officers of the Spanish army, as a foreigner he had many envious enemies, and all his ability as a soldier, with the sweetness and insinuating flexibility of his manner, was no guarantee to him among such a people as the Spaniards, who are ever cool and averse to strangers.

His pupil, JOACHIM BLAKE, afterwards Captain-General of Aragon and four other provinces, was the son of an eminent Irish merchant who had settled at Velez, near Malaga, and was descended from an ancient family in the

---

* The reader will remember the mistake of Donna Julia,—

"Was it for this that General Count O'Reilly,
Who took *Algiers*, declares I used him vilely?"
Don Juan, Canto i.

county of Galway. His mother was the daughter of a wealthy Spanish banker named Joyes.

At an early age young Blake manifested an ardent predilection for the profession of arms—a predilection inherent in his race, which had given Ireland many proofs of high valour during two centuries. While yet a boy he applied himself to the science of mathematics with great success, and was soon appointed Superintendent of Cadets in the military school established by Count O'Reilly, at Puerto de Santa Maria. In 1773, Blake commenced his military career as a volunteer in the Regiment of America, for it has long been an established principle in the Spanish armies that candidates for commissions must learn the art of war in the ranks; and for some years subsequent to this he served as lieutenant and adjutant to the battalion, so great was the progress he had made in his profession, and so intimate was his knowledge of regimental economy. At the beginning of the war waged by France against Spain, he was appointed Major of the Volunteers of Castile, without serving the intermediate rank of captain; a favour never before granted to any officer, even to a Spaniard. In this capacity he led his battalion with distinguished bravery during the campaigns of 1793 and 1794, in Roussillon and Catalonia, and was wounded when storming the heights of San Lorenzo de la Maga. He was appointed colonel in 1802, without passing through the grade of lieutenant-colonel, and obtained command of a newly-raised battalion, styled *Los Volontarios de la Corona* —the Volunteers of the Crown; and from thenceforward he bore a prominent part in all the warlike and political broils of Spain.

After the peace in 1802, Blake was made brigadier or Mariscal de Campo, by Charles IV., and on his volunteer regiment being numbered with the Spanish line, he was further confirmed in command of it. This position he occupied until the invasion of Spain by Bonaparte and the imprisonment of the king; after which ensued the great contest known as the Peninsula War, during which, by the unanimous voice of the Galicians, he was summoned to the chief command of their valuable and extensive province.

During the second operations of Marshal Bessières (Duke of Istria) in Spain, the army of Blake—twenty thousand strong—united with the ten thousand Castilian recruits of old Don Gregorio de la Cuesta, at Benevente in July, 1808, for the purpose of opposing him; but they soon disagreed; for, contrary to the wishes of Blake, whose fiery energy consorted ill with the indolence of Cuesta, that officer left a strong division to protect stores at Benevente, and led only twenty-five thousand infantry, a few hundred horse, and thirty pieces of cannon, towards Palencia, in the beautiful Tierra de Campos. *Contrary to his judgment*, a battle was risked (14th July, 1808) at Medina del Rio Seco, against the French under General Lasolles.

There, on that day, so fatal to Spain, notwithstanding all the energy of Blake, General Lasolles, with fifteen thousand men and thirty cannon, routed the soldiers of Castile and Galicia, with the loss of seven thousand two hundred of their number, killed, wounded, or taken; and the survivors fled with such absurd precipitation, that the French, in crossing the bed of the Sequillo in pursuit, and finding it dry and stony, exclaimed: "Diable! Why, Spanish rivers run away, too!"

The generals of the two Juntas separated in anger; but Blake had discovered such talents in the lost battle, that he was appointed Governor and Captain-General of the Kingdom of Galicia, and President of the Royal Audience.

He retreated towards the mountains, and Bessières then entered the city of Leon.

Meanwhile the Junta of that province and of Castile sided with Blake, to whom Marshal Bessières sent twelve hundred of the prisoners taken at Rio Seco; and believing it to be a favourable opportunity to tamper with their leaders, he wrote urging them to obey the act of abdication, and acknowledge Joseph Bonaparte, in whose name he offered Blake high rank and honours if he would enter the French service, like Colonel O'Meara of the Irish

Brigade, Clarke the Duc de Feltre, General Kilmaine, Marshal MacCarthy, and other Irishmen; while to Cuesta he very *liberally* offered the Viceroyalty of Mexico; but both the Spanish cavalier and the Irish soldier of fortune repelled his offers with disdain.

On the 17th September the latter advanced against the enemy with six columns, each five thousand strong. Descending from La Montana towards the Upper Ebro, he sent one division to menace the French in the Castle of Burgos, and turn the flank of Marshal Bessières; he left another at Villarcayo to preserve a communication with Reynosa and cover his retreat. He received supplies from General Broderick, who in his despatches complained bitterly that Blake treated him with hauteur, and declined to afford any information as to the nature of his intended operations. The French having abandoned Bilbao, it was regarrisoned by Marshal Ney; and after various evolutions, it was attacked on the 12th October by Blake, at the head of eighteen thousand men. Merlin, with three thousand French, abandoned the fortress and retreated, fighting every foot of the way until he reached Zornosa, where he was succoured by General Verdier, who checked the fury of Blake's pursuit. The winter was now approaching, and his troops began to be in want. Seldom have soldiers endured greater privations than those suffered by the poor Spaniards of Blake. They were destitute of caps, boots, and stockings, and had been constantly in the open air for months, without tents or proper food; yet not a murmur escaped them, nor a wish was uttered but to conquer for their country.

While the well appointed forces of France were hourly increasing, Blake, fearing neither difficulty nor danger, boldly ascended the valley of El Darongo to assail two divisions of the Fourth corps (Lefebre, Duke of Dantzig's), which occupied the neighbouring villages. Full of hope he advanced, and anticipating, if successful, to capture Marshal Ney's corps of sixteen thousand men, fearlessly with only eighteen thousand Spaniards, and almost without artillery, he hastened to engage twenty-five thousand Frenchmen of all arms!

Favoured by a dense mist, the Spaniards entered the valley, and for a time nothing was heard but the shots of their skirmishers ringing between the mountain peaks, till Vilatte's corps suddenly fell on Blake's vanguard, and hurled it back upon the third division at the bayonet's point. Then, on came the dark columns of Sebastiani and Laval, each looming in succession through the mist, while a fire of round and grape-shot from their artillery (to which Blake could not reply) swept through the rocky vale, heaping his ranks against each other, and strewing them on the grass.

Madly and bravely Blake, with his infantry and Guerillas, sought to defend every rock and pass of the valley; but they were driven back in full flight towards Bilbao, and crossing the Salcedon, took up a position at Nava, watched by seven thousand French under Vilatte.

After the battle of Gamonal, Soult resolved to make an effort for ever *to cut off Blake*, who, without cavalry, clothing, or food, had reached Espinosa with six divisions and only six pieces of cannon, which he posted in rear of the town at Aguilar del Campo. He had now only twenty-five thousand bayonets, but strongly and skilfully posted. His left wing, composed of Asturians, and his old favourite division occupied the heights above the road to St. Andero; another covered the road to Reynosa, and Romano's soldiers filled a wood two miles in his front.

He was attacked at two o'clock on the 10th November by Marshal Victor, whose soldiers carried the wood at the point of the bayonet, forced his centre, turned his left flank, and he had the mortification to see San Romano and Don Luiz de Riquelmé, his two best brigadiers, fall mortally wounded. His Spaniards were hurled in masses upon each other, and utterly routed. Romano's corps were all taken to a man; the rest fled through Castile, Leon, Galicia, and Asturia, carrying everywhere the tidings of their defeat and the terror of the French name; and poor Blake, jaded, weary, exasperated, and disheartened, reached Reynosa on the 12th, with only seven thousand men—his old division—without artillery, without arms, without spirit, and without hope!

R

Such was the battle of Espinosa. Blake, in this terrible condition, was attacked by the vanguard of Soult, and after losing two thousand men, retired through the vale of Caburniego, and reached Arnedo in the heart of the Asturian Sierras.

Spain was now nearly prostrate at the feet of France!

In 1809, Blake was appointed Captain-General of the *Coronilla*, or Lesser Crown; a title given to the union of Valencia, Aragon, and Catalonia. In the latter he succeeded General Romano. Gathering his forces in April, restless and indefatigable, he advanced to Alcanitz, from whence the French retired to Samper and Ixar. On this Marshal Suchet advanced against him with the third corps, and on the 23rd of May they fought the battle of Alcanitz.

Blake was skilfully posted in front of the town with twelve thousand men. The bridge of Guadaloupe was in his rear; a pool of water covered his left, but his right was without protection; his centre occupied a hill. With only eight thousand foot and seven hundred horse Suchet attacked him, but without success. Rendered desperate by reverses, the Spaniards stood firm, and fought with their ancient rather than their modern bravery. Suchet was wounded and compelled to retreat; this retreat became a panic, and in great confusion the French reached Samper in the night. This small success was a cause for rejoicing all over Spain. "The victory at Alcanitz," was in every man's mouth, and the Supreme Junta gave Blake an estate, and added the ancient kingdom of Murcia to his command. He now hoped to recover the far-famed Zaragossa, and turning all his thoughts to Aragon, neglected the defence of Catalonia.

After the late victory his little army was augmented by more than twenty thousand men, and full of new hope and enthusiasm he marched with these to Ixar and Samper.

Suchet hovered near Zaragossa, but left a column under General Faber at Villa Muel, near the Sierra of Daroca, to watch Blake, who, hoping to cut that officer off, marched through Carinena, so famed for its vineyards, and sent General Arisayo with a detachment to Bottorio, with orders to capture a convoy of French provisions on the Huerba. This movement was successful, and lack of food forced Faber to retreat towards Plascencia.

The advanced guards exchanged shots on the 14th of June at Bottorio, and Blake, full of confidence, made a vigorous attempt to surround the French by pushing a column to Maria on the plains of Zaragossa; on the 15th he formed his troops in order of battle, but slowly and unskilfully, as they were raw soldiers, who had but recently relinquished the vinedresser's knife for the musket and sword. Occupying both banks of the Huerba, towards 2 p.m. he extended his left flank to overlap the French right; but Suchet, who was unexpectedly joined by Faber's brigade and another from Tudela, paralysed the movement by a furious attack of cavalry and voltigeurs. Blake's left fell back at the very moment that he was triumphantly leading on his centre, and he became involved in a desperate sword-in-hand conflict, in which the leading columns of Suchet were repulsed. He would have achieved more but for a violent storm which arose at that moment, and so darkened the air that the adverse lines could scarcely see each other, and for a time the action ceased. Blake's position was ill chosen (according to the memoirs of Suchet); he was surrounded by deep ravines, and had only one line of retreat by the bridge of Maria, which crossed the Huerba near his right wing.

Marshal Suchet observed this error, and on the storm lulling, selected some cavalry and two regiments of infantry, and forming them, all drenched as they were by rain, in solid column, by a vigorous effort he broke through Blake's brigade of horse, siezed the bridge, and cut off his retreat!

Undaunted by this fatal event, Blake, at all times brave and decided, formed his infantry of the left and centre into solid masses, and fought desperately for victory; but was repulsed with great loss, and defeated, leaving one general, twenty-five guns, and many colours on that rough and rocky field, from which he was driven about dusk, when the darkness was so dense that few prisoners were taken. Suchet had Harispe wounded and a thousand men slain.

Favoured by the obscurity of the night, Blake's men fled by the ravines to Bottorio, where he made incredible efforts to rally and remodel them next day. Then he received tidings that a French brigade, under Laval, was marching by the Ebro to cut off his retreat. To anticipate this movement Blake fell back on the night of the 16th, and after skirmishing with Suchet next day at Torrecilla, *again* formed line of battle on the 18th, to meet him at Belchite, a small town in Aragon. Blake had on this day only fourteen thousand men, dispirited by recent repulse and the loss of nearly all their artillery. Suchet had twenty-two battalions and seven squadrons, with a fine artillery corps, all flushed by recent success, and making fifteen thousand men; thus the result may be anticipated—a defeat!

He had four thousand of his men taken, with the remainder of his artillery, all his baggage and ammunition. He had many difficulties to contend with as leader of an undisciplined army, and stung to the soul by this second defeat, he reproached the Spaniards with great bitterness as shameless cowards; and, after demanding an inquiry into his own conduct, "with a strong and sincere emotion of honour," restored to the Junta the estate which had been conferred upon him after the victorious battle of Alcanitz.

Following up the victory of Belchite, Marshal Suchet sent detachments as far as Morella on the Valencian frontier; but no man in arms appeared to meet them, for Blake's dispersion was signal and complete. His march towards Zaragossa, and his attempt to wrest Aragon from the foe, were fatal to the Spanish cause in Catalonia, where St. Cyr, with more than forty thousand men, occupied the country between Figueras and the city of Gerona, which was blockaded by eighteen thousand Frenchmen, who pressed with vigour one of the most memorable sieges suffered by this ancient ducal city, which was bravely defended by its intrepid Catalans. Blake was ordered by the central Junta of Seville to succour them, as the garrison were defending half-ruined walls with a valour and obstinacy which filled the city with a thousand scenes of horror and distress. He marched accordingly at the head of a weak and irregular force, which was thoroughly dispirited by the result of the two last battles; and thus he resolved to confine his operations simply to supplying the town with men and provisions, rather than risk his strength by attempting to raise a siege which, if essayed with success, would save Gerona, and with it all Catalonia.

Collecting two thousand mules laden with flour, he sent them with four thousand foot and five hundred horse, under Henry O'Donnel and Garcia Condé, towards this strong and picturesque little city, which they reached after a furious encounter with the enemy during a dark and stormy night; but the provisions received did not amount to much more than eight days' food for the starving Geronese and their garrison, which was encumbered rather than aided by Garcia Condé's reinforcement, St. Cyr now resolved to seek out Blake and destroy him for ever; but rendered wary by misfortune, he retired into the mountains, and thus ended his first attempt to relieve the city of Gerona.

Soon after, still hovering near the French, and threatening them, he advanced to the position of St. Hilario; and on St. Cyr preparing to storm the post called Calvary, Blake, from the 20th to the 25th of September, 1809, made movements as if he meant to force the blockade; but being incapable of doing so, his whole object was merely to introduce another convoy; and, watching an opportunity, while drawing the attention of St. Cyr towards the heights of San Sadurnia, on which he had posted a column, he sent 10,000 men under Wimphen towards Gerona. O'Donnel led the vanguard. A dreadful conflict took place on Wimphen's attempting to force the French lines. He was defeated; and in the twilight Blake failed to succour him; but Henry O'Donnel, another gallant Irish soldier of fortune, succeeded in hewing a passage into Gerona with 1000 men and 200 laden mules. Irritated by Blake's second attempt to succour Gerona, St. Cyr marched a column to menace his communication with the citadel of Hostalric, a depôt of magazines on the Tordera. On this he was forced to retreat, leaving to its fate the noble little city of Gerona, which, as its heroic captain, General Alvarez, said, " if not succoured again by all Catalonia, will soon be but a heap of carcases and ruins."

Again, on the 29th October, we find the unwearied Blake hovering on the heights of Brunola, watching the siege of Gerona, and while he was thus occupied, Hostalric was stormed by the French, and 2000 Spaniards, with all his magazines, were taken therein. On the 10th November Gerona capitulated, and Alvarez, its brave and veteran governor, died of a broken heart at Figueras, when on the march towards France, a prisoner of war. Blake now retired to Tarragona, leaving the remains of his army under Henry O'Donnel, who drove Marshal Augereau into Gerona, and received command of the troops at Vich, on Blake being called into Andalusia.

In May the seaport of Tarragona was besieged, taken, and sacked by Suchet, in a manner discreditable alike to his talents as a soldier and his humanity as a man. During the horrors of that affair, which covered the French with infamy, Blake was in Valencia, having sailed for that province on the 16th of May, in search for succour; but Tarragona was lost, and then he assumed command of the Murcian army, which was 22,000 strong, and had remained inactive ever since General O'Mahy's appointment. In June, 1811, the firmness and activity of Wellington formed a strong contrast to the wavering and indolent demeanour of the Spanish generals, until Blake marched to Condado de Niebla, on concerting a movement down the right bank of the Guadiana with the British general, who delivered to him the pontoons lately used at Badajoz. He marched on the 18th, crossed the Guadiana on the 22nd, at the ancient town of Mertola, where the stream first becomes navigable : but halted at Castillegos on the 30th, and sent his siege train to Ayamonte by water. Then, instead of moving his whole force directly on the great city of Seville, he sent only a small column of cavalry, under the gallant Conde de Penne Villamur, in that direction; and, unfortunately, consumed two entire days in besieging the castle of Niebla—a small fortress, which gave the title of count to the eldest son of the Duke of Medina, and was garrisoned by 300 Swiss, who had deserted from the Spanish army at the commencement of the war, and whom he was most anxious to capture and punish. The absence of his siege train rendered the attack futile; and Soult, on hearing of it, sent a detachment from Monasterio to relieve the Swiss, who defended themselves with great valour, while General Conraux crossed the mountains by the Aracena road, to cut off all communication between Blake and his artillery at Ayamonte. Thus he was compelled to abandon the siege, and by a precipitate march reach a pontoon bridge which was thrown across the stream for him by Colonel Austin at San Lucar de Guadiana, from whence he took shelter in Portugal.

Still indefatigable, he projected an assault upon San Lucar de Barameda; but the sudden appearance of Soult's advanced guard disconcerted his troops, who retreated to Ayamonte, and from thence to the Isle of Camelas, where a Spanish frigate and 300 transports fortunately arrived in time to afford him the means of escape. Early in July he embarked all his troops, and sailed to Cadiz, as the French had reinforced San Lucar and taken possession of Ayamonte.

Landing at Almeria, Blake formed a junction with Freire, and proposed to invest Granada; but deeming it necessary first to visit Valencia, where the factious Marquis del Palacio was acting most unwisely, he left his army, now 27,000 strong, under Freire, and before he could return it had utterly dispersed!

After the rout of the Murcians at Baza in Granada, he rallied the fugitives, and in virtue of his authority as regent assumed the chief direction of the war in Valencia, where his noble efforts were nearly rendered futile by the villany of Palacio's faction, who opposed him and endeavoured to detach the soldiers and people from his authority, and proposed to inundate the plains that lie round the black marble mountain of Murviedro; but on Suchet invading the province, Blake concentrated his ill-armed and undisciplined but brave horde of peasantry to meet him. Exclusive of 5000 infantry and 700 Murcian horsemen, under O'Mahy, at Cuença, and 2000 men under Bassecour at Riguena, in September, he had 20,000 foot and 2000 horse; but, as a foreigner by name and race, he was unpopular both in Murcia and Valencia, "and the regency of which he formed a part was tottering," adds General Napier, in the fourth volume of his history. "The Cortes had quashed O'Mahy's command of the Murcian army, and even recalled Blake himself; but the order, which did not reach him until he was engaged with Suchet, was not obeyed. Meanwhile that part of the Murcian army which should have formed a reserve after O'Mahy's division had marched for Cuença, fell into the greatest disorder; above 8000 men deserted in a few weeks, and those who remained were exceedingly dispirited."

Suchet's army entered in three columns, passed Castellon de la Plana, masked Pensicola, invested Oropesa, and skirmished at Almansora, where a few French, by bravely routing a great body of Spaniards, made Blake doubt seriously the firmness of his troops; and thus leaving four thousand men under O'Donnel at Segorbe, he retired beyond the Guadalquiver, leaving Valencia in confusion. Suchet then invested the town of Saguntum, and again turning all his attention to destroy Blake, after much manœuvring, they fought their disastrous battle of the 25th October, 1811.

On the level and fertile plain which lies between Murviedro and Valencia, and is intersected by torrents and ravines, fringed by olive-trees, Suchet drew out his lines of battle before the ramparts of Saguntum, where Blake was defeated, with the loss of 5000 men; and on the Emperor Napoleon reinforcing Suchet with 15,000 men, under General Reille (a Reilly of Irish parentage), the position of Blake and his Andalusians became more than ever desperate.

He had now fought *five pitched battles* as a general, and had under his command 22,000 foot and 3000 horse. In November, Suchet advanced towards the Guadalquiver with a force diminished to 18,000 men by garrisons and detachments. Though Blake had destroyed two of the bridges, and manned the houses, and was in hourly expectation of a general rising of the Valencians, the French fearlessly stormed his defences, crossed the river, menaced his front, and harassed his rear, until he was compelled to form an intrenched camp five miles in extent, enclosing the city of Valencia and three of its suburbs. A twelve-feet ditch surrounded this camp, the slope of which was so high as to require ladders.

The battle of Valencia, fought in December, 1811, followed. O'Mahy was defeated, and fled to Alcira, leaving Blake blocked up in the fortified camp with eighteen thousand men in want of provisions, while the French were well and freely supplied by the *Valencians*, who, as Blake reports, "were a bad people." On the 2nd December he made a bold effort to break through Suchet's lines, and sallied out at the head of ten thousand men; but was repulsed, and Suchet pushed more vigorously than ever the siege of the city, knowing well that it was impossible for Blake to remain long in a camp which included a starving population of fifty thousand souls. The fire of sixty great guns drove Blake into the city, abandoning his camp on the 5th December to the foe, who found in it eighty pieces of cannon. In the evening Suchet summoned Valencia; but Blake declined to yield. Then skirmishes, assaults, and bombarding continued till the 9th, when the citizens were on the point of insurging against Blake, and insisted that he should surrender. He complained bitterly of their cowardice, and required leave to march with his soldiers to Alicant with their baggage, colours, and only four pieces of cannon.

These terms were refused him.

The Valencians opened their gates, and the brave but unfortunate Blake was compelled to surrender his sword.

and march out at the head of twenty-two generals, eight hundred and ninety-three other officers, and eighteen thousand men, as prisoners of war; leaving in the hands of the enemy eighty stand of colours, two thousand horses, three hundred and ninety pieces of cannon, forty thousand stand of arms, one hundred and eighty thousand pounds of powder, and three millions of ball-cartridges, with a vast store of other warlike munition.

After the fall of Valencia he had no opportunity of achieving anything of importance; and in May, 1812, the Regent Charles O'Donnel, Conde de Abispal, bestowed the command of the Valencian forces upon his own brother Joseph, who rallied at Alicant the remains of Blake's army, four thousand of whom escaped from Suchet's guards.

For his last important capture, Suchet was created Duke of Albufera; and poor Blake, as a prisoner of war too important to be exchanged, was ordered into France with his two aides-de-camp.

The preceding has been but a brief outline of the career, services, and struggles of Blake, whose popularity, by a combination of circumstances over which he had no control, was almost destroyed for ever in Spain.

He was accompanied to the Spanish frontier by the Adjutant-General Florestan Pipi, who was then sent to Naples. On entering France he was sent to Paris, and from thence to the strong Château de Vincennes, where he remained a close prisoner until the fall of the Imperial Government; but this captivity did not prevent the Cortes from appointing him a Counsellor of State when naming the regency. The triumph of the allies having broken his fetters in 1814, after receiving many marks of favour from the Emperor Alexander, he returned into Spain under the ministry of Ballasteros, and was appointed Director-General of the Corps of Engineers. He occupied this honourable post until the revolution of 1820, when, in exchange, he received a seat in the Council of State. When war was threatened between France and Spain in 1823 he was appointed, on the 7th February, one of the committee of five generals who were ordered to concert measures for defending the kingdom. In the French army which entered Spain in that year, under the Marquis of Lauriston (an officer of *Scottish* parentage), we find two lieutenant-generals of *Irish* descent—Count Bourke and Viscount O'Donoughue; the Duke of Angoulême was General-in-Chief, and to him, the Duke of Berwick and Alba, a Spanish grandee of the Stuart blood, gave his adherence. The restoration caused by the French intervention under the Marshal Lauriston was fatal to Blake; for being suspected by the royalists of constitutional principles, he was only able to avoid prosecution by great care and solicitude: but his career was drawing to a close, as he died at Valladolid in 1827, regretted by all the Spanish army, and eulogized by the people in their songs and stories of "the War of Independence."

The military men who had borne arms under him, says a French writer, recognised and admitted his positive talent, his great knowledge and perspicacité of tactiques; but agreed that he failed in two essential points—the prompt *coup d'œil* which decides at once the fortune of a battle, and that art of manner by which it is necessary to excite the enthusiasm of the soldier.

A distinguished branch of the old Celtic sept of O'DONNEL has borne a prominent part in the Spanish annals during the last fifty years; but so early as the days of Philip of Anjou and Charles of Spain, we find an O'Donnel fighting in the ranks of their armies.

Soon after the accession of James VI. to the English throne, he was engaged in the last struggle of the Crown against the houses of O'Donnel and O'Neil. An earldom was bestowed as a peace-offering upon the chief of the former; but his plots against the king soon deprived him of it: his estates were seized, an English colony planted in the land of his tribe, and he fled to the Court of Spain, between which and the Irish there had been a close connexion during the animosity of Philip II. and Elizabeth. He was welcomed with all the honours of a Castilian grandee, and attained a high rank under King Charles.

Eighty years after this we find his descendant, Baldearg O'Donnel, still remembering the days when the chiefs, or petty princes of his race, were solemnly inaugurated as the successors of St. Columba on the Rock of Kilmacrenan. He resigned his commission in the service of Philip V., of whom he begged permission to join the Irish, then in arms against William of Orange. Philip refused; but the O'Donnel fled by a route so circuitous that he visited Turkey, and after enduring many privations, landed at Kinsale in 1690, where seven thousand armed Ulster-men hailed him with joy, as the *Red O'Donnel* of an ancient Celtic prophecy.

From Baldearg O'Donnel is descended General Count O'Donnel, who commanded the army of Maria Theresa on the fall of Count Lacy at the great battle of Toorgau in 1761; and also General O'Donnel, Vice-Governor of Lombardy, who was attacked by the Milanese during the Austrian revolution of 1848, when his palace was stormed and himself taken prisoner. There was also a Count O'Donnel in the Hungarian service, who died at Brussels in 1767, after reaching the patriarchal age of one hundred and two years.

Of this ancient Celtic family there are now, or were lately, four general officers of the highest rank in the service of Great Britain, Spain, Austria, and America; but of these the most distinguished is Leopold O'Donnel, Conde de Lucena and Marshal in the service of Donna Isabella II.

The four O'Donnels, Henry, Charles, Joseph, and Alexander, who attained such distinction in Spain during the Peninsula War, were the sons of Irish gentlemen who emigrated to that country during the latter end of the last century; and of their services and honours our limits will allow but a brief outline; while General Sarsfield, Colonel O'Ronan, A.D.C. to the Marquis de Campo Verde, or such partisan soldiers as MacDonel, the unfortunate Guerilla chief who fell in action, Captain Flinter the Christino, or General O'Doyle and his brother, a captain, who were taken prisoners at the last battle of Vittoria, and shot in cold blood by Zumalacarregui, can only be indicated here by name.

CHARLES (afterwards) COUNT O'DONNEL first became known to history in 1810, when commanding at Albuquerque, from whence, on the 14th March, he made a vigorous attempt to surprise General Foy, but was driven into Casceres. Marching towards the ancient city of Merida on the 2nd April, he drove back General Regnier and made an attempt to surprise Truxillo (the birthplace of Pizarro), which is situated on a mountain. Here he was repulsed, and with difficulty effected a retreat to Albuquerque; but three months after we find him at Truxillo again, co-operating with Don Carlos de España, with whom he cut off the French at Rio Monte. In May he had lent two thousand infantry and two hundred cannoneers to Blake, to enable that officer to conduct the siege of Tarragona, receiving in return from Captain Codrington two thousand British muskets to equip a new levy. He allowed four thousand of his best Valencians to embark with Miranda to fight at Tarragona, but not until he received a pledge that the British would bring back all who survived the siege.

Charles served long with Blake, and was in most of the battles just recounted; thus, to rehearse his earlier services would be to enumerate those of Blake a second time.

In September, 1811, when the latter was forced to retire beyond the Guadalaviar, he left Charles O'Donnel with four thousand men on the side of Segorbe; and on investing Saguntum in October, he sent him with Villa Campo's division and San Juan's cavalry to Betera. There O'Donnel was attacked by Harispe, though well posted in rear of a canal, and having his centre protected by a chapel and some houses; but the French advanced with such fury, that the Spaniards were swept away by the first fire.

In the war of 1823, General O'Donnel commanded a corps of Royalists, which were destroyed by the troops of Torrijos, the Constitutionalist; and soon after, his wife, the Condesa de O'Donnel, had a narrow escape from a party of the Empecinado, who were sent to Valladolid to take her prisoner, but were repulsed by the troops of the Marshal Duke of Reggio.

Charles O'Donnel was now Captain-General of Old Castile, and as such, in the month of August, he summoned and took from its insurgent garrison, under General Jalon, the citadel of Ciudad Rodrigo. By the convention between them, it appears that the governor of the fortress undertook to obey any orders he might receive direct from the king; but displayed great distrust of the royalists and the Irish commander. After this, the latter marched into Estremadura, everywhere crushing the Constitutionalists, and enforcing the supremacy of the king. In August his head-quarters were at Salamanca, and in October at Algesiras. This war, in which the absolute power of Ferdinand was fatally enforced by the bayonets of France under Marshal Lauriston, the Duke of Reggio, and others, soon ended; but though smothered for a time, the restless spirit of the Spaniards soon again broke forth into a flame, and most fatally for the house of O'Donnel, as shall be shown in the sequel.

JOSEPH O'DONNEL, who had been serving with his brothers against the common enemy, was appointed by the regent, the Conde de Abispal, to succeed Blake in command of the Murcians and Valencians in May, 1812. He collected the remains of these two armies, remodelled them with great energy, raised new levies, and during the illness of Marshal Suchet mustered fourteen thousand men in the neighbourhood of Alicant.

These operations, with others in Catalonia, brought on the battle of Castalla in July, when, with 6000 foot, 700 horse, and eight guns, he fought General Harispe on the mountains; but on the rough pathway and a narrow bridge near Biar, the Spanish infantry were borne down by the weight and fury of the French cuirassiers, and forced to retreat, leaving 3000 slain on the field. O'Donnel, who had made incredible exertions to gain the day, and had fired two pieces of cannon at the bridge with his own hands, attributed his defeat to the disobedience and inability of San Estevan, who commanded his cavalry, and who, by holding that force aloof, took no share in the battle. Pursued by the French cuirassiers, Joseph fled by the Jumella road, and reached the city of Murcia, where he was joined by General Maitland's armament from Sicily, and thus saved from destruction; but he unwisely required that officer to abstain from all requisitions for forage and rations from the neighbouring country. Maitland assented, and immediately sank under the unnecessary difficulties thus created. In August, when O'Donnel was at Yecla with 6000 men, the Cortes passed a severe censure upon him for his conduct at the battle of Castalla; so severe, indeed, that his brother, the Conde de Abispal, a proud and haughty soldier, resigned his high command during the campaign, which ended in Wellington's retreat from Burgos; and then the weakness of the Spanish Government became more than ever apparent.

On the 6th of December, when at Malaga, Joseph wrote a long letter to General Donkin, concerning the *malheur* at Castalla, in which we find his knowledge of English so imperfect that he was obliged, after a dozen of lines, to adopt and end it in French; and after this unfortunate defeat we hear no more of him.

ALEXANDER O'DONNEL, the third brother, was colonel of a regiment of Spanish infantry, and served with it in the Danish Isles under Romana. Attacked there by overwhelming numbers, they effected their escape in 1808; but on being made captives at Espinosa, they entered the French ranks to the number of 4500, and served in Napoleon's Continental war, until they were all taken prisoners by the Russians on the retreat from Moscow, when they were brought back to Spain in British ships, under he care of Captain Hill of the Royal Navy. One of the Spanish corps which returned after this strange career of military service was the regiment of Don Alexander O'Donnel, which had been fully equipped by the Emperor Alexander in 1812, and for which the daughter of General Betancourt embroidered a pair of colours. It was styled the *Imperial Alexander Regiment*, and under O'Donnel distinguished itself in the national cause till after the disasters of 1823.

HENRY O'DONNEL, Conde de Abispal, who, like his brother, had been serving with success and distinction in the battles of the Peninsula, was a brave, reckless, and determined soldier, possessed of military talents of a very high order, together with a heedlessness of his own life and of the lives of others. Passing, with honour to himself, through all the subaltern ranks, he was a colonel of Spanish infantry in 1809, when Blake ordered him to command in the attack upon Sauham's posts near Brunola, where, on the 31st August, he had the mortification of seeing the place retaken, after he had carried it at the point of the bayonet.

On the 26th September, as related in the memoir of Blake, he led the advanced guard in the brilliant attempt to relieve Gerona. On the 13th October he broke out of the city, sword in hand, hewed a passage through the French blockade, and, falling on Sauham's quarters sabre à la main, forced that general to fly in his shirt, and successfully achieved one of the most daring enterprises of that memorable siege. In 1810, on succeeding Blake in command of the Catalonians—an appointment bestowed by the provincial Junta, who heard of his high reputation—he attacked Marshal Augereau with great fury, and drove him into Gerona. He took up a position at Vich, but on the approach of the French retired to the Col de Sespina, where he led a charge so fierce and decisive, that Sauham's battalions were hurled from the hills in confusion upon the plain. Marching to Manresa, he summoned the Miguelets from Lerida to his colours. These were a species of banditti who infested the mountains, and were armed with pistols, daggers, and blunderbusses. With 12,000 men, Henry O'Donnel took up a position at Maya in February, and harassed the French before Vich, where he fought and lost a severe battle, and was forced to retreat to the Sierras, and from thence to Tarragona, leaving a fourth of his men dead on the field.

O'Donnel, "whose energy and military talents," says Napier, "were superior to all his predecessors," now sent Caro with 6000 men against the French at Villa Franca, where unfortunately they were all killed or captured; and being wounded, he was compelled for a time to resign the command to General Gasca.

On the 6th April, he harassed the French, then retreating from Tarragona towards Barcelona; and after retiring from Vich with an army discomfited by only 5000 Frenchmen, with the same discomfited men he baffled Augereau, who led 20,000 bayonets; forced him to abandon Lower Catalonia, and to retreat in disgrace to Gerona, where Marshal Macdonald, a Scotsman, was sent by Napoleon to succeed him. During the investment of Hostalric by the French, Henry O'Donnel collected many convoys for its relief; he attacked the blockade at several points with the Miguelets, and particularly distinguished himself in a noble and dashing attempt to relieve the brave Julian Estrada, on the night of the 12th May, when this strong citadel fell. During the siege of Lerida by Suchet, O'Donnel collected two divisions of 4000 each; with these and 600 cavalry he skilfully passed the defile of Momblanch, and fought the contest of Margalef, where his troops were defeated; but he rallied, and led them again upon the columns of the Duc d'Albufera. The struggle was terrible; but he was forced to retreat through the passes, leaving one general, eight colonels, 5000 men, and three guns in the hands of the foe. His force was now 1400 strong, well supplied by the active Miguelets; and by the bravery of his soldiers and his own unwearying zeal he long prevented the siege of Tortoza, and found full employment for the enemy during the remainder of the year.

"After the battle of Margalef, Henry O'Donnel reunited his forces, and being of a stern, unyielding disposition, not only repressed the discontents occasioned by that defeat, but forced the reluctant (and lawless) Miguelets to supply his ranks and submit to discipline." Thus, in July he had twenty-two thousand men when Marshals Macdonald and Suchet combined to crush him, and when Napoleon's order to invest Tortoza arrived. On this O'Donnel, after making a skilful feint towards Trivisa, suddenly threw himself with ten thousand men into the fated city, from whence, upon the noon of the 3rd July, he fell furiously upon the French entrenchments, and made a fearful slaughter of the troops of Laval. After this he retired to Tarragona. Having cut off Macdonald's communication with the walled city of Ampurias, he now conceived and executed the most skilful and vigorous plan which had yet graced the Spanish arms.

Leaving Campo Verde in the valley of Aro, on the 14th. he marched rapidly down from Casa de Silva upon Abispal, where the French, under Swartz, were entrenched. He attacked them, slew two hundred, and, taking the rest, embarked them for Tarragona, whither he retired soon after, to take a little repose, being troubled by his last wound; yet in January, 1811, we find him again in arms, directing the movements of the army, and harassing Marshals Macdonald and Suchet, though unable to ride or appear in the field; and on his being created Conde de Abispal, he resigned the command of his Catalonians, three thousand in number, to Campo Verde, being so disabled by wounds that he was quite unable to conduct the siege of Tortoza.

In October, 1812, he was appointed to that situation, which several Irish soldiers of fortune have held—Captain-General of Andalusia,—and on Wellington reaching Cadiz in December of that year, after the retreat from Burgos, on his making a complete reorganization of the Spanish forces, the first reserve corps was given to the Conde de Abispal, and the second reserve to Lacy. Thus they both served in the new campaign which ended so gloriously on the field of Vittoria. After this signal victory, the task of reducing the forts near the tremendous pass of Pancorbo, which secured the approach to the Ebro, was given to the Irish Conde and his Andalusians, to whom they fell partly by storm and partly by capitulation.

On the 14th July, 1813, to O'Donnel and his reserve of five thousand was permanently entrusted the important duty of blocking up the French garrison in Pampeluna, now almost the last stronghold of Napoleon in Spain. This task he conducted with great vigour, while Wellington secured the passes of the Pyrenees and pushed the siege of San Sebastian; but on Soult forcing the passes on the 25th July, such an alarm reached Pampeluna, that the Conde de Abispal spiked some of his cannon, blew up his magazines, abandoned the trenches, and but for Picton's victorious stand at Huarte, was prepared to retreat. On the fortunate arrival of a small Spanish division under Don Carlos d'Espana, the blockade was resumed and the siege pressed with renewed vigour.

O'Donnel was posted on the right of Marshal Murillo at the great and decisive battle of Pampeluna, so absurdly and obstinately styled by the British *the battle of the Pyrenees*, from which it is nearly thirty miles distant. Soult was completely overthrown, and in August O'Donnel reinforced the seventh division in occupying the important passes of Exhallar and Zugaramurdi. After this, being again troubled by old wounds, he fell ill and resigned his command for a time to Giron. In November he resumed it again, and occupied the beautiful valley of the Bastan, prior to the invasion of France under Wellington.

In February, 1814, he led six thousand men at the passage of the Gaves, and was engaged in all the operations on the Lower Pyrenees with the Spaniards under the Prince of Anglona. He served in that victorious campaign which terminated at the blood-stained hill of Toulouse, where, as General Napier so pithily remarks, " the war terminated, *and with it all remembrance of the veterans' services.*"

In the Constitutional war which ensued in Spain nine years after, and during the invasion of that country by monarchical France in 1823, the O'Donnels bore a prominent part, and adhered to Ferdinand VII. The Conde de Abispal was appointed a field-marshal, with the office of governor and political chief at Madrid, and on the 25th March he issued a proclamation announcing that the amnesty granted by the Cortes to those in arms against the king was about to expire, and concluded by a brief warning to the factious and the Constitutionalists to lay down their arms. On the 17th April he published his able orders and propositions to the militia of the capital, together with the following declaration of his political principles :—

"*Don Henry O'Donnel, Knight Grand Cross, &c., General of the 3rd Corps, &c.*

"Having learned that some ill-disposed persons have confounded my *private opinion* with those sacred obligations *which my oath and duty impose upon me,* and have given out that I am unwilling to support the Constitution of 1812 even to the last extremity, and until the national representation, lawfully constituted, should have made certain changes therein; I do declare that *I am resolved to defend it,* according to my oath, until it shall be altered by those means which the Constitution itself prescribes, and that I deem as traitors all Spaniards who, deviating from the path of duty traced out by law, shall cease to obey the same. Such were my sentiments when, in answer to an address from M. Montijo, I wrote a letter which they charge me with having published, and such will ever be my sentiments. But my *opinion* as an individual shall never prevent me from fulfilling my *duty* as a general and a citizen of Spain.

"Madrid, 17th May, 1823."

But ere long he found the difficulty of reconciling his private sentiments and conviction with his duty to a king who had become the tool of France. Abispal proved the Talleyrand of Spain, and lost all favour by his indecision and vacillation; for, after receiving the Grand Cordon of the Order of Carlos III. from the hands of Ferdinand VII., he passed over to the Constitutionalists. From that day his power declined, and he was glad to seek shelter from the fury and clamour of the people at Montpelier in France, where he lived in retirement and much reduced in circumstances.

His son, LEOPOLD COUNT O'DONNEL, remained in Spain, and had attained the rank of colonel when the civil war broke out between the Carlists and Christinos, a step in which the children of the four elder O'Donnels were strangely divided, brother against brother, and cousin against cousin.

Thus, on the 2nd May, 1835, when Quesada was attacked by Don Tomas Zumalacarregui (the Claverhouse of Spanish loyalty), his division would have been annihilated but for the timely succour he received from Colonel Leopold O'Donnel de Abispal, who unfortunately was taken prisoner by the Navarrese while vainly struggling to rally the Royal Guards. All who were captured were barbarously shot by the Carlists, and of all who perished none was more regretted than the young, handsome, and chivalric O'Donnel. Though a colonel in the service, he was merely accompanying Quesada to profit by his escort so far as Pampeluna, where he was about to celebrate his nuptials with a beautiful Spanish girl of high rank, and the heiress of an old and wealthy family. A noble ransom was offered, but Don Tomas was inexorable.

His father, Henry O'Donnel, then in his old age, died of a broken heart at Montpelier, on hearing of his son's disastrous fate.

COLONEL JOHN O'DONNEL (a cousin of Leopold's) commanded the 2nd regiment of Castilian infantry, while his brother Charles led the insurgent cavalry of Don Tomas, and at the head of his own corps, the heavily-armed and ferocious lancers of Navarre, performed in his twenty-fifth year the most brilliant feats of the Constitutional war. For his romantic victory over Lopez, in fair battle on one of the immense plains of Old Castile, he was made Knight of San Ferdinando. Soon after, he was mortally wounded in action near Pampeluna, and as he expired in agony, he exclaimed: "I wish some one would send a bullet through me and end this misery!—I have but a short time to live. Already four O'Donnels have perished in this war; and their blood has been shed on the right side as well as on the wrong!"

He referred to Leopold, who was shot in cold blood at Alsassua; to his second brother, who lost a leg at Arguijas, and died under the amputation; to Charles, who lay on a bed of sickness from which he never rose; and to John, who was wounded in battle at Mendigorra; and being dragged from bed by a mob at Barcelona, was cruelly murdered in the streets and literally cut *into ounce pieces*. He and Charles left wives and children in France.

LEOPOLD, the Conde de Lucena, and his brother Colonel HENRY O'DONNEL, who in the Spanish affairs of the present time have borne so prominent a part, are of the same warlike stock; but their adventures are too recent to require a record here.

Marshal Baron Loudon.

ON the summit of a rising ground, by the side of a brook in the parish of Loudon in Ayrshire, stand the ruins of the ancient Castle of Loudon, which was destroyed about three hundred and fifty years ago by the clan Kennedy, headed by their chief, the Earl of Cassilis. This old Scottish stronghold was the seat of a family from which sprung Gideon Ernest Baron Loudon, or *de Laudohn*, a distinguished general of the Continental wars.

Loudon of that ilk was one of the oldest families in the kingdom of Scotland.

Lambin was proprietor of the lands and barony of Loudon during the reign of David I., who succeeded to the throne in 1124. James of Loudon, *dominus de eodem*, or of that ilk, obtained a charter of the same barony from Richard de Morville, Constable of the Kingdom; *Jacobo filio Lambin*, &c., also obtained a charter from William de Morville, as *Jacobo de Loudon, terrarum baroniæ de Loudon*. Both these documents were granted during the reign of William the Lion, who succeeded to the throne in 1165, and are, says Sir Robert Douglas, a proof that he took his sirname from these lands, according to the custom of those early times; and his armorial bearings were, argent, three escutcheons sable. His daughter, Margaret of Loudon, was married to Sir Reginald Crawford, High Sheriff of Ayr, and became the grandmother of Sir William Wallace, the heroic defender of the liberties of his country.

In later times, a branch of this old family had left

"Loudon's bonnie woods and braes,"

so famed in Scottish song, and settled in Livonia, where their bravery and services had won them several fiefs and baronies, of which, however, they were dispossessed by Charles XI. of Sweden, after the peace of Oliva, when the Polish Republic gave up its right to the old Teutonic province.

During the reign of his successor, the famous Charles XII., the Livonian nobles made a vigorous effort to regain their patrimonies and privileges; but the Swedish king having put to death their representative, the celebrated general, John Raynold Patkul, an officer in the service of Augustus, King of Poland, by cruelly breaking him alive upon the wheel, where he received sixteen blows, enduring the longest and greatest tortures that can be conceived, all hope of restoring Livonian liberty died ; and with many other noble families, the Loudons dedicated themselves to the profession of arms : one became a captain in the Royal Swedish Guards, and was uncle of the subject of this memoir.

GIDEON ERNEST LOUDON was born at Tootzen, in Livonia, in the year 1716.

In consequence of the war and troubles in which his native province was involved, his education was much neglected ; and though his great military genius in after years enabled him in some degree to supply the deficiency, he never ceased to regret the loss he had sustained, by those circumstances over which he had no control, but which, fortunately for himself, forced him to earn his bread by his sword as a soldier of fortune. He had learned little more than to read and to write, with a smattering of geography and geometry, when in 1731 he entered the Russian service as a cadet.

He was then in his fifteenth year, and Anne, daughter of Ivan II., niece of Peter the Great, and consort of the Duke of Courland, was Czarina of Russia. The corps to which young Loudon was attached was a battalion of infantry; and after being two years in garrison with it, an opportunity was afforded him of making an essay in arms, when the war of the Double Election created disturbances in northern Europe.

In 1733 Stanislaus Leczinski, whom Charles XII. had

invested with the Sovereignty of Poland in 1704, and whom Peter the Great had dethroned, was chosen king a second time on his daughter being married to Louis XV., from whom he received a paltry succour, cousisting of only four battalions of infantry; but the Austrian Emperor, on being assisted by the Russians, compelled the Poles to make *another* selection, and the Elector of Saxony was raised to their throne by the name of Augustus III., while poor King Stanislaus was driven into Dantzig, where the Russians followed aud besieged him.

Loudon's regiment served with the blockading force, at the investment of this populous city, which is the capital of Western Prussia, and at that time had a population of two hundred thousand. Loudon was present during the siege and capture of Dantzig, from which, however, the ex-King of Poland made an escape, and renounced for ever the poor distinction of being monarch of a republic plunged in anarchy.

In the year 1734, his regiment formed part of the army which was sent by the Empress Anne towards the Low Countries, and spread a terror along the frontier of Germany. In this campaign he marched from the banks of the Wolga to those of the Rhine. A peace being signed at Vienna, the forces marched to the Dnieper, the scene of so many sanguinary encounters between the Russ and Turk. This movement was to repel the Osmanlies and punish the Tartars of the Crimea, who had made an irruption into the southern province of Russia, and committed unparalleled outrages.

In the army under Marshal the Count de Munich, young Loudon served in the long campaign from 1736 to 1739, and was present in that barbarous warfare in the Crimea, which is already detailed in the memoirs of the Counts Lacy and Brown, including the capture of Azoph; the storming of the lines at Perecop; the assault and capture of Oczackow, Staveoctochane and Choczim, with the general ravage and subjugation of the Tartar peninsula down to the extreme verge of the Tauric range, and to the Symbolorum Portus of Strabo—the harbour of Balaclava.

In his position, which was then so subordinate, the share borne by Loudon in those brilliant operations was necessarily obscure ; but, for his ability and attention to duty, he was soon raised from the rank of cadet to the commissions of a second, and then first lieutenant; a proof that the germ of an able officer had been discerned by his colonel in the foreign volunteer. The treaty which ceded Azoph to Russia in 1739 secured a brief peace to Europe, and the Empress Anne Ivanowna began to disband her unwieldly forces.

On this occurring, Lieutenant Loudon repaired to St. Petersburg in 1740, for the double purpose of complaining to the Empress that he had been unjustly treated during the war, having served nine years and being still a subaltern ; and also to solicit from her further employment and promotion. Disappointed in both these objects, he resigned his commission in her service with disgust, and quitted the Russian capital, resolving to make an offer of his sword to the Empress Queen of Hungary, Maria Theresa, who had succeeded her father Charles VI. on the Austrian throne, and found it assailed on all sides by hostile armies.

As he passed through Berlin he fell in with several officers, principally Scots and Irishmen, with whom he had served under Marshal Munich in the late campaigns ; and some of these recommended him to join the Prussian service, in which they had all accepted commissions ; and one was kind enough to offer him an introduction to the warlike Frederick II., with whom, after some weeks' delay, he had the honour of an interview. Loudon modestly stated his nine years' service, his junior rank and wishes, adding that, as he had held a lieutenantcy under the Empress Anne, he ventured to hope that his Majesty would bestow upon him the command of a company. Frederick keenly scrutinized his face, which "was serious, cold, severe, reserved, pensive, and reflecting" (for he was a man schooled in danger and adversity), and it did not prepossess the royal martinet of Prussia in his favour, for he had the rudeness to turn his back upon the military stranger, and say to some officers near him,—

"*The physiognomy of this man does not please me.*"

In anger and mortification young Loudon, then in his twenty-fourth year, quitted his presence with a swelling heart; but he could not then foresee the time when he would become the most formidable enemy that ever met the Prussian monarch in the field.

In very poor circumstances he reached Vienna in 1742, and being furnished with a strong recommendatory letter from the Austrian ambassador, repaired to the Imperial palace in search of military employment. While he was lingering unknown and unnoticed in the ante-chamber, a gentleman accosted him, inquiring his name and business. Loudon having mentioned both, and expressed great desire to see the Empress, this person said, "I will do all in my power to assist you, sir," and passed directly *into* the cabinet. In a few minutes "Lieutenant Loudon" was summoned by name, and on entering, was astonished to discover in his unknown protector the husband of the beautiful Maria Theresa, Francis Stephen, Grand Duke of Tuscany and First Emperor of the House of Lorraine-Austria! Under auspices so favourable, his request was at once granted, and he obtained a company in the Free Corps of Pandours raised by Baron Trenck, who had known Loudon in Russia, and was well pleased to have under him so gallant an officer.

These Pandours were Sclavonians from the banks of the Drave, a river of Germany which rises in the Tyrol and empties itself into the Danube near Effeck in Hungary. This regiment, which was raised chiefly in the village of Pandour or Szent Istevan, wore long coats girt by a waist-belt, in which each man carried a sabre, four or five pistols, and a poniard. On service they always acted as irregular cavalry. This corps had originally been infantry, and were styled the Regiment of Ruitza. Their chief occupation had been to clear the roads of brigands and freebooters; and though the biographer of Baron Trenck endeavours to conceal the fact, history proves that in their new organization the Pandours were a mere military banditti, whose pay was plunder, and whose duty was devastation.

Little as he must have liked the service, Captain Loudon commenced a campaign in their ranks, in the war which ensued on Louis XV. and the King of Prussia leaguing together for the partition of the Austrian Empire. A French army under the Marshal Dukes de Belleisle and de Broglie, entered Germany, where the Bavarian Elector formed a junction with them ; reduced Lintz, the capital of Upper Austria, and threatened Vienna. Kevenhüller recovered Lintz; the battle of Czaslau, in which the Pandours and Croats charged with such effect and fury was fought ; Prague was besieged, and all northern Europe found itself engaged in a general strife.

At the head of his Pandours Baron Trenck acted the part of a bold partisan. He stormed the Isle of Rheinmarck, put its garrison to the sword, and with his own sabre slew the commandant, the Comte de Creveceur. Mentzel with four thousand Croats and Pandours broke into Lorraine and Luxembourg, where they committed terrible devastations.

In 1744, when Prince Charles of Lorraine forced his famous passage over the Rhine, Gideon Loudon led his company in the *foremost* boat, and was the *first* who landed on French ground; but in a skirmish with the advanced picquets of the French near Zabern, a city built on the summit of a rock, and defended by a strong castle of the Bishops of Strasburg, he was struck by a musket-ball when fighting bravely at the head of his men. It entered his right breast and came out behind near the shoulder-blade, and thus incapacitated him for farther service for some time. He fell—was taken prisoner, and conveyed to a neighbouring cottage. A few days afterwards the Austrian army advanced ; the Pandours drove the enemy ; Loudon was restored to liberty, and had the satisfaction of saving from pillage the dwelling of the peasant with whom he had found shelter and by whom he had been benevolently treated.

Meantime the King of Prussia, sick of his bloody victories, signed the treaty of Breslau, which filled France with consternation, and forced her marshals, Belleisle and

LOUDON STUDYING THE MAP OF GERMANY.

Broglie, to retire towards Prague; but the close of 1745 saw tranquillity restored to Germany for a time.

Disgusted with the reckless regiment of Trenck, Loudon quitted it and returned to Vienna, where he resigned his commission and was preparing to leave the Austrian dominions in search of fortune elsewhere, when some of his military friends advised him to remain, and procured for him a majority in the regiment of Liccaner, which at that time was garrisoning a town on the Croatian frontier. His old corps the Pandours were disbanded, but were afterwards re-organized in 1750 as regular troops, and became of great service in the war of 1756, and in those of the first French Revolution.

This new appointment and its emoluments enabled him to espouse Clara de Hagen, the daughter of a brave Hungarian officer who resided at Pæsing. He was sincerely attached to this lady, and they had one child, a daughter, who died in infancy.

During ten years that he remained in the garrison towns of Croatia he spent all his leisure hours in perfecting his military education, and completing the study of fortification, geography, and geometry. He procured a vast number of maps and plans of fortified places, such as castles and barrier towns; and, as if he had some intuitive presentiment of the part he was yet to perform in the great game of war, he pored over them incessantly. Having once obtained a German map of unusual size, he spread it over the floor of his barrack-room, and *sat down* upon it, to pursue his study of it with greater ease, and was thus occupied when Madame Loudon entered.

"My dear major," said she, "still as ever, occupied by these horrid plans and perpetual studies!"

"Never mind my present labours," said he, cheerfully; "they will be of great service to me, my dear Clara, when I obtain the bâton of a field-marshal."

Madame Loudon laughed, for her husband was then eight-and-thirty, and the bâton of a marshal seemed yet to be a long way off.

In 1756 the Seven Years' War was threatened. A

league was formed by the Court of Vienna for stripping the King of Prussia of his dominions. The French threatened the electorate of Hanover, and formed an alliance with Sweden and Austria against Britain and Prussia, the king of which, on receiving evasive answers from Vienna as to the object of the Austrian armaments, prepared for immediate strife.

Anxious for employment, and remembering, perhaps, the manner in which Frederick II. had insulted him at his levée in Berlin, the enterprising spirit of Loudon induced him to visit Vienna and solicit a command against Prussia; but having left his regiment without obtaining leave of absence, he was on the point of being reprimanded and ordered back to Croatia, when by good fortune he obtained the friendship and patronage of Prince Kaunitz, the head of a noble family, whose possessions lie on the Iglau in Moravia. By the prince's interest he was appointed Lieutenant-Colonel of eight hundred Croats. These wild and hardy troops were destined to be ordered on every desperate service, and as their mode of fighting resembled in every respect that of the Pandours, Loudon was well fitted to command them; more especially as he had acquired their dialect while quartered in their native province. They were all clad in short waistcoats with sleeves, long white breeches, light boots, and rough huzzar caps. They had each a long firelock with a rifle barrel and short bayonet, a crooked sabre, and brace of pistols. This corps formed part of five thousand Croats levied by the Empress-Queen for the new war against Prussia. Like the Pandours of Baron Trenck, they had no pay or provisions, but such as their swords and the terror of their presence won them; and as irregular troops they were a scourge wherever they marched.

On the 29th of August, 1756, the King of Prussia entered Saxony at the head of seventy battalions of foot and eighty squadrons of horse, in three columns, which marched by three different routes, but formed a junction at Dresden and captured it. The Elector, who was King of Poland by the title of Augustus III., took refuge in a camp at Pirna, while Frederick marched into Bohemia and found the Austrians encamped at Lowositz under Marshal Count Brown, who was defeated there in October; and after a long and bloody contest forced to retire in rear of Egra.

It was at this time that Loudon with his Croats joined the Austrian army; and in the disastrous retreat which ensued after Lowositz, he narrowly escaped when a hundred of his grenadiers were slain by the Prussian hussars. During Marshal Brown's retreat out of Saxony, Loudon took by surprise the town of Estchen at the head of five hundred men, and destroyed two squadrons of Prussian hussars. This was his first exploit, and it was deemed the most brilliant of the Austrian campaign.

He distinguished himself again at Hirschfeld, on the Bohemian frontier; and for his bravery on that occasion was appointed colonel in February, 1757.

On the 20th of that month his corps had formed part of the six thousand Austrians who attacked the Prussian position at four in the morning. Loudon fought with incredible bravery, and slew many of the enemy with his own hand. In August he attacked the Schriekstein and captured three hundred newly raised soldiers. He now obtained an increased command—a small division, six thousand strong, consisting of Croats and Pandours. With these he attacked and defeated a body of the enemy at Erfurth, a garrison town of Saxony. He then joined the now allied French and Imperialists, who marched to Weissenfels, a city in the centre of Thuringia. By this time the Swedes were pushing on the war in Pomerania and had besieged Stettin. Marshal Richelieu with eighty battalions and one hundred squadrons of French had entered Halberstadt, and was everywhere levying contributions with fire and sword, while the Austrians had made themselves masters of Lignitz and most of Silesia; and after laying siege to Schwiednitz, were preparing to pass the Oder. Everywhere the tide of war had turned upon the King of Prussia.

Loudon was now with what was named the *Combined Army*. The Prince de Soubise commanded the French; the Prince of Hildburghausen led the Austrians, and their united and immediate object was to clear Saxony of the Prussians. Frederick left a division to cover Silesia, and approached this Combined Army, which passed the Sala and established its head-quarters at Weissenfels; from whence the Comte de Mailly was sent to summon Leipzig. On the 5th November, the King of Prussia gave battle to this Combined Army, then fifty thousand strong, at Rosbach, a village of Prussian Saxony, at eleven o'clock in the morning. The allies were formed in line with their cavalry in front. The impetuosity of the Prussian infantry, whose charge was admirably sustained by a fire of artillery and advance of horse, broke the allied line, and, notwithstanding all the efforts of the Prince de Soubise, Frederick obtained a complete victory with the loss of three hundred men only; while the Combined Army lost no less than eleven generals, three hundred other officers, nine thousand killed, wounded, and prisoners, sixty-three guns, twenty-nine colours, and one pair of kettle-drums. With the battle of Rosbach terminated the campaign in Saxony.

Loudon was with the Combined Army during all these operations; and the Prince of Hildburghausen, desirous of signalizing his own authority by some grand stroke, proposed to the Prince de Soubise the project of dislodging the Prussians from the petty principality of Gotha, where Seidlitz commanded. They began their march accordingly with their grenadiers and Austrian heavy cavalry, while Loudon led the Pandours and French light dragoons. They dispatched one column of cavalry over the heights which led to Thuringia; another on the left, preceded by hussars, approached Gotha from the side of Langensaltza; while Loudon with the Pandours, dragoons, and a body of grenadiers, formed the column of the centre.

Seidlitz was ready to receive them. He was in order of battle, and had all the defiles secured by horse and cannon. A desultory conflict ensued among the woods and mountains; and though the Prince de Soubise cut a passage to the castle wall of Gotha, he was obliged to retreat and leave three officers and one hundred and sixty soldiers in the hands of Seidlitz. The Prussian column under the Prince of Bavern attempted to cover Breslau, which surrendered on the 22nd November to the Austrian generals, by whom he was made prisoner; while the remnant of his army joined Frederick, and on the 5th December the battle of Lissa, where he gained a signal victory, was fought in Silesia. Such was the severity of the season that many hundreds of soldiers were found dead on their posts; and the German generals were reproached with heartlessly exposing their men to the extremity of cold; for a campaign in winter is alike opposed to the dictates of humanity and the common rules of war, as the operations of our own troops in the Crimea have given terrible proof.

In these arduous duties, though always at the head of his Croats and Pandours, Loudon never received another wound, though exposed almost daily to balls, bayonets, and sabres; and it is worthy of remark that the musket-shot received at Zabern was the only scar of his long military career.

In the campaign of 1758 he received the Imperial military Order of Maria Theresa, which was instituted by the Empress Queen in the June of the preceding year. In this Order it is an inviolable principle that no officer whatsoever, "on account of his high birth, long service, wounds, or former merits, much less from mere favour, or the recommendation of others, be received; but that those only who have signalized themselves by some particular act of valour, or have aided the Imperial service by able and beneficial councils, and contributed to their execution by distinguished bravery, shall be admitted."

In the operations of the new year the King of Prussia recovered Schwiednitz from the Imperialists on the 16th April; entered Moravia on the 27th May; invested Olmutz, which was stoutly defended by the governor, General Marshall, a Scotsman; while Marshal Daun, under whom Loudon held a command, took post on the adjacent mountains, to intercept and cut off the Prussian convoys. The siege had now been open for four weeks, and the trenches were pushed with great vigour by the

T

Scottish exile—the gallant Marshal Keith—notwithstanding the great difficulties attending it; for Loudon, bravely, and at incalculable hazard, in the defiles of Damstadt, in the principality of Lichenstien, intercepted a convoy of four hundred waggons, and obliged General Zeithen, who escorted them with twenty squadrons and three battalions, after a five hours' encounter, to retire on Trappau. This loss was irreparable, for General Putkammer, eight hundred men, and the *military chest* were taken.

The King of Prussia was compelled to raise the siege, and effected one of the most able retreats ever seen in Germany; he then marched to oppose the Russians, who had broken into Brandenburg under Generals Brown and Farmer, two Scotsmen, whom he met in battle at Zorndorf, defeated on the 25th August, and drove them into Poland.

Had Loudon (who was ably seconded by Daun) *not* intercepted General Zeithen, " the town of Olmutz must have been taken in a fortnight," says Frederick, who styles it the Battle of the Convoy; "for the third parallel was finished, and the besiegers had begun to open the saps." For this service Loudon received the rank of lieutenant-field-marshal.

He had now won the reputation of being the first cavalry officer in the service of the Empress-Queen; and he was of great use to Daun in galling and incommoding the King of Prussia during the retreat from Olmutz.

With four thousand men he took post in the wood of Opotshno, a Bohemian town, fifteen miles north-east of Koningengratz, where he intended to attack the Baron de la Mothe Fouque, who with thirty-two battalions and squadrons was conveying the heavy siege train. But there Loudon was unexpectedly assailed by Frederick, who had heard of his projected ambush, and marched to attack him in it, and he was forced to retire through the forest with the loss of a hundred Croatian troopers. He retreated towards Holitz, and thus the siege train passed unmolested to Glatz.

Loudon and General St. Ignan followed Frederick

closely; at Koningengratz their Pandours slew General Saldern, Colonel Blankenzee, and seventy men, but were checked by the sabres of Putkammer's hussars; and to prevent this harassing of the rear-guard, Frederick prepared an ambuscade on a narrow path which lies through a wood at Metau. In this defile he concealed ten battalions and twenty squadrons, under whose fire the Austrians were drawn by a few flying skirmishers. "Loudon, who was very easily heated," to quote Frederick, "resolved on an assault;" but the Prussian cavalry poured upon him like a torrent, a fire opened upon his men from every point of the rocks and pass, three hundred were shot dead, and he was forced to retire. Soon after this he was lured again, by the Volunteers of Le Noble, into a ravine near Skalitz, where he was suddenly assailed by six battalions in the night, and had to give way, with the loss of six officers and seventy men.

He took possession of Peitz, a town in the Duchy of Brandenburg, on the right bank of the Matx, and left no means untried to fulfil with signal success his duty of covering Daun's left flank during the whole of the Austrian advance and Prussian retreat. Daun posted himself at Stolpen, to the eastward of the Elbe, on one hand to preserve a communication with a column which he had detached to Koningstien, and on the other to favour the active operations of Marshal Loudon, who had advanced through Lower Lusatia to the frontier of Brandenburg.

At the battle of Hochkirchen, which was fought on the 13th October, the defeat of the Prussians was solely attributed to Loudon's skill and bravery. On the 12th he had attacked a great convoy, but was repulsed by Marshal the Honourable James Keith, with the loss of eighty men, among whom was the Prince de Lichenstien, lieutenant-colonel of the regiment of Löwenstien. After this Loudon assembled his dispersed troops and took ground in a woody mountain, which was a long quarter of a league, German measure, beyond the Prussian right, facing the village of Hochkirchen. A marsh separated the flank of Frederick from this height. Daun secretly prepared a road for four columns to form a junction with

Loudon, who on the night of the 13th glided down with his swift Pandours to the rear of the Prussian position, and set on fire the village of Hochkirchen, driving out by the edge of the sabre the battalions quartered there, and seizing on a battery which defended an angle of the place; while the gallant Major Lang, with the regiment of the Margrave Charles, threw himself into the churchyard, and in the dark opened a blaze of musketry on the Pandours, whose light uniforms were soon too fatally visible by the flames of the burning village. Around this conflagration the whole tide of battle rolled at midnight. The aged Marshal Keith and Prince Ferdinand of Brunswick were killed, and the Prussians were defeated with the loss of seven thousand men and most of their camp equipage.

Marshal Daun filled his despatch (which detailed this victory) with the highest encomiums on Loudon, whom he sent immediately towards Silesia in pursuit of Frederick, whose forces he was to exclude from Lusatia; and so he followed and galled them with untiring zeal and vigour, though he was then suffering from a severe and chronic disease in the stomach; but on his march towards the Saxon capital, the Prussian monarch made one vigorous stand and repulsed him; after which he retired to Zittau.

Reinforced by 12,000 men, the marshal concealed himself in the forest of Schonberg, where he again attacked the Prussians, whose whole line of march became "one battle;" but Prince Henry, Frederick's brother, commanded the rearguard; and so excellent were his dispositions, that only Lieutenant-General Bulow and 215 soldiers fell.

On the 1st November, Frederick began his march for Silesia. Loudon, still pressing on, fell with such fury on the rearguard, that he was nearly taken prisoner by the Prussian hussars. He then brought up his cannon; but these were dismounted by the heavier pieces of Frederick, which at the same time threw the Austrian foot into disorder. Thrice Loudon rallied them; and thrice, sword in hand, he led them to the charge: but the approach of the noble Putkammer hussars compelled him to fall back; and thus, amid skirmishes, night marches, toil, starvation, plunder, and devastation, the campaign of the year was closed by the Austrians raising the sieges of Neiss and Dresden, and the King of Prussia retiring to winter quarters at Breslau.

The generals of the Imperial army usually spent the winter in the Austrian capital; and now the Empress expressed a strong desire to see Marshal Loudon, of whom Count Daun had written so favourably in all his despatches and letters. Thus he prepared to return to Vienna, but was compelled to remain for some time at Dœplitz in Bohemia, in consequence of a return of his illness: and there Madame Loudon, who had remained at Vienna during the whole war, arrived to attend him. As soon as he was sufficiently restored, they travelled together to the capital, where they arrived on the 24th of February, 1759. The streets were crowded by dense masses of persons, all anxious to behold and to welcome the hero of whom they had heard so much, and his reception was most enthusiastic. Only two years had elapsed since he left that city as a field-officer of Croats, and now he returned to it a Lieutenant-Field-Marshal and Knight of Maria Theresa.

From the fair Empress he received the most flattering distinction; and she commanded her own physician, the Baron Von Swieten, to attend him until his health was completely re-established. She bestowed upon him the Grand Cross of her Order, and created him a Baron of the Holy Roman Empire.

The moment his physician permitted him, he resumed his command; and no general of the Seven Years' War bore a more distinguished part in the campaign of 1759 than Baron Loudon, though Frederick II., who had imbibed an animosity to him, always mentions his name slightingly in his works.

The Prussian monarch, in the beginning of the year, had great success; but his chief embarrassment was the approach of the Russians, who defeated him in Silesia on the 23rd July, and spread their outposts along the banks of the Oder. On the frontiers of Bohemia nothing of importance occurred, though Loudon, who occupied Trautenau, was continually in motion, alarming the Prussian posts and cutting off their supplies.

He made an attack on General Seidlitz near Frederick's strong camp at Schmuckseiffen, and lost 150 men. Immediately after this, the Court of Vienna gave him command of 20,000 men, 1200 of whom were dragoons, to give vigour to their Russian allies, who were destitute of cavalry. By the way of Greiffenberg he marched through Silesia, foiling, deceiving, and skirmishing with the horse of Prince Henry, till he took up a position on the heights of Laubau, where he had fought the Prussians in the preceding year. He chose this ground with the intention of being in advance of them now, when he should receive orders to join the Russians under Count Soltikow.

With this general he achieved a junction, and together they took up a position at Cunnersdorff, opposite Frankfort-on-the-Oder, and gave battle to Frederick at eleven o'clock, A.M., on the 12th of August. The Russians had their intrenchments stormed amid great slaughter; a starfort erected by them on two sand hills, to cover their right flank, was carried at the point of the bayonet, and a dreadful massacre of them ensued in the churchyard of Cunnersdorff. Under the glare of a burning sun, and sore with many a wound, the brave King of Prussia led on his troops; and for two hours the infantry fought hand to hand. The Jews' Cemetery, seven redoubts, and 180 pieces of cannon, were already taken, when Loudon, perceiving that the Russians were unable to maintain their ground, brought up his well-chosen reserves, and fired his field-pieces loaded with case-shot, to sweep the Prussian line. He then charged on both flanks with his fine Austrian cavalry, who bore down all before them. The Prussians fell into confusion, and their rout became total. Frederick had two horses shot under him, and his blue uniform literally torn to rags by bullets and sword-cuts. The struggle was awful, and night came down on a field where 30,000 men lay dead or dying, and of these more than the half were Prussians. The brave

Putkammer was slain, and ten other generals lay killed or wounded near him.

The movements of Frederick after this most signal defeat were of a masterly description. He soon compelled Loudon and Soltikow to act on the defensive, and recovered every place in the Saxon Electorate except Dresden. Forcing the Russians to retire into Poland, he joined his brother Prince Henry in Saxony, compelled Marshal Daun to retreat as far as Plawen, and forced him to take shelter in the camp at Pirna; after which he retired into winter quarters in November.

For his victory at Cunnersdorff Loudon was raised to the rank of *General-velt-zeug-Meister;* but he drew off from Soltikow with all his cavalry immediately after the battle.

In the campaign of 1760 he received command of the army destined for service in Silesia. It consisted of 40,000 men, and in all operations he was to be seconded by the Russians, who, according to an agreement made by the two Empresses, were to fight their way along the banks of the Oder, while Daun carried on the war in Saxony. This army was light, and as unencumbered by baggage as a Pandour leader could desire. At its head Loudon left the camp in which he had passed the winter, and after attacking and repulsing General Goltze at the head of his horse, he left Draskowitz with 6000 men at Neustadt, and took the road to Bohemia, after menacing in succession Silesia, into which he penetrated with two corps, the new Marche of Brandenburg, Breslau, even Berlin and Schwiednitz. At last he fixed upon the latter, and General the Baron de la Mothe Fouque (who had weakened his forces by detaching the brigades of the Scottish General Grant and General Zeithen), deceived by an artful feint, marched towards it with all his troops leaving the garrison in Glatz quite unprotected.

The able Loudon at once perceived the success of his feint, or stratagem, and immediately had recourse to another. He took possession of Landshut, and left there a small body of troops, who were immediately assailed and driven out by the Baron de la Mothe. While the latter was thus occupied in recovering this trivial post, Loudon made himself master of several important positions, and passed in triumph through Johannesberg and Wisstengersdorff, and at Schwarzwalde routed the hussars of Malachowski, and thus surrounded the baron's little army of Prussians. The latter did everything requisite to secure their position against the superior force of Loudon, who early in June attacked them with irresistible fury.

On the night of the 23rd he seized two heights on the right, and formed there two batteries, which swept the Prussian front and rear. He then stormed their intrenchments at the head of 28,000 men, and drove out the enemy, who formed solid squares to repel his cavalry, which pushed them in disordered masses on the Balkenhayn-road. Their squares were broken, and 4000 men were slain. Among them fell the gallant baron, pierced by two mortal wounds. Seven thousand men surrendered, and Glatz, the most important place between Silesia and Bohemia, as it stands in a narrow vale between two lofty hills, was the immediate consequence of the victory. The Gersdorff hussars and dragoons of Platen cut a passage to Breslau with 1500 of the infantry.

Pushing on, the victorious Loudon prepared to besiege that place, where he expected to be joined by the Russians, and thus enabled to complete the conquest of Silesia, the great object of the war. Encouraged by his success at Glatz, he assailed the Silesian capital, and bombarded it with great success on the 30th July. He set forth in his summons to surrender, "that his forces consisted of fifty battalions and eighty squadrons, most of which were within three days' march; that it was in vain for the governor to expect succour from the King of Prussia, now on the other side of the Elbe, and still more vain to look for relief from Prince Henry, who must sink beneath the Russian sword if he attempted to obstruct its progress; and that the inhabitants must resign all hope of terms or quarter if they ventured to defend the town."

The reply of the governor was firm and noble. Loudon

showered bombs and red-hot balls on one side, while attempting an assault on the other.

Prince Henry, one of the most accomplished of the Prussian generals, advanced to its relief by a forced march of one hundred and twenty English miles in five days, resolving to give the Baron battle before the Russians joined him; and on his approach Loudon prudently raised the siege and retired, though he still kept Neiss and Schwiednitz under blockade. The King of Prussia by this time was on his memorable march to prevent the junction of the Russian and Imperial armies in Silesia ; and with this intention had encamped at Lignitz, where, while encompassed by three hostile columns, he gave battle to Loudon. Attacking him at three o'clock, A.M., on the 15th August, near Lignitz, he repulsed him with loss before Daun could come to his assistance ; and further secured his own rear effectually by a strong *corps de reserve* and park of artillery posted on the heights of Paffendorf.

Frederick obtained some information as to Loudon's disposition of force from an Austrian officer, an Irishman, who had deserted. "He was so intoxicated," says Frederick, in his own *History*, "that he could only stammer out he had a secret to reveal. After making him swallow some basins of warm water to relieve his stomach, he affirmed what had been divined, that Daun meant to attack the king that very day." Loudon made incredible efforts, on foot and on horseback, to maintain his ground. After receiving five consecutive charges of five lines of five battalions each, the confusion of the Austrians became general, and they fled towards Binowitz. The battle of Paffendorf cost Loudon ten thousand men ; the field, which sloped like a glacis, was occupied by the Prussians, who took two generals, eighty other officers, six thousand soldiers, twenty-three pairs of colours, and eighty-two pieces of cannon !

We next find the indefatigable Loudon in position at Hohenfriedberg, a small Silesian town, which he had to abandon on the night of the 11th September, finding his flank turned by the Prussian vanguard on their gaining the pass of Kauder. On the 18th he occupied the defiles of Giersdorf, and that night, by a cannonade prevented the enemy from advancing to Wahlenburg. He next laid siege to the strong and important fortress of Kosel, seventy-three miles distant from Breslau, and threatened the whole province with subjection.

The Russians and Austrians now effected their junction again, and together made themselves masters of Berlin on the 4th October; after which the affairs of the great Frederick seemed desperate; but he resolved to retrieve them by some decided effort. Crossing the Elbe, he hurried into Saxony, followed by Daun with eighty thousand men, whom he routed at Toorgau on the 23rd November. By this he recovered all that he had previously lost; the Russians retired into Poland, the Austrians evacuated the desolated province of Silesia, and the Swedes took refuge on the shores of the Baltic. By the defeat of Daun, Loudon was compelled abruptly to raise the siege of Kosel and retire out of the province.

In 1760, Bohemia, Silesia, and other parts of Germany presented a lamentable aspect. Cities were empty, villages desolate, and castles in ruins. The fields were ravaged and destroyed, till a famine was at hand; wives and children had perished; husbands and fathers had been driven into the ranks of adverse armies, to fight for bare subsistence rather than their blackened hearths and rifled homes; trade was neglected; the seats of learning abandoned; the land untilled: and all this curse had fallen upon the people by the mad ambition of their kings and princes.

During the winter Loudon's activity prevented Frederick from obtaining recruits, provisions, or forage from the principalities or circles of Neiss, Groskau, Frankestien, Strehlen, Neustadt, and Oppelen.

In January he repaired to Vienna, to assist at the councils of war and arrange the plan of the new campaign.

In this year (1761) he was destined by the Court of Vienna to undertake a war of sieges in Silesia, where he was to be supported by the Russians; and on the 10th of

March he resumed the command of his division. In April he wrote to the Empress stating that since the 18th instant he had revoked the truce made with General Goltze, and intended to fix his head-quarters at Caretau, a league from Glatz. In May he patrolled the country about Lignitz and Jauer to levy contributions, and eighty-seven of his men were cut off by General Tatter at Rostock. About the 12th May, on Frederick's approach, he retired into Bohemia, by the way of Gattesberg, before eighty thousand men, and on the 6th of June established his head-quarters at Hauptmonsdorf.

Frederick was resolved to act solely on the defensive, being tired of the war.

On the 21st July he was encamped at Pulzen, when Loudon, who occupied the opposite mountains, descended by the defile of Steinkunzerdorf, feigning to attack the fortress of Neiss. This drew Frederick out; and they engaged on the heights of Munsterberg, where a warm cannonade ensued. On the 23rd Loudon encamped at Ober Pomsdorf; "and either from native restlessness, or a habit of commanding detachments, in eight days he changed his position six times; for which no satisfactory reason could be given." On the 17th July the whole of the Prussian army received the communion, and sixty rounds of ball per man.

Loudon's force, after he was joined by General Brettano from Saxony, amounted to eighty thousand men. He was also joined by a column of Russians under General Czernicheff. He received a letter from Maria Theresa, wherein she somewhat needlessly " gave him full power to give or decline battle as he chose; and this power was to extend to all his military operations in general." In the first days of August he transmitted to her a letter which he had received from Frederick of Prussia, and written by his own hand, in which he offered him great sums " if he would agree to act *faintly* in this campaign." Loudon at the same time sent the Empress a copy of his answer, importing, "that being accountable to God and to his sovereign for his conduct, all the treasures of the earth should not tempt him from his duty to either; and that he begged his Prussian Majesty would make him no more proposals so repugnant to his duty, and so injurious to his honour."

On the 15th August he detached forty-three squadrons of horse to join a Russian column which had passed the Oder; but Frederick met them on their march near Parchwitz, and defeated them, taking all their colours and cannon. These troops were horse grenadiers—the flower of the Austrian cavalry. The march of Loudon to form a junction "with the Russians," say the London papers for 10th September, 1761, " is alone sufficient to raise his reputation as a general as high as even a victory could have done. He had marched seven hours before the enemy had the least suspicion of his design, and had a conference with Marshal Butterlin near this place (Lignitz); on his return from which he narrowly escaped being taken prisoner by the fleetness of his horse, his escort being attacked smartly by a strong detachment of Prussians." The allies afterwards separated; and the Hamburg journals asserted that it "was owing to a pique and jealously between Laudohn and Butturlin about the command, and the open antipathy of their respective troops to each other."

After a long series of marches, manœuvres, and feigned attacks, in which he had completely the better of the great Frederick, Loudon suddenly appeared before Schwiednitz, the ancient and fortified capital of a principality situated among the hills of Lower Silesia. Its walls were manned by a brave Prussian garrison; but, to cut off all succour, Loudon posted twenty battalions on the heights of Kunzendorf, which are so steep that they cannot be taken from any troops who possess them.

Frederick's army, consisting of sixty-six battalions, one hundred and forty-three squadrons, and four hundred and six pieces of cannon, encamped at Bunzelwitz, in a place surrounded by chevaux-de-frize, abattis, mines, and palisades. Loudon made a partial attack upon this formidable post; but, pushing on, he resolved to take Schwiednitz by surprise. Previous to the advance, says an officer of his army, in one of his letters, "his Excellency our general having assembled upon the Limelberg, the troops destined to scale the walls of Schwiednitz harangued them there, and promised them a reward of one hundred thousand florins if the place was taken without pillage.

"'No, no!' exclaimed the Walloon grenadiers; 'lead us on, and we will follow to glory; but we will take no money from you, our father Loudon!'

"Then the Count de Wallace, colonel of the regiment of Loudon Fusiliers, after being twice repulsed by two battalions of the brave regiment of Treskow, said to his soldiers,—

"'I must carry this fort or die! I have promised it to Loudon; *remember that our regiment bears his name—it must conquer or perish!*'

"This short speech produced a surprising effect. An entire battalion sprung furiously into the ditch. The officers themselves fixed the scaling-ladders, and were the first that mounted. M. de Wallace had the glory of forcing the most difficult point of attack, and taking prisoners two battalions, who made the most courageous defence."*

Twenty battalions had been distributed to the four points of attack. One column advanced to the Breslau gate, a second on the Strigau gate, a third to the fort of Bockendorf, and a fourth on the redoubt of Eau. On the 1st October, at three in the morning, favoured by a dense fog, Loudon and Wallace led their soldiers to the assault; and the escalade was made with such rapidity, that the garrison had only time to fire *twelve* cannon shot. Lieutenant-General Zastrow, the governor, who had been at a ball, hurried his troops to arms; but the contest was short; a few volleys were exchanged, when a magazine blew up and killed eight hundred Prussians in the fort of Bockendorf. Taking advantage of the confusion, Wallace rushed on, burst open the gates of the town, and with the loss of only six hundred men, Loudon was master of the place before daybreak. Zastrow and three thou-

* Letter from an officer to a friend at Ratisbon, Oct. 25th, 1761.

sand men were taken, with a great store of all the munition of war. This was a severe blow to the pride of Frederick, who was weak enough to attribute the success of Loudon to the treachery of Major Rocca, an Italian prisoner; but an officer named De Beville made a noble defence in the redoubt of Eau.

Loudon garrisoned the town by ten battalions, under General Butler, an Irishman; and after remaining long encamped at Freyburg, in December he sent O'Donnel into Saxony after a body of Prussians, and cantoned his own troops among the mountains, while the Russians wintered in Pomerania.

During the winter of 1761 an epidemic malady made great ravages in the army of Loudon. It was a kind of leprosy, the progress of which was so rapid, that it soon thinned his ranks, and filled the hospitals and cemeteries.

The year 1762 saw a fortunate change in the affairs of Prussia; Peter III., a peaceful prince, succeeded to the Russian throne, and formed an alliance *with* Frederick, who did not fail to profit by it, and retook Schwiednitz, though garrisoned by 9000 men, in spite of the utmost efforts made by Daun and Loudon to prevent him. After this he concluded with Maria Theresa a cessation of hostilities in Saxony and Silesia; and soon after peace was secured to Germany by the treaty of Hubertsbourg, on the 16th of February, 1763.

In the seven campaigns of the *Seven Years' War* seventeen pitched battles had been fought; three sieges had been undertaken and five sustained by Prussia, with innumerable skirmishes. Austria took 40,000 Prussian prisoners, and Prussia took the same number of Austrians. The hospitals were full of maimed and suffering soldiers In each regiment, on an average, only eight officers, and less than 100 men, were alive who had witnessed the commencement of the war. Loudon was the only officer, not born a prince or of an illustrious family, who had risen to such high rank during that sanguinary struggle. He was, moreover, a stranger, *a foreigner*, and a soldier of fortune. At the peace the Empress presented him with the lordship of Klien Betchwar, not far from Kolin. On this he built a strong and beautiful castle, with the revenues which he derived from a barony in Bohemia; and there he retired to enjoy a few years of repose and peace, and to overlook the cultivation and improvement of his estate.

In 1766 the grateful Empress made him Aulic Councillor of War; in 1767 the highest nobles of the Empire received him as one of their members; and in 1769 he was appointed Commandant-General in Moravia.

In 1770 he was present at the interview between the Emperor Joseph and his old antagonist Frederick the Great of Prussia. Dissembling that ungenerous animosity which he had imbibed against the fortunate Loudon, Frederick always addressed him as "M. Velt-Maréschal," though he had not attained that rank in full; and when Loudon, with his natural reserve, was about to seat himself at the foot of the royal table,—

"Sit next to me, M. de Loudon," said his Prussian Majesty; "for, be assured, I love better to see you by my side than *opposite* to me."

At his departure he presented the baron with two horses, the finest of his stud.

In 1778 Loudon was gazetted to the rank of Field-Marshal, and was placed at the head of an army 50,000 strong, to defend the interests of Austria in the new war which broke out between the great powers of Germany, on the death of Maximilian Joseph, the Elector of Bavaria.

He posted the army of the Emperor behind the Elbe, in strongly fortified positions; and distributed his own corps among the secure posts of the Riechenberg (on the same ground where the Austrians were defeated by the Duke of Brunswick in 1757); of Gabelona, a fortified town which occupies an important pass; of Schlukenau, thirty miles from Dresden, and towards Lusatia; but the main body of his troops he skilfully distributed between Leutmeritz, a well-fortified town; Lowositz, in the same circle, but four miles distant from it; Dux and Töplitz. The King of Prussia took the field with all his force, to prevent the Emperor from co-operating with Loudon, to whom he opposed the column of Prince Henry: and now ensued a campaign full of interest only to those who study brilliant manœuvres and subtle tactics.

Loudon's posts at Schlukenau, Rumberg, and Gabelona were taken by the prince, who forced him to abandon Aussig and Dux, with the fortifications and magazine at Leutmeritz, and, indeed, all the left bank of the Elbe; but falling back on the Iser, he skilfully secured its passages by strong detachments. In short, so equal was the distribution of strength, numbers, skill, and discipline, that the war was a mere succession of able movements, but barren of striking events; and after a year of marches and skirmishes, the Emperor relinquished Lower Bavaria, on which he had seized unjustly, and a peace was concluded on the 13th May, 1779, the birthday of the Empress-Queen.

After this Loudon returned to his sequestered castle; and once more, for eight years, resumed the peace and pleasure of a country life.

In 1787, when in his seventy-first year, he was again summoned to the field by the Emperor, to lead the Austrian armies against the Turks; and a series of brilliant captures and encounters realized all that had been hoped from his old valour and experience.

He poured his hosts along the Croatian and the Bosnian frontiers; and in August, 1788, after two fruitless assaults, in one of which 430 of his men were killed and wounded, he received by capitulation the fortress of Dubitzar, on the right bank of the Unna. On the 20th the Turks had attacked his camp, but were repulsed; after which he again ordered an immediate assault; but, as it failed, he ordered the town to be fired, and it burned till the morning of the 24th. He then opened several mines, and by the 25th his sappers were within ten feet of the walls. The Turks then "capitulated to Marshal Loudon, whose principal terms were:—

"That the officers might march out with swords, but their troops were to lay down all arms and surrender as prisoners of war.

"That the women and children might go to Roczaracz,

attended by five Turkish soldiers, for whose return the commandant should be answerable."

Novi-bazar, a Bosnian Sanjak, the capital of a province, with its castle, next fell into his possession; then Gradiska, a strong Turkish fortress which had been erected fifteen years before by French engineers, at the junction of the Virbas with the Saave; then Belgrade, the most important town and fortress on the Austrian frontier of the Turkish empire. Its citadel occupies a commanding position on the summit of a precipitous rock which rises in the centre of the streets and is surrounded by a lofty wall, a triple fosse with flanking towers, and an esplanade 400 paces broad. These works were principally constructed by Benjamin Swinburne, a native of Staffordshire, who had embraced Islamism, adopted the name of Mustapha, and risen to high rank in the Turkish artillery. Led on by Loudon, the Austrians overcame every obstacle, and captured this famous Belgrade.

In that town he found a fine funeral monument of white marble, covered with Turkish inscriptions, arabesqued ornaments, and sculptured garlands of flowers. He had this great sarcophagus carefully taken to pieces and sent to his estate of Hadersdorf, to form a tomb for himself.

In this war of carnage, as it was justly named, for no quarter was given on either side, the Imperialists numbered at first 218,000 bayonets and sabres; but they were soon reduced to half that number by the resistance of the Turks.

Neu-Orchova, a small town and fortress of Wallachia situated on an island on the Danube, was his last capture after he had defeated the Bashaw of Travernick and was repulsed in turn from two practicable breaches; but he reduced it by a regular siege; and with this ended the Turkish war, which he had conducted with glory to Austria and ended with honour to himself.

In 1790 he returned to the army in Moravia.

He was now seventy-four years of age, and his health was failing fast. During the latter part of his life he had been much afflicted with rheumatism, gout, and colic, the fruit of military toil and hardship. All these attacked him regularly every spring and autumn.

On the 26th of June he dined with Prince Lichnowski, at Böhmisch Gratzen, and was seized on that night by a fever, from which he predicted he would never recover, and about the 6th of July he was in a dying state. Observing around his bed many of his old brother officers in tears, he endeavoured to console and reassure them by the calmness of his own demeanour.

"I implore you," said he, "to unite true religion to that high courage which I know you to possess, and to defend your minds from the approaches of atheism. All the success I have had in this world I owe to my confidence in God, as well as the glorious consolation which I now experience, in this awful time, when I am so soon to appear before Him." On the 10th, he requested the sacrament, and begged the Marshals Colloredo and Botta to be present at the reading of his will, and to bear his dying blessing and remembrances to the old officers and soldiers who had served under him. Then perceiving his favourite nephew, Alexander Loudon, weeping at his bedside, he said,—

"Arise—be a man and a Christian—love God and your fellow-creatures."

He lingered on until the 14th of July, when he expired in great agony.

Thus died, in the year 1790, Field-Marshal Baron Loudon, one of the greatest generals of the eighteenth century. "It was but seldom that a smile was seen to unwrinkle his lofty forehead," says a writer of his own time. "He was as little acquainted with the real laugh as Cato. As to his character, he knew how to diversify it wonderfully. Loudon on horseback and at the head of an army appeared to be quite another man, and was indeed a complete contrast to Loudon in the country or the town. His conduct agreed perfectly with what his cold and reserved physiognomy announced, for he spoke but little, and slowly. From his early youth he constantly avoided the society of women; he was uncommonly timid in their company, and was a very good husband. Accustomed to find himself punctually obeyed by thousands in the field, at the least sign indicated by him, he required the same docility of his vassals and servants, and he acted with severity to them—perhaps more than ought to have been used to men who were unaccustomed to military discipline."

As a souvenir of the many perils he had passed through, he carefully preserved at Hadersdorf a musket-ball which had been cut in two on the pommel of his saddle, and also his Croatian sabre, which had been struck from his hand by a bomb, and bent so that no armourer could ever straighten it.

His remains were enclosed in a double coffin, adorned by gorgeous mountings and handles, and were solemnly borne from Böhmisch Gratzen to his estate of Hadersdorf, a small town of Lower Austria, near the Klein-Kamp, and five miles west of Vienna.

In the park he had once selected a spot shaded by many fine trees, under which he had expressed a wish to be buried; but, on his return from the Turkish campaign, he selected another place, and planted it with shrubs and flowers in imitation of a Moslem sepulchre; and this he was wont to term his Turkish Garden, for therein he had reconstructed the marble sarcophagus which had been conveyed from Belgrade.

There he now lies in peace, shaded by some stately old trees and in the centre of a green meadow. His funeral monument, which is one of great magnificence, is securely walled round; and among the sculpture with which the Austrian Government adorned it, there may still be traced the shield *argent*, charged with three escutcheons *sable;* the old heraldic cognizance which the Loudons of that ilk carried on their pennons in the wars of the Scottish kings.

Count O'Reilly,

CHAMBERLAIN OF THE EMPIRE.

WERE we to choose a hero for a military romance, he would be Andrew O'Reilly, who bore the high reputation of being the first cavalry officer in the Austrian service.

This distinguished Irish soldier of fortune, the *last* of the *éleves* of the Lacys and others whose achievements in the third Silesian war and the Turkish campaign have already been recorded, obtained the rank of General in the Austrian army, Chamberlain, and Commander of the Imperial and Military Order of Maria Theresa, with the rank of Colonel Proprietaire of the 3rd Regiment of Light Horse.

He was born in 1740, and was the second son of James O'Reilly, of Ballincough, in the county of Westmeath, and of Barbara, daughter of Thomas Nugent, Esquire, of Dysart (grand-daughter of Thomas, fourth Earl of Westmeath). His brother Hugh was created a Baronet by George III., and subsequently assumed the name of Nugent. His only sister married Lord Talbot de Malahide.

Entering the Imperial service early in life, O'Reilly filled in succession all the military grades save that of Field-Marshal; but of those events in his stirring life which led to his elevation to a coronet, we barely afford a summary. One of the most important incidents in his early career is connected with his marriage; and while it illustrates the manners of the last century, is worthy of notice, for the remnant of old romance and chivalry it displays. He and a brother officer, Count Klebelsberg, uncle of Francis Count de Klebelsberg, who, in 1831, was President of the Government of Lower Austria, were rivals for the hand of the Countess Wuyrlena, a rich and beautiful Bohemian heiress; and aware that *both* could not succeed, they determined to solve the difficulty of selection by a combat *à l'outrance*. The intended duel was, however, reported to the authorities, and both O'Reilly and Klebelsberg were placed under close arrest by the Director General of the High Police; but, resolved to achieve their purpose, they secretly left Vienna, and travelled post together to Poland, and meeting in the neutral territory of Cracow, fought their remarkable combat. The duel lasted long, for both were perfect swordsmen, active, skilful, and wary; but at length O'Reilly ran Klebelsberg through the body, after receiving many dangerous wounds in his own person.

The affections of the countess, with her hand and fortune, were the immediate reward of the soldier of fortune.

Rejoining the army, he served with great brilliance in the war between France and Austria. The forces of the latter were commanded by the Archduke Charles.

On the 14th June, 1800, he fought under General Melas, at the battle of Marengo. "Melas," says M. Thiers, in his *History of the Consulate and Empire*, "placed General O'Reilly on the left, and Generals Kaim and Haddick on the right, to gain the road to Piacenza, the object of so many efforts and the salvation of the Austrian army."

On the 2nd December, 1805, that great day when "the sun of Austerlitz arose," and eighty thousand Frenchmen, flushed by rapid conquests, by the capitulation of Ulm, and the recent capture of Vienna, met the Austro-Russian army in one of the bloodiest battles on record—a battle, which, as General Rapp has it, " was a veritable butchery, where we fought man to man, and so mingled together, that the infantry on either side dared not fire lest they should kill their own men"—the star of Napoleon bore all before it; and the French, though losing thirteen thousand men, totally routed their allied enemies, with the loss of thrice that number, taking all their colours, baggage, ammunition, and one hundred and twenty pieces of cannon. On that terrible day, the political result of which was an almost immediate cessation of hostilities between France and Austria, it was universally admitted that a succession of daring and brilliant charges made by the Light Dragoons of O'Reilly, "alone saved the Austrian army from total annihilation."

The Emperor Alexander declined the overtures of Bonaparte, and renewed the war next year. The field of Eylau gave his Russians a partial revenge; and ere long they reaped the fulness of it amid the flames of Moscow and the slaughter of Smolensko.

On the 12th of May, 1809, O'Reilly, for his services at Austerlitz and elsewhere, was appointed Governor of Vienna, with a powerful garrison; and in a few days after, the Eagles of Napoleon were at its gates. Shut up in the city with the troops, the Archduke Ferdinand resolved to defend it, though the French had already stormed and carried all the suburbs. In vain were flags of truce sent in; the bearers were not only refused admittance, but, despite the orders of O'Reilly, were even maltreated, and in some instances massacred by the people. The bombardment followed, and soon Vienna was wrapped in flames; but the Emperor Napoleon, being informed by O'Reilly that one of the archduchesses had remained in Vienna detained by illness, gave orders to cease firing.

"Strange destiny of Napoleon!" exclaims old General Bourrienne; "this archduchess was Maria Louisa!"—the future Empress of France.

On O'Reilly devolved the difficult and trying task of obtaining honourable terms for the capital of the Empire, from an enemy flushed by victory and the pride of a hundred hard-fought fields. He accordingly deputed the Prince of Dietrechstien, the Burgomaster, and the chief citizens to Napoleon, who inveighed bitterly against the obstinacy of the gallant Archduke Ferdinand, but lauded the coolness, bravery, and great presence of mind of the governor, whom he emphatically terms "*le respectable General O'Reilly*," and accepted all the terms proposed by him; but in the fourteenth clause stipulated that O'Reilly should be the bearer of the treaty to his master, to the end that he should honestly and faithfully lay before him the true position of the now half-conquered Austrian Empire—and this duty O'Reilly ably performed.

He served in the great battle fought near Aspern on the Marchfeld, during the 21st and 22nd of May, between the French under Napoleon, and the Austrians under the Archduke Charles.

In the prince's plan of the attack "to be made upon the hostile army, on its march between Essling and Aspern," it was ordered " that the cavalry brigade under the command of Veesy will be attached to the second column, and the *Regiment O'Reilly* to the third." This regiment consisted of eight squadrons of Light Dragoons, and the column to which it was attached comprised twenty-two battalions.

O'Reilly, with his cavalry, followed the column which marched from Seiring, by the road of Sussenbrunn and Breitenbe. Here O'Reilly, with several troops of Light Horse and Chasseurs formed the advanced guard, which met the enemy's cavalry at three o'clock in the afternoon, near Hirschstettin, while the other columns of the Austrian army drew back upon their position between Esslingen and Aspern, and while Lieutenant-General Hohenzollern ordered up his batteries, and the battle became general on all sides.

In close column of battalions, the line of the third column was advancing with great bravery, when the French cavalry fell upon them, sabre in hand, with such fury, that they were repulsed, and nearly lost their cannon. At this moment the regiments of Zach, Colloredo, Zetwitz, and the second battalion of the legion of the Archduke Charles, led by Lieutenant-General Brady, an Irish officer, " demonstrated with unparalleled fortitude what the fixed determination to conquer or die is capable of effecting against the most impetuous attacks."

The splendid cavalry of France turned both flanks of Brady's column, and penetrating between them, repulsed the Light Horse of O'Reilly, who came up at full speed to succour the soldiers of his countryman. Surrounded, the Regiment O'Reilly were summoned to lay down their arms; but a destructive fire of carbines was the answer to this degrading proposition, and the French cavalry gave way.

The Regiment O'Reilly passed the night on the field of battle, which was lost by the Austrians. The market town of Aspern, on the north side of the Danube, was destroyed, and the loss of the Imperialists was frightful.

After a two days' conflict, there lay on that field the flower of the Austrian army; 87 field-officers, 4199 sub-alterns and privates, 12 generals (including the Prince de Rohan), 663 officers, and 15,651 soldiers were wounded; of these, Field-Marshal Webber, with 8 officers, and 329 men were taken prisoners, with 3 pieces of cannon, 7 powder waggons, 17,000 muskets, and 3000 corslets. The loss of the French was terrible! 7000 men and an immense number of horses were buried on the field; 29,773 wounded men strewed the streets and suburbs of Vienna; hundreds of corpses, gashed and shattered, floated down the rapid Danube and were flung upon its shores, where they lay unburied and decaying, filling the air with pestilence and the place with horror.

In October peace was signed at the camp of Schoenbrunn, and, divorcing the woman who had loved him when he had only his sword and his epaulettes, Napoleon espoused Maria Louisa of Austria; and Prince Charles, who by his accumulated blunders at the battle of Aspern, had thrown away the fortunes of Continental Europe, received from his Imperial conqueror the Grand Riband of the Legion of Honour. O'Reilly came in for a full share of the honours and decorations which were showered upon the Austrian army.

At the general peace of 1814 the Empire, exhausted by a war of five-and-twenty years, reduced her vast military establishments to 58 regiments of the line, 12 battalions of chasseurs, and 5 garrison battalions—in all, 1044 companies of fusiliers, and 116 of grenadiers. The cavalry were reduced to 36 regiments of cuirassiers, light dragoons, hulans and hussars. Of the third regiment of light horse O'Reilly was colonel and proprietor. He was also High Chamberlain of the Empire.

At this time Louis Count Taaffe, a noble of Irish parentage, was Second President of the Austrian High Court of Justice, and General Count O'Donnel was Military Governor of Austrian Lombardy. One of the Emperor's most distinguished officers was General Count Nugent, who in the war of 1847-8 led 30,000 Austrian infantry to succour Marshal Radetzki, who was then opposed to the troops of Charles Albert.* Count Taaffe was a member of the new ministry formed on the 21st of March, in the year of the Austrian revolution; but he retired from office shortly before the appearance of the chartered constitution on the 19th of April.

O'Reilly lived to see Austria affected by the commotions which pervaded Europe after the French Revolution of 1830, when the Duke of Modena and the Archduke of Parma were obliged to quit these states, and a formidable insurrection broke out in the Patrimony of St. Peter—an insurrection to quell which 18,000 Austrian troops were marched towards the frontier; but O'Reilly was too far advanced in years to draw his sword again in the service of the House of Hapsburg. He died in October, 1833, at Vienna, after attaining the patriarchal age of *ninety-two*. He had long survived his countess, and died childless.

* Nugent, a field-marshal in 1858, commanded 25,000 Austrian troops at the funeral of Marshal Radetzki, and acted as chief mourner.

Count O'Connell,

KNIGHT OF ST. LOUIS, AND COLONEL OF THE IRISH BRIGADE.

THE life of this military wanderer presents, in his chequered career, the curious anomaly of a general and his soldiers being received into the service of their native country and native monarch, against whom they had previously fought with a bravery that too often gave the laurels of victory to his enemies.

Count Daniel O'Connell was of the same family as the famous political agitator who bore his name, and he sprang from an old Milesian race who held the rank of Toparchs in their own province. He was the son of Daniel O'Connell of Derrynane, and of Mary, daughter of Duffe O'Donoghue, of Anwys in the county Kerry, Ireland, and was born at Derrynane Abbey, in 1742. At the early age of fifteen, like others whose fortunes I have recorded, he left his native country to seek foreign military service, and in 1757 was appointed a Sub-Lieutenant of the Irish Brigade in the French service, in the battalion known as the Infantry regiment of O'Brien, or Lord Clare, and which bore the title of Clare until its dissolution, thirty-five years after.

In the preceding year war had been declared between France and Britain respecting their mutual territorial claims in North America. The former prepared a vast military armament to carry on the strife; and in the army formed on the 12th July, 1759, to be led by the Maréchal Princes of Condé and Soubise, were the *Irish* and *Scottish* Brigades; and in the former was the Regiment of Clare, with which young O'Connell was serving as a subaltern. From this period, for some time, little is known of him, save that he served throughout the Seven

Years' War, and at its close, for his good conduct, was promoted into a new corps which had recently been embodied.

In 1779, when France espoused the cause of America, and sought to harass the mother country in Europe, O'Connell was engaged in the expedition against Portmahon, which is the principal town in Minorca, situated on a rocky promontory, difficult of access from the landward, and defended by Fort San Philipo, in which there was a resolute garrison. O'Connell, with his new regiment, served under the Duc de Crillon at the siege, and conducted himself with such honour as to be specially noticed. The operations were severe and protracted, but in three years the Spaniards and their allies recaptured the whole island of Minorca, which at the peace of 1763 had been formally ceded to Britain.

In 1782, O'Connell served with the combined French and Spanish armament which blockaded Gibraltar, during that memorable siege which had commenced on the 12th of January in the preceding year. Having shown considerable skill as an engineer at Minorca, he was one of the council-of-war appointed to assist the Chevalier d'Arcon in conducting the grand attempt in which France and Spain had resolved to try their full strength for the capture of that celebrated rock, the key of the Mediterranean; and for this purpose, as already related in the memoir of the Lacys, 40,000 soldiers, with 200 pieces of cannon and 80 mortars, pressed the attack by land, while 47 sail of the line, 10 battering ships, and a multitude of frigates, mounting 1000 guns and having 12,000 chosen soldiers added to their crews, lay before the fortress by sea—and in that fortress, to meet all this warlike preparation, were only 7000 British soldiers!

The French army was commanded by Louis Duc de Crillon-Mahon, the representative of an ancient noble family in the Vaucluse, who had commenced his military career in the Grey musketeers, and served under Marshal Villars in Italy. He had direction of the whole attack; his engineers were the most expert in Europe, and brave volunteers came from all quarters to take part in a siege which attracted the attention and raised the expectation of all Continental Europe.

As a member of the council-of-war, O'Connell repeatedly opposed the plans of the Duc de Crillon and of the Chevalier d'Arcon, and declared their system of attack "worthless;" and the sequel, in the triumph of General Elliot, proved that his observations were correct.

In the grand attack he accepted command of one of the floating batteries.

Ten of these, mounting from ten to twenty-eight guns, had been built under the orders of M. d'Arcon. Their bottoms were of solid timber, their sides were sheathed with wetted cork, and filled with damp sand between the timbers. They had sloping roofs of raw hides and network to receive the bombs, which thus exploded harmlessly over the heads of the besiegers. These floating batteries were exposed during the whole time to that terrible fire of red-hot shot—a suggestion of General Boyd—which ultimately, by firing the great ship of Buenaventura de Moreno, struck the Spaniards with confusion and dismay.

O'Connell had one of his ears torn off by a cannon-ball; and by the explosion of a shell, which by its weight penetrated the roof of skins, he was covered with wounds and bruises of minor importance.

His services, during this futile and disastrous siege, were considered so valuable by the King of France, that, on the recommendation of the Duc de Crillon, he was rewarded with the colonelcy of the Regiment de Salm-Salm; a German corps raised in the principality of that name; but this post he held for a short period, being removed to the regiment of Royal Swedish Infantry.

After this, in 1787, the government of France having resolved that the military economy of their army should undergo a complete revision and remodelling, appointed a military board, consisting of four generals and *one* colonel to prepare reports and recommend alterations where necessary. The colonel chosen was O'Connell, who drew up a system of regimental economy, and a code of tactics, which were afterwards used with brilliant success against himself and his loyal comrades during the first campaigns of the revolution. When the labours of the board ceased, he was appointed to the onerous situation of Inspector-General of Infantry, with the duty of regulating the new uniforms and equipment of the Line, when many alterations and improvements were adopted in 1791.

He was succeeded as colonel of the Swedish regiment by Count Pherson, afterwards one of the principal agents in the escape of Louis XVI. from Paris.

O'Connell now enjoyed the reputation of being one of the most distinguished officers in France.

Besides his very extensive knowledge of mathematics and military strategy, says a French writer, he was well versed in the study of languages; and although Latin and Greek were to him alike familiar, he spoke with equal fluency French, English, Italian, and German. He had conceived a great predilection for the Erse (*gallique*) of the mountains of Kerry, and he was never more happy than when he could converse in this dear old idiom, of which he could so well appreciate the beauties.*

Now came the fatal, the culminating, point of the once splendid monarchy of France—the dark days of the Revolution; of the captivity and death of the weak, but unhappy Louis; of the flight or destruction of his nobles. Before the final catastrophe of the royal execution, a proposal was made by the National Assembly, which deeply interested Count O'Connell and others who had made France the land of their adoption. This was the intended expulsion from her soil of all foreign officers and soldiers who had served King Louis, including Irish, Scots, and Switzers. While this ungenerous measure was being debated, the gallant Duke of Fitzjames, in February, 1791, addressed to Louis XVI. a letter on behalf of the exiles; and this document is so remarkable in its tenor, that I may be pardoned in quoting from it one or two paragraphs. After briefly and modestly stating the services rendered by his father and grandfather to the line of St. Louis, he thus advanced the claims of the Irish in France:—

"Sire, my grandfather came not alone into France! His brave companions are now mine, and the dearest friends

* *Biographie Universelle.*

of my heart! He was accompanied by THIRTY THOUSAND IRISHMEN, who abandoned home, fortune, and honour to follow their unfortunate king. For the descendants of those brave men, whom your ancestors deemed so worthy of protection because they had been faithful to their sovereign, I now entreat the same bounty from the great-grandson of Louis XIV. It is reported that the National Assembly propose disbanding the Irish regiments as foreign troops. The blood they have shed in the cause of France ought to have procured them the right of being denizens of that kingdom, even though their capitulation had not entitled them to that privilege.

"Sire, permit me to lay at your Majesty's feet the ardent wish of the Irish regiments, who are as much attached to France by gratitude as formerly they were to the *House of Stuart* by love and duty. If the Assembly now reject their services, they implore your Majesty's *recommendation* to the prince of your family now reigning in Spain, presuming to assure you that the present will be worthy of being made by a King of France, and of being favourably received by a prince of your royal race.

"Fidelity and valour are their titles to recommendation! Of the former they expect an authentic testimonial from the French nation, as they have never ONCE failed in their duty during a century, and wherever they have fought their valour has been conspicuous in battle.

"Sire, I entreat you to listen to their request; for myself I ask no compensation—for me there is none! The honour of commanding *them* cannot be repaid. It secures my glory, as to lead them against a foe ensures immediate victory!"

But this spirited and touching letter failed to stay the popular clamour against these military strangers in the sequel.

In July the Assembly decreed that the standards of the Irish, German, and Liegoise infantry should be the tricolour, inscribed "Discipline and obedience to the law;" but when the princes, Monsieur of France (or Comte de Provence) and Charles Philippe, the Count d'Artois, fled to Coblentz, the formal defection of several Irish officers hastened the destruction of the old brigade of immortal memory; and with it, after the 10th of August, disappeared the ancient Swiss, German, Italian, Scottish, and Catalonian regiments of the monarchy.

During the crumbling of that monarchy, O'Connell, though in secret communication with the princes at Coblentz, lingered in Paris until the close of 1791, when that strange convention was held at Pilnitz between the Emperor Leopold and the Prussian king, who formed a league to invade France and remodel its government. In a letter from Pavia, dated 6th July, the Emperor had already openly avowed his intentions in this new war, and invited all European powers to co-operate with him. At this crisis the French government proposed to place O'Connell at the head of one of their many armies levied to meet this European combination; but the count, despite the earnest recommendations of Carnot and of his friend the celebrated General Dumouriez, declined; and then, unable to withstand the issue of the suspicions which this refusal excited in Paris after the terrible 10th of August, 1792, when the attack of the Tuileries and massacre of the Swiss took place, he secretly left the city, and repairing to the princes, offered to them his sword and fealty at Coblentz; which, being within the Prussian frontier, became the head-quarters of all those emigrants and Prussian troops destined to form the army of the Prince of Conti, who vainly hoped to restore the line of St. Louis to the throne of his forefathers. His chief aid-de-camp was the Comte de Macarthy, an emigrant officer of distinction, a marshal-de-camp of horse in 1791.

O'Connell, relinquishing his higher claims among the crowd of noble applicants for service, accepted the command of a regiment as colonel, and left nothing undone to improve its discipline and efficiency, for his whole energies and enthusiasm were devoted to the reconstitution of the French monarchy.

The first of the French troops to proffer their loyalty, on this occasion, were the Scottish and Irish soldiers of the old Regiment de Berwick. The depôt of this corps was then quartered at the strong town of Givet, on the frontiers of France, under the command of Sir Charles MacCarthy-Lyragh, who immediately marched his men to Coblentz, and joined the battalion. Sir Charles afterwards passed into the British service, when he was made a Colonel and Governor of Senegal, where in 1824 he fought a battle with the Ashantees, by whom he was slain and beheaded. The loyalty of the Irish brigade met with a warm response from the fugitive princes. "This offer," replied Monsieur to the deputation who came to proffer fealty, "will mitigate the sufferings of the king, who will receive from you with pleasure the same mark of fidelity which James II. received from your ancestors. This double epoch ought for ever to furnish a device for the Regiment de Berwick! It will henceforth be seen upon your colours; every faithful subject will there read his duty, and behold the model he ought to imitate."

"The colours of Berwick," added Charles Philippe the Comte d'Artois, "are, and always will be, in the path to honour, and we will march at their head!"*

The king perished, and then followed the campaign of 1793, a period most disastrous to the emigrants; but amid all the slaughter and merciless butchery, with which the republicans inspired the war—a war, to maintain which, the fiery zeal of Carnot enrolled no less than *fourteen* armies, mustering 1,400,000 men—O'Connell led his battalion with honour to himself and to the cause he served, till all hope was lost, and then with others he fled to England in the beginning of 1794.

Among those condemned by Robespierre's tribunal in that year, were two distinguished officers of the Irish brigade—General O'Moran, who defended Dunkirk against the Duke of York; and John O'Donoghue, General de Brigade in the Army of the Rhine.

At the same time were condemned, M. Murdoch, a Scotsman in the service of the Comte de Montmorin; and W. Newton, an English colonel of the Dragoon Regiment de Liberté, and formerly an officer in the Russian service.

* *Scots' Magazine*, 1791.

In reduced circumstances O'Connell reached London, where he resided for a time in comparative obscurity; and where, for many reasons, his residence was far from being a pleasant one. Still, undiscouraged by the aspect of affairs in France, and by the numerous bloody defeats and massacres sustained by the emigrant troops and other supporters of the Bourbons, he took a warm interest in the attempts meditated in 1794; but fresh conflicts seemed only to fire the zeal of the republicans anew, till the French armies, following their victories, drove their enemies across the Meuse and then beyond the Rhine; after which they penetrated into Holland, revolutionized it, and succeeded in detaching Prussia from its alliance with Britain.

At this epoch O'Connell laid before William Pitt the plan of a new campaign, which so pleased that minister, that he made the count, then in his fifty-second year, an offer of military service under the British government. This he at once accepted, and proposed to form a new brigade to be named *the Irish*, and to be raised principally from remnants of the regiments of Clare, Lally, Dillon, Berwick, &c., emigrant officers, and men who represented the old brigade of King James; but here O'Connell's religion, which was strictly Catholic, prevented him, in those days of intolerance, prior to the Emancipation Act, attaining in the British service a higher rank than Colonel; and this rank he held till the day of his death.

The brigade consisted of six battalions, each of the strength usual on a war establishment; but O'Connell had the mortification to find himself gazetted by the Horse Guards Colonel of the *fourth* regiment instead of the first, to which he was justly entitled, by his previous position and general military character.

His commission was dated 1st October, 1794.*

The list of colonels was as follows:—

1st Regiment—the Duke of Fitzjames.
2nd Regiment—Anthony, Count Walsh de Serrant.

* War-Office Records—communicated

3rd Regiment—Honourable Henry Dillon.
4th Regiment—Count Daniel O'Connell.
5th Regiment—Charles, Viscount Walsh de Serrant.
6th Regiment—James Henry, Count Conway.*

Several of his old friends were appointed to the corps ; among these were Bartholomew, Count O'Mahoney, Colonel, 1st January, 1801 ; John O'Toole, Colonel, 1805 ; and Colonel James O'Moore, who was appointed Major-General in 1801.

This brigade, which was embodied under circumstances so singular, instead of being sent to fight upon the continent of Europe, as O'Connell and his brother emigrants had fondly anticipated, after many changes in its constitution and organization, was ordered to Nova Scotia, to Cape Breton, and to the then pestilential West India Isles. The snows of America and the burning sun of the tropics soon had a fatal effect upon these unfortunate wanderers, and they were nearly all swept away by disease and death.

Of the six regiments, only thirty-four officers of all ranks were alive in 1818, on the Irish half-pay.

On the 25th December, 1797, O'Connell, weary of a service so heartless, and so little conducive to the welfare of the cause he loved so much, retired upon the full-pay of colonel unattached, and returned home.†

In 1802 he profited by the Treaty of Amiens, when peace was negotiated between Great Britain and France, to return to the latter ; but the frail bond of unity was soon broken, and he was comprehended in the harsh decree which seized, as prisoners of war, all British subjects remaining in France.

At the restoration of the Bourbons in 1814 he regained his liberty, and Louis XVIII. restored to him his rank of General, and with it the Colonelcy of a regiment and the pension and Grand Cross of St. Louis, which he enjoyed with his retired full pay as a British Colonel. This was after the decree of the 16th July, by which the whole of the old army was disbanded, and the command conferred

* War-Office Record. † Ibid.

upon Marshal Macdonald, who remodelled a new army from the wreck of Napoleon's veterans.

O'Connell lived in tranquillity and honour, a remnant of other days and of old romantic sympathies, until 1830, when he was again deprived of his French emoluments for his unwavering fidelity to Charles X. and the elder branch of the Bourbons. After this he retired to his château at Meudon, near Blois, where he died, on the 9th of July, 1833, in the ninety-first year of his age, the oldest Colonel of the British army, and the senior general of the French.

Such was the chequered career of one of the last of the brave old Irish Brigade.

Marshal Macdonald.

STEPHEN JAMES JOSEPH MACDONALD, Marshal of France and Duke of Tarentum, was the son of Neil MacEachin Macdonald (a gentleman sprung from the branch of the Clanranald in Uist), who served in France as a lieutenant in the Scottish Regiment of Ogilvie, to which he had been appointed by the recommendation of Prince Charles Edward Stuart, whom he had served bravely and loyally even after the close of his disastrous campaign in Scotland, and whom he had followed into exile after materially contributing to that deliverance which was effected by the celebrated Flora Macdonald. He was one of the hundred and thirty Highlanders who gathered on the shore of Loch nan Uamh after the horrors of Culloden, and embarked with Prince Charles for France.

Neil MacEachin (*i.e.*, the son of Hugh) had been a preceptor in the family of his chief, Clanranald, and being originally designed for the Catholic Church, had been educated at the Scottish College in Paris. He spoke French with great fluency, and to the exiled prince proved a faithful adherent, friend, and solace, in all his wanderings; and when Charles was so ungenerously committed to a dungeon at Vincennes by order of the French government, his captivity was shared alone by the brave islesman from Uist. According to Mr. Chambers, there is every reason to believe that he was the author of a little work entitled *Alexis*, in which he preserved a minute record of the prince's wanderings. and dangers in the Western Isles of Scotland.

His son, the future Marshal of the Empire, was born on the 17th of November, 1765, in the old fortified town of Sedan, in the departement of the Ardennes.

Destining him for the profession of arms, he had him educated with the greatest care, and in his nineteenth year enrolled him as a cadet in the Legion of Maillebois, which was to enter Holland, and second a revolution there—a movement neutralized by the influence of Prussia.

In 1784 young Macdonald was appointed a Sub-lieutenant in Dillon's Regiment, a battalion of the Irish Brigade, which now included in its rank many Scottish emigrants and their descendants; and in this corps he remained a subaltern until the Revolution in 1792, when his colonel, the brave, loyal, and unfortunate Dillon, was murdered at Lisle, where his body was literally torn to pieces by the revolted soldiers and infuriated mob.

Although, like the 4th Hussars and the Regiment of Berwick, Dillon's battalion emigrated entire and joined the fugitive French princes, Macdonald remained in France; *not* because he did not share the loyal sentiments of his comrades, but because he loved the beautiful Mademoiselle Jacob, whose father had joined the popular party against the monarchy. This lady he afterwards married; and the influence of her family led him to embrace, or at least to adopt, the principles of the revolutionists, while he avoided their crimes and excesses.

The new government soon discovered that Macdonald was a bold, active, and intelligent officer, and at once gave him employment. He made the first campaign of the revolutionary war as Staff-major, under de Bournonville, and served afterwards in the same capacity with General Dumourier, acquitting himself so much to the satisfaction of these distinguished leaders, that, on the 1st of March, 1793, he was appointed Colonel of the Regiment de Picardie, the second regiment of the old French line, which was then in garrison at Thionville; and this ancient corps (which was originally raised by Charles IX. in 1562) he commanded in the first campaign in Belgium.

He was sincerely attached to Dumourier; but, on the defection of that general from the Republic, after his fruitless attempts on behalf of the king, his retreat to the camp at Maulde, and the attempt to assassinate him on the 5th April, Macdonald did not accompany him in his flight to the Austrians, but remained with the army, in which he was soon after named a General of Brigade. Under the celebrated Pichegreu he served with this rank in the Army of the North against the combined forces of Britain and Austria, and particularly signalized himself at Werwick and Comines.

The column of Pichegreu consisted of fifty thousand men. It penetrated to Courtrai, which was surrendered by a garrison that found it indefensible. Macdonald was next at the investment of Menin on the Lys, where a formidable resistance was made. The battle before this place lasted from eight a.m., until four in the afternoon, when the Germans, who had advanced to the relief, retired, and left Menin to its fate. A few months after saw all the Austrian Netherlands overrun by the victorious French, and the allies who had come to protect the province retiring in disorder beyond the Meuse. On this retreat the British and Hanoverians were particularly pressed by Macdonald, who followed them into Holland.

At the passage of the Meuse a Scottish officer named Macdonald came to Pichegreu's army with a flag of truce, and during the parley—

"You have," said he, "among you a general of my name; we wish much to take him prisoner."

"Have a care, monsieur," replied a French officer, "that he does not take *you*."

And next day this officer, with a party, was nearly captured by the column of Macdonald.*

The passage of the Waal on the ice, under the heavy batteries of Nimeguen, when leading the right wing of the Army of the North, was one of Macdonald's most brilliant achievements.

* "General Macdonald, who has come forward with so much *éclat* as commander of a French column, is the descendant of a Mr. Macdonald of Argyleshire. His uncle is Mr. Macdonald of Kinlochmoidart. He preserves his clannish affections, and in the campaign of Pichegreu in Flanders and Holland, having command of a brigade which had to press on a British brigade, where he discovered a *namesake*, he supplied his countryman during the memorable retreat with every comfort which a camp could afford."—*Edinburgh Herald,* 10th January, 1799.

After many desultory movements, the discomfited allies had taken up a position beyond this river, which is a branch of the Rhine, and contested the passage with the French during the severe winter of 1794. The stream was a mass of ice, as the frost was unusually intense; thus the sufferings of the soldiers were great.

Resolved to avail themselves of the advantage which these sufferings gave them, the French had made repeated attempts to force the passage of the river. On the night of the 26th December, when an unusual gloom had settled over the frozen stream and snow-clad scenery, Pichegreu, with all his forces, advanced towards the boundary with such rapidity that he lost several cannon and soldiers. Next day he ventured on the ice and the swamps that bordered it, making a general assault upon the posts of the allies. Macdonald, with the right wing, pushed boldly between Fort St. Andre and the walls and batteries of the ancient town of Nimeguen, in which there lay a strong garrison. His orders were "to act as an army of observation, and prevent the British and Germans from supporting the Dutch, as the main attacks were to be made by the left and centre."

The latter, numbering 16,000 bayonets, crossed the Meuse in three columns, near the village of Driel, and invested Fort St. Andre and the fortifications in the Isle of Bommel; while Macdonald achieved with signal success the passage elsewhere, and formed his battalions in position beyond the frozen stream. Taken by surprise, the inert Dutch soldiers in the Bommeler-waard made but a show of resistance. They were driven out by the charged bayonet, and 600 of them were captured.

The French left wing advanced towards Breda with equal success, and stormed the lines between that city and Gertrudenberg in Northern Brabant; forced the entrenchments at Capellan in Gueldreland, and stormed Waspick. In this series of reverses the allied British, Dutch, and Austrians lost one hundred pieces of cannon, and had more than a thousand prisoners taken; while the French securely established themselves far beyond the contested river. Ere long all resistance to their progress ceased.

every fortress, city, and castle submitted to them in succession, till the desperation of his affairs compelled the Stadtholder to seek refuge in Britain, while his allies retreated by the way of Amersfort to cross the Issel, abandoning Holland to its fate, and to the armies of Pichegreu and Macdonald.

For his services in this campaign the latter was now made a General of Division. Every officer under whom he served mentioned him with honour in their reports to the Directory; but while, with that openness which is characteristic of soldiers, his comrades thus rendered every justice and tribute to his worth and bravery, the suspicious representatives of the people, who followed the Army of the North, and thrust their officious counsels upon its generals, occasioned him constant anxiety. Their dislike of his Scottish name was never concealed, and his natural frankness unfortunately laid him but too open to their insidious attacks; till ultimately their animosity was gratified by the Directory *depriving* him of his command. Of this injustice Pichegreu complained bitterly, and said, "My army will soon become disorganized, if thus wantonly deprived of its best officer."

"We have dismissed Macdonald," was the coarse reply of the Deputy St. Just, "because neither his *face* nor his *name* are republican; but we will restore him, Pichegreu, to thee, and with thy head shalt thou answer for him."

This opinion of the Committee of Public Safety so far influenced the Directory, that, until he replaced Championnet in Italy, Macdonald was never entrusted with an independent command. Soon after this mortification in Holland, the convention for a peace between France and Austria was held at Leoben, and on its conclusion he repaired to Cologne, and, quitting the army of the Rhine, joined that of Italy, where the bright star of Napoleon was now in the ascendant. By the nature of his frontier service Macdonald had hitherto little or no correspondence with the future Emperor, who having also imbibed the suspicions of the Directory, was long in discovering the worth or relying on the fidelity of the only Scottish soldier in his service. Macdonald appeared in Italy too late to bear any part in the first events of the campaign of 1797, when the armies of the aggressive republic marched to spread their new political principles throughout the Italian peninsula; but in the following year he was at the invasion of the Papal States, with the terrible Massena and with Berthier, who proclaimed the republic at Rome, on which the Pope fled to Florence. One of the early measures of the French generals was the suppression of the English, Scottish, and Irish colleges, all the effects in which were seized and the students dispersed.

To the Pope they sent a tricoloured cockade and the offer of a pension, to which he made the following reply:—

"I acknowledge no uniform save that with which the Church has adorned me. My life is at your disposal, but my soul is beyond your power. I cannot be ignorant of the hand whence the scourge proceeds which chastises the sheep and afflicts the pastor for the errors of his flock; but I submit to the Divine will. Your pension I need not. A staff and scrip are sufficient for an old man who must pass the remainder of his days in sackcloth and ashes. Rob, pillage, burn as you please, and destroy the monuments of antiquity, *but religion you cannot destroy:* it will, in defiance of your efforts, exist to the end of time!"

Macdonald's Scottish surname was a puzzle to the Italians, who styled him Maldonaldo, Mardona, and every possible variety of the original. After occupying the States of the Church, and leaving Macdonald with his corps to overawe them, the French armies, whose line of march was everywhere marked by flames, plunder, and barbarity, advanced into Naples to expel the old Bourbon king, and erect an affiliated republic on the ruins of his throne. On this service our hero commanded under Championnet. Prior to this he had been charged with the duty of repressing the insurrections which broke out among the Romans, who massacred or assassinated the French soldiers whenever an opportunity of doing so occurred. The most serious of these risings was at Froisinone, a village in the valley of the Apennines. This he suppressed with great severity, and, to strike terror into the peasantry, shot all prisoners taken in arms. The barbarities of the French, during their brief ascendency, are still remembered with horror in Italy. They and their partisans hunted and destroyed the Neapolitan royalists like wild beasts, and made a desert of all Apulia. It was in this province that Ettore Caraffa, Conti di Ruvo, and heir of the Duke of Andria, joined the invaders of his native country, and, after storming and reducing to ashes Andria, a prosperous and populous city in the province of Bari, he was so extolled by the Directory for his generous republicanism, that "when General Broussier carried the town of Trani by storm, Caraffa recommended that it should be burned also—and burned it was, with nearly all that were in it—the wounded and the dead, with those that were living and unhurt. They made, in fact, a hell of all that smiling Adriatic coast long before Cardinal Ruffo had passed the first defile in the Calabrias."

At Froisinone the Roman insurgents murdered the son of the Consul Mathei merely because his father was at the head of the new government. Macdonald offered from fifty to five hundred piastres for the chiefs of the insurrection, dead or alive. He issued a proclamation to the Romans inviting them to obedience and respect for the new authorities put over them, as being the only means of raising the Roman Republic to the rank she should occupy; and he concludes thus: "The great nation wills it so, and its will must be executed.—MACDONALD."

Towards the end of 1798, as Commander-in-chief of the Roman territory, he ordained the Consulate to raise two regiments of horse and a battalion of infantry in each department.

The Court of Naples had now been subverted; under the protection of a British fleet and army, the king retired to Sicily, and a republic was supposed to be quietly established at the extremity of the peninsula. when the brave Calabrese, a race of hardy mountaineers, who were living in wild places in all the simple civilization of three centuries ago, rose in arms, and, uniting with the Apulians from the plains, poured against the French in tumultuary hordes—half robbers and wholly patriots. Then began a war of torture and extermination. These new insurgents demanded a general from their foolish and feeble king; but, instead of a soldier, he sent them a priest—a man of peace to oppose armies led by such men as Championnet, Macdonald, Berthier, and Massena!

This was the celebrated Cardinal Ruffo, a descendant of the ancient princes of Ruffo-Scilla, whose now ruined castle crowns that rock so famed in ancient story, and opposite to the fabled whirlpool upon the Sicilian shore. In a remote corner of Calabria he unfurled the banner of Bourbon, with the cry of " Viva Ferdinand and our Holy Faith !"

This brought to the muster-place thousands, who swore upon their knives, daggers, crosses, and relics, to clear their native land of those lawless Jacobins and infidel republicans who were violating and desecrating everything, whether sacred or profane. The mountain robbers, who knew well the secret passes of that romantic and beautiful country—men who under their own government had subsisted by rapine and slaughter, led the van of the new movement. The cardinal cared little for the morals of his followers. Provided they were stanch, brave, good marksmen, and well armed, he received them all with an apostolical benediction, and left the rest to Providence and gunpowder. He marched at their head direct for Naples, where the French army under Championnet was cantoned; and, as he advanced, his wild and tumultuary army was increased, in every town and valley through which he marched, by sturdy peasants armed with muskets, daggers, and weapons of every description.

The fury with which these irregular hordes, clad in their picturesque costume, their Italian hats, and shaggy zammaras, assailed Championnet at Naples, with the advance of another column under General Mack from another point, forced Macdonald to march with his division, four thousand strong, from Rome, and retire to Ottricoli, a small town on a hill near the Tiber, about thirty-six miles distant. He left a garrison in the Castle of St. Angelo, which was summoned by Mack to surrender. He sent a copy of this document, which was imperious in its tenor, to General Championnet, who empowered Macdonald to reply, which he did in the following terms:—

HEAD-QUARTERS, MONTEROZI, 29th November, 1798.

"The Commander-in-chief, sir, has sufficient confidence in me to recognise as his own the reply which I make to your letter of the 28th November. I well know that he has not given any answer to your letters concerning the evacuation of the forts and strong places; and one of these, we consider the Castle of St. Angelo. The silence of contempt alone was due to your insolent menaces on this subject, and this was the only answer that could be expected consistently with the dignity of the French name. You mention a regard for treaties, and yet you invade the territory of a Republic in alliance with France, and do so without provocation, and without its having given you the least reason for such conduct.

"You have attacked the French troops, who trusted in the most sacred defences—the law of nations and the security of treaties.

"You have shot at our flags of truce which were proceeding from Tivoli to Vicavero, and you have made the French garrison at Rieti prisoners of war.

"You have attacked our troops on the heights of Terni, and yet you do not call that a declaration of war!

"Force alone, sir, constrained us to retire from Rome (and you, sir, know better than any one the truth of what I say), that the conquerors of Europe will avenge such proceedings! At present, I confine myself merely to stating our injuries; the French army will do the rest. I declare to you, sir, that I place our sick, Valville the commissary of war, and the other Frenchmen who have remained at Rome, under the care of all the soldiers whom you command. If a hair of their heads be touched, it shall be a signal for *the death of the whole Neapolitan army!* The French Republican soldiers are not assassins; but the Neapolitan generals, the officers and soldiers who were taken prisoners of war, on the day before yesterday, on the heights of Terni, shall answer with their heads for the safety of my wounded. Your summons to the commander of Fort St. Angelo is of such a nature, that I have made it public, in order to add to the indignation and to the horror which your threats inspire, and which we despise as much as we think there is little to be dreaded from them.

"MACDONALD."

In his position at Civita Castellana, near Ottricoli, he was attacked by Mack with great determination. Championnet, in his despatch, states that the enemy were forty thousand strong, and advanced in five columns. "General Macdonald, surrounded on all sides, gave proof of his great talents. He received the attack with that courage which distinguishes the man of firm character, and by his able dispositions entirely disconcerted the enemy." His advanced guard, under Kellerman, consisted only of three squadrons of the 19th chasseurs à cheval, the first battalion of the 11th regiment, and two pieces of flying artillery. This handful of brave fellows routed Mack's first column, slew four hundred, and took fifteen pieces of cannon, fifty caissons, and two thousand prisoners, while they had but *thirty* killed.

The Italians of De Mert retired to the heights of Calvi, a steep mountain range, where, after a midnight march, during a severe December storm, Macdonald surrounded and attacked them a few days after, and by a flag of truce summoned them to capitulate. To this they made some ridiculous propositions, but he sent the following ultimatum:—

"The column shall surrender prisoners at discretion, or be put to the sword!"

On this they surrendered at once to the number of five thousand, with all their arms, fifteen standards, eight guns, and three hundred horses. Among the prisoners were the Marshal De Mert and Don Carello. After this, he returned to Rome, re-established the Republic, and then taking the route to Capua followed Mack's Neapolitans.

who fled before him. Mack was an Austrian general who had entered the service of Ferdinand of Naples to organize the patriots. For this purpose he had brought with him from Vienna fourteen experienced officers.

On the march to Capua Macdonald's soldiers suffered greatly from the constant rain and storms of snow, by the overflow of the mountain torrents, the destruction of all the bridges, and by the rifles of the armed peasantry, who mercilessly slew every straggler. The bravest men in the Neapolitan army were the mountain banditti; and many of these romantic desperadoes, who led armed bands, received the commission of colonel, and were decorated with knightly orders.

Fra Diavolo, a brigand by profession, was a colonel in the infantry, and cavaliere of San Constantino; the Abate Proni, a ferocious monk of the Abruzzi; Gaetano Mammone, a miller from Sora; and Benedetto Mangone—three outlaws and brigands, covered themselves with distinction in this horrible war against the French; but Benedetto was a veritable monster. "He never spared the life of a Frenchman who fell into his power; and it is said that he butchered with his own hand four hundred Frenchmen and Neapolitan republicans; and that it was his custom to have a human head placed upon the table when he dined, as other people would have a vase of flowers."

In March, 1799, a picquet of sixty Polish soldiers was captured between Capua and Fondi by the Calabrese, who put every one of them to death. In the Campagna Frenchmen were roasted alive by the peasantry, or tied naked to trees and left to be devoured by dogs and wolves. Stragglers were destroyed by every means barbarity could devise.

The King of Naples, who had come from Sicily, fled again; and General Mack, before he was blocked up in Capua, wrote in these terms:—

"Sire, of forty thousand men with whom I entered the Roman territory, only twelve thousand remain; and, of these, many are going over daily to the French."

Macdonald, with Championnet, laid siege to capua.

where Mack made a vigorous resistance and repulsed them; but the attack was renewed with fresh fury; the city was won by assault, and the remains of the Neapolitan army, who had gathered courage from despair, and whom shame for past defeats inspired with a glow of double vengeance, perished under the bayonets of the French. Their bodies choked the bed of the Volturno; and for six leagues from thence the road to Naples was strewed with their dead and dying, till even the conquerors grew tired of slaughter. When Mack yielded himself a prisoner of war to the General of Division, he proffered his sword, a handsome weapon, which had been presented to him by the King of Great Britain in 1795.

Championnet laughed, and returned it to him, saying—
"Keep your sword, M. le General, the laws of the Republic prohibit the use of British manufactures."

At this time the rage of the French army against their peculating commissaries was great, for they had suffered severely by the scarcity of provisions; but Championnet and Macdonald skilfully turned this discontent against the enemy.

"Soldiers," they exclaimed, after the fall of Capua, "your magazines are at Naples!"

"Let us march, then—to Naples lead us!" was the reply, and to the capital the fugitives of Mack's army were pursued. A dreadful slaughter was made among the Lazzaroni, for a fresh struggle ensued at Naples, and every house from which the troops were fired on was burned to the ground, and its inmates bayoneted.

Macdonald had distinguished himself in every engagement with the unfortunate Mack; but now a series of disputes ensued between him and Championnet, who had many troubles to contend with. Irritated by the devastations committed by the Sieur Faitpoult, Commissary of the Directory, the general commanding ordered him to quit Naples, with his horde of plunderers, within twenty-four hours. Faitpoult, instead of obeying, raised the standard of mutiny against Championnet, but was forced to retire.

The coarse reproaches of the Deputy St. Just still

rankled in the memory of Macdonald, who left nothing undone to gain the confidence of the Directory, and persuade the members of it that he respected their authority, while it is but too probable that he despised them in his heart. The Sieur Faitpoult had friends in the Directory; thus the firmness of Championnet in expelling him from Naples was styled mutiny to the Republic, and he was ordered to quit the peninsula, and resign his command to General Macdonald. Poor Championnet was placed under arrest; and, relinquishing his bâton to his more fortunate second in command, had to appear before a court-martial at Turin.

With confidence Macdonald accepted this new position, which was one of great difficulty; for the revolted state of Naples, and, above all, the turbulence and ferocity of the Lazzaroni, were sources of incessant alarm. To travel, or pass from town to town, without an armed escort, was at that time impossible; fighting, skirmishing, solitary assassinations, and wholesale massacres, were of daily occurrence, particularly in the province of Otranto, where the embers of revolt were still fanned by the presence of the brave old Cardinal Ruffo, who appeared at the head of his followers, clad in full pontificals, wearing his scarlet hat, and carrying his pastoral staff surmounted by a cross; and thus attired, in a sacred costume so well calculated to rouse the enthusiasm of Italians to frenzy, he led them to battle. Thus he gave them his benediction before it, and thus he said mass for the souls of those dead braves who died for "Ferdinand and the Holy Faith;" thus attired, at many a siege, he sprinkled the battering guns, like his drums and banners, with holy water, mingling, as it were, the smoke of the censer with the smoke of battle. Though the fiery spirit thus roused was restless and abroad, Macdonald ultimately forced the whole kingdom to submit, and completely mastered the capital, which he governed with firmness and moderation.

His order of the day, issued on the 4th March, 1799, amply details the many dangers which surrounded him, and the wise measures he took to guard against them. He threatened to make the clergy responsible for the violence of the populace; but concluded by declaring his reverence for, and attachment to, religion, and his determination to protect all pastors and magistrates who conformed to the laws of the new republic. Five days after this, being informed that King Ferdinand had an intention of landing again, he published a proclamation, in which he somewhat oddly invited the people of Naples to rise against their native prince, and unite with France. Acting in concert with the Commissioner Abrial, he lowered the taxes levied on the people; and, filled by a just admiration for the memory of Tasso, he saved from destruction the poet's native town, Sorrento, on the southern side of the Gulf of Naples, where an insurrection had taken place. After this, the provisional government made him a rash and pompous offer of forty thousand auxiliaries.

In April, he generously released and sent to Captain Trowbridge, a British officer and eleven seamen, who had been cast ashore at Castellamare, during a tempest. He had treated them with every kindness as his countrymen. They were the crew of a prize, the *Championnet*, privateer.

The entire command of the army in Italy was now bestowed upon General Sherer; and when that officer was defeated between the Lake of Garda and the Adige, on the 26th of March, he sent a despatch to Macdonald, desiring him to form a junction with his troops in northern Italy by forced marches. On hearing of the battle near the Adige, the Neapolitans again rose in arms; and the massacres of the French by wandering bands were again of daily occurrence; but, in spite of every natural and human obstacle, Macdonald effected the junction according to his orders. As his retreat from Naples would have been dangerous without an attempt to overawe the armed masses who hovered on the mountains, he attacked and took Lacava, Castella, and the gloomy little town of Avellino, before his departure. On the 26th May, he was in Tuscany, and united with the divisions detached by General Moreau. There were not wanting those who blamed him for losing time in combining his force with that of Moreau; but those who did so were ignorant of the nature of the country he had to traverse with his trains of artillery and baggage.

"General Macdonald has been here since the 5th instant," says a French letter from Florence. "We deem him the saviour of the French in Italy, and our confidence in him will not be disappointed. His army, which has advanced by forced marches, assembled here yesterday. It is full of ardour, and its zeal, which a few reverses have only fired anew, is a happy presage in our favour."

On the 13th June, he attacked Modena, and in less than two hours dispersed the Austrian division of Count Hohenzollern, which was in position upon the glacis of the place; and two thousand prisoners were taken by his French grenadiers. In an account of this affair, General Sarrazen, who led these grenadiers, mentions that when Macdonald was pressing on with the infantry of the line against the *cavalry*, he said to him—

"Macdonald, I shall remain with my grenadiers, and think you had better do the same."

"Do you not see, M. Sarrazen, that I have them all, as if caught in a mousetrap," replied the commander, joyously; and, when within a hundred paces of the Austrian horse, he required them to surrender.

"We yield," replied an officer, sheathing his sabre and riding confidently forward. Macdonald continued to approach until within pistol-shot of their line, when the treacherous German suddenly exclaimed, while unsheathing his weapon,—

"Draw sabres—charge!"

He threw himself at full speed upon Macdonald, who was far from anticipating a movement so sudden, and, after receiving three sword-cuts on the head, was thrown from his horse covered with blood. This was all done in a moment, and the German officer mingled with his squadron, which instantly took to flight. They were, however, overtaken and captured, and their leader, a youth of eighteen, was slain. Macdonald was at first supposed to be dead, for he lay stunned on the ground, having three deep wounds, with a contusion by the fall from his horse; yet he was in his saddle, and at the head of his column on the 17th, when the advanced guard of the Russians under Suwarrow, forced the French into position on the right bank of the Trebia, so celebrated for the victory of Hannibal over the forces of the consul Sempronius; and there, on this classic ground, ensued one of the bloodiest battles of the Italian campaign.

Macdonald had advanced by Reggio and Modena, to effect a junction with the army of Moreau, or to relieve Mantua; but being without pontoons, he found the passage of the Po impossible, as that river was swollen by recent rains, and, moreover, was defended by General Kray, with 10,000 irregulars, and twice that number of armed peasantry. On the 17th, his advanced guard was at Placentia; next day, he attacked and repulsed General Ott, near San Giovanni; but the advance of the Russians, under Suwarrow, changed the fortune of the field.

General Sarrazen states Macdonald's force at 40,000 strong; M. de Segur gives it at 28,000. On the bank of that stream, the most rapid and impetuous in Cisalpine Gaul, the contest was fierce and desperate; but the daring attempts of Macdonald to cross, at the head of his troops, were repulsed.

"On the 18th and 19th," says a journal of the time, " the battles were very murderous The French formed a square four men deep and fought desperately, till a column of Russians passed the river up to their necks in the water, broke through with the bayonet, and made a dreadful carnage among them. On the whole, the French are supposed to have lost, since the 11th instant, 15,000 men in killed, wounded, and prisoners. Macdonald himself has received two sabre-wounds from a Hungarian hussar. Among the prisoners taken are 4 generals and 700 officers. Our loss consists of 4000 men killed and wounded, and 400 prisoners; but the latter were rescued in the pursuit, and 40 waggons with French wounded were taken at the same time."

The fury of the Russian advance threw Macdonald's centre into confusion. Sabre in hand, he strove to enforce order under a heavy fire of cannon and musketry; but was swept away with the panic-stricken mass of the 5th regiment of light infantry, among whom he became entangled, and who were flying in disorder, abandoning their muskets, knapsacks, canteens, and blankets in their eagerness to escape. By them he was hurried into the current of the Trebia, and narrowly escaped being drowned. This confusion was caused by a brilliant charge of 500 Cossacks, who rushed with their lances in the rest through a cloud of dust. A terrified French chasseur exclaimed,—

"The whole Russian cavalry are upon us—fly!"

Then it was that the 5th gave way, and the centre was broken, but still the flanks fought desperately; and had the division of Moreau been in the field, it must have been won for France; but on that day he was attempting to raise the siege of Tortosa. Three standards were laid at the feet of Suwarrow.

At Trebia, according to M. de Segur, who once served on Macdonald's staff, "during three days of a battle, the most desperate in our annals, twenty-eight thousand French withstood fifty thousand Russians, held the fortunes of the day in balance, and gave vainly to Moreau the time to strike a blow for France. The victory remained finally with Suwarrow; but, in his astonishment, the rude Muscovite exclaimed,—

"One more such success, and we shall lose the Peninsula!"

Meanwhile, Macdonald had been deceived in his expectations; his army was exhausted; he was severely wounded, and when it was necessary that he should retire, a torrent of foes behind opposed his retreat. Beyond this torrent, other foes awaited him. The courage of his soldiers failed; *but* he, calm and serene, encouraged them, saying,—

"Be of good cheer, for nothing is impossible to the brave!"

With the remains of his shattered army he retired towards Tuscany and Bologna; and at Piacenza a great quantity of his ammunition and baggage fell into the hands of his pursuers. In the Directory there were men who now reproached him with having wished to gain a battle alone, or at least without the participation of

Moreau; but it was by the express command of that
general, on whose part he fully expected assistance, that
he attempted to force the passage of the Trebia, and break
the left wing of the Austro-Russian army. Notwithstanding the desperation of his circumstances, he was not
without hopes of making another stand; but, on being
deserted by General Lahoz, a Cisalpiner, and his corps,
which united with twenty thousand insurgents to gall his
flight, Macdonald relinquished all idea of again giving
battle, and continued his retreat towards the mountains of
Genoa, followed by the troops of Generals Ott, Klenau,
Lahoz, and Count Hohenzollern, and by hordes of brigands
and guerillas, who murdered his men on all hands, and
massacred them in the mountain passes.

With a flag of truce, he sent an officer to the Austrian
general Melas, praying that he would treat with mercy
the wounded Frenchmen whom he had been compelled to
abandon in Piacenza.

"The request is needless," replied Melas; "Austrian
soldiers know too well the duties of humanity to require
such advice."

Wounds and fatigue had so severely impaired Macdonald's health, that he was fain to ask Suwarrow's
permission to visit the baths of Pisa. This, the Russian
with chivalry and courtesy granted at once; but, instead
of visiting the celebrated Bagni di Pisa, the general
returned to France, relinquishing the command of his
column, after uniting it to the army of Moreau; and immediately on his arrival in Paris he was entrusted by
Napoleon with the command at Versailles.

By this time the French had abandoned the whole
coast of the Adriatic, and lost their conquests in Naples,
where nothing remained of them but the graves of the
slain.

During the past hostilities the domestic relations of
the Republic had not improved in character or in spirit;
and the feeble condition of the Directory afforded an
admirable path by which the ambition of Napoleon might
lead to a newer and firmer form of government. Returning
hastily from his unsuccessful Egyptian campaign, he had

reached Paris; and entering at once into the schemes of Talleyrand and his friend Sieyes, a military conspiracy was formed to remodel the Republic as a Consulate, of which *he* should be the head. Whatever may have been the motives, or secret ambitions, which led the military chiefs to revolutionize France again, it cannot be denied that she benefited thereby; and the energy with which the essay was made, and the success it had, were a sure guarantee for the decision of future affairs.

Macdonald was in command at Versailles while these plans were maturing, and when Napoleon arrived at the Palace of St. Cloud. Though not actually in the conspiracy, he was in the secret, and knew that opposition to Napoleon would neither be for the interests of France, the army, or himself; thus he took the lead in the matter, and by suddenly closing or dispersing the political club at Versailles, made the inhabitants aware that he, at least, deemed the time had come, " when a just administration should obliterate the horrors of the last few years, and the fatal vacillation of the weak Directory."

On the 18th Brumaire, the attempt was to be made; and Napoleon, accompanied by Macdonald, De Bournouville, and Moreau, inspected in the gardens of the Tuileries ten thousand chosen soldiers on whose faith they could depend, and there Augereau, the future Duke of Castiglione, joined them.

"M. le Général," said he, embracing Napoleon, "you have not called for *me*, but I have come to join you."

" You are welcome," replied Napoleon.

It was a perilous task they had undertaken, to overthrow the political incubus that had pressed so long upon France; and while the startled Directory, who had already discovered the designs of those without, were debating about their own safety, and while Moulins urged that a battalion should be sent to seize Napoleon, the latter suddenly appeared, sword in hand, at the door of the hall, and entered with his grenadiers, three deep, at a time when the projected Consulate was being discussed by some of the Directory with very little chance of success. He decided the matter at once, by ordering his drummers to beat a *pas de charge*, and by dismissing the judges with a promptitude worthy of Cromwell, and with a courage which evinced that, on his part, nothing would be wanting to retain the power he had won.

When an army was formed for the re-conquest of Naples, in 1800, Napoleon offered Macdonald the command of the *corps de reserve*. He did this to testify his pleasure for his adherence to the revolution of the 18th Brumaire; but the general, who felt piqued by the offer of a command so subordinate, in a country where he had before led an army, urged illness and wounds as a reason for remaining in France. The penetration of Napoleon was too keen for the true sentiments of Macdonald to escape him; thus on the 24th of August, in the same year, he was appointed to command the army of Switzerland, which was destined to penetrate into the Tyrol, to second the operations of the army of Italy and favour the columns of Moreau (who was then warring in Germany) by compelling the Austrians to employ at least thirty thousand of their best men among the Tyrolean mountains—the bulwark of the German empire.

Macdonald marched from Bearn in September, with forty thousand men,* towards Helvetia, accompanied by General Matthew Dumas, chief of the staff, a soldier who used his pen better than his sword. His first desire was that a corps of Helvetians should be formed to cooperate with the French against the Austrians; but this request the Swiss government declined; and he soon found his campaign to consist of a series of arduous marches among the mountains, where, as the season advanced and the winter drew on, his soldiers endured every misery that toil, hunger, and cold could inflict.

In the passage of the Alps, when one of his columns, composed of the 80th Regiment, with some cavalry, artillery, sappers, and guides, under Laboissière, attempted to cross the Splugen, in the country of the Grisons, a dreadful avalanche suddenly came thundering down from the mountains to bar their march, and swept forty-two

---

* General Sarrazen says *fifteen* thousand (?)

of the 10th Dragoons, with their horses, over a precipice. His other columns met with equal difficulties. A letter in the Paris papers, dated "Head-quarters, Chicavenna, 7th December, 1800," relates:—

"It was necessary to traverse the Splugen and Mount Carduiet. These mountains, even in July, present all the horrors of winter; judge what they are in December! Threatening and inaccessible rocks, seas of snow on all sides, torrents of avalanches falling with a noise equally terrible. Since our first march, two hundred men, with their horses, have been swallowed up. After unheard-of labour, we succeeded in disengaging all of them except three. There was not the least trace of a road; but by labour and constancy we opened a narrow path, bordered by precipices which the eye could not fathom nor the foot always avoid."

Two-thirds of the pass, which leads towards Como had been traversed, the troops in front, with muskets slung, digging a path for their comrades in the rear, till the column, exhausted by cold and fatigue, began to retire without orders, though the dangers behind—snow, hunger, and avalanches—were the same as those in front. Macdonald galloped towards his sinking soldiers, and his presence had an immediate effect on them. They halted; he entreated and threatened; but they listened in sullen silence.

Then he dismounted, seized a shovel, and proceeded to dig the snow, exclaiming—

"My comrades, I would rather perish in the abyss than stoop to turn my steps on perils such as these!"

"Vive M. le Général!" cried the soldiers of the 80th. Confidence was inspired anew; again the muskets were slung, the shovels resumed, and after three days of labour, danger, and toil, the passage was achieved, and the troops of Macdonald debouched from that terrible gorge, where the frozen precipices seemed to hang from heaven, and where whirlwinds of hail, tempests of snow, with death in its most frightful form, had been encountered.

The resistance he experienced from the Austrian troops was trivial; and on the 7th of January, 1801, he made himself master of the circle and city of Trent; but the armistice concluded at Treviso on the 16th of the same month put an end to the war. After this he remained for some time at Isola, suffering from an illness caused by the fatigues he had undergone at Splugen, and Delmas commanded in the interim.

At the close of the campaign he returned to Paris, where his opposition to some of the arbitrary measures of the First Consul made that haughty personage resolve on politely getting rid of a troublesome mentor, by sending him on a distant mission. He was accordingly dispatched to Denmark, as Minister Plenipotentiary from France to the Court of Christian VII. There he resided for three years, and there he encountered so many disagreeables, as his presence was unwelcome in Copenhagen, that he frequently solicited his recal; but Napoleon was jealous of Moreau, who was Macdonald's chief friend: thus he was only recalled when the First Consul was about to exchange the consular staff for an imperial sceptre.

It was about this time that the famous conspiracy of General Pichegreu and Georges Cadoudal, and their correspondence with the Prince of Condé, were discovered. In that correspondence Moreau was compromised to a dangerous extent; thus his friend Macdonald was received with greater coldness at the Tuileries.

The high indignation which he had the temerity to express after the mock trial and banishment of his brother soldier Moreau, who fled to America, completed the displeasure of the new Emperor, who withdrew all countenance from Macdonald, and, notwithstanding his past services, bravery, and endurance, his name was omitted from the list of marshals of the Empire who were then created.

He retired to the country, inspired by a mortification which he could not repress; and remained in seclusion, unnoticed, during the early part of the new war against Spain and Austria, and until 1809 would seem to have been forgotten; but he had perhaps the consolation of remembering "that he must not fear who thirsts for glory; and although we often find that true merit is eclipsed for a time, we have never known it to be entirely lost; it bursts at last through the clouds which environ it, and appears resplendent in its bright and genuine colours."

These were the words of Fabius Maximus to Emilius when, with Varro, he went to lead the Roman army; and thus the "true merit," the coolness and intrepidity of Macdonald, were destined to shine again, for he was remembered by Napoleon when that monarch became entangled with the Italian and Peninsula wars—when the great armies of Austria pressed him on one hand and the distant hordes of Russia were gathering on the other; then, but not till then, did he seem to remember the brave soldier whom petty quarrels and court intrigues had compelled him to overlook. This was in that year when the perfidy of Napoleon to the royal family of Spain and to the whole Spanish nation excited such indignation, not only at the Court of Vienna, but throughout the whole of Germany and Europe generally.

Macdonald was now offered the command of a division in that corps of the army of Italy led by Prince Eugene Beauharnois, who was then evincing his usual intrepidity, but was experiencing severe checks from the Archduke John of Austria. This offer he at once accepted, for he had grown weary alike of peace and of retirement. He joined Prince Eugene; and from that period was deemed his mentor rather than his second in command.

At the head of the right wing he crossed the Isola on the 14th and 15th of April, 1809, and drove the Austrians from their strong positions at Goritz, capturing eleven of their guns and much munition of war.

These successes led to those at Raab and at Laybach, both of which were the result of Macdonald's combinations and manœuvres; and pushing on vigorously, without leisure or delay, with his division, he joined the grand army of the Emperor before the gates of Vienna.

On the 5th and 6th of July he was at the famous battle of Wagram, where he led two divisions of infantry, some of which were battalions of the Garde Impériale. With these he advanced under a fire, when two hundred pieces of cannon were engaged on both sides, and when the roar of the conflict was the greatest ever heard even by the oldest veteran of these warlike armies. Three-fourths of his column perished under the storm of shot by which it was assailed as he advanced to break the Austrian centre, the task assigned to him by the Emperor.

The fury with which his troops came on was irresistible. He drove back the brigades of the archduke with immense loss, and a total rout of the Austrians ensued, thus terminating a two days' conflict which will ever be remembered in the annals of carnage—for few prisoners were taken on either side, which proved the resolution of both—to conquer or die!

Thirty-six thousand, seven hundred and seventy-three officers and soldiers of both armies lay killed or wounded on the field and round the walls of Vienna; while, as related in the memoir of Count O'Reilly, corpses in every variety of uniform, gashed and bloody, floated in hundreds down the dark waters of the Danube, or were daily thrown upon its shores to feed the wolves or to fester and decay. Such was the field of Wagram, and it was the culminating point in the fortunes of Stephen Macdonald.

Napoleon, though little disposed to view him with favour, when the field was won, sprang from his horse, and embraced him with ardour, exclaiming,—

"Now, Macdonald, we are together for life and death!"

He complimented him before his staff, extolled him in the bulletin, and on the field of battle made him at last a Marshal of the Empire.

Of all the French marshals he was the only one who thus received a bâton in the field, and soon after he was created Duke of Tarentum, from a town of that name in Naples.

"Among all the marshals of France," says the editor of Bourienne's *Memoirs*, "there is not one so pure from every stain on the soldier's character—so daringly honest with Napoleon in his prosperity—so lastingly true to him in his adversity, as this, his only Scottish officer."

Napoleon thus bore honourable testimony to the value of his service at Wagram, the glory of which another marshal sought to appropriate to himself.

"As his majesty commands his army in person," says Napoleon, in a private order, dated Camp of Schœnbrunn, 9th of July, 1809, " to him belongs the exclusive right of assigning the degree of glory which each merits. His majesty owes the success of his arms to the French troops, and not to strangers. Prince Ponte Corvo's order of the day, tending to give false pretensions to troops, at best not above mediocrity, is contrary to truth, to discipline, and to national honour. The corps of the Prince of Ponte Corvo did not remain immovable as iron. It was the first to retreat. His majesty was obliged to cover it by the corps of the Guard and the division commanded by Marshal Macdonald, by the division of heavy cavalry commanded by General Nautsonby, and by a part of the cavalry of the Guard. *To Marshal Macdonald belongs the praise which the Prince of Ponte Corvo arrogates to himself.* His majesty desires that this testimony of his displeasure may serve as an example to every marshal not to attribute to himself the glory which belongs to others."*

After Wagram he commanded in the duchy of Gratz, and maintained in his army a discipline so severe in repressing plunder and outrage, that on his departure at the peace with Austria, before his division began its homeward march for France, the States prayed him to accept an offering of two hundred thousand francs, but he resolutely declined them.

"Messieurs," said he, " I am a soldier—I have done but my duty."

Then the deputies offered him a jewel-box of great value. as a bridal gift for one of his daughters; and to the bearers he made the following reply :—

" Gentlemen, if you believe that you owe me anything, you shall have the means of repaying me amply, by the care you will take of three hundred poor invalid soldiers, whom I shall leave in your city."

* Bourienne.

Napoleon was now in the zenith of his power; his marriage with Maria Louisa—an espousal more politic than honourable—had been celebrated at the close of the year of Wagram; and in the year following, Holland, the Valais, and the Hanse Towns were annexed to France; territories which, with those of Rome, gave to the new empire an augmentation of nearly 5,000,000 of subjects.

The war was now raging in the Peninsula, and there the feeble measures of Augereau in Catalonia made Napoleon resolve to supersede him. The Duke of Tarentum was named his successor, and, as such, he soon restored order among the Catalans. In their mountainous province, more than in any other part of Spain, military talent and energy were required; as the entire population —a brave, resolute, and hardy race—were in arms against the invaders. Augereau's losses in the desultory warfare maintained by the Guerillas were so severe that they more than counterbalanced his success in the sieges he undertook; and these losses were so indicative of mismanagement that they ensured his recal to France. He marched for the frontier laden with the plunder of Barcelona, and of all the officers who formed its escort, General Chabran was the only one—as the Catalan journals remarked—who did *not* pillage the house in which he had been quartered; but returned to the Patron de Caza the silver spoons he had used at table.

At this time rapine was the order of the day in the French army; a hammer and a small saw invariably formed a portion of a soldier's accoutrements, that he might have tools at hand to break open every lock-fast place, when the work of pillage began.

In Catalonia, Macdonald found himself at the head of 17,000 men; in the adjoining province of Aragon, Suchet led 16,000; and the Spanish corps of O'Donnel were the only regular troops opposed to them both.

On Suchet laying siege to Tortosa, a fortified city on the left bank of the Ebro, Macdonald marched with 12,000 men to secure the entrance of a convoy of provisions into Barcelona; and this he achieved in triumph, defeating a vigorous attempt of the Spaniards to intercept it.

O'Donnel, general of the Spaniards, now directed his main efforts to relieve Tortosa, where the Conde de Alacha Miguel Lili, with 7800 brave fellows, who had survived or escaped from the battle of Tudela, made a stout resistance. O'Donnel left nothing undone to impede the operations of the besiegers and raise the blockade; till Macdonald, to distract his attention and favour the operations of Suchet, marched upon Tarragona, a seaport near the mouth of the Francoli. It is picturesquely situated upon a hill, and is surrounded by old Moorish walls, having turrets at intervals. As it is a place of importance, the Spaniards were anxious to preserve it, and pressed Macdonald so severely that he was forced to take up a position in sight of the town, in a plain so near the sea that one of his flanks was exposed to a cannonade from a British frigate. Finding this position untenable, after a sharp encounter, and reaping no other advantage from his march than the plunder of Reus, a wealthy little manufacturing town, he retreated across the plains of Tarragona, harassed on both flanks by the troops of Sarsfield and Ibarrola, who slew 300 of his soldiers, captured 130, and retook most of the pillage found in Reus and elsewhere.

As a central point, from whence he could cover Suchet's operations against Tortosa, and command a space of country capable of supplying the troops with food and forage, Macdonald chose a strong position near Cervera, in sight of the Mediterranean. Finding him secure here, O'Donnel, instead of attacking him, turned the attention of his own troops against the French elsewhere, and cut off several of their small garrisons, until he received a wound which disabled him.

On the 13th December, Macdonald received a welcome reinforcement of ten thousand men; but, notwithstanding, Eroles, Sarsfield, and Campoverde, at the head of the Spanish regiments of the line and Guerillas of Catalonia, fought him successfully in almost every instance. Yet his movements so completely covered the siege of Tortosa that, after five months' delay, Suchet was able to break ground before it, and the Conde Lili surrendered at discretion; for which sentence of death was pronounced against him by the Spanish authorities; and with great solemnity, in the market-place of Tarragona, the head was struck from his *effigy* by the public executioner.

In 1811, Macdonald possessed himself of Figueras, a small Catalonian town situated in a fertile plain, not far from the frontier of France. On an eminence it has a magnificent castle, with bomb-proof towers and undermined approaches. This important strength had been taken by the French three years before; but on the night of the 10th April, 1811, some Catalonians who had been forced into the ranks of a French regiment, finding themselves, by a lucky coincidence, all on guard together, resolved to have their revenge. They opened a sally-port to their countrymen, who entering the castle sword in hand, made the garrison, to the number of four thousand men, prisoners, without a shot being exchanged. On the 19th of the following August, Macdonald, after meeting with a determined resistance from these Catalonians, retook the castle of Figueras, by capitulation, and garrisoned it again for Joseph Bonaparte.

After this recapture, Catalonia seemed to be subjugated to the yoke of France; yet, for some reason unknown, Macdonald was withdrawn from the command of the army there, and it was bestowed upon General Decaen. It is supposed that Napoleon, who disliked that any one should assume the part of monitor or judge of his soldiers, was piqued at the tenor of an obscure passage in Macdonald's report, in which he detailed to Marshal Berthier the recapture of Figueras. It ran thus:—

"*I please myself in rendering justice* to the army, in the hope that the Emperor will view with an eye of favour these brave fellows, entreating your excellency *to cause it to be remarked* to his Majesty that his army in Catalonia is a stranger to the event which has re-united it in this place."

"How happens it," said General Sarrazen, "that Macdonald, who does not want for good sense, should have permitted himself to use such awkward observations?"

In the disastrous invasion of Russia he had command of the 10th Corps, of which the Prussians formed a part. The details of that terrible winter campaign are too well known to all the world to require recapitulation in these memoirs.

The Emperor led his army to Smolensko, on the great road to Moscow, and crossed the Niemann on the 27th of June.

Macdonald crossed the same river, on the same day, at Tilsit, by a bridge of boats, and at the head of his French and Prussians (the Corps d'Yorck) seized Dunabourg, while Kowno, in Lithuania, fell without a struggle, and the great army of the Empire marched through it in splendid order, with all its bands playing and colours flying. How different was the aspect of the few surviving fugitives of that army when they repassed Kowno in December following!

With orders to occupy the line of Riga, and if it was captured, to threaten St. Petersburg, Macdonald marched towards the capital of Livonia, which was occupied by a numerous garrison, whose defensive measures were ably seconded by a British naval force. Napoleon conceived that if the main body of the Russians fell back on St. Petersburg, he would, when following them, be able to effect a junction with the 10th Corps under Macdonald, after which they could push on together; but though the latter burned the suburbs of Riga, his operations against the place were long retarded by the bravery of the besieged. Though not regularly fortified, the town has considerable means of defence, being encircled by an earthen rampart, and having a citadel, while a fortress guards the entrance of the Duna or Dwina.

The project of Napoleon became a failure, when the route pursued by the retreating Russians proved different from the one he anticipated. Thus he was obliged to advance after them to Moscow, while Macdonald remained for a time before Riga, on which he could make no impression, though he fought under its walls a series of bloody conflicts, in futile assaults and repulsing desperate sorties. Suspicion of the faith of his Prussian regiments was not his least source of anxiety. When St. Cyr was alarmed that his flanks might be turned by the Russians from Finland, he wrote an urgent letter to Macdonald requesting him to oppose the march of those troops who were led by Wittgenstien and Steinheil, and whose line of march lay in front of the position before Riga; adding that if he (Macdonald) objected to detach any part of his forces from the blockade, to come and assume command of St. Cyr's division in person, and meet this army from Finland " But Macdonald," adds Count Segur, " did not conceive hmself justified in making so important a movement without express orders. He distrusted Yorck, the Prussian general, whom he suspected of intending to deliver up to the Russians his park of siege artillery. He replied, that to defend it was his first and most indispensable duty, and he declined to quit his station."

Macdonald's suspicions soon proved correct; for on the 13th December, 1812, when in presence of the enemy, he was abandoned by the whole of the Prussians under General Yorck; and was thus compelled to retire, though resisting with indomitable energy the attack of the Russians, who followed him closely, when sword in hand he sought to hew a passage to the rear. By this time all was lost elsewhere.

He survived the perils of that frightful campaign, in which out of 300,000 soldiers, who, in June, passed the Niemann in all the pomp of war and pride of former victories, scarcely 50,000 escaped out of Russia; and of these the greater number had suffered so dreadfully from wounds, hunger and frost, as to be quite unfit for future service.

With 1131 pieces of cannon, there were taken by the Russians 41 generals, 1298 officers, 167,410 sergeants and rank and file. The *rest* were accounted for by the frost and snow, the Cossack lances, the bullet and the sabre, rendering the paths across the whitened wastes of Russia impassable with the bodies of the dying and the dead. Never in all the annals of war were greater sufferings detailed than those endured by the miserable French on their retreat from flaming Moscow.

In 1813, Macdonald commanded a corps in Saxony, where, on the 29th April, he had the satisfaction of routing at Mercebourg the division of General Yorck, composed of the *same* Prussians who had abandoned him at Riga during the previous year; and at Lutzen, where, on the 2nd May, the combined forces of Russia and Prussia met the French in battle, led by the Emperor in person, he attacked the Prussian reserve, and after a long and severe engagement cut it to pieces.

"Now," said he, "I have fully avenged the desertion of General Yorck."

After this Napoleon retired and established his headquarters at Dresden, while Leipzig and Breslau were also occupied by his troops. On being reinforced by the Saxons, whose king he held as a species of hostage for his people, he resolved on attacking the northern allies near Bautzen; and Macdonald hastened with his division across the Spree, to share in the battle which ensued in June. The French triumphed, and their foes had to retreat, but in fine order, into Silesia. Macdonald was despatched by the Emperor in pursuit; but was compelled to fall back, as the roads by which he must have marched were almost inundated.

Nowhere did he attain more distinction than during the horrors of the three days of Leipzig.

This Saxon city, which is situated in a fertile plain, has suffered in many wars, but by none so much as the campaign of 1813. In that year Napoleon made it the general hospital for the sick and wounded of his army; thus its beautiful environs soon became the sad scene of many important events. In several battles and skirmishes the allies had defeated the French during the months of August and September; but Napoleon, who, with his characteristic obstinacy, adhered to Dresden as the centre of his position, found himself out-manœuvred, when eighty miles *in his rear* he heard of Marshal Blucher passing the Black Elster, and that Bernadotte, a prince of his own making, but now in arms against him, had arrived, after a long and circuitous march, near the suburbs of Leipzig, while Schwartzenbourg drew near that city from the south-east.

This was in the month of October.

The French numbered 160,000 bayonets and sabres; the allies 240,000. The outposts were soon engaged on the 16th; the following day was spent in skirmishes and manœuvres till the three allied armies formed a junction, and the stern conflict of the 18th began with all its terrors over an extent of line that covered seven miles. A little village on the French right, where Napoleon had posted himself, was lost and retaken again and again at the bayonet's point under a storm of round and grape shot. Noon arrived, but the battle was still undecided, when all breathless with speed, an officer, with his uniform torn and bloody, rushed towards the Emperor.

"Sire," he exclaimed, "the left wing has given way; the Saxon cavalry and artillery have gone over to the enemy!"

"Silence!" replied Napoleon, sternly; "silence!"

The intelligence was kept secret from the right and centre, and still the strife went on.

By three p.m. came the still more alarming tidings that the Saxon infantry had deserted *en masse* to the allies. This also was kept a secret from the French troops, though the Imperial Guard was ordered to take their place; but the power thus attained by the allies was no longer to be withstood, and a precipitate retreat towards the Rhine became the first thought of the vanquished Emperor.

At nightfall he gave the order to fall back, leaving the environs of Leipzig strewed with dead and dying; but his order was tardily executed, as all the French fugitives with their baggage, cannon, and wounded, on horseback, on foot, or in waggons, were compelled to take *one* road, every other being occupied by the cavalry and horse artillery of the victors; consequently, the sufferings and slaughter of the French, even after the field was lost, became dreadful. Napoleon, before retiring, had ordered that the bridge of the White Elster should be undermined, and directed Macdonald and Prince Joseph Poniatowski, with their divisions, to defend a portion of the suburbs that lay between the advancing enemy and the Borna road; and to leave nothing undone to maintain their post to the last, that the retreat of the army and baggage might be fully covered.

Poniatowski was brave as a lion. He was nephew of Stanislaus Augustus, the last King of Poland, and was animated alike by the purest patriotism and hatred of the Russians; hence he served France against them as the oppressors of his house and native country. He had 2000 Polish infantry and a few horse with him; and seeing the desperation of affairs, as the waggons of wounded, dripping with blood, the heavy artillery with their tumbrils, and the masses of fugitive soldiery exhausted by three days of fighting and excitement, pressed in close ranks across the bridge of the Elster, he drew his sabre and turning to his countrymen—

"Gentlemen," said he, "here we must win or lose our honour!—Forward!" and at the head of a few Polish cuirassiers he made a rush towards the enemy. At that moment the bridge of the Elster was *blown up*, and his retreat cut off for ever!

Macdonald was similarly circumstanced, as his troops had manned and enfiladed the suburbs, where they were firing briskly to keep the foe in check from walls, houses, and hedgerows.

According to the *Moniteur*, it was the intention of Napoleon to have the bridge blown up only at the last moment, and when all his troops had passed the stream. General Dussaussoy had remitted this duty to Colonel Montfort, who, in turn, had remitted it to a corporal and four sappers. On the first appearance of the enemy upon the road, and when the cuirassiers of Poniatowski charged, the startled corporal fired the train, and a dark cloud of dust and stones ascending into the air with a mighty roar, announced the destruction of the bridge; while Macdonald and his whole corps, with eighty pieces of cannon, all their eagles, and several hundred carriages laden with powder, baggage, and wounded men, were on the *wrong* side of the river. A shout of astonishment and dismay arose from those who had crossed; and many an anxious eye was turned back to Leipzig, where the roar of musketry was yet heard in the rear.

The attention of Napoleon, who had left the city by the road which led by the bridge to Lindenau (the direct route for France) was arrested by the explosion, and one of his aides-de-camp exclaimed,

"Sire—sire—they have blown up the bridge of the Elster, and Macdonald's corps is *yet in Leipzig !*"

"At that time," to quote Bourienne, "Napoleon was accused of having given orders for the destruction of the bridge, immediately *after* his own passage, to secure his retreat from the active pursuit of the enemy. The English journals were unanimous on this point, and there were few of the inhabitants of Leipzig who doubted the fact."

If this be true, it was a baseness only equalled by the strangulation of Pichegreu, the torture of Captain Wright in the Temple, and the lonely butchery of the hapless Duc d'Enghien.

Finding all lost, and that his retreat was cut off, Macdonald sheathed his sword, and calling on his soldiers to escape as they best could, threw himself into the river, the waters of which were darkening as the night drew on. He swam across, and reached the other side in safety. Poor Poniatowski, though bleeding and severely wounded, imitated his example; but he was pierced by a bullet from one of the enemy's skirmishers, who had now lined the steep bank of the Elster, and opened a murderous fire upon the mass of unfortunate fugitives, the wreck of Macdonald's corps, who were struggling in the stream. In the dark, the unfortunate prince was swept away with his charger and drowned. Five days after, his corpse was found by a fisherman, and interred on the bank of the stream. A granite sarcophagus, surrounded by acacias and weeping-willows, marks the place where he lies.

Colonel Montfort, the corporal, and the four sappers, were delivered over to a court-martial.

Such was the closing episode of that terrible day at Leipzig, the anniversary of the more glorious events of Ulm and of Jena—a day that cost France nearly forty thousand men.

Napoleon continued his retreat to Mayence, with an

army exhausted by toil, crushed by defeat, and savage in spirit, but lacking the stamina to make one more vigorous stand for France, save at Hanau; for French soldiers, more than any other, are the worst to retrieve a disaster.

"The *defensive* system," to quote the *Memoirs* of Marshal Ney, "accords ill with the disposition of the French soldier, at least if it is not to be maintained by successive diversions and excursions; in a word, if you are not constantly occupied in that little warfare, inactivity destroys the force of troops who rest continually on the defensive. They are obliged to be constantly on the alert night and day; while, on the other hand, offensive expeditions wisely combined raise the spirit of the soldier, and prevent him from having time to ponder on the real cause of his dangerous situation. It is in the *offensive* that you find the French soldier inexhaustible in resources. His active disposition and valour in assaults double his power. A general should never hesitate to march with the bayonet against an enemy, if the ground is favourable for the use of that weapon. It is in the *attack*, in fine, that you accustom the French soldier to every species of warfare— alike to brave the enemy's fire, and to leave the field open to the development of his intelligence and courage."

But now the spirit of the French soldiers was almost dead for a time; and so ill was this retreat conducted, that the rear-guard, with 20,000 sick and wounded, fell into the hands of the enemy.

Macdonald was at the battle of Hanau, the last stand made by this discomfited host in Hesse Cassel. There the French were attacked by the Austrians and Bavarians, whom they routed, and then continued retreating, the whole of their cavalry hewing a passage, sword in hand, through the lines of the enemy.

He was now despatched by the Emperor to Cologne, with orders to organize a new army. These instructions he found the impossibility of fulfilling, so he abandoned the Rhine, along the banks of which the bayonets of the allies were glittering everywhere, and falling back into the interior of ancient France, with the war-worn veterans of his shattered column, he formed the left wing of the retreating army; and at its head, during the campaign of 1814, he gave more than one severe repulse to the Prussians, who were pressing towards Paris under Marshal Blucher. These encounters were chiefly on the banks of the Marne, and especially at Nangis, in the north of France, where he fought a severe action with the allies on the 17th of February; but these struggles and all the valour of the French Imperialists were vain, for ere long the capital was taken; then Germany found itself freed from oppression; Holland rang with acclamations on the downfall of Napoleon; and Wellington had halted in his long career of victory, on the banks of the Garonne, and by the hill of Toulouse.

Macdonald adhered to the fallen Emperor—the child of Destiny—and was with him in the old palace of Fontainebleau at the time of his abdication from the most splendid of European thrones. Hope had fled. His army was dispersed and crumbling to pieces; its great officers and leaders had abandoned him; and such is the instability of human affairs, that the people of whose blood he had been so lavish—the people to whom he had been a demigod—were turning with ardour to another monarch, and welcomed the foemen against whom they had struggled for more than twenty years of war and carnage that were without parallel.

"The wreck of the army assembled at Fontainebleau," says General Bourienne, "the remains of a million of men levied in fifteen months—comprising the corps of Marshals Oudinot, Ney, Macdonald, and General Gerard—did not exceed twenty-five thousand."

Various interviews that took place between Napoleon and the Duke of Tarentum about this time are carefully detailed by this gossiping old soldier, in the supplement to the *Biographie Universelle*, and other memoirs.

Macdonald with his corps had marched in with all speed from Montereau, on receipt of an order from the Emperor, that he meant to march on Paris—a resolution that filled his officers with consternation. On the marshal's arrival at the palace, the generals waited on him in a body, to request that he would place before the Emperor, the rashness and desperation of attempting to recapture Paris from the allies.

"Messieurs," said he, "in the present juncture, such advice might displease his Majesty—leave the matter to me."

As soon as he presented himself before Napoleon—

"Well, marshal," said he, "how do things go?"

"Very ill, sire."

"What! Very ill? How is your division disposed?"

"It is completely discouraged, sire; recent events at Paris have spread consternation through its ranks."

"Think you," asked the Emperor, "it will join with me in a movement upon Paris?"

"Trust not to that, sire," was the desponding answer; "should I give such an order, I should hazard being disobeyed."

"But what are we to do?" said the Emperor, passionately. "I cannot remain as I am! I shall march against Paris; I will punish these inconstant Parisians, and the folly of the senate! Woe to the government they have plastered up waiting the return of their Bourbons. To-morrow I shall place myself at the head of my Old Guard, and to-morrow we shall be in the Tuileries!"

"Sire," urged Macdonald, "are you ignorant that a provisional government has been established?"

"I know it."

"Then, sire, read this—a letter from Marshal Bournonville, announcing the sentence of forfeiture pronounced by the senate, and the resolution of the allied generals not to treat with you."

The countenance of Napoleon became violently contracted. After a pause, he exclaimed, furiously,

"I shall march upon Paris!"

"March upon Paris, sire," reiterated Macdonald; "that design must be renounced, for not a sword will leave its scabbard to follow you."

Finding all indeed over, the bitter subject of his abdication came to be gravely considered, and he handed to the marshal a document, on the 4th April, stating that he was ready to quit the throne of France.

The tender and honourable part acted by Macdonald at this humiliating but memorable time was duly appreciated by the Emperor, who has done him ample justice. With Marshal Ney and the Duke of Vicenza, he was named one of the commissioners sent by Napoleon to the Emperor Alexander.

"Well, Duke of Tarentum," said the former, before the marshal left Fontainebleau, "do you think a regency is the only thing possible?"

"Yes, sire."

"Well," continued Napoleon, who had now recovered his composure; "I charge you with my message to the Emperor Alexander; you will go with Ney instead of Marmont. *I rely on you*, and I hope you have entirely forgotten the circumstances which separated us so long?"

"Oh, sire, I have never once thought of them since 1809."

"I rejoice to hear it," replied Napoleon with emotion; "but marshal—I must now make the acknowledgment—*I was wrong*."

"Sire!" exclaimed Macdonald; the Emperor pressed his hand and faltered out but one word,

"Go."*

Macdonald vehemently urged that a regency should be established in France, in the person of Maria Louisa, in favour of her son, the young King of Rome, and violent altercations took place at the conference.

"Speak not to me, sir," said he to Bournonville, who opposed him; "your conduct has made me forget the friendship of thirty years!" "As for *you*, sir," he added, turning to Dupont, "your behaviour towards the Emperor is not generous. I acknowledge that he may have been unjust to you in the affair of Baylen; but how long has it been the fashion to avenge a personal wrong at the expense of the country?"

"Gentlemen," exclaimed the Duke of Vicenza, "do not forget that you are in the presence of the Emperor of Russia."

The energy with which Macdonald urged the cause of

* *Bourienne.*

Napoleon embarrassed the Emperor of Russia; but neither the eloquence with which he spoke of the military glory of France, and the resolution of himself and his comrades never to abandon the family of one who had led them so often to victory, and with whom they had shared so many perils in war, nor the arguments with which he sought to enforce the regency, were successful; and at midnight on the 6th, he returned in dejection to Fontainebleau, to render, with Ney and Caulaincourt, an account of his mission. Napoleon again exhibited much emotion, and said, with a sigh,

"I know, marshal, all you have done for me—with what warmth you have pleaded the cause of my son. They desire my simple and unconditional abdication? Well—act on my behalf. Go, and again defend my interests and those of my family."

Bourienne and others thus relate their last interview.

"Alas!" said Napoleon, "I am no longer rich enough to recompense your last service, Macdonald; but I can perceive how unwisely I was formerly prejudiced against you. I can also see the designs of those who inspired me with that prejudice."

"Sire," replied the marshal, "I have already had the honour to assure you, that since 1809 I have been yours in life and death!"

"Since I can no longer recompense you as I would wish, I pray you to remember that I shall NEVER forget the faithful service you have rendered me!"

Napoleon then turned to Caulaincourt, saying,

"Duke of Vicenza, bring my sabre."

Caulaincourt brought the weapon, which was one of exquisite workmanship, and placed it in the hands of the Emperor.

"Behold," said he, "a recompence, Macdonald, which, I believe, will give you pleasure. This sabre, which was given to me by Murad Bey, in Egypt, after we had won the battle of Mount Tabor, accept, my friend—a gift which, I believe, will gratify you."

"Sire," replied the marshal, whose voice trembled as he received the sabre from the Emperor; "if ever I have a

NAPOLEON AND MACDONALD.

son, this weapon shall be his noblest heritage; and as such I will guard it with my life."

"Give me your hand, and embrace me!" exclaimed Napoleon; and throwing themselves into each other's arms, they parted in tears—parted never to meet again as friends.*

In obedience to the commands of the fallen Emperor, the marshal, on the day succeeding this impressive farewell, sent in his adhesion to the new government.

"Now," he wrote, "that I am freed from my allegiance to the Emperor Napoleon, I have the honour to announce to you—the provisional government—that I accord with the national wish which recals the dynasty of Bourbon to the throne of France."

On the 6th May, he was named member of the Council of War, and Chevalier of St. Louis. This was an order instituted by Louis XIV. in 1693, and, until the revolution, it remained entirely in possession of the French army. The badge was a gold cross of eight points, hung from a broad crimson ribbon. On the 6th June, he was created a peer of the realm by the surviving descendant of the Capet family, Louis XVIII., who seemed now firmly seated on the throne of France. But this monarch, as soon as order was duly established, was sufficiently rash and unwise to raise doubts about the validity of that law by which, during the stormy days of the republic, the property of the emigrant noblesse had been confiscated and sold. This was an unpleasant topic to broach at a time when Napoleon, like a caged lion, in Elba was watching for the moment to break forth; and Macdonald foresaw that misfortunes might ensue from its discussion; thus, on the 3rd December, 1814, he made an oration which succeeded in tranquillizing the fears of those who had made fortunes amid the anarchy of the republic, or with the growth of the late military empire. He had, moreover, the amiable intention of succouring the aged nobles and chevaliers of St. Louis, who were returning home after twenty-two years

* "The sabre I recognised at once; only since I had last seen it, the following words had been engraved on the blade:—*Sabre worn by the Emperor on the day of the battle of Mount Tabor.*"—*Bourienne*, vol. iv.

of exile, and the families of those whose fidelity to the ancient monarchy had involved them in penury, expatriation, and ruin.

His proposition was to raise twelve millions of annual rents, to be divided in proportions according to the rank and necessities of the claimants. His motion was received by all honourable men with favour, and with lively gratitude by those whose cause he had undertaken. He also advocated the hard case of his old comrades, the veteran soldiers of the Empire, who had lost their pay and pensions by the success of the restoration.

Macdonald won the hearts of all by these proposed measures; but they were brought forward too late in the year to have any practical or beneficial result; for now the eyes of all men were turned towards the little isle of Elba, from whence the *Violet*, as his soldiers named Napoleon, was confidently expected to come with the spring.

About this time, learning that Madame Moreau, the widow of his old friend and brother soldier, had secretly applied in his favour to an influential friend at Naples, to the effect that the revenues of the dukedom of Tarentum, which had been long withheld, should be continued to him, he wrote to the French plenipotentiary at the court of Ferdinand, praying that, with all gratitude to Madame Moreau, there might be no interference in the matter.

"Ferdinand of Naples," said he, with noble spirit, "owes me nothing, for having routed his armies, revolutionized his kingdom, and forced him to seek refuge in Sicily."

"Had I not laid it down as a principle," replied Ferdinand, "not to maintain one of the French endowments, I would assuredly have made an exception in favour of Marshal Macdonald."

On the 1st of March, 1815, the Emperor landed from Elba, and again Europe vibrated with war. The followers of the Bourbons were struck with consternation, and the soldiers to whom Louis XVIII. looked for protection and defence, were naturally enough flocking to the standard of their old leader; and he could turn to none, in his desertion and dismay, save a few officers of high rank, whose spirit of honour made them adhere to their oath of allegiance. The first to whom he addressed himself was Marshal Macdonald. He sent that officer to Lyons, where he arrived on the 8th of March, and found the Comte d'Artois in despair at the sullen and mutinous spirit exhibited by the troops he commanded.

Macdonald, of course, could not be surprised at this conduct in the soldiers, while his own heart led him towards the Emperor, and an *oath* tied him to the throne of the Bourbons; but he ordered a general parade of all the troops, and reviewed them before the prince. Still the same sullenness and the same silence, so unusual in French soldiers during a time of excitement, were apparent in the officers and men. So strong did this feeling become, that the Comte d'Artois (according to the *Voice from St. Helena*) had to withdraw in haste from Lyons, accompanied by *one* solitary dragoon, while Macdonald marched with a regiment of cavalry and two battalions of infantry of the line towards the bridge of the Rhone, which Napoleon was approaching at the head of a few soldiers of the Old Guard and a force increasing every hour by the regiments which deserted as they were despatched against him.

The marshal seized and barricaded the bridge, his soldiers still obeying in silence, till the brass drums of the Emperor were heard ringing on the highway; again the old tricolour was seen, and the eagles that had spread their gilded wings over so many fatal fields were glittering in the sun. The marshal ordered his troops to fix bayonets and load with ball-cartridge.

Where was then the memory of that farewell at Fontainebleau? and where the sword of Murad Bey—the souvenir of Mount Tabor? The marshal was deeply moved at that moment, but he remembered the oath he had sworn to Louis XVIII.

The 4th Hussars, who formed the imperial advanced guard, dashed boldly up to the bridge at full speed, and, brandishing their sabres, shouted their old battle-cry, "*Vive l'Empereur!*"

The effect was electric. The soldiers of Macdonald

could no longer restrain their long-smothered enthusiasm. They, at least, had sworn no fealty to King Louis. With a shout they responded, and, waving their caps and muskets in welcome, tore aside the barricade, and rushed to meet the Emperor, leaving the marshal on horseback, and by the roadside *alone*.

The 4th Hussars wished to seize and deliver him to the Emperor, but, animated by a high sense of chivalry, his own dragoons, who had come with him from Lyons, would by no means permit this, and drew their ranks across the road until he escaped. He returned immediately to Paris, and was desired by Louis XVIII. to command in the army formed under the Duc de Berri. This army proved, however, but a phantom, as the soldiers composing it almost to a man joined the banner of the Emperor.

Left thus alone, Macdonald repaired to the unfortunate king, and on the night of the 20th of March accompanied him on his retreat to Menin; but he again returned to Paris, where pleading his oath of fidelity, sworn by the Emperor's desire to the Bourbons, he declined to serve the imperial cause or become one of the Chamber of Peers under it—a refusal, doubtless, most painful to one who knew that he owed all his rank and honours to Napoleon. Relinquishing all these, as it were, for a time, the marshal duke enrolled himself as a simple grenadier in the National Guard of Paris, and as such did military duty during the usurpation, as it was named; and in the plain uniform of this corps, divested of medals, crosses, and epaulettes, he appeared as a private sentinel before Louis XVIII. on his return to the Tuileries.

On the capitulation of Paris to the allies the remains of Napoleon's army, then encamped beyond the Loire, were placed under the command of Macdonald, whose instructions were to remodel and re-organize the regiments, a difficult and arduous mission, which he accomplished with equal fidelity and address; but the soldiers, dispirited by the defeat at Waterloo, awed into submission by the flight of their idol Napoleon, and the presence of the overwhelming masses of the allies, obeyed him in silence and dejection. All was over now with the Bonapartists. The army of the Empire was broken and scattered, like the marshal dukes who had led it to those glories and conquests of which there remained but the memory now!

In the words of M. Fleury de Chabulon, "Marshal Ney was the first to give the alarm and despair of the safety of his country. Marshal Soult had abjured his command, Mashal Massena, exhausted by victory, had no longer the strength required by circumstances; Marshal Macdonald, deaf to the war-cry of his old companions, left his sword peacefully in its scabbard; Marshal Jourdan was on the Rhine; Marshal Mortier had the gout at Beaumont; Marshal Suchet evinced repugnance and irresolution; and finally, the Marshals Davoust and Grouchy no longer enjoyed the confidence of the army."

Thus the throne that had been so long propped by bayonets and by the splendid chivalry of the Old Guard and of the whole imperial army, had crumbled into dust at last!

For his talent in organizing the army of the Loire Macdonald received the office of Grand Chancellor of the Legion of Honour, succeeding the Abbé de Pradt on the 10th of January, 1816, and on the 3rd of May, in that year, he was appointed Knight Commander of St. Louis.

It is related that, when dining one day at the Tuileries, Charles X. said to him—

"How came it to pass, marshal, that when serving in our Irish regiment of Dillon, which emigrated *with us* entirely, you still remained in France?"

"Sire," he replied, "because I was in love with Mademoiselle Jacob; and I applaud myself for it, since to that girl's love I owe the honour of being this day at table with your Majesty."

"How so?"

"Because, had I emigrated, I might have lived in penury and died of despair; but now, sire, I am a duke and marshal of France."

This reply was so frank and politic, that the king questioned him no more on that subject. He was one of the four marshals who had command of the Royal Guard;

and as one of a commission appointed to inquire into the recruiting of the army, on the 24th of February, 1818, he made an able report upon the oppressive law of conscription, urging upon the French ministry the British system of voluntary enlistment.

Four years after this, by a royal ordinance, he procured the reversion of his rank and titles to the Marquis de Rochedragon, his son-in-law; but this ordinance was useless, as there was no prospect of that noble having any family. Thus, the marshal being anxious to have a male heir—all his children being daughters—he married, in his fifty-eighth year, Mademoiselle de Bourgoing, and from that period led a quiet and retired life. Soon after his marriage he came to Scotland, the land of his forefathers.

Accompanied by his aide-de-camp, Colonel Count Couessin, a nobleman who was descended from an ancient family in Brittany, and was the husband of his niece, Macdonald arrived in Edinburgh about the middle of June, 1825. He remained at an hotel, where he received the cards of all persons of distinction in the vicinity, and was visited by every gentleman in the city who bore his name. He attended mass in the Catholic church of St. Mary, and viewed all the great "sights" of the Scottish metropolis. A Mr. Macdonald Buchanan invited him to a dinner at which Sir Walter Scott, Lord Jeffrey, and Henry Cockburn, were present, with several gentlemen who claimed the marshal as a clansman and relation. "From what I see of you, gentlemen," said he, when returning thanks after his health had been proposed, "and from what I have remarked of this country, I feel more pride than ever in having Scottish blood in my veins."

With great interest he visited the battle-field of Prestonpans, and viewed the ground from the Thorntree, where Colonel Gardiner was slain by the Highlanders. After being *fêted* at Hopeton House, he left Edinburgh for the Highlands, with the intention of visiting every part of the country in which his father had accompanied Prince Charles Edward, during their flight and concealment after Culloden.

On his way north, he visited the field of Bannockburn,

on the 24th of June, the anniversary of the battle; and, after surveying the ground with a soldier's eye, he praised the dispositions and the valour of Robert Bruce. Everywhere he expressed himself " enraptured with the beauty of the country; and above all, of the metropolis of Scotland." He visited the " fair city" of Perth; and accompanied by Macdonald of Staffa, reached Inverness early in July, and went immediately to the field of Culloden, where his father's sword had been drawn for the last of the Stuarts. There he gazed about him long and thoughtfully, surveying the desert moor, which is yet dotted by the green graves of the loyal and brave men who fell there.

He expressed astonishment that the prince, with his slender army of swordsmen, destitute alike of horse and artillery, should have fought twice the number of regular troops on such ground, instead of retiring into the mountains, and harassing the army of Cumberland by a guerilla warfare.

In the ill-fated *Comet* (a steamer which was wrecked a short time after, under distressing circumstances) he left the Highland capital for the wild mountain-shore of Arisaig; and to a large dinner-party on board he made an address expressive of his admiration for the Scottish clans, "than whom," said he, "no people, I think, deserve to be more esteemed for their national character and uniform good conduct." Everywhere he was *fêted* and welcomed with Highland ardour and hospitality, and in many instances by old Highland soldiers and retired officers, who had served against him in Holland, Germany, and Spain.

On his landing under the walls of Armidale Castle in Sleat, on the southern shore of Skye, he was saluted by fifteen pieces of cannon, and was received by a body of his clansmen in full Highland arms and array, under Lord Macdonald.

At the beautiful ruins of Castle Tiorm, in " the country of Clanranald," there was presented to him an aged clansman, named Alaster Macdonald, then in his hundredth year, who had known his father, and remembered the melancholy embarkation of Prince Charles and his fugitive followers, seventy-nine years before. With this old namesake the marshal conversed long, and asked him many questions about the personal appearance, &c., of Prince Charles Edward.

He left the Scottish isles in a government ship, and reached Dublin on the 16th of July; and there he again met Sir Walter Scott, who had arrived in the same city on the previous day.

"Respecting his visit (to Scotland) a singular tradition is preserved in France," says Dr. Memes; "namely, that, on being introduced to Sir Walter Scott, the marshal offered to place at the disposal of the historian authentic and unpublished intelligence on certain important and misrepresented events. Sir Walter declined the proffered aid, with the remark, 'Thank you, marshal; but I prefer taking my materials from popular and current reports.' We relegate this to the class of fables."

After his return to France, he led a life of quiet and retirement, and for nearly twenty-five years his name was rarely heard. He grew rapidly feeble; for his long career of war in almost every country in Europe, and the numerous severe wounds he had received, brought age quickly upon him.

He died in his seventy-fifth year, on the 24th of September, 1840, at his country house near Courcelles. A noble and generous eulogy was pronounced upon him by General Count Philip de Segur, author of a history of Napoleon's Russian expedition, and who in former days had been the aide-de-camp of Macdonald.

The latter was pure in spirit and generous in heart, faithful and benevolent in peace, as he was brave and true in battle. Sarrazen thus describes him:—

"The Duke of Tarentum is of a good size, of a slender make, but robust and pale-faced, with eyes full of fire; his smile is sardonic, his bearing military, and his manners polished. I believe him to be a sincere friend; and although he showed a weakness of character in the council of war which occasioned the loss of the battle of Trebia, we cannot but allow him to have all the firmness necessary to a good general."

It has been already shown that the misfortune on the banks of the Trebia arose from circumstances over which the marshal had no control; but it was a battle that he fought long and gallantly.

He was thrice married; first to Mademoiselle Jacob, one of the most beautiful girls in France, by whom he had two daughters, one of whom married Sylvester Rene, Duke of Massa, in Italy; and the youngest to Alphonse Comte de Perregaux. He married secondly, Madame Joubert, formerly Mademoiselle de Montholon, widow of his comrade the brave General Joubert, who was slain in battle against Suwarrow at Novi, on the 16th of August, 1799. By her the marshal had an only daughter, afterwards the Marchioness de Rochedragon. He married thirdly, Madame de Bourgoing, daughter of the superintendent of the Royal Hospital at St. Denis, and widow of the Ambassador Baron de Bourgoing.*

They had two children : to the joy of the old marshal one of these was a son, whom he named Alexander, and who in October, 1824, was held at the baptismal font by his Majesty Charles X. and Madame the Dauphinesse, and who now inherits the dukedom of Tarentum, and the sabre of Mont Tabor.

Such was the career of Stephen Macdonald, the son of an obscure Scottish fugitive from the field of Culloden, who thus became a Marshal Duke of the Empire, and by his worth and bravery shed a glory on his father's name and on the rank he won.

* *Biographie Universelle*, &c.

Thomas Dalyell,

OF BINNS, GENERAL OF THE SCOTTISH ARMY, AND FIRST COLONEL OF THE SCOTS GREY DRAGOONS.

IN my novel of *The Scottish Cavalier* I have endeavoured to portray the character of this celebrated cavalier officer, with all that military sternness and ferocity of disposition which has generally been attributed to him, but chiefly by his enemies, for the poor man seems never to have found a single friend among the many historians of the Covenant. Thus, notwithstanding his unwavering loyalty to the House of Stuart in the days of its declension, by his extreme severity when that House was in the zenith of its power, he became so unpopular in Scotland, that his memory is still execrated there. He is stigmatized as a "persecutor," as the *Bloody Dalyell*, whose spirit is yet averred to haunt the fields where he routed or slew the children of the Covenant—who had sold himself to the devil; one who was shot-proof, and

"Whose form no darkening shadow traced
Upon the sunny wall;"

one who, when he spat, burned a hole in the earth; one in whose military boots water would boil, and whose spectre, habited in a buff coat and morion, wearing that voluminous white beard for which he was so remarkable, still haunts the house in which he was born and the tomb in which he lies.

Descended from an old baronial family, which was afterwards ennobled by the Earldom of Carnwath, and which acquired its estates about the end of the sixteenth century he was the son of Thomas Dalyell, of the Binns, in West Lothian, and of the Honourable Janet Bruce, a daughter of the first Lord Bruce of Kinloss, the eminent minister of James VI.—a peer whose skill in statecraft, in conjunction with the Earl of Mar, was of great service in securing James's peaceful accession to the English throne in 1603.

Thomas Dalyell, the younger, is said to have been born about the year 1599, during the reign of James VI. in Scotland, at his father's house of Binns, in the parish of Abercorn, Linlithgowshire. The ancient name is Dalyell; but the *z* has since crept in, by the corruption of the letter *y* in old Scottish orthography, and hence the pronunciation of it so puzzling to an English tongue.

Dalyell is first heard of as an officer of those auxiliary Scottish troops sent to Ireland by their native Parliament, at the request of Charles I., to protect the Ulster colonists, and assist in repressing the rebellion under Sir Phelim O'Neil and Macguire, when the dreadful massacre of the English took place.

For this service the Parliament of Scotland levied eight battalions of infantry, of whom two thousand five hundred were Highlanders. Arms for three thousand men were offered to the Irish Protestants, and the castles of Craigmore and Carrickfergus, two small strongholds in the north of Ireland, were supplied with all requisite munitions of war from the magazines at Dumbarton.

The colonels of the eight Scottish regiments which mustered in November, 1641, were as follow:—

Archibald, Earl of Argyle, afterwards executed for treason in 1660.

Sir Duncan Campbell, of Auchinbreck, who was afterwards slain at the battle of Inverlochy.

Sir Mungo Campbell, of Lawers. These three had Highland battalions.

Alexander Lord Forbes, who had served the King of Sweden.

William, Earl of Lothian.

Alexander, Earl of Eglinton.

Lord Sinclair.

The Earl of Lindesay.

Major-General Sir David Leslie, of Pitcairly, was to command the whole. Argyle deputed the leading of his regiment to its lieutenant-colonel, James Wallace, of Auchans; Lord Sinclair's was led by his major, Sir James Turner, the celebrated military memorialist, and that of the Lord Lindesay was led by Major Borthwick.

Thomas Dalyell was an officer in these forces, but to which corps he was attached is not clearly known. He was with the first column of those auxiliaries which, under Major-General Munro—an officer who had long served with distinction in Germany, at the head of Lord Reay's Highlanders—embarked on the 2nd of April, 1642, for Ireland. He had with him three thousand infantry, six hundred cavalry, and a train of guns. Landing in the north of Ireland, he took possession of Carrickfergus, and in it placed a garrison under young Dalyell's command.

The second column sailed for Ireland on the 27th of July under Sir David Leslie, the same general who afterwards commanded the Scottish army at the battle of Dunbar, and for his services was raised to the peerage as Lord Newark.

At Carrickfergus Munro shot thirty Irish prisoners who were accused of committing outrages upon the Protestants. Local tradition has swelled this number to *three thousand*, and adds that they were thrown over certain rocks named the Gobbins.

On the 28th and 29th of April Munro was joined at Carrickfergus by Lord Conway and Colonel Chichester, with eighteen hundred English infantry, five troops of horse, and two of dragoons; and in May he succeeded in effecting a junction with Sir Henry Tichbourne of Beaulieu, when their united forces mustered only two thousand horse and twelve thousand infantry. At this time the pay of an English colonel was 3*l.* a week; of a captain, 2*l.*; of a private, 3*s.* 6*d.* In 1645 more troops were required in Scotland to oppose the Cavaliers on the one hand, and the Irish on the other; thus, on the 27th of February, the Scottish shires and boroughs mustered a great force, whose pay was 6*s.* Scots per day.

It is not improbable that Dalyell was at the battle of Benburb, a village of Tyrone, where, in the spring of 1646, General Munro was defeated by the Irish, and forced to retire, with the loss of three thousand four hundred and twenty-three slain; Lord Montgomerie, twenty-one other officers, a hundred and fifty privates, the Scottish artillery, twenty stand of colours, and fifteen hundred baggage and cavalry horses taken. "In vain did Lord Blaney take pike in hand, and stand in the ranks. Though exposed to the play of Munro's guns and musketry, the Irish infantry charged up hill without firing a shot. They met a gallant resistance; but Blaney and his men held their ground long, till the superior vivacity and freshness of the Irish clansmen bore him down."

In 1648 we still find Dalyell, then a colonel, in command at Carrickfergus, when that little fortress was surprised by General Monk, who took possession of it in the name of the English Parliament, and made both Munro and Dalyell prisoners of war. The former he sent to London.

Henry Guthry, Bishop of Dunkeld, in his Memoirs, asserts that the castle was surrendered to Monk treacherously, by the Earl of Glencairn's regiment, which formed the garrison.

Dalyell was so deeply imbued by the Cavalier loyalty of the period, that about this time, on the death of Charles I., to testify his grief, he made a vow never to shave his beard until he had avenged him; and he cultivated this appendage to his stern visage until it attained great length and volume, for it covered his whole breast and descended below his girdle, as we may still see by the portraits of him. At this period *vow beards*, as they were named, were not unusual with the more resolute and enthusiastic of the Cavaliers. The comb with which Dalyell was wont to dress his hair is still preserved at Binns, "and it gives a vast idea of the extent of beard and of the majestic character of Dalyell in general, being no less than *twelve* inches broad, while the teeth are at least six inches deep."

Dalyell was too enterprising and restless a spirit to

remain long a prisoner; for he soon achieved his liberty, and, on returning to Scotland, was appointed major-general, and held that rank in the army, which consisted of eleven regiments of horse and twenty battalions of infantry, with fourteen field pieces, and which was led by Charles II. into England in 1651. At the head of his brigade he fought bravely at the fatal field of Worcester, where, on the defeat of the Scots, he had the misfortune to be again taken prisoner, and, with other officers and captives of rank, was marched, under a sure guard, to London, and committed to the Tower.

Sir Walter Scott, in his history of Scotland, mentions (but I know not on what authority) that he had previously served in the wars of Montrose.

For his loyalty and service in England his estates were declared, by the dominant party in Scotland, to be forfeited, and his name was specially excluded from the general Act of Indemnity. But Dalyell was not to be withheld even by the guards or gates of the Tower of London, for he soon after effected his escape again—*how* is not recorded; but after lurking somewhere on the Continent, he suddenly made his appearance, in March, 1654, off the northern coast of Scotland, in a small vessel, at a time when the Lowlands were overawed by eighteen of Cromwell's garrisons and by ten thousand regular forces maintained by him, by Argyle, and his adherents.

This was in anticipation of the Restoration, and at a time when the cause of royalty in Britain seemed most desperate. Being joined by a Colonel Blackadder and a slender band of loyalists, he took possession of the castle of Skelko, and, wherever he went, boldly proclaimed the king, and denounced Argyle and Cromwell as rebels and regicides. To stimulate his exertions, he received the following characteristic letter from the young king, Charles II. :—

"TOM DALYELL,

"Though I need say nothing to you by this honest bearer, Captain Mewes, who can tell you all I would have said, yet I am willing to give it to you under my own hand,

that I am very much pleased to hear how constant you
are in your affection to me, and in your endeavours to advance my service. We have all a hard work to do; yet
I doubt not God will carry us through it : and you can
never fear that I will forget the good part you have acted,
which, trust me, shall be rewarded, whenever it shall be
in the power of your affectionate friend,
"CHARLES R." *
"Colen, 30th Dec. 1654."

This attempt of Dalyell's had been made in unison
with the Earl of Glencairn's rash but gallant expedition
to the Highlands, when Glengarry, Lochiel, Struan, and
other chiefs, whose swords were never in the scabbard
when Scotland or her king required them, met in the
wilds of Lochearn, and made an arrangement to rise in
arms and attempt a restoration ; but all hope of success
soon proved desperate, and they dispersed. Dalyell abandoned the castle he had taken, and retired once more to
the Continent, where he obtained from the exiled king a
letter or certificate, in which his bravery, loyalty, and
faith, were warmly extolled and recommended.

Furnished with this, and having nothing else in the
world now but his sword and his stout heart, the penniless cavalier resolved to seek his fortune in foreign wars.
Proceeding to Russia, which has ever formed so ample a
field for Scottish enterprise and valour, he visited the barbarous court of the czar, and applied for military service.

The sovereign then reigning was Alexis Michailowitch,
grandson of the patriarch Fedor Romanoff, who in his fifteenth year had succeeded in 1645 to the title of czar;
and is chiefly remarkable as being the father of Peter the
Great, who raised the Muscovites from the depths of barbarism to a state of comparative civilization.

The letter of Charles II. at once procured for Dalyell
the rank of lieutenant-general in the service of Muscovy;
but great obscurity involves his career in that country,
for even the wars in which he was engaged were little
noted by the rest of Europe.

* Chambers' *Eminent Scotsmen*.

He was now in his fifty-fifth year.

Alexis invited several other Scots to join his army being anxious to introduce a more regular system of discipline into his ranks; but the most eminent of these were General Drummond, Governor of Smolensko, and the two Gordons,* who, under Peter the Great, brought to perfection the standing forces of Russia, which however were so few, that in 1687 they amounted to no more than ten thousand men. An old topographical work, published at the Savoy in London, in 1711, mentions that "the Russians endeavoured to bring their soldiers under better discipline; for which end they made use of a great many Scots and German officers, who instruct them in all the warlike exercises that are practised by other European nations."

At that time—the beginning of the last century—their infantry were armed with a musket, sword, and an axe, which were slung behind; their cavalry were clad in steel morions and cuirasses, and were armed with bows, arrows, iron mouls, sabres, targets, and spears; and in the epoch of Dalyell, their army had a great battle-drum, which was fastened to the backs of four horses abreast, and had eight drummers to beat upon it.

His first active service was against the Poles, with whom Alexis Michailowitch had gone to war in 1653, and from whom he captured Smolensko, which he united to Russia, and Kiow, after committing frightful devastations

---

* Alexander Gordon, of Auchintoul, major-general in the service of the czar, wrote a life of Peter I., which was published at Aberdeen in 1755. "On the 30th November, this year," says this work, "died also General Patrick Gordon, much regretted by the czar and the whole nation. His majesty visited him five times during his illness —was present at the moment he expired, and shut his eyes with his own hands. He was buried also in great state. He was son to John Gordon, Esq., of Achlenchries in the county of Aberdeen, whose grandfather was a son of the family of Haddo, now Earls of Aberdeen." This officer entered the Russian service in the reign of Alexis; and Alexander Gordon joined it in 1693. Both served at the capture of Azof; the younger was at the battle of Narva, and was long a prisoner in the hands of the Swedes. In his old age, he returned to Scotland, and closed his days in peace in his native place.

in Lithuania. The Russian armies then invaded Livonia, stormed Dorpt, Kokenhausen, and other places, but were obliged to retire from before Riga with severe loss.

Dalyell was now raised to the rank of full general, and commanded against the Tartars, and the Turkish armies of Mohammed IV.—the son of the debauched Sultan Ibrahim—against whom Alexis declared war about this time (1654-5); and in these contests, waged at the head of barbarous hordes against hordes equally barbarous, the wanderer must have acquired much of that unyielding sternness, if not ferocity, which characterized his future proceedings in his own country. In these campaigns quarter was never asked nor given; prisoners were shot, beheaded, impaled, or put to death by slow fires, and by every species of torture that Muscovite brutality, or the most refined cruelty of the Oriental mind could suggest; and in this terrible arena of foreign service was schooled the future commander-in-chief of the Scottish troops—the scourge of the Covenanters—he to whom was given full power to crush and to destroy the men who struggled for freedom of religious opinion, for liberty of conscience, and who, as they phrased it, "drew the sword for an oppressed Kirk and broken Covenant."

After eleven years of service in these wild and snow-covered regions, Dalyell requested permission, by desire of Charles II., to return to Scotland. The king had now been restored; Cromwell was in his grave; the Parliament and great officers of state had once more taken upon them the *mis*government of Scotland, and a wicked war was maintained there against the Presbyterian Church, which Lauderdale and his ministry were leaving nothing undone to subvert and to suppress. The Laird of Binns now requested from the czar a certificate of his faithful service in Russia, and a missive to that effect was passed under the great seal of the empire.

"Part of this document," says Chambers, "was conceived in the following terms:—

"That he formerly came hither to serve our great Czarian Majesty: whilst he was with us, he stood against our enemies and fought valiantly. The military men that were under his command, he regulated and disciplined, and himself led them to battle: and he did and performed everything faithfully, as a noble commander. And for his trusty services we were pleased to order the said lieutenant-general to be a general. And now having petitioned us to give him leave to return to his own country, *We*, the great Sovereign and Czarian Majesty, were pleased to order, that the said noble General, Thomas, the son of Thomas Dalyell, should have leave to go to his own country.

"And by this patent of our Czarian Majesty, we do testify of him, that he is a man of virtue and honour, and of great experience in military affairs. And in case he should be willing *again* to serve our Czarian Majesty, he is to let us know of it beforehand, and he shall come into the dominions of our Czarian Majesty, with proper passports. Given at our Court, in the Metropolitan City of Moscow, in the year from the Creation of the World 7173, January 6."*

From Russia he was accompanied by his countryman and old fellow-soldier, who had served with him in Ireland, General Drummond, who was also summoned by Charles II. and obeyed the royal behest. In an Act passed by the Scottish Parliament in 1686, granting this officer the lands of Torwoodie, it is stated "that upon a call from his majesty's royal brother, after his restoration, he left a splendid and honourable employment under the Emperor of Russia to give obedience to his native prince, and since his return to this kingdom, he did good and signal service as major-general, in the defeat of the rebels and suppression of the rebellion raised in 1686."

From a passage in Burnet it would seem, that when the nonjuring exiles at Rotterdam and other Covenanters, were preparing to rise in arms in 1665, and when Charles II. found the necessity of raising more troops, he formally summoned Dalyell home.

"Two gallant officers," continues the Bishop, in the "History of his own Times," "that had served him in the wars, and when these were over had gone with his letters

* This must be the Russian computation of time.

to serve in Muscovy, where one of them, Dalyell, was raised to be a general, and the other was advanced to be a lieutenant-general and Governor of Smolensko, were now, but *not without great difficulty*, sent back by the czar."

There can be little doubt that Dalyell returned to Scotland, with a heart boiling with rancour against those who had sold and destroyed the king; and who had brought so many of his brother soldiers—the Scottish Cavaliers of Montrose, of Hamilton and Munro —and so many of his own kinsmen, to the scaffold. With this sentiment may have been a longing for vengeance upon those who had been so long dominant in the land; who had deprived him of his estate and driven him into exile; and all these bitter sentiments were doubtless fostered by the inborn prejudice of class, religion, education, and the foreign service of years. To all these must be attributed many of the fierce and relentless acts which are related of him by the historians of the Covenant. Many of these dark deeds must, however, be doubted; and many accepted with caution.

After the Restoration, the Parliament of Scotland, which was presided over by Lieutenant-General the Earl of Middleton as High Commissioner, proved a very pliant and complying body. They granted to Charles II. a revenue of 40,000*l.* for life, and rescinded all the acts passed by their wiser predecessors for defining or *restricting* the royal prerogative. The Solemn League and Covenant was pronounced a treasonable and seditious bond; and they passed other acts, by which the Earl of Lauderdale, Secretary of State for Scotland, gradually prepared a way for the abolition of Presbytery, and the restoration of an Episcopal Hierarchy. Alarmed by these measures, the Scottish Kirk sent James Sharpe, one of their most eminent divines, to expostulate with Charles II.; but Sharpe abandoned his colours, and betrayed their cause by accepting the Archbishopric of St. Andrews, while the Marquis of Argyle, James Guthrie, and Johnstone of Warriston, who had conspired with Cromwell, and directly, or indirectly, abetted the sale and execution of Charles I., were consigned to the headsman. Such was the new aspect of affairs, and it made religion and rancour grow side by side in the land.

The rash king next enjoined the Scottish privy council openly to establish Episcopacy, and bishops for the new dioceses were consecrated in England; while Fairfowl, Archbishop of Glasgow, was insane enough to solicit an act of council to eject all recusant ministers, and close their churches until episcopally ordained incumbents could be procured: and by this act, *three hundred and fifty* parishes, about a third of those in the kingdom, were declared to be vacant; and this tyranny was attempted after all the wars, battles, and bloodshed in defence of the Covenant — after all the armies levied and lives lost since 1638, and after the king himself had perished in attempting to subvert the rights of the people! Now, the Scots became justly more than ever inflamed against the cruelty and injustice of their own government.

Finding their churches closed, they met in arms on the green hill sides, and in lonely muirs, to hold what were termed field conventicles, where the oppression they endured for conscience sake, the recollection of their present danger, and the memory of their struggles made in years gone by, together with the grandeur of the solemn scenery by which they were surrounded, filled their hearts with a splendid enthusiasm and with a purity of soul, as, with the sword by their sides, they worshipped God in those wild places, which, since the days of the Romans, had been the best stronghold of their forefathers.

As a ballad (which I quote from memory) has it:—

"Oh, sad and dreary was the lot of Scotland's true ones then,
A famine-stricken remnant with scarce the guise of men;
They burrowed few and lonely mid the chill dark mountain caves,
For those who once had sheltered them were in their martyr-graves.

"A sword had rested on the land! it did not pass away;
Long had they watched and waited; but there dawned no brighter day,
And many had gone back from them, who owned the truth of old,
Because of much iniquity their love was waxen cold."

To crush this growing enthusiasm (which was so great

at times, that an angel was more that once averred to have been seen in mid air, overhanging a conventicle), to suppress these armed religious meetings, and enforce Episcopacy on the people, was now the ungrateful task assigned to Dalyell, to Drummond, and the Scottish standing forces, who were all commanded by officers of high Cavalier principles, and were usually men without much scruple in obeying the orders of the king and council.

Alarmed at the spirit of resistance evinced by the people, and remembering perhaps the fate of his father, Charles II. changed the Scottish ministry. Lauderdale had begun to persuade him that more lenient measures were necessary, and Sharpe, whom the Covenanters received as a Judas, retired from the administration of ecclesiastical affairs; but the change came *too late*, for again the banner which had been displayed so victoriously of old, "for an oppressed Kirk and broken Covenant,' was unfurled, and a body of the Presbyterians rose in arms.

Lieutenant-colonel Sir James Turner, author of a little treatise on the art of war, and of his own Memoirs, from which we may learn that he was a fierce and unscrupulous *sabreur*, was captured with his troops at Ayr, by the Lairds of Corsack and Barscob at the head of a few followers. Another party of soldiers were routed by them at Dalry, and these insurgents began at once their march for Edinburgh, the seat of government, in the autumn of 1666.

They first proposed to put Turner to death; but spared his life on Corsack discovering that his conduct to the people had been much less severe than the written *orders*, which were found on his person, had inculcated.

Dalyell at this crisis commanded the king's troops in the capital. He concentrated all the detachments which were dispersed throughout the adjacent country, and marched westward, by the Glasgow road, to meet those insurgents, whose strength was ever varying, and whose numbers were greatly exaggerated.

"A great many came to the rebels who were called

Whiggs," says Bishop Burnet; at Lanark, in Clydesdale, they held a solemn fast day, in which, after much praying, they renewed the Covenant and set out their manifesto, in which they denied that they rose against the King, but complained of the oppressions under which they groaned; they desired that Episcopacy might be put down, that the Covenant might be set up, their ministers restored to them; and then they promised that they would be, in all other things, *the king's most obedient subjects.*"

Such were the simple and just demands of these poor people. Dalyell followed them closely from place to place with his cavalry, the flower of which were the high-spirited Scottish Life Guards. He published a proclamation, offering pardon to all who within twenty-four hours returned to their own houses; but he threatened with death all who were taken in arms after that brief period. He found the whole country so completely in the interest of the revolters, that he could obtain no intelligence of their number, intention, or movements, save the rumours brought to head quarters by his own parties and horse-patrols; and thus, while *he* was hovering in the west, by a sudden march, they appeared unexpectedly within four miles of Edinburgh.

Their number had considerably augmented during their march; but few men of any influence or property joined them; as most of the Covenanting gentry had been committed to various castles and prisons, on the plausible pretext that it was necessary to insure their neutrality in case of a war with the Dutch.

On reaching the vicinity of the Pentland Hills, they numbered about three thousand horse and foot, ill armed and totally undisciplined.

Colonel James Wallace, of Auchans, a descendant of the Wallaces of Dundonald, a brave officer, who had served with distinction in former wars, and been lieutenant-colonel of Argyle's Highland regiment in Ireland—a veteran soldier, who had seen the battles of Benburb, Kilsythe, and Dunbar, when he was lieutenant-colonel of the Scottish Foot Guards*—took command of the whole,

* Raised for Charles II. in 1650, and disbanded after Worcester.

and, knowing how slender was his force, how destitute of succour, and how desperate in purpose and position, he left nothing undone to ensure a victory, or at least a death that should avenge their defeat and fall.

On reaching the secluded village of Colinton, which lies in a deep and wooded hollow, they learned that in Edinburgh, where they confidently expected a great accession, the citizens, under their provost, Sir Andrew Ramsay, were in arms against them, and had made vigorous preparations for a defence. The barrier gates were shut and fortified by cannon; the gentlemen of the neighbouring shires had been summoned to defend the walls; the College of Justice had formed a corps of cavalry, and all gentlemen in the city who possessed horses were ordered to mount, and appear in arms in the Meal Market, under the young Marquis of Montrose, to await the orders of General Dalyell.

The latter sent Alexander Seton, Viscount Kingston, with a body of the Guards, to the old quarries in Bruntsfield Links, with orders to lie there concealed, as across these links lay the direct road to the quarters of the insurgents, who had many friends in the capital; but overawed by the active measures of the Cavalier government, they—according to Kirkton—" could only fast and pray for them."

On learning all this, Colonel Wallace marched along the slope of the Pentland Hills, in the hope of being able to effect a retreat towards Biggar. The season was the dreary month of November. Dogged by Dalyell and battered by a storm of wind and rain, the hapless Covenanters had been losing heart, and as their spirit diminished, so did their numbers, which, from three thousand dwindled down to nine hundred hungry, wet, and famished creatures, " who looked more like dying men than soldiers going to conquer."

Wallace began to see the hopelessness of the cause he had undertaken; but the spirit of the few who adhered to him never flinched.

" We are not unwilling to die for religion and liberty," said these brave fellows; " yea, we would esteem a testimony for the Lord and our country a sufficient reward for all our loss and labour."

They wrote to General Dalyell a long and pathetic letter, setting forth their religious grievances; but no answer was returned to it, save the sound of his trumpets and the clash of the kettle-drums, when, on the afternoon of the 28th of November, his cavalry and infantry—upwards of three thousand strong,—after a fortnight's constant marching, were seen traversing the western slope of the beautiful Pentland range, and, descending, with all their standards displayed, towards Rullion Green, where these nine hundred devoted men, with their swords and Bibles, awaited them. As Dalyell approached, they sang the seventy-fourth and seventy-eighth Psalms.

Wallace drew up his little band in line, with a few of his toil-worn horsemen covering the right flank, which was somewhat exposed. Desperation and religious enthusiasm enhanced their natural bravery, and twice they repulsed the attack of the royal troops; but it was renewed by Dalyell's horse, the finest cavalry in Scotland, being principally cavaliers of the Life Guards, nobly mounted and richly accoutred. Dalyell led them on, and, by a single charge, they bore down horse and foot alike, at sword's point. This was when the dusk was closing on these lofty and heath-clad mountains. Fifty Covenanters were slain, including two eminent Irish divines—Andrew MacCormick and John Crookshanks—who had joined them, and who perished in the front rank.

In this conflict Dalyell and the famous Covenanter, Captain John Paton, of Meadowhead, met hand to hand on horseback, and exchanged several blows before they were separated by the pressure of their soldiers. Paton then discharged his pistols at Dalyell, off whose person the balls were seen *to recoil.* On perceiving this (and knowing him to be shot-proof, according to a superstitious historian), the captain loaded his pistol with a *silver coin,* a manœuvre observed by Dalyell; he stepped behind a soldier, who fell, pierced by the coin which was supposed to be proof to any spell; but the same legend is related of Claverhouse at Killycrankie. Paton was among the last who left the field. Dalyell perceived him retiring, and sent three well-mounted troopers in pursuit, and these came to blows with him when he was urging his horse to leap a deep ditch. By a back-handed stroke he clove in two the head and helmet of his first assailant; the other two fell headlong into the ditch, where they lay struggling under their fallen chargers.

"Take my compliments to Dalyell, your master," said Paton, tauntingly, as he rode off; "tell him that I am not going home with him to-night."

John Nesbit, of Hardhill, a tall and powerful Covenanter, fell on the field, covered with wounds, but was found to be alive next day, when he was stripped and about to be interred with the dead. He was a brave man, and had served in foreign wars, for which he was made a captain of Musketeers at Bothwell some years after.

The gloom of the November night, and a sentiment of chivalry—of pity, perhaps, for their poor and persecuted countrymen—inspired the Life Guards to spare the fugitives, the mass of whom escaped and dispersed; but eighty prisoners—among whom was Neilson, the unfortunate Laird of Corsack—were taken, and these were next day marched in triumph through the streets of Edinburgh, while cannon thundered a salute from the castle, and the bells rang in every steeple; while the streets resounded with the tramp of the cavalry, who, with standards advanced and kettle-drums beating, escorted them to prison. "It is recorded that Andrew Murray, an aged Presbyterian minister, when he beheld the ferocious Dalyell in his rusted head-piece, buff coat, and long waving beard, riding at the head of his cavalier squadrons, who, flushed with victory, surrounded the manacled prisoners with drawn swords and cocked carbines—and when he heard the shouts of acclamation from the people, was so overpowered with grief for what he deemed the downfall for ever of *God's Covenanted Kirk*, that he became ill, and expired."

The dead were buried on the field, and there may yet be seen, within a small and rude enclosure, which is overshadowed by a few trees, a monument bearing an inscription to the memory of Crookshanks, MacCormick, and others who lie where they fell. At the back of the Pentland Hills runs a rivulet named the Deadman's-grain, from the circumstance of a wounded Covenanter falling there when pursued by a cavalier trooper. Drawing a pistol from his holsters, he fired it at his pursuer underneath his bridle arm, but, missing, shot his own horse in the flank. The animal fell, and his rider was immediately slain, where his green grave is yet shown by the side of the mountain burn.

At Easton, in Dunsyre, there was long visible a lonely grave, in which, according to a tradition transmitted from father to son, there lay a Covenanter who had expired of wounds received at Rullion Green. It was opened in 1817, and found to contain the skeleton of a tall man, with two silver coins dated 1620. On being touched, the bones crumbled to dust.

Colonel Wallace, on seeing all lost, left the field, accompanied by Mr. John Welsh, and, favoured by the darkness, took a north-westerly direction among the hills, and escaped. After long concealment and enduring many privations, he reached the Continent, and died in penury, at Rotterdam, in 1678.

It is a strange circumstance that, after the rout of his followers, many of them were slain by the Lothian peasantry.

Of the unfortunate prisoners, the servile and barbarous Scottish Privy Council made a severe example. Twenty were executed at Edinburgh, ten being hanged upon the same gibbet at once; seven were executed at Ayr, and many were hanged before their own doors in other parts of the country. The heads of those who perished at Edinburgh were fixed above the city gates, and their right arms and the hands with which they subscribed the Covenant were affixed to the Tolbooths of Lanark and other towns.

When Gordon, of Knockbreck, and his brother were hanged on the same gibbet, they clasped each other in their arms, that together, and at once, they might endure the pangs of death.

Like all Covenanters, the whole of these men maintained, with their dying breath, that they had taken up arms *not* against the king, but against the insupportable tyranny of the Episcopal prelates. And that these men, and such as these, did not die in vain, the future history of their country has shown, for their last words left an echo that lingers yet in the hearts of the people.

Dalyell was highly complimented by the Council for this victory, and Neilson of Corsack, the most important of his prisoners, was ordered to be tortured in that dark, panelled room under the Parliament Hall, wherein sat the Council, over which the Duke of Rothes presided.

Neilson of Corsack was a country laird, who had been long distinguished for gentleness and amiability of disposition; but rage at the ill treatment he received from the new clergy alone drove him to despair, and from despair to arms. On his refusal to become an Episcopalian, by the information (or at the instance) of the curate of his parish, he was dragged from his house, fined, and imprisoned, while his delicate wife and little children had been driven as outcasts into the mountains. Soldiers were then quartered on his lands, and his cattle were carried off. This was scarcely such treatment as a Scottish gentleman of the seventeenth century would endure with calmness. Rendered desperate, Corsack took to his sword, and commanded the party which surprised Sir James Turner, whose life he subsequently saved. That officer was not ungrateful for the act, and did all in his power to obtain mercy for him, but in vain. The Council were inexorable, and "Corsack was so cruelly tortured by the iron boots, that his shrieks were sufficient to move the heart of a stone."

The *thumbikins* were the favourite instrument of torture most generally resorted to by the Lords of Council. These were small steel screws which compressed the thumb-joint, or whole hand if necessary, and were an invention brought to Scotland by General Dalyell from the Continent.

Charles II. distinctly, by letter, ordained the Privy Council to substitute banishment for torture and death; but his *missive was concealed*, and in his name the work of cruelty still went on, and still unsated by the daily horrors furnished by the result of the conflict at Rullion Green, Generals Dalyell and Drummond were ordered into the Shires of Ayr, Dumfries, and Galloway, to complete the destruction of any Covenanters or recusants who might remain in these districts.

In this year, and most probably for that duty, he raised a regiment of infantry; but it has long ceased to exist, and was probably one of the many Scottish corps disbanded at the peace of Ryswick.

While on this new service the enemies of Dalyell record innumerable instances of cruelty perpetrated by him; and though his temper was hot and his character undoubtedly fierce and resolute, these stories must be accepted under reservation.

"The forces were ordered to lie in the west," says Burnet, "where Dalyell acted the Muscovite too grossly. He threatened to *spit* men and to *roast* them, and he killed some in cold blood, or rather hot blood, for he was then drunk, when he ordered one to be hanged because he would not tell where his father was, for whom he was in search. When he heard of any who did not go to church, he did not trouble himself to set a fine upon him, but sent as many soldiers as might eat him up in a night. And the clergy were so delighted with it, that they used to speak of that time as the poets do of the golden age. They looked upon the soldiery as their patrons. They were ever in their company, and complying with them in their excesses, and, if they are not much wronged, they rather led them into them, than checked them for them. *Dalyell* himself and his officers were so disgusted with them, that they increased the complaints, that had now more credit from them than from those of the country, who were looked on as their enemies. Things of so strange a pitch in vice were told of them, that they seemed scarce credible."

And this severe picture of the Episcopal Clergy is given by a Scottish Bishop, which renders it the more worthy of credence.

It is recorded of Dalyell, that once, when inflamed by passion, he struck a prisoner on the face with the hilt of his dagger so severely that blood flowed from the wound but it must be remembered that this person had boldly taunted the fierce old man, as " a Muscovite beast who used to roast men alive !" He established his head-quarters at Lanark for some weeks, and there he imprisoned many Covenanters in a damp dungeon, which was so narrow that, owing to their number, they could neither sit nor lie at length with comfort ; and where they were deprived of all accommodation for preserving cleanliness or decency.

While his troops were in this town, a peasant when passing through the streets was seized by a patrol, and brought before him ; and because this man either could not, or would not, give such information as would commit some of the prisoners, he was condemned to instant death. He begged one night's reprieve, that he might prepare to die, and make his peace with Heaven ; but even this was denied him, and, according to the historians of the Kirk, he was dragged into a neighbouring field, shot dead by a platoon of carbines, stripped and left nude upon the ground.

On another occasion, we are told that he ordered a woman, who had aided the escape of a fugitive, to be cast into a hole filled with toads and reptiles, where she died in great misery.

Such stories seem exceedingly improbable, yet they pass current in Scotland, and are still believed to the present day.

In Dumfries the soldiers were accused of " having tied a man neck and heels to a pole, and turned him like a joint of meat before a great fire." In Kilmarnock, the men of Dalyell's regiment placed an old recusant in a dungeon, which was destitute of vent or chimney, and there tortured him by the smoke of a coal fire. When almost suffocated he was borne forth, amid laughter and derision, to the open air, and permitted to revive. After this he was imprisoned again ; and this torture was continued for several nights and days.

At Dalry, Sir William Bannatyne, one of Dalyell's officers, ordered a woman who had been accessory to the escape of her husband, to be tortured by having lighted musket-matches tied between her clenched fingers, a cruelty by which she lost one hand entirely, and some days afterwards expired of torture. A farmer, whom this officer was dragooning, and from whom he was extorting money, asked why he was thus fined.

"Because," replied Sir William, with provoking candour, "you have great gear, and I must have part of it."

And on service so barbarous as this, the year 1667 passed away; and the estates of the forfeited Wallace of Auchans and others were bestowed by Parliament upon Dalyell and Drummond, or were retained by the grasping officers of State to enrich themselves. Thus for a time the unhappy Covenanters seemed to be completely crushed. Upon Dalyell was conferred the valuable estate of Mure of Caldwell, who had been accessory to that revolt which terminated at the Pentland hills; but of this property his family were deprived by the Revolution of 1688. Those who made peace with the Government, by interest, bribery, or fines, received protections, of which the following, in my own possession, granted the year before Bothwell, may serve as an example :—

"At Glasgow, the twenty day of March, 1678.

"For saemeikelas Major Alexander Coult of Garturke, in the parish of Monkland, hath signed the bond appoynted by the Lords of His Maties Privy Councell ffor himself and all such who live under him, ffor their peaceable and orderlie deportment; the Comitty of His Maties Privy Councell do hereby take the said Major Alexander Coult under their special protection and safeguard: and hereby discharge all officers and souldiers to trouble or molest the said Major Alexander Coult, his house, famillie, tenants, cottars or servants, or any belonging to him, in their personal gudes or estate, as they will be answerable at their highest perill, and allows him *to have and wear his wearing sword and pistolls.*   GLENCAIRNE,
"STRATHMORE,   WIGTOUNE,
"AIRLIE,   CAITHNESS."

Captain John Creichton, the celebrated cavalier trooper, who served long, both as a private and officer, under Dalyell in Scotland, and whose interesting memoirs were published by Dean Swift, has left us the following portrait of his stern leader, and it is so graphic that I may be pardoned quoting it entire.

"He was bred up very hardy from his youth, both in diet and clothing. He never wore boots, nor above one coat, which was close to his body, with close sleeves like those we call jockey coats. He never wore a peruke, nor did he shave his beard since the murder of King Charles the First. In my time his head was bald, which he covered only with a beaver hat, the brim of which was not above three inches broad. His beard was white and bushy, and yet reached down almost to his girdle. He usually went to London once or twice in a year to kiss the King's hand, who had a great esteem for his valor and worth. His unusual dress and figure, when he was in London, never failed to draw after him a great crowd of boys and other young people, who constantly attended at his lodgings, and followed him with huzzas, as he went to court and returned from it. As he was a man of humour, he would always thank them for their civilities when he left them at the door to go to the King, and would let them know exactly at what hour he intended to come out again and return to his lodgings.

"When the King walked in the park attended by some of his courtiers, and Dalziel in his company, the same crowds would always be after him, shewing their admiration at his beard and dress, so that the King could hardly pass on for the crowd, upon which his Majesty bade '*the devil take Dalziel for bringing such a rabble of boys together to have their guts squeezed out*,' while they gaped at his long beard and antique habit, requesting him at the same time—as Dalziel used to express it—'*to shave and dress like other Christians, and keep the poor bairns out of danger*.' All this could never prevail on him to part with his beard; but yet, in compliance to his Majesty, he went once to Court in the very height of the fashion; but as soon as the King and those about him had laughed sufficiently at the strange figure he made, he resumed his usual habit, to the great joy of the boys, who had not discovered him in his fashionable dress."

From this it would appear that Dalyell had been much

of a wag, that he loved to humour children, and enjoyed their fun and amazement at the sight of his huge beard, and by appearing once in the gaudy frippery of a Cavalier had striven to ridicule the foppery of the Court of Charles II.—three points of character very different from those usually attributed to him.

He was appointed a Privy Councillor, and soon after represented the county of Linlithgow in Parliament, and in 1670 an act of ratification, confirming all his estates and honours, was passed. In this document he is designated "His Majesties right trustie and weel-beloved Generall Thomas Dalyell, of Binns, late Lieutenant-Generall of His Majesties late forces within this ancient kingdome." From this it would appear that promotion, as well as profit, had resulted to him after the affair at Rullion Green and dragooning the Westland Whigs. He represented his native county in the Scottish Parliament from 1678 to 1685.

To assist in the security of Episcopacy in Scotland, and still further to fortify the royal authority and the power of that tyrannical Council, which committed so many atrocities in the king's name, Lauderdale, who was created a duke when at the head of the Scottish affairs, obtained the formation of a militia consisting of two thousand cavalry and sixteen thousand infantry; and as the northern kingdom swarmed with experienced and high-spirited officers all lacking military employment, these troops were soon disciplined and equipped; but the flower of the national troops were the standing forces of the country.

These, at this time, were as follows:—

1. The Royal Life Guards, the regiment of the famous John Grahame of Claverhouse, Viscount of Dundee, were raised after the Restoration, in 1661. The privates were styled, *par excellence*, gentlemen, and usually appear to have been cadets of good families. The Sieur de la Roche, a French Protestant refugee, who was slain in a tavern brawl at Leith by John Master of Tarbet and an Ensign Mowat, is styled in their indictment, "a gentleman of his Majesty's troop of Guards." Under Claverhouse, this Scottish patrician band served at Bothwell

Bridge, at Drumclog, and in all the unhappy contentions of the period. Mr. Francis Stuart, afterwards a captain of the Guards, grandson of the Earl of Bothwell, was, says Captain Creichton, " a private *gentleman* in the Horse Guards, like myself." In this trooper the reader will no doubt recognise the Serjeant Bothwell of *Old Mortality*.

"On the 2nd of April, 1661," according to Wodrow, "the King's Life Guard was formed. By their constitution they were to consist of noblemen and gentlemen's sons, and were to be one hundred and twenty in number, under command of the Lord Newburgh. After taking an oath to be loyal to his Majesty, they made a parade through the town of Edinburgh, with carbines at their saddles and swords drawn."

The maimed and old veteran officers, adds Kirkton, in his secret history, "the poor colonels, majors, and captains who expected great promotion (at the Restoration) were preferred to be troopers in the King's troop of Life Guards. This goodly employment obliged them to spend with one another the small remnant of the stock their miseries had left them, but more they could not have after all their hopes and sufferings" (he means) during the days of Cromwell.

In 1674 these Life Guards consisted of four squadrons, and were commanded by the Marquis of Athole.

After the Union, in 1707, this corps was removed to London, and is now represented by the 2nd troop of the 1st Life Guards.*

2. The Scottish Foot Guards, raised in November, 1660, were commanded by George, Earl of Linlithgow, and were, as they are still, named Fusiliers, being armed with the *fusil*, a light French musket; and by the Scottish Privy Council, in their orders to the army in 1667, it was ordained that the field officers of this corps should command in chief, and give orders in field and garrison, to all troops whatsoever. In 1707 these Guards were placed upon the united British establishment; in February, 1712,

* War-office communicated.

they were marched to London; in the following year they shared the duties for the *first* time with the English Guards, and have *never been in Scotland since.**

3. The Royal Regiment, known of old as the Scottish Archers in France, was at this time abroad at Tangiers, and did not return until 1682, when it arrived in Rochester, reduced to sixteen companies, and after the battle of Sedgemoor was sent into Holland.

4. The Earl of Mar's regiment, which served at Bothwell Bridge, was remodelled in 1689, and now known as the 21st Fusiliers.

5. The infantry regiment of Dalyell is no longer in existence, but Leven's Scottish regiment is now known as the 25th, or Royal Borderers; Angus's Foot—the regiment of our old friend, Uncle Toby—is numbered as the 26th, or Cameronians; and the regiment of Argyle, infamous as the perpetrators of the Glencoe tragedy, is no longer in the service.

6. The Scottish train of artillery, commanded by the Laird of Lundin in 1687, was disbanded at the Union, when Lord Leven was its general, and the last survivor of it, then an old man, served as a volunteer, with Sir John Cope's army, at Preston Pans. In this corps was a strange rank, named "gentlemen of the cannon," as we may learn from a letter of Viscount Teviot, dated 1699, and printed among Carstare's State Papers.

At the union with England, in 1707, it would seem to have been arranged that Scotland should have the first regiment of infantry, theirs being the oldest, and that England should have the first regiment of Dragoons.

The severity with which Dalyell and Drummond treated the Covenanters with these regular troops drove them frantic.

In February, 1677, the former despatched John Creichton, one of his most active, favourite, and relentless

---

* The Royal Horse Guards of Scotland were raised at Edinburgh in 1702. The Duke of Argyle, who came over in 1688, was their first colonel. Lord Polwarth's Horse (now the 7th Hussars) then the only Scottish regiment of Light Dragoons, were embodied in 1689.

troopers, with an ensign and fifty soldiers of the Foot Guards, to seize Adam Stobie, of Luscar, near Culross, in Fife, "a fellow who," as the captain says, "had gone through the west, endeavouring to stir up sedition in the people by his great skill in canting and praying."

After surrounding his house in the night, the unfortunate Covenanter was discovered in concealment under some straw in a lime-kiln, from whence he was at once dragged forth. His daughter, in tears and terror, besought mercy of Creichton, and offered to ransom her father for two hundred dollars; but the trooper knew too well the inflexibility of his general, and, though not always insensible either to the voice of a woman or the offer of a handsome sum, he marched back to Edinburgh, and presented Stobie to Dalyell, together with four other recusants, who had been found in Culross by the Ensign of the Guards.

On the 22nd of February, the General brought his prisoners before the Privy Council, who fined Stobie three thousand marks for keeping conventicles and *conversing* with intercommuned persons. After paying this he was to be transported; but he saved their lordships further trouble on his account by breaking from his prison and escaping in the night. After this he joined in the next rising, and is believed to have been slain at Bothwell Bridge, as he was never heard of afterwards.

About this time Francis Stuart, the Earl of Bothwell's grandson, was recommended by Dalyell to Charles II. for a commission, and was appointed Captain of Horse with John Creichton, who had hitherto been with him in the Life Guards, as his lieutenant, and these officers served under Colonel Graham, of Claverhouse, at the battle of Drumclog; for after the murder of Archbishop Sharpe on Magus Muir, the armed field conventicles had increased in every part of the country, and discontent, with sullen desperation, were rapidly moulding the people into a mass that was ready for revolt. Conflicts with the soldiers were of daily occurrence, and many of them were barbarously murdered, in lonely billets and solitary parts of the country, by the more savage or fanatical of the hill men, as the recusants were named, from their habit of usually lurking in the mountains.

Superstition was not wanting to lend a darker and more terrible hue to the events of the time, as Scotland is peculiarly the land of omens. Atmospheric visions were everywhere visible, if we are to believe such old memorialists as Law and others.

At Kilbryde, near Glasgow, two armies were seen in the sky, firing platoons of musketry at each other; "the fyre and smock were seen, but without noise or crak." On the slope of a lonely hill near Eastwood Muir, the tall apparition of a blood-red spectre was seen to tower suddenly between the terrified beholders and the blue sky, while a dreadful voice exclaimed—

"Woe! Woe unto the land!"

At a conventicle, suppressed in Fife by Adam Masterton of Grange, an officer of the Life Guards, the fugitive women, who observed the conflict from a distance, asserted that they could perceive, to their awe and terror, "the form of a tall man of majestic stature," hovering in mid air "above the people all the while of the soldiers shooting."

In August, 1678, the devil, who seemed always in those days to take a deep interest in Scottish affairs, held a great meeting of witches and warlocks in Lothian, "where," saith the veracious Law, "there was a warlock who formerly had been admitted to the ministry in the Presbyterian times, and who, when the bishops came in, conformed with *them;* but being deposed, he now turns under the devil, a preacher of hellish doctrine." In the March of the same year, he adds, a tremendous voice was heard in the ancient and half-ruined Abbey of Paisley, exclaiming—

"Woe, woe, woe! Pray, pray, pray!"

Showers of blood and of Highland bonnets, afforded the crones, elsewhere, ample matter for discussion and wonder.

Amid all this absurdity, while the tyrant Lords of Council tortured and hung peasants and preachers, or ruined honourable and long-descended families, for worshipping God as their hearts desired, and for doing so, in wild and sequestered places, or for refusing to say God save a King, who was *uncovenanted;* while Dalyell had every satanic power attributed to him, and the black charger of Claverhouse was believed to be the veritable devil himself, the efforts of some to promote godliness in the land were alike melancholy and amusing; thus people were punished for taking snuff in time of sermon, for carrying water on the Sabbath day, and for a thousand charges equally frivolous.

To repress the conventicles which began to assume a more formidable aspect, from the number of armed men who attended them, additional garrisons were established. Two peers and ten barons, who were obnoxious to Lauderdale, were lawlessly dispossessed of their mansions, which were converted into military stations. In each of these Dalyell placed a company of infantry and ten troopers, who were supplied with everything by provincial assessment or military contribution. Fathers were made responsible for their children; husbands for their wives; magistrates for their citizens; landlords for their tenants; and thus, by a network of military tyranny, it was resolved that at the sword's point, Scotland should become a highly episcopal country. Five hundred marks were offered for the seizure of any one who held a religious meeting; and four thousand pounds sterling was an ordinary price for the head of a good preacher. Others were valued according to their reputation among the people; and under such laws as these the troops of his sacred Majesty King Charles made plenty of prize-money and plunder.

The barbarities to which the people were subjected at last attracted the attention of the English House of Commons, who appointed a committee to inquire into these affairs, and into the Act empowering the Privy Council at Edinburgh to march the Scottish army wheresoever they chose; but there the matter ended. The Government was then *federal,* and any interference might have caused another national rupture.

Roused at last to more open resistance, a body of these

poor people appealed again to that which of old was ever the Scotsman's best and most ready argument—the sword—and the defeat of Claverhouse's cavalry at Drumclog was deemed a sure omen of great events to come. They established their camp at Hamilton, and unfurled a standard, which is still preserved at Edinburgh. It is blue, crossed by the white saltire of St. Andrew, and is inscribed—

"COVENANTS—RELIGION—KING AND KINGDOMES."

Robert Hamilton, of Preston, a brave but intolerant and injudicious man, assumed the command. He was without experience as a leader, and his followers were destitute of all discipline as soldiers; hence dissensions were of hourly occurrence in the camp.

Alarmed by the tidings of this rising, the end of which no one could then foresee, the King sent his son James, Duke of Monmouth and Buccleugh, to assume command of the Scottish troops, and enforce the restoration of order. The duke brought with him four troops of English horse, commanded by a Major Main, a novelty which did not increase his popularity in Scotland, where English troops had not been seen since Cromwell's time. At the head of ten thousand men, with a fine park of artillery, he marched westward at midsummer, against the insurgents.

"Upon the duke being made commander-in-chief, Dalyell refused to serve under him," says Captain Creichton, "and remained at his lodgings in Edinburgh, till his Grace was superseded, which happened about a fortnight after."

The principal officers in the kingdom attended the duke on this expedition. Among them were the Earl of Linlithgow, with his regiment of Foot Guards; the Earl of Mar, with his regiment of Fusiliers; the Marquis of Montrose, the Earls of Airley and Home, and Graham of Claverhouse, all commanders of horse; while a host of cavalier nobles and gentlemen attended him to serve as he might require.

On the 22nd of June, he found the Covenanters in position at the bridge of Bothwell, where the Clyde is seventy-one yards wide. This picturesque old bridge was twelve feet broad, and one hundred and twenty feet long, with a rise of twenty in the centre, where there was a barrier gate, which was removed in 1826. This gate Preston had barricaded, while flanking the approaches with musketry. To three hundred stout hearts led by Hackston of Rathillet, and the stern John Balfour of Kinloch, otherwise styled of Burley, was confided the keeping of the bridge, and well these brave men kept it too, under a heavy fire of cannon and musketry, to which the flankers of the bridge replied by firing briskly from behind the thickets of alder and hazel trees which clothed the banks of the stream.

Under cover of a cannonade, Lord Livingstone led the assault, at the head of his father's regiment, the Scottish Foot Guards, and despite its barricade of stones and timber, and all the efforts of its desperate defenders, the gate was stormed by the infantry, and the bridge was carried by the clubbed musket and levelled pike, after a fierce contest. Then a body of the Lennox Highlanders, led, say some authorities, by General Dalyell; by their own chief, Macfarlane, say others, raised the war-cry of *Lochsloy* and flung themselves, claymore in hand, on the main body of the Covenanters, while Claverhouse with the Life Guards—all burning to avenge their recent defeat at Drumclog—defiled across the bridge at full speed, and forming in squadron on the opposite side, swept all before them, as they might have driven a flock of sheep. Main's English dragoons and the Highlanders are accused of behaving with great barbarity in slaughtering the fugitives. The aged Laird of Earlstone prayed for quarter from Major Main, who ran him through the body and slew him on the spot.

When the charge was over, the gentlemen of the Scottish Life Guards became so exasperated on seeing the Covenanters treated thus by Englishmen, that they fell, sword in hand, upon Main's dragoons, and cut many of them down, "being grieved," as the Rev. John Blackadder has it, "to see Englishmen delighting so much to shed their countrymen's blood."

In the streets of Hamilton the reckless Balfour of Burley made a bold attempt to rally the fugitives; but a musket-ball broke his sword arm, as his troopers reined up their horses in the thoroughfare.

"Withered be the hand that fired the shot—I can fight no longer now!" he exclaimed in bitterness, as the weapon fell from his grasp, and once more the flight was renewed.

Four hundred Covenanters were slain on the field, and twelve hundred were made prisoners; these, on the evening after the battle, were marched to Edinburgh, where they were thrust into the Greyfriars churchyard, like sheep penned in a fold. Some were selected for the scaffold, the rest were banished to the plantations, and of these many perished miserably at sea.

The pursuit was scarcely over and the troops returned to their various colours, when old General Dalyell, on horseback and in fiery haste, lest the fighting should all be over, arrived from Edinburgh, with a new commission appointing *him* commander-in-chief. This document, which he had received by express from London, was dated 22nd June, 1679, the very day of the encounter. It did not, however, entirely supersede the authority of the Duke of Monmouth, who by the Privy Council was styled "Lord General." Dalyell is said to have publicly upbraided the gentle duke with his clemency to the prisoners, and for the tenor of the orders he issued before the battle. These were, to yield quarter to all who asked it, to make as many prisoners as possible, and to spare life.

"Had *my* commission come *before* the battle," said Dalyell, grimly, "these rogues should never more have troubled the king or country."

He marched the troops to Glasgow, and three days afterwards—the insurrection being deemed at an end— they were dispersed in detachments throughout the Lowlands, most of them being sent to where they were far from welcome—their old quarters.

After the battle, Dalyell captured the Reverend John King, a preacher who had once been chaplain to the exiled Lord Cardross. This gentleman he sent in irons to Edinburgh, escorted by a guard of Main's dragoons, and on their march from Glasgow there occurred a strange accident, which the people believed to be a visitation of Heaven. One of these troopers, at a wayside alehouse, drank, "Confusion to the Covenant!" and being asked "where he was going,"

"I am carrying King to hell," said he, an answer likely enough to be made by a reckless soldier.

"The judgment of Heaven did not linger on this wretch," records the superstitious Wodrow; "he had not proceeded many paces on his journey, when his horse stumbled, his carbine went off and shot him dead."

King perished on the gibbet soon after, and had his head and right hand cut off.

In the winter after the battle, Dalyell quartered himself at Kilmarnock, with one battalion of Linlithgow's Foot Guards, and the horse troops of the Earl of Airlie and Captain Francis Stuart of Bothwell.

"Here," says Captain Creichton, "the general, one day happening to look on while I was exercising the troop of dragoons, asked me when I had done, whether I knew any one of my men who was skilful in praying well in the style and tone of the Covenanters? I immediately thought upon one named James Gibb, who had been born in Ireland, and whom I had made a dragoon. This man I brought to the general, assuring his Excellency 'that if I had raked hell, I could not find his match in mimicking the Covenanters.' Whereupon the general gave him five pounds to buy him a greatcoat and a bonnet, and commanded him to find out the rebels, but be sure to take care of himself among them.

"The dragoon went eight miles off that very night, and got admittance into the house of a notorious rebel, pretending he had come from Ireland out of zeal for the cause, to assist at the fight of Bothwell Bridge, and could not find an opportunity since of returning with safety; and therefore, after bewitching the family with his gifts of praying, he was conveyed in the dusk of the evening by a guide to the house of the next adjoining rebel, and thus in the same manner from one to another, till in a month's time he got through the principal of them in the west, telling the general at his return, that he 'made the old wives, in their devout fits, tear off their biggonets and mutches ;' he likewise gave the general a list of their names and places of abode, and into the bargain brought back a good purse of money in his pocket."

"How used you to pray among them?" asked Dalyell.

"It was my custom in my prayers," replied the trooper, "to send the king, the ministers of state, the officers of the army, with all their soldiers and the episcopal clergy, all at one broadside to hell; but particularly our general himself."

"What," exclaimed the general, "did you also send *me* to hell, sir?"

"Yea," replied the unabashed dragoon, "you at the head of them as their leader."

This discreditable abuse of hospitality and breach of faith in the soldier is recorded as a piece of admirable tact and strategy by Creichton, and doubtless Dalyell would make good use of the notes supplied to him.

In the month of July, in the following year, 1680, Dalyell sent Creichton with thirty of Airlie's horse, and fifty of Strachan's dragoons, under Captain Bruce of Earlshall, to capture or kill a hundred and fifty Covenanters, who, since the fight at Bothwell, had been lurking in the wilds of Galloway. These unfortunates, after being tracked from place to place by Bruce and Creichton, made a stand against them at Airsmoss, near Muirkirk, on the 22nd July, and there these desperate men fought as only the homeless and the outlawed, the brave and the foredoomed, can fight; but they were routed, and fourteen of them were taken prisoners. Among these was David Hackston, of Rathillet, who had been present at the murder of the Archbishop of St. Andrews. Sixty were slain, and one of these was Richard Cameron, a preacher, and formerly a schoolmaster at Falkland, for whose capture five thousand marks had long been offered by the government at Edinburgh.

"Lord!" he exclaimed, before the cavalry charged; "Lord, spare the green and take the ripe! Come on," he added, drawing his sword, "let us fight it out to the last.

This is the day I longed for! This is the death I have prayed for; to die fighting against the avowed enemies of the Lord."

He was shot and buried in the moss, where his grave is still shown; but his head and hands were conveyed by Creichton to head-quarters. So perished this enthusiast; but he bequeathed his name to a sect from which the 26th Scottish Regiment of the Line still takes its title of *the Cameronians*.

With a barbarity worthy of the Sepoy mutineers his head and hands were exhibited to his aged father, then a prisoner in the gloomy Tolbooth of Edinburgh, and tauntingly he was asked, if he knew to whom they had belonged.

"Oh yes," said the old man, as he wept and kissed the bloody relics; "they are my son's—my dear son's—but good is the will of the Lord!"

After this revolting incident, they were fixed to the Netherbow-porte, the eastern gate of Edinburgh.

Captains Bruce and Creichton had also brought with them from Airsmoss the Laird of Rathillet, who had received many wounds in the skirmish. He was personally questioned by Dalyell, who is said to have threatened to roast him, because his answers to certain queries were brief, sullen, and unsatisfactory. Covenanting writers add, that the general refused to permit Hackston's wounds to be dressed, and ordered him to be chained to the floor of his dungeon till he was conveyed to Edinburgh, where he was executed by prolonged tortures with a barbarity that had never been equalled, even in those days.

Among others seized by Dalyell was John Spreul, an apothecary in Glasgow, whom he brought before the Council, and accused of being concerned in the fight at Bothwell. His leg was put in the iron boot, and at each query the headsman gave the wedges five strokes with a mallet. "Dalyell," says Wodrow, "complained that he did not strike strongly enough; upon which, he (the torturer) offered himself the mallet, saying he struck with all his might." Spreul was afterwards imprisoned on the Bass Rock, where he remained for six years.

Amid the many instances of severity attributed to Dalyell, I must not omit to record one of a different kind. The most celebrated prisoner taken at Bothwell was Captain John Paton, of Meadowhead, who served under Gustavus Adolphus, and had fought at Kilsythe against Montrose, where he had displayed remarkable bravery and skill in the use of his sword. Dalyell was present when this fine old veteran was examined before the Privy Council. On this occasion a soldier had the rudeness to taunt him with being "a rebel."

"Sir," retorted Paton, "I have done more for the King perhaps than you have done — I fought for him at Worcester."

Some humane impression or soldierly emotion stirred the heart of Dalyell at these words.

"Yes, John, you are right—that is true," said he: and striking the soldier with his cane, added, "I will teach you, sirrah, other manners, than to abuse a prisoner such as this." He then expressed sorrow for Paton's situation, and said he would have set him at liberty had his actions not been subject to the control of others; "but," he added, "I will yet write to the King, and crave at least your life."

"I thank you," replied the unmoved Covenanter; "but you will not be heard."

It is said that he obtained a reprieve for Paton, but was unable to save his life; for though willing to take the test, the Captain was hanged, by sentence of a quorum of the Council, in the Grassmarket, on the 9th May. In August, 1853, a monument to his memory was erected in the churchyard of Ayr.

Undaunted by all that had passed and was still passing around him, in the September of that year, Donald Cargill, one of the most determined preachers of the Covenant, and one who had long escaped the fangs of the Council, held a conventicle in the Torwood, near Stirling, and with all solemnity and bitterness excommunicated the King, the Dukes of York, Monmouth, and Lauderdale, General Dalyell and others, an act of daring which, at such a time, made a deep impression on the Government;

but in the following year he paid for his enthusiasm by the forfeit of his life, being captured by General Dalyell, and executed by the authorities.

Tyranny and local misgovernment had now rendered the condition of poor Scotland sad beyond description.

Through the lonely mosses, the pathless moors, and pastoral mountain districts of their native land, the unhappy Covenanters were hunted like beasts of prey, without a refuge or a resting place but such as Heaven accords to wild animals; and wherever found, captivity or death was the penalty. During twenty-eight years of this military persecution, it has been calculated that eighteen thousand persons suffered death in the field, or by the utmost extremities of torture that the Council could inflict; seventeen hundred were banished to the plantations, and two hundred perished on the scaffold alone; seven thousand are said to have fled to foreign countries, and four hundred and ninety-eight were slain in cold blood, or in casual encounters; and all this was done in the name of God, of Religion, and Law!

In September, 1679, there was a stormy debate in the Scottish Privy Council. By an act of indemnity, his Majesty pardoned all who had been at Bothwell Bridge, ministers and lesser barons excepted, provided they appeared before such persons as the Council should appoint, and signed a bond that never again would they rise in arms against the government. It may readily be believed that very few gave this promise; and from the minutes it would appear that Dalyell and Sir George Mackenzie of Roschaugh, urged that all who had *not* done so should be proceeded against as rebels. The President and others pled that to proceed to further extremities would be cruel, as more than four thousand persons, many of whom might be sick or ignorant of the King's letter, were involved in the measure proposed, and ultimately Dalyell, and those who adhered to him, agreed that the King should once more be addressed on the subject.

The next entry connected with the General runs thus:—

November 6, 1679. "At Privy Council there is a letter read from his Majesty, nominating Lieutenant-General

Dalziel commander-in-chief of all the forces of Scotland, with power to him *to act as he shall think fit*, and only be liable and accountable and judgeable by his Majesty himself; for Dalziel would not accept of it otherways ; only he promised and declared, that in difficult exigents he should take the advice of his Majesty's Privy Council." (*Fountainhall*, vol. i.) On the 3rd June, 1680, the Council received a letter from Charles on this subject. It declared that when he gifted forfeitures, he always reserved for his own use the houses standing on the forfeited lands. He also gave Dalyell a Commission of Justiciary, with the advice of nine others, to execute justice on all who were in arms at Bothwell, or failed to take the bond within the period stated, since the 1st of January.

In 1680, the Duke of York and Albany arrived in Edinburgh, to supersede Lauderdale, and took up his residence at Holyrood. Dalyell received him at the head of the troops and a body of armed citizens, consisting of sixty men chosen from the sixteen companies of the Trained Bands which lined the streets. After his arrival, he and his Duchess, Marie d'Este of Modena, so celebrated for her beauty, left nothing undone to ingratiate themselves with the Scottish people, to the end that, if excluded by the Act of Succession from the English throne, they might for themselves secure the ancient crown of Scotland. Everything was studied, done, and adopted to ensure popularity; and one fact is certain, that after the Duke's arrival the persecution of the Covenanters was much less severe than before. By ostentatious pageants, he revived in the nation what it was even then beginning to forget, the memory of its regal independence and the pride of better days; and thus he sought to make his family less abhorred in the hearts of the people. He projected many improvements at Edinburgh. Among others, the plan for building a bridge across the North Loch, and having a new town built upon the northern ridge; and the Holyrood parties, where *tea* was seen for the first time in Scotland, the balls and masques of the Ladies Anne, afterwards of Denmark, and Mary, afterwards of Orange, were long the theme of aged demoiselles and stately dow-

sgers in Edinburgh, where the beauty and charming
suavity of the young princesses, with their natural gaiety,
brightened the gloomy towers and tapestried rooms of the
ancient palace: and the memory of these things was
transmitted by many a mother and grandmother to their
little ones, when the last of that old royal race was far
away in hopeless exile and obscurity, and the first grass of
spring was sprouting on the graves of Culloden.

The Duke of York and his Duchess are said to have
been warned of the lofty spirit and haughty punctilio of
the old Scottish aristocracy from a speech of General
Dalyell.

James had invited this stern and bearded cavalier to
dine with them at Holyrood soon after his arrival; but
the Duchess Mary, as a daughter of the ducal Prince of
Modena, seemed to consider it somewhat derogatory to
her rank to sit with a subject at table, and declined to
take her place.

"Madam," said the old veteran, "I have dined at a
table where *your* father must have stood at *my* back."

In this instance it is supposed that he alluded to the
board of the Emperor of Germany, whom the Duke of
Modena, if summoned, must have attended as an officer
of the household. Abashed by the firm retort of this
grim old man, the haughty princess at once took her seat,
and from thenceforward she and her husband resolved, in
their intercourse with the Scottish noblesse, to exercise
all the suavity and affability they could command. By various acts of leniency the Duke also sought to win favour.

"General Dalyell," says old Lord Fountainhall in his
Diary, "having caused to be condemned by court martial
a sentinel who had been found sleeping at one of the gates
of the Abbey, the Duke caused him to be remitted and
forgiven all punishment."

In this year, soon after the Duke's arrival, the services
of the General were required to repress a dangerous demonstration among the students of the Edinburgh University. Being deeply imbued with the sentiments of the
Covenanters, on Christmas Day, 1680, these young men
resolved to manifest publicly their horror of all prelacy,

by burning an effigy of the Pope, a ceremony eminently calculated to offend the royal Duke, as a zealous Catholic; and the magistrates, having resolved at all hazards to prevent this impolitic display, immediately communicated with General Dalyell, that he might have the troops in readiness to overawe the city. In furtherance of their daring scheme, the students posted on all the gates and public places of Edinburgh the following curious placard:—

"AN ADVERTISEMENT.

"These are to give notice to all noblemen, gentlemen, and citizens, that we, the students in the Royal College of Edinburgh (to show our detestation and abhorrence of the Romish religion, and our zeal and fervency for the Protestant), do resolve to burn the effigies of *Antichrist, the Pope of Rome*, at the Mercat-cross of Edinburgh, at twelve o'clock in the forenoon—being the festival of our Saviour's nativity. And since we hate tumults as we do superstition, we do hereby, under pain of death, discharge all plunderers, robbers, thieves, whores, and bawds to come within forty paces of our company, and such as shall be found disobedient to these our commands, *sibi caveant.*

"By our special command, ROBERT BROWN, Secretary to all our Theatrical and Extra-Literal Divertisements."

By an oath, the students bound themselves to stand by each other, under a penalty, and employed a carver in wood to make them an effigy of his Holiness, "with clothes, triple crown, keys, and other necessary habiliments."

The Lord Provost, Sir James Dick, reported their intentions to the Duke of York, and threatened that "he would make it a bloody Christmas for them;" while Dalyell marched all the troops from Leith into the Canongate. The Grassmarket, an old quaint street lying to the south of the Castle rock, was filled with troops, whose patrols scoured all the wynds and closes, as the narrow alleys of the ancient city are named. The militia, or trained bands of Edinburgh, occupied the High-street; guards were placed on the College, which stood without the walls, and those at the palace were doubled for additional security to the royal duke and his family.

Undismayed by all these warlike preparations, the students, many of whom were armed with swords and pistols in their belts, mustered in the High School yard, and with loud shouts bore, shoulder high, an effigy of the Holy Father, clad in pontifical robes, with mitre and keys, down the narrow wynd that led from the school to the wynd of the Blackfriars, from whence they boldly issued by an archway into the lower end of the High-street; and there, after reading an accusation and sentence, amid a general cry of *Pareat Papa!* they set fire to the effigy, which was hollow and filled with gunpowder. To these proceedings the city militia offered no opposition; but, according to the history of this affair, published in Paternoster-row in 1681, " on the first report of what was doing, General Dalyell galloped in with his dragoons through the Netherbow-porte, and was followed by the infantry under the Earl of Mar."

A scuffle ensued. The Earl of Linlithgow, a Catholic peer, with a few of his Foot Guards, dispersed the students sword in hand, and in making a pass at one of them, fell, amid loud laughter, prostrate before the blazing figure, which was burned to the complete satisfaction of all concerned therein. Many students were captured and threatened with torture by the Council; but for his loyalty in this affair, the house of the Lord Provost, an old manor at Priestfield, near Duddingstone, was one night set on fire by ignited powder-balls, and burned to the ground. A proclamation was issued, banishing all students fifteen miles from the capital, and for closing the gates of the university; but the circumstance of a gunpowder barrel, bearing the Edinburgh Castle mark, being found near Priestfield, caused a general suspicion that some officers of the garrison had a hand in the affair. A reward of two hundred merks was offered for each of the leaders in these outrages; but it was to the honour of the students that not one was betrayed by his comrades.

The civil commotions were now of a nature so serious, that the local government forced the magistrates of Edinburgh to *number* the inhabitants of the city and its suburbs, and to make accurate lists of all men and women between the ages of sixteen and sixty, for the information of the Lords of Council. The name, rank, or profession of persons in lodgings or hostelries, and of all strangers in the city, were to be delivered nightly by the bailies to the captain of the city guard, who, under a penalty of 100*l.* Scots, was to send it to the commander-in-chief, or officer next in command.

On the 15th of November, 1681, Dalyell raised that celebrated dragoon regiment, so well known in military history as the Scots Greys, from the peculiar colour of their horses. They were a corps of horse-grenadiers, and were recruited almost exclusively among the sons of the Cavalier gentry and their tenants.* The regiment is now numbered as the 2nd Cavalry of the Line. They wore the old heavy-skirted buff coat; and it is worthy of remark, that the *last time* such a garment was worn in the British service was by the colonel who commanded them at Minden, seventy-four years after.

Captain Creichton mentions that, when he was lying in his lodgings at Edinburgh, suffering from sword wounds received at Airsmoss, Dalyell was wont to visit him daily, as he went to the Duke's Court at Holyrood, and once "did me the honour," he continues, "to mention me and my services to His Royal Highness, who was desirous to see me. I was admitted to kiss his hand, and ordered to sit down in consequence of my honourable wounds, which would not suffer me to stand without great pain."

About this time the Reverend John Blackadder, a pious and good man, who had long continued preaching in solitary places, revisited his native country, after having been in Holland, and was captured by a party of soldiers, and brought to Edinburgh, where Johnstone, the town major, at once conveyed him, under escort, to the house of Dalyell, in the Canongate. The account of their interview, and of the examination of Blackadder before

---

* In a muster-roll of Captain Murray's Scottish company, at this time, I find "*Corporall* Sir David Livingstone."

the inexorable Lords of Council, are graphically detailed in the memoirs of that unfortunate Covenanter.

The Major conducted him down that long and ancient street to where the General lived, near the old palace porch, which has now been demolished. The prisoner was accompanied by his son Thomas, who in after years died a merchant in New England. It chanced that the dreaded Dalyell, whose white vow-beard and lofty bald head impressed with fear and respect all on whom he bent his stern grey eye, opened the door as they approached, being probably about to walk forth.

"I have brought you a prisoner," said Major Johnstone.

"Take him to the guard," replied Dalyell, briefly.

On this the poor minister, whose emotions on finding himself confronted by the scourge of the Covenanters must have been far from enviable, stepped up the stair, and said timidly—

"Sir, may I speak with you a little?"

"You, sir, have spoken too much already," replied Dalyell, in anger, for he never controlled his wrath at the sight of a Covenanter. "I should hang you with my own hands, over that outshot!"

At that moment Dalyell knew not who Blackadder really was; but finding him in a mood so sullen, and aware that the old man's anger was not to be trifled with, the Major took his prisoner away. Instead, however, of consigning him to the common guard-house—for Blackadder was a man alike venerable by his years and character—he gave him a room in the house of Captain Murray, of Philiphaugh, where he remained until he was brought to the dread Council chamber for examination before the Duke of Rothes, then Lord High Chancellor of Scotland; Sir George Mackenzie, of Rosehaugh, King's Advocate; General Dalyell, and Paterson, the last Bishop of Edinburgh.

"Are you a minister?" asked Rothes.

"I am," replied Blackadder.

"Where?"

"At Troqueer, in Galloway."

"How long since?"

"Since 1653."

"Did you excommunicate the King at the Torwood, or were you there at the time?" continued the Chancellor.

"I have not been at the Torwood for these four years."

"But what do you *think* of it (the excommunication)? Do you *approve* of it?"

He was asked the usual ensnaring questions (and, like other prisoners, had the instruments of torture on the table before him) as to whether he approved of the execution of Charles I.; if he had preached in the fields and on the hill-sides, and so forth; but his answers proved unsatisfactory, and, after a long examination, he was sent back to Philiphaugh's apartments at Holyrood.

On the morning of the next day he sent his son Thomas to a kinsman named Blackadder, who bore the rank of colonel, and had been Dalyell's comrade in the expedition at Skelko Castle in 1654, and who now exerted himself in his favour, and made such interest with the stern General, that he received the recusant divine with great politeness in the forenoon, when he was again brought before the Council.

"Mr. Blackadder," said he, "of what family are you—the House of Tulliallan?"

"Yes, General, I am the nearest alive now, to represent that family, although it is now ruined and brought so low."

Dalyell was also allied by blood to the family of Tulliallan.

"Are you the son of Sir John Blackadder?" asked Bishop Paterson; but the inflexible Covenanter declined *his* authority as a spiritual lord, and would not reply even to this trivial question.

In the sequel, he was sent prisoner to the Bass, escorted by three Life Guardsmen, and an officer named Rollock, who threatened to pistol him at Fisher-row, when the people gathered to see him pass. On that dreary rock, which was then the home of many a broken heart, the old man died in his seventieth year, and he now lies in the churchyard of North Berwick.*

* See Crichton's *Memoirs of Blackadder.*

The publication of a stern and high-toned manifesto against *Charles Stuart*, and all supporters of his authority, together with the secret murder of two gentlemen of the Life Guards, who had been particularly active in discovering conventicles, and who were assassinated a few nights after its appearance in November, 1684, excited great alarm in the minds of the Scottish ministry. An oath, abjuring the principles inculcated by this document, was ordained to be put to all persons above sixteen years of age, and capital punishment was the penalty of all who refused it. Dalyell took measures still more decisive with the parish where the guardsmen were murdered; and he marched a body of troops to Livingstone, where the officers had authority to summon before them the inhabitants of that parish, and of five others adjacent, that they might be interrogated upon the late seditious manifesto.

Those who owned it were instantly to be shot; and those who refused to answer were also to be shot. Officers and soldiers were sent through Edinburgh—particularly to the Calton, where the poorest and most humble class of citizens resided—to enforce the oath of abjuration and ask ensnaring questions, as to whether the rising at Bothwell was a *rebellion*, and the slaying of Archbishop Sharpe a *murder?* "Old women were taken from their wheels, and journeymen and apprentices from the forge, to answer these teazing and captious questions," and the thumbikins were always at hand to freshen their memories.

A document preserved in the General Register House at Edinburgh, signed by Charles II. at Windsor, 16th of June, 1684, and printed by a literary club, affords us a list of the Scottish standing forces, then commanded by Dalyell, and irrespective of the militia which formed the main strength of the country.

Reduced since Bothwell, the Life Guards then consisted of a hundred men; each officer was furnished with two horses; the pay, sterling, of a captain was 1*l.* per diem; of the lieutenants 12*s.*; of the cornets 7*s.*; of the troopers 2*s.* 6*d.*

His Majesty's regiment of Foot Guards, still com

manded by Lieut.-General George, Earl of Linlithgow, consisted of ten companies, each consisting of three officers, two sergeants, two drummers, and seventy-three rank and file, making a total strength, staff included, of eight hundred and seven men.

The grenadiers of the Foot Guard were the same in number as the ten preceding companies.

The Earl of Mar's regiment consisted of eleven companies of eighty strong. The pay of a captain of infantry was 8*s.* sterling per diem; the privates received 5*d.*

A regiment of horse (armed with sword and pistol), consisting of five troops of fifty men each, including officers and men.

A regiment of dragoons (armed with sword, pistol, and *musket,* for service on horseback or on foot), the *Scots Greys,* consisting of "six companies," also of fifty-nine each, including officers. All troopers received 1*s.* per diem.

The garrison of Edinburgh Castle consisted of 5 officers and 121 soldiers; of Stirling Castle, 3 officers and 47 soldiers; of Dunbarton Castle, 3 officers and 32 soldiers; of the Bass Rock, 1 officer and 28 soldiers.

The train of artillery was commanded by a Master of the Ordnance, whose pay was 120*l.* per annum, with a conductor, engineer, fireworker, and master gunners.— (*Miscellany of the Maitland Club.*)

Dalyell's pay as a Scottish General was 400*l.* per annum.

Assisted by a militia, this small force proved sufficient, for a time, to coerce all the Lowlands of Scotland.

In July, this year, Mr. William Spence, a follower of the recently forfeited Marquis of Argyle, was tortured by the Privy Council, that he might be forced to reveal all he knew of that noble's intrigues with the English, and to read certain letters in cypher, which were placed before him by Major Holmes; but on the torture failing to produce the desired effect, "he was," according to Lord Fountainhall, "*put in General Dalyell's hands;* and it was reported that by a hair shirt and pricking (*i. e.,* with a needle), as the witches are used, he was five nights kept from sleep, till he was half distracted. He ate very little that he might require less sleep; yet all this while he discovered nothing; though had he done so, little credit was to be given to what he should say at such a time."

After this is the following entry :—

"August 7th, 1684. At Privy Council, Spence (mentioned 26th July) is again tortured, and has his thumbs crushed with thumbiekins. It is a new invention used among the colliers when transgressors, and discovered by General Dalziell and Drummond, they having seen them used in Muscovy. After this, when they were about to put him in the boots, he, being frightened, desired time, and he would declare what he knew; whereon they gave him some time, and sequestrated him in the Castle of Edinburgh, as a place where he would be free from any bad advice or impression to be obstinate in not revealing."

There is something alike quaint and horrible in the quiet and matter-of-fact way in which this old senator records such extra-judicial barbarities; but instruments of torture were then as necessary to the Privy Council as the pen and ink with which their minutes were recorded.

To repress the reviving spirit of the Covenanters, four Commissions of Lieutenancy were, in September, ordained to meet at Glasgow, Ayr, Dumfries, and Dunse. The first, as Dalyell ordered, to be guarded by Lord Ross's troop of Horse and Captain Inglis's Dragoons; the second by the troop of Guards and his own Grey Dragoons; the third by the Horse of Claverhouse, Drumlanrig, and Strachan; the fourth by the Horse of Balcarris and Lord Charles Murray's Dragoons; but now the horrors of this civil and military persecution received a check by the death of Charles II. on the 6th February 1685, and on the accession of his brother, who was immediately proclaimed at Edinburgh, James VII. of Scotland, by the Lyon King and magistrates, and Dalyell received a new commission as commander-in-chief of the kingdom; but the Catholic tendencies of the new court—tendencies to which, with all his hatred of Covenanters and Low Churchmen, "the old Muscovite" was rigidly averse—would not have permitted him to retain his authority long.

Death now, however, solved the important problem of how he was to act at this peculiarly dangerous juncture; he was thus, to use the words of his comrade Creichton, "rescued from the difficulties he was likely to be under, between the notions he had of duty to his prince on one side, and true zeal for his religion on the other;" as he expired suddenly at his house in the Canongate of Edinburgh, in the month of July, 1685.

On the 7th August, while the minute-guns boomed from the dark portholes of the ancient half-moon battery of the castle, his body, in a magnificent hearse, drawn by plumed horses, and having six pieces of brass cannon, his led charger, his suit of armour, and his many trophies, sword, spurs, helmet, and gauntlets, and his general's bâton, all borne by officers of rank, and escorted by all the standing forces in Edinburgh, with drums muffled, standards craped, and arms reversed, was slowly conveyed through the western gate of the city to Linlithgowshire, and interred in the family vault of the Dalyells at Binns, in the parish of Abercorn.

There the persecuting Cavalier rests in peace, though the superstitious peasantry still aver that his tall, thin, and venerable figure, in buff coat and head-piece, with his vast white beard floating from his grim visage to his military girdle, is seen "in glimpses of the moon," flitting, like an unquiet spirit, about the old manor house, or in the avenues and parks which were formed by himself around it.

He died in his eighty-fifth year.

The hearts of the Covenanters gathered hope, and held jubilee at his death; and if all be true that is recorded of him, it can scarcely be a matter for wonder that his name and memory are still execrated in Scotland, and that the reputation he has left behind him is not one to be envied.

General Drummond, his old Russian comrade, succeeded him as Commander-in-Chief of the Scottish army; Charles, Earl of Dunmore, was appointed Colonel of the Scots Greys, and the Laird of Livingstone filled the seat left vacant by him, as Commissioner in Parliament for the shire of Linlithgow.

His son Thomas, who succeeded him, was created a baronet of Nova Scotia, and left a daughter, Magdalene Dalyell, who, by her marriage with James Menteith, of Auldcathie, transmitted the property to her son, who thus represented the ancient line of the Earls of Menteith.

In reviewing the life of this singular officer, I cannot do better than quote the words of one of the most temperate and popular of Scottish writers:—

"There are *two* ways of contemplating the character even of so blood-stained a persecutor as Dalyell. He had, it must be remarked, served royalty upon principle in its *worst* days, and seen a monarch beheaded by a small party of his rebellious subjects, and a great part of the community, including himself, deprived of their property, and obliged to fly for their lives to foreign lands; and all this was on account of *one particular way* of viewing politics and religion. When the usual authorities of the land regained their ascendancy, Dalyell must naturally have been disposed to justify and support very severe measures, in order to prevent the *recurrence* of such a period as the Civil War and the Usurpation. Thus all his cruelties are resolved into an abstract principle, to the relief of his personal character, which otherwise, we do not doubt, might be very good. How often do we see, even in modern times, actions justified upon general views, which would be shuddered at if they stood upon their naked merits, and were to be performed upon the sole responsibility of the individual!"

Such was the chequered military career of the first colonel of the old Scots Greys, certainly one of the most remarkable men of a time replete with bloodshed and cruelty.

The persecuted and the persecutor—the fiery Cavalier and the stern Covenanter—are alike in their quiet graves, and the grass of nearly two hundred years has grown and withered over them. Their strife is becoming, indeed, a tale of the times of old; yet few Scotsmen can look back without emotions of sorrow and compassion to those dark days of religious madness and political misrule when, with all their bravery, their forefathers perpetrated such deeds as made "the angels weep." But, happily for us, time and the grave mellow the memory of all things.

THE END.

www.ingramcontent.com/pod-product-compliance
Lightning Source LLC
Chambersburg PA
CBHW031248230426
43670CB00005B/91